eLearning with
Dreamweaver® MX

Building Online Learning Applications

Betsy Bruce

Building Online Learning Applications

macromedia®
PRESS

eLearning with Dreamweaver® MX: Building Online Learning Applications

Copyright © 2003 by New Riders Publishing

 Published by Macromedia Press, in association with New Riders Publishing, a division of Pearson Education

FIRST EDITION: November, 2002

International Standard Book Number: 0-7357-1274-3

Library of Congress Catalog Card Number: *2001099274*

06 05 04 03 02   7 6 5 4 3 2 1

Interpretation of the printing code: The rightmost double-digit number is the year of the book's printing; the rightmost single-digit number is the number of the book's printing. For example, the printing code 02-1 shows that the first printing of the book occurred in 2002.

Trademarks

Warning and Disclaimer

Publisher
David Dwyer

Associate Publisher
Stephanie Wall

Production Manager
Gina Kanouse

Acquisitions Editors
Kate Small
Todd Zellers

Development Editor
Susan Hobbs

Senior Marketing Manager
Tammy Detrich

Publicity Manager
Susan Nixon

Project Editor
Tonya Simpson

Copy Editor
Lisa Lord

Indexer
Chris Morris

Manufacturing Coordinator
Jim Conway
Dan Uhrig

Book Designer
Chris Wil

Cover Designer
Alan Clements

Composition
Scan Communications Group, Inc.

Contents At a Glance

Table of Contents

Part VII Appendixes

About the Author

 Betsy Bruce (betsy@betsybruce.com) specializes in creating training applications using Macromedia products, especially Dreamweaver and Authorware. Formerly a senior developer for MediaPro, Inc. in the Seattle, WA area, she is now an independent consultant and trainer holding certifications as a developer and trainer for Dreamweaver, CourseBuilder for Dreamweaver, Authorware, and Flash. She is also a frequent presenter at both technology and training conferences. She's presented at Macromedia UCON and DevCon, ASTD TechKnowledge, Online Learning, and many other conferences.

Betsy provides clients both large and small with carefully tailored solutions implementing best-practice recommendations for creating eLearning applications. Recent clients include Canon USA, Portland General Electric, and Apex Online Learning. She enjoys working individually with clients to craft templates and custom CourseBuilder objects that enhance the group's eLearning development along with training and ongoing mentorship to make each project a success.

An accomplished author, Betsy has written the *Sams Teach Yourself Dreamweaver in 24 Hours* series, the most recent of which is *Sams Teach Yourself Dreamweaver MX in 24 Hours*. She also contributed to *Macromedia Web Publishing Unleashed* (Que) and co-authored *Getting Started with eLearning* (Macromedia). Betsy acted as one of the Subject Matter Experts for the Macromedia Dreamweaver MX Certification Exam.

Born and raised in Iowa, Betsy now lives on the West Coast. In her free time, she enjoys reading, cooking, home remodeling projects, movies, and digital music. Be sure to visit Betsy's web site at http://www.betsybruce.com/.

About the Technical Reviewers

These reviewers contributed their considerable hands-on expertise to the entire development process for *eLearning with Dreamweaver MX: Building Online Learning Applications*. As the book was being written, these dedicated professionals reviewed all the material for technical content, organization, and flow. Their feedback was critical to ensuring that the material fits our reader's need for the highest-quality technical information.

Robyn Ness holds a master's degree in psychology with a specialization in judgment and decision making. She currently works as a Web developer for the department of Communications and Technology at The Ohio State University, focusing on issues of usability and content design.

Lon Coley (LonColey@ariadne-webdesign.co.uk) is an information-technology professional specializing in Internet solutions and the Internet in education. She has been active professionally within the Internet sector for five years, working with companies and colleges looking to understand and expand into the Internet in the modern working environment. As an experienced teacher and trainer, Lon writes and develops dedicated customized training courses for both business and education. For more information, visit Lon's site at http://www.ariadne-webdesign.co.uk.

Dedication

This book is dedicated to my parents, John (deceased) and Pat Bruce, both educators. You always advised me not to be a teacher because you wanted me to make more money! However, I just couldn't stay out of education. You are extraordinary role models, as both people and professionals.

Acknowledgments

I'm lucky to know some very talented folks who design and create learning applications. I greatly appreciate the input of Scott Urstad and Mark Steiner, who both helped me see the bigger picture. Thank you to Dana Joy, Mark Moore, Kathleen Peppers, Jennifer Henry, Brandon Carson, Penny Carson, and Ruppi Barnickel for helping me explore their roles as instructional team members.

I'd like to acknowledge Ron Gilster, my former supervisor at the Communications Technology Center for Washington's Community and Technical Colleges, who dropped a copy of Authorware on my desk and started my career in learning application development. Thanks to Craig Kitterman for being my own private ASP guru.

Thank you, Kate Small, Suz Hobbs, and Lisa Lord, my editors. Your support, intelligence, and talent helped me make this the best book I could write. My thanks to the entire team.

Thanks to my many inspirational clients. I often learn as much from you as you learn from me. I've had you in mind while writing this book and have attempted to capture the knowledge and techniques necessary to help others follow in your pioneering "eLearning footsteps."

Special thanks to Dana, who is always supportive, flexible, kind, and full of humor. Siberian huskies Shasta and Nikko deserve a long run in their favorite canyon for keeping me company while writing this book. Also, thank you to Cappy, who always encourages me with wise insight and practical counsel.

This book was powered by:

Beverages: Starbucks French Roast and Diet Pepsi

Music: Michelle Branch, *The Spirit Room*; Diana Krall, *The Look of Love*; Tori Amos, *Strange Little Girls*; Collective Soul, *Collective Soul*; and various MP3s downloaded from the Internet to evaluate for future purchase.

Computers and peripherals: Compaq Presario 1800T laptop with 320MB RAM and docking station running Windows 2000 Professional, an Apple iMac 600Mhz Graphite running OS X, a Lexmark Z51 printer, an HP external CD-RW drive, and an HP ScanJet 5370C scanner.

Tell Us What You Think

As the reader of this book, you are the most important critic and commentator. We value your opinion and want to know what we're doing right, what we could do better, what areas you'd like to see us publish in, and any other words of wisdom you're willing to pass our way.

As the Associate Publisher for New Riders Publishing, I welcome your comments. You can fax, email, or write me directly to let me know what you did or didn't like about this book—as well as what we can do to make our books stronger.

Please note that I cannot help you with technical problems related to the topic of this book, and that due to the high volume of mail I receive, I might not be able to reply to every message.

When you write, please be sure to include this book's title and author as well as your name and phone or fax number. I will carefully review your comments and share them with the author and editors who worked on the book.

Fax: 317-581-4663

Email: stephanie.wall@newriders.com

Mail: Stephanie Wall
              Associate Publisher
              New Riders Publishing
              201 West 103rd Street
              Indianapolis, IN 46290 USA

Introduction

WITH THE COST OF COMPUTER TECHNOLOGY decreasing and the speed of bandwidth increasing, online learning applications are becoming a popular and feasible way to provide learning. The exponential growth of the Internet has enabled people to connect, do business, and accomplish tasks in ways that weren't imagined even a few years ago. Most of us were taught in educational settings of schools and campuses, instructors and fellow students. Today it's possible to deliver effective courses to a diverse population over the Internet.

Learners discover the advantages and disadvantages of online learning when they take their first online courses. The advantages to online learning are many: The ability to learn when it fits into your schedule, interacting with the course wherever you are in the world, and progressing through the materials at your own pace are the major advantages.

The first time I took an online course, I discovered I missed the eye-to-eye communication with the instructor and my fellow students. That minor disadvantage can be eased by adding e-mail, listserv, or chat components to an online course. I suggest that every online learning developer take an online class so you can experience what other learners experience when they take one of your courses.

eLearning with Dreamweaver MX: Building Online Learning Applications enables you to develop and deploy online training and eLearning applications by using Dreamweaver, a powerful Web-editing software package. You'll explore the planning, development, and fine-tuning processes of creating an online learning application. This book will teach you the processes that real-world eLearning developers use to develop and maintain effective online learning applications.

Who Should Read This Book

I've written this book to enable readers from diverse backgrounds to develop an online training application with Dreamweaver MX. Four main groups will be interested in this material:

- Novice to experienced Web developers who want to develop online learning applications.

- Traditional computer-based training developers—Authorware programmers, for example—who want to develop online learning applications in HTML.

- Those new to both training and Web development who would like to understand online learning application development. This book would be useful after they have completed a Dreamweaver fundamentals class or after reading a Dreamweaver hands-on book.

- Students of instructional design or educational technology who need to understand the development phase of creating online learning applications.

What This Book Covers

The subject of this book is developing online learning applications (also called eLearning applications) with Macromedia Dreamweaver. You'll also explore many powerful extensions to Dreamweaver, including the CourseBuilder and Learning Site extensions.

Throughout the book, starting with Chapter 4, "Creating a New Site Definition," you'll build a sample online learning application. You'll start by defining the site in Dreamweaver and you'll end with creating a tracking database using Learning Site. All the assets used to create the application can be downloaded from my Web site at

www.betsybruce.com/elearning_book/

You can also download the assets from the New Riders Web site:

www.newriders.com/. Search for the book page at 0735712743 and select downloads.

Book Goals

The six main sections of this book are divided into areas that roughly approximate the development cycle of an online learning application. In the following list you'll find what you can expect to understand in each of the sections of this book.

Part I, "Planning Your Project," will help you

- Understand the five steps in the ADDIE instructional method and name some of the deliverables in each step

- Interpret design documents, such as scripts, storyboards, and lists of assets

- Identify team members in an instructional project and understand their roles

Part II, "Creating a Prototype," will help you

- Understand the technical issues in creating a specification ("spec") for an online learning project
- Create standard CSS and CSS-P (positioning) styles and understand how to link a single external stylesheet to all the Web pages in a site
- Create functional buttons, menus, and other interface elements in Dreamweaver

Part III, "Inserting Content," will help you

- Organize and access the course assets by using the Assets panel in Dreamweaver
- Create, use, and edit reusable templates and library items
- Create custom interactions and insert JavaScript into Web pages by using Dreamweaver Behaviors
- Insert and control rich media elements, such as Flash, Shockwave, and Authorware content
- Understand how plug-ins work and which plug-ins are necessary for the rich media used. Help users find the plug-ins they need for the course

Part IV, "Using CourseBuilder," will help you

- Become familiar with the interactions and controls available through CourseBuilder
- Understand how to use the tabbed wizard interface to insert CourseBuilder objects into a Web page
- Modify a CourseBuilder object and save the custom object to the CourseBuilder Gallery for later use
- Understand how to add complex scripting by using Course-Builder's Action Manager
- Place multiple CourseBuilder objects on a Web page to create a quiz and track that quiz with CourseBuilder's tracking frameset
- Use various techniques to hide quiz answers from students

Part V, "Tracking the User," will help you

- Understand how to use ASP to authenticate users

- Track comments to a database by using ASP

- Understand how to use the tracking capabilities of Learning Site, a free extension to Dreamweaver from Macromedia

- Understand what learning management system software is and some of the common functions it performs

- Name the popular tracking standards

- Understand how to use CourseBuilder's Knowledge Track option to track users

Part VI, "Collaboration and Optimization," will help you

- Understand how to upload and share the online learning application to a remote site

- Understand Dreamweaver's check in/out capabilities, as well as how to use Microsoft Visual SourceSafe and WebDAV to access and share the remote site with team members

- Understand how to use the Synchronize command

- Create, interpret, and save Dreamweaver reports

- Understand how the Dreamweaver interface is controlled through the Configuration folder

- Create and modify parts of the Dreamweaver interface

- Download and install extensions from the Macromedia Exchange

What This Book Doesn't Cover

This book is not an introduction to Dreamweaver. There are numerous introductions to Dreamweaver, including my book *Sams Teach Yourself Macromedia Dreamweaver MX in 24 Hours*. I assume that you have a working knowledge of the Dreamweaver interface. I also assume that you have already created a few Web pages containing text and images.

The information contained in this book demonstrates practical, real-world methods of developing instructionally sound and technically sturdy online learning applications. This book is not a theoretical text on instructional development. Check Appendix A, "Resources," for books on instructional theories.

Software Requirements

You'll need Dreamweaver and a connection to the Internet to accomplish the exercises in this book. This book focuses on the most recent version of Dreamweaver, Dreamweaver MX, but most of the exercises (probably 98%) can be accomplished with Dreamweaver 4. An Internet connection is necessary to download the two extensions you'll explore: the CourseBuilder and Learning Site extensions. You can find a trial version of Dreamweaver MX at

www.macromedia.com/software/dreamweaver/trial/

Another type of software used to log and track an online learning application user, called a learning management system, will be discussed in Part V. This complicated software application is not something that typical users have sitting on their shelves of software boxes. Because a learning management system is a server application with a database back end, it is usually complicated to set up. I've used WBT Manager as the example in this book. If you are interested in trying this software, you can download a demo at

www.wbtmanager.com/wbt/trial/

Why Use Dreamweaver?

Dreamweaver excels at interactivity. In online learning, interactivity helps engage the user and provide simulations of real-life job activities. No other Web editing programs in existence (as of this writing) enable a developer to quickly create click interactions—for example, simulating the selection of a button in a software application—or drag-and-drop or multiple-choice question interactions.

Dreamweaver is also the premier professional Web-editing application. Dreamweaver not only enables you to create Web pages, cascading stylesheets, Dynamic HTML, and JavaScript, but it also facilitates uploading and safely sharing an online learning application with a development team. Many specialized features that aren't built in to Dreamweaver are available as free extensions to the program.

Have fun using Dreamweaver to create the sample online learning application in this book! Creating online learning applications is a rewarding and exciting application of the World Wide Web. I hope this book helps augment your valuable contributions to the growing field of online learning.

Part I

Planning Your Project

IN THIS CHAPTER

chapter 1

Instructional Design 101

AN INSTRUCTIONAL TEAM SPENDS MOST OF ITS TIME designing and planning (*not* developing) an online training or eLearning application. Although this book covers the development of online learning applications, this chapter introduces you to instructional concepts and instructional design. Because all the instructional phases are interdependent, it's important that you are familiar with and have respect for the phases that others carry out. The success of your instructional project requires attention to more than just the development phase, the main subject of this book.

If you are working in a team, this chapter helps you understand how your teammates created the documents you will use as a map to develop the project. If you are working by yourself as a one-person team, this chapter introduces you to instructional concepts that will help you design your project so that the development goes smoothly and your application is instructionally sound.

In this chapter, you will understand the following:

- The ADDIE instructional design model

- The order and dependencies of the instructional design process

- The documents produced during the instructional design process

Introducing the ADDIE Instructional Design Model

Good instruction doesn't just happen, so you'll want to use proven instructional design models to guide you. Instructional design is a complex set of concepts and methodologies that cannot be covered in only one chapter. If you'd like to learn more, and I hope you do, check out the information in Appendix A, "Resources."

Creating eLearning applications using proven instructional methods has numerous benefits:

- Learners retain more information.

- Observable and measurable learning results are produced.

- Learners complete the entire eLearning course because the content is engaging and interesting.

- Learners intuitively understand how to accomplish tasks in the well-designed eLearning application.

In this chapter, you'll explore the concepts behind the ADDIE instructional model and look at examples of documents produced to support the instructional design process. The ADDIE model is one of the most popular instructional models; many eLearning professionals consider it the standard instructional model. It has been documented and examined extensively and has been used successfully by many instructional teams over the years. ADDIE is an acronym that stands for

Analysis

Design

Development

Implementation

Evaluation

As this chapter progresses, you'll explore each of the five phases of the ADDIE model, starting with analysis.

Exploring Analysis: The A in ADDIE

During the analysis phase of the ADDIE model, your team conducts an investigation of the client, assessing the problems to be addressed. The goal of the analysis phase is to identify the problems correctly and prepare a list of goals to remedy the problems. You also can analyze the intended audience during this phase. During the analysis phase, the following documents are produced:

- A performance analysis report identifying the performance problems and suggesting solutions

- A list of goals

- An audience analysis report

Identifying Performance Problems and Creating Goals

Identifying the actual performance problems is sometimes difficult, and the results of analysis are often surprising. Let's say that many employees at your company enter data into the wrong fields of a database application. A supervisor has asked you to develop a training course to eliminate the problems. You'll want to analyze the performance problems first, conducting a *performance analysis*. Creating training materials without analyzing the problem can be an expensive mistake.

Identifying the Problems and Solutions with Performance Analysis

Power User Tip

If you'd like to know more about performance analysis, you should read *Analyzing Performance Problems,* by Robert F. Mager and Peter Pipe (more information on this book is in Appendix A). The book presents a simple and effective method of evaluating any type of problem.

Conducting a performance analysis requires you to collect information about the problem. You conduct interviews, observe employees at their jobs, request feedback from employees who excel at their jobs, and review data sources. Let's pretend you've been asked to create a learning application because there are many errors in a company database. Conducting an interview with an employee might sound like this:

You: Could you show me how you use the database?

Tom: Well, I have a paper form that a client has filled out. I enter the data into the computer.

You: Tell me about how you enter the data.

Tom: I read the paper and then enter the information in the database.

Here's the first, middle, and last name at the top of the page. I scroll down a ways and enter the name. Then I read the next line on the paper, company name, and scroll back up to the company section of the form on the computer. I continue until I've entered all the information, and then I save the record.

You: What are your challenges with this task?

Tom: Our old system was easier. We entered each client into a spreadsheet. I didn't even have to look at the screen. I could just type, hit the Tab key, type, hit the Tab key.

You: Thanks, Tom, for your help.

Is training on the new database application going to help Tom? Probably not! This probably is not a training problem. After your performance analysis, you decide that the database application is not designed to efficiently record data from the existing forms. You recommend that the paper form be redesigned so that Tom and others can enter the data quickly and efficiently without having to scroll up and down the screen.

You might say, "But we're the training department and we provide training. Why should I recommend another solution?" Because throwing training solutions at a problem that can't be solved by training is a waste of time and resources. And, most of all, it won't solve the problem! You want to concentrate on addressing problems that training can effectively solve.

So let's look at a different interview for the same database entry problem that your hypothetical company is experiencing:

You: Tell me about how you use the database.

Tom: I get a stack of forms to enter, and then I enter the information into the database.

You: Tell me how you enter the data.

Tom: Here, I'll show you. I get one of these forms and first enter the name. But sometimes I have questions, like this guy has "Jr." after his name. Where do I put that? Do I add "Jr." to his last name? Do I use a comma? I'm new to the department and although everyone here is very helpful, they're busy and I hate to interrupt them.

You: What are your challenges with this task?

Tom: There are many variations on the forms that I don't know how to address. I run into some variations often, some not as often, and I forget where I'm supposed to put the data. I'm certainly not stupid, but it's a lot to remember. I'm embarrassed to ask the same questions over and over.

You: Thanks, Tom. You've been very helpful.

Can your training department help Tom with his task? As you investigate, you find out that the techniques for using the new database application have not been documented. The employees who have been doing this task for a while switched over to the new application and applied the techniques that they knew from before. Tom needs some training, and he needs references to use when he encounters ambiguous data. In this case, you've identified a performance problem, created a list of performance barriers, and a list of recommendations, as shown in Figure 1.1.

Figure 1.1

A list of performance barriers and solutions in the performance analysis report.

Performance Analysis Report

Introduction

The data entry department receives completed forms from clients containing client information to be entered in the company's database. Numerous data entry errors have occurred, including data entered into incorrect fields. Some employees are entering the data more slowly than expected.

Sources
* Interview with the manager overseeing data entry
* Interviews with data entry staff
* Interviews with selected clients who have filled out the forms
* Examination of reports on the number of errors in the database and the time that it takes employees to enter the data
* Examination of any documentation on the current database application

Optimals and Actuals

The manager overseeing the data entry process would like to see at least a 99% accuracy rate for data entry from the client forms. Interviews with the data entry staff revealed they were motivated to be accurate and speedy. They would all like to thoroughly understand the database application that they use for their jobs. Data entry staff would like to be more self-reliant, causing fewer interruptions to experienced staff members.

Currently, the data entry staff encounters problems entering the data from approximately 25% of the forms they receive. Some of the forms have been written illegibly (approximately 5%). Some of the forms have data written in the margins or in an inappropriate field on the form.

Over the years, the department has developed standard ways to deal with this ambiguous data but these methods have not been documented. Employees must pause their data entry work and seek out experienced co-workers to consult with when they encounter ambiguous data that they don't know how to handle. This interrupts experienced employees and requires that they accompany the person to their desk to examine the data in question.

Clients interviewed said that they were sometimes unclear where to place necessary information on the form. The clients felt it was better to put the information on the form in an incorrect place than to omit it. The manager of the data entry area said that data entry employees must enter all of the data from the form because the forms are not preserved.

Recommendations	Recommendation
Barrier The data entry staff receives illegible client forms.	Add a notice at the top of the client form requesting that the form be entered legibly in printed letters.
The data entry staff does not know how to address some client forms that contain ambiguous data.	Create a database cheat sheet that data entry employees can consult when they have questions about where data should be entered. Create training on how to use the cheat sheet.
Clients sometimes do not understand where to place necessary data on the client form.	Identify additional fields that are necessary on the client form and redesign the form. Redesign the form to be logical, have good instructions, and be easy to use.
Data entry staff must leave their desks to consult on ambiguous data. Experienced employees are interrupted with questions.	Train data entry staff how to use the data entry cheat sheet. Develop a procedure for questions where the data entry employee puts the form they have questions about aside and consults with an experienced employee during a set time period.

Creating Instructional Goals

After the performance barriers and recommendations have been identified, and assuming that some sort of training is recommended, you need to create a list of instructional goals. The solutions you've documented that involve training will be further developed through the rest of the ADDIE model. The list of goals, shown in Figure 1.2, should be observable and should always focus on what learners will be able to accomplish after they've completed the training.

Know Your Audience: Audience Analysis

Would you want to create an online training course for a senior citizen's center that includes techno music and MTV-style effects? How about a course for the company sales force that is totally in English when more than 50% of the salespeople are in Mexico? It doesn't take much guesswork to say "probably not" to both of these scenarios.

What kind of colors, music, technical tone, photographs, and language should you use in the online learning application? Should you guess? Unfortunately, many instructional teams do just that, not because they are lazy, but because they think they already know the audience. You'll often be surprised at audience analysis results.

During the analysis phase, you analyze many factors that will affect the design of your training application. The tone, language, color scheme, amount of user control, and even the font size of the text on the screen can all be design elements you'll want to analyze up front. These elements influence the effectiveness of your training and vary from group to group.

Instructional Goals

Goal 1
Data entry employees can identify data that has been entered into the incorrect field in the client form.

Goal 2
Data entry employees can use the database cheat sheet to correctly classify commonly encountered ambiguous data types.

Goal 3
Data entry staff can apply the correct procedural steps to client forms that contain ambiguous data not covered in the database cheat sheet.

Figure 1.2
A list of instructional goals is produced to eliminate the performance barriers.

You might want to create a questionnaire, like the one shown in Figure 1.3, asking your audience what they like and don't like. Be sure your questionnaire is written in a nonthreatening way and that your audience knows what the information will be used for. If many in your audience express a like for mystery TV shows, maybe you can design your online training application with clues that allow the learner to play detective, uncovering information just like the detectives on mystery TV shows. If many in your audience are country music fans, maybe you can hire a country music artist as voice talent to introduce your training application.

After collecting the questionnaires from your audience, you can then create an audience analysis report based on your findings. Is it important to understand your audience's tastes? Yes! You want your audience to spend time in the eLearning application and have a comfortable learning experience, one that feels natural to them. Learners have better retention levels when eLearning applications incorporate the types of music and media they enjoy.

Figure 1.3

An audience analysis questionnaire is useful when collecting information to create an audience analysis report.

Exploring Design: The First D in ADDIE

In the design phase of the ADDIE instructional model, an instructional designer creates documents that are eventually handed off to the development team. The designer might or might not be available during the development process, so these documents must be as complete as possible. With clear design documents, the developers will be able to carry out the training design accurately and effectively. During the design phase, the following documents are produced:

- A list of instructional objectives

- A list of assessment (test) questions

- A storyboard containing information about interactive elements, media elements, and the complete text script for the eLearning application

During the design phase, the goals produced during the analysis phase are used to craft a set of instructional objectives for the course. The instructional goals are refined into clear-cut and measurable learning results called instructional objectives. The objectives form the basis for all the course materials. Assessment questions are written from the instructional objectives and determine whether the learner successfully accomplishes the objectives.

After the objectives and assessment questions are created, the course is drafted to give the learner the information and experiences necessary to fulfill the objectives. The instructional designer creates a document called a *storyboard*, a visual representation of what the learner will see on the computer screen during the online training. The storyboard contains the text that will appear, along with descriptions of images and interactive elements.

Creating Learning Objectives and Assessment Questions

During the analysis phase of the ADDIE model, your team produces a list of instructional goals for the online learning application. In the design phase, the list of goals gets broken down into distinct, measurable learning objectives. These objectives become the foundation of the design and development phases.

Objectives should be written clearly and succinctly, describing a single *learning outcome*, the intended knowledge that the learner acquires. You could write an objective such as this:

> Data entry personnel will know how to enter the data from the paper form into the database application and will be able to do it quickly.

There is no way to measure this objective, and it describes two learning outcomes (accuracy and speed). A good objective can be measured, such as

> Data entry personnel will enter data from a sample paper form into the database application with no more than a single error.

> Given a list of ambiguous data, data entry personnel, using the database application "cheat sheet," will identify the correct field and format for each example on the list.

Objectives should have meaningful instructional intent. Pure memorization of facts is not generally useful for true understanding of a topic. It's important that the instructional objectives represent the knowledge that the learner will need to understand to master the topic of the online learning application. It's also essential that the objectives provide a measurement for mastery of the topic.

How do you know when learners have mastered the objective? You'll assess their proficiency with assessment questions in a test or quiz. The assessment questions are designed alongside the instructional objectives so that each objective has a corresponding assessment question. Here are some assessments for the objectives defined above:

> Enter the data on sample form A from the course packet into the data entry form below.

> Use the database application cheat sheet from the course packet to correctly match the 10 data items below to the appropriate field in the database application.

Designing the Storyboard

The most time-consuming document produced during the ADDIE design phase is the storyboard. It's the blueprint for eLearning development. The storyboard addresses the facts, concepts, processes, procedures, and principles identified in the objectives.

To design the storyboard, an instructional designer works with a *subject matter expert*, or *SME* (pronounced "smee"). The SME is the person who understands the skills and knowledge the learner needs to meet the objectives. The SME should understand *best practices*—strategies and approaches to the job that have been shown to be especially effective. SMEs should be the advisors and sounding boards during the design phase and subsequent phases of the project.

The storyboard includes the text, media elements, and interactive elements that present the concepts and skills necessary to understand the objectives. Throughout the design phase, the audience profile is considered so that the storyboard always "speaks the audience's language." The SME answers questions and demonstrates the skills that are incorporated into the training.

There are many ways to create a storyboard. You can use a software tool that can export storyboard elements directly into your finished training application. I've used desktop publishing tools (such as Adobe FrameMaker or PageMaker), drawing tools (such as Macromedia Freehand or Adobe Illustrator), presentation tools (such as Microsoft PowerPoint, shown in Figure 1.4), and word processing tools (such as Microsoft Word or Corel WordPerfect).

Power User Tip

If you are working on a large training project, you might want to invest in creating macros or software tools that can export the storyboard elements. For example, Dreamweaver templates can import XML, eXtensible Markup Language (see Chapter 7, "Building Reusable Templates and Library Items"). If you export text and other elements from the storyboard into XML files, you can import them directly into a Dreamweaver template.

Figure 1.4

An example of a storyboard created in Microsoft PowerPoint.

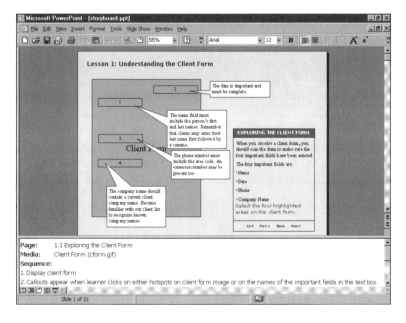

I've used plain old paper and pencil, too, as shown in Figure 1.5. Whatever works best for you is the perfect storyboarding tool.

Figure 1.5

An example of a storyboard created by hand with pencil and paper.

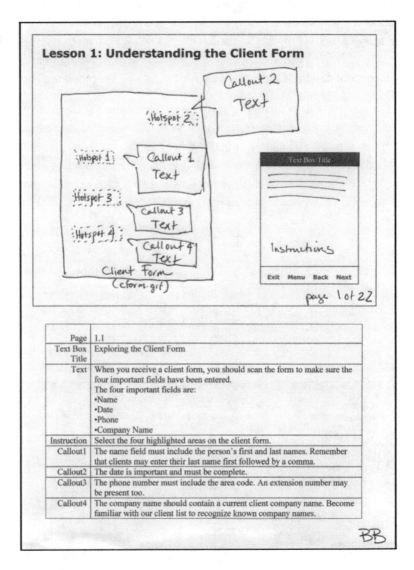

Don't worry about artistic skills. This is a plan, not a work of art. Who cares if the folks in the next cubicle snicker at your drawings? If you communicate the screen's action and intent with stick people and arrows, your team will understand exactly how to implement your design. Your graphics designer can make up for your artistic inadequacies in the final course. While creating the storyboard, also create a list of media elements. All the graphical elements, movies, and sounds in each page of your storyboard will need to be acquired or created.

When creating the storyboard, strive for a consistent design by repeating set interactions and page types. Effective instruction presents text and media elements in a consistent and predictable (but still interesting!) way. Once learners have encountered instructions for completing a task, they should be able to instantly recognize new instructions. The instructions should occur in the same area of the screen, in the same font and point size, in the same color, and be worded similarly. You might even want to create a map of the screen, as shown in Figure 1.6, outlining the consistent elements of your training application.

Power User Tip

Even if you *are* artistically inclined, don't spend a lot of time drawing nicely on the storyboard; you'll be crushed when you decide to throw out a page of the storyboard with your beautiful drawing.

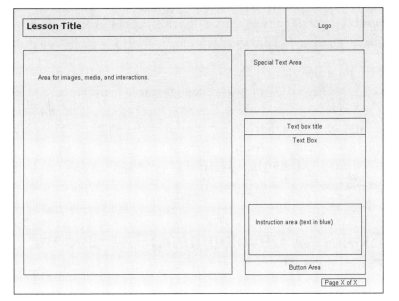

Figure 1.6
A map of the screen defines consistent elements.

During the design phase, you identify logical groups for the pages you create in the storyboard. Here's a description of some storyboard pages:

Page 1—A multiple-choice question to assess the learner's knowledge of the topic before the lesson

Page 2—An informational page, requiring the learner to read some text, look at a graphic, and then go on to the next page

Page 3—This page requires the learner to read instructions and then click on the correct area (a hot spot) on the screen.

Page 4—Another information page

Page 5—Another hot-spot click

Page 6—A multiple-choice question assessing the learner's understanding of the current learning objective

These six pages fall into three logical groups: an information page group (pages 2 and 4), multiple-choice questions (pages 1 and 6), and hot-spot interactions (pages 3 and 5). Similar pages should be presented to the learner in similar ways. To ensure this continuity, your team will create templates for these logical groups during the development phase. Using templates to develop training applications helps guarantee consistent presentation and usually speeds up development.

Even though evaluation is the last phase in the instructional process, you'll want to do a little evaluating right now. You can put together a focus group and describe to them the interactions you are thinking about including in the training. Show some target learners your storyboard and elicit feedback from them. Use the feedback you receive to improve the storyboard and address design flaws before the project goes into development.

Exploring Development: The Second D in ADDIE

During the development phase of the ADDIE model, the development team creates the Hypertext Markup Language (HTML) code for the eLearning application. Templates and reusable elements are created, and then a portion of the online training application is developed into a pilot project or proof of concept. Graphics designers and asset specialists create all the media elements the storyboard calls for.

When the pilot project has been approved, the project moves into *production*. During production, the processes and tools have been defined and created, and the project has an assembly-line–type efficiency.

This book details the development process for an eLearning application. During the development phase, the following documents and elements are produced:

- Templates and reusable elements

- Media elements, such as images, movies, and sound files

- A pilot project that is a small portion of the storyboard design

- A finished Web site containing the entire online learning application

Developing Templates and Course Structure

During development, you'll use the storyboard as your map for creating the online learning application. You'll likely receive parts of the storyboard before the entire document is complete. The developers work with the instructional designer to implement the course. The beginning of the development phase is spent creating the templates and course structure that will be used to produce the training application.

Power User Tip

The phases in the ADDIE model don't necessarily happen sequentially. There is often an overlap between the phases.

The course structure is the code, graphical elements, headings, and text that form the "stage" where the instruction is presented. You will create the *user interface*, the portion of the online learning application that enables the learner to control and interact with the course. For example, the next and back buttons and the lesson title are examples of interface elements. The user interface is part of the course structure.

Templates are files used as a starting point to create the course. The goal is to create a group of templates that are strict enough to enforce consistency but flexible enough to address inconsistencies. That's a tall order! It requires creatively envisioning what the final course will look like and how inconsistencies will be addressed. It also requires deciding how the text and media elements (graphics, movies, sounds) are going to be imported into course pages.

After the logical groups of pages are identified in the design phase, you'll have a list of templates that need to be developed. You'll also want examples of how the finished pages created with the templates are supposed to look. How much text will the average page display? What happens on pages where the text is a little too long? Are graphics centered in the defined area, or do they always align in the upper-left corner of the defined area? Your templates will help answer these questions and ensure consistency.

Developing Media Elements

The storyboard calls for graphics, photos, movies, sounds, or other elements to be included. These elements need to be created or acquired by purchasing the rights. Another term for media elements is *assets*; You'll explore assets further in Chapter 7.

Graphics designers work with the design documents, the instructional designer, and the developer to create appropriate graphics for the course. The saying goes, "A picture is worth a thousand words," so your graphics designer saves you from displaying lots of text that learners often don't want to read anyway! Because this book addresses developing online training, delivered on the Internet or an intranet, the graphics designer should be adept at optimizing graphics so that they are as small as possible and download quickly.

Some media elements might require the user to have third-party players installed, such as the Flash, Shockwave, or Authorware players. Luckily, many users already have these popular players installed. There are also a number of players available for sounds, special graphic formats, and movies such as the QuickTime, Real, and LiquidAudio players.

Developing the Pilot Project

It's important that the course structure works properly and addresses the instructional needs of the targeted learners. You should create a *pilot project*, a slice of the entire course that's indicative of average course content, to evaluate before you develop the entire course. You might revise your pilot project many times, so it's important to keep the following guidelines in mind:

- Don't get attached to it! You should stay open to the changes that might be required.

- Look at all the available design documents. Will the application require any out-of-the-ordinary content?

- Put the pilot project through rigorous tests. Let your co-workers and real users run the pilot project. Listen to their comments and recognize repeated mistakes and points of confusion.

Fix problems now! Don't get caught in the trap of thinking, "Oh, we can fix that later." You might end up passing the project off to others who are not aware of the problem, or you might even forget about it.

Producing the Online Learning Application Web Site

After the pilot project is approved, you move into the production stage of development. Because your templates, media elements, and pilot project are complete, you can work quickly and efficiently to pour the storyboard design into pages of information that are connected by the course structure. This is where your preparation pays off: You should create an assembly line–like atmosphere of well-organized production. Henry Ford would be proud!

Exploring Implementation: The I in ADDIE

You now have a completed online training application ready to go. How are learners going to access it? To implement your course, you will have to distribute it to learners. Because this book is about online training, I'll assume you are distributing your course via a

Web browser. During the implementation phase, the following elements are produced:

- Online training application located on a server where learners can access it over the Internet or on an intranet

- The online training application running from a learning management system, if required

Delivering the Course to the Learner

Delivering your course requires that you upload your course elements to a central location where learners can access it. This location will probably be a server that is running Web server software. Learners enter a Uniform Resource Locator (URL) or click on a hyperlink to request the course from the server; it's the same process you perform every time you look at a Web page. Learners can access the course over the Internet or within the closed environment of an intranet.

You'll want to be sure that learners have the software programs necessary to view the course and the media it contains. The course might require players or a certain browser or browser version, so you should build into your course a method of automatically determining whether the learner has the proper setup to view the course. This method should detect whether learners have the correct players and browser and link them to download sites if they don't.

Power User Tip

If you are implementing your online training application on an intranet, your network administrator might be able to automatically install required players onto learners' computers.

If you are tracking user progress, you will want to have the learners log in to the application so that you can identify individual learners. There are different levels of tracking and different methods and technologies that you can use, which are covered in Part V, "Tracking the User."

Understanding Learning Management Systems

Your company or client might have purchased specialized software called a *learning management system*, or *LMS*. There are many different brands of LMS software (sometimes it's called other names, such as computer-managed instruction, or CMI). This software accomplishes two major purposes:

- It tracks enrollment and learner progress through courses.

- It manages courses, learners, assessments, and other learning resources.

Tracking the learner in an LMS requires the addition of specialized code that passes data from your course to the LMS. We'll explore the standards for these tracking systems and how to build this code into your courses in Chapter 15, "Using a Learning Management System."

Exploring Evaluation: The E in ADDIE

If you've created measurable objectives and effectively trained learners to those objectives, it should be easy to evaluate your results. It might take some patience to wait for learners to take your online training course and put what they've learned into action. Don't get sidetracked and skip this step, though, because it's an important one!

Although the evaluation phase is discussed at the end of the ADDIE cycle, you will actually be conducting evaluations throughout all the phases. Maybe you should think of this phase as the time you collect data and further evaluate what you've done to this point. In this iterative process, you prepare to possibly revisit some of the earlier phases in the cycle. During the evaluation phase, the following documents are produced:

- A return on investment report
- Summative analysis report
- List of revisions and updates

Determining Return on Investment

In today's competitive market, you always want to maintain data demonstrating what a benefit you and your department are to your employer. If you are a vendor creating training applications for clients, you'll want to build in a way for your client to gauge the effectiveness of the product you've sold them, right? Then your clients will want to hire you to create more training!

Online training applications aren't free. Large resource investments of time and money go into creating training applications. You want to evaluate whether the resources delivered benefits that outweigh the costs, making your effort an excellent investment. You'll want to show how the return on investment (ROI) for your project is a positive number. I'm not talking smiley faces here! You know the bean counters want hard numbers.

Evaluating Data

When you designed your objectives, you made them measurable. Now is the time to collect data hopefully showing positive differences between those who have taken the course and those who have not, or showing quantifiable differences between performance before and after taking the course. I hope that the numbers will demonstrate that your course was effective in addressing the performance issues. If you get mixed results, that's okay, too; you can confidently improve and refine your course during a *revision cycle*.

Don't guess during this evaluation phase. Hard facts win every time. Set yourself up for success by properly evaluating the effectiveness of your courses. It may be best to get a neutral person to evaluate your course and the data. At the end of the evaluation phase, a summative analysis report evaluating the project is produced.

The data you collect on your course might show that learners don't understand some of the concepts presented in the training application. Think of these results as an opportunity to make the course even better! You should continue to fine-tune your course so that it's as effective and clear as it can be.

Planning for Revisions and Updates

Information changes so quickly that it would be unreasonable to expect to design and develop an online learning application that does not require any changes or revisions. You should continue to evaluate the content, making sure it hasn't exceeded its shelf life. For this task, you will probably depend on the SME who helped you with the design phase.

To document errors, revisions, and updates you will want to maintain a database or spreadsheet where future changes will be logged. Usually, this is called an error log or revision log. When the time is right to start the revision process, you can refer to this document and implement the updates.

Summary

In this chapter, you looked at the "big picture" of designing, creating, and implementing an online learning application. You familiarized yourself with the ADDIE instructional design process and what happens in each step of the process. You learned about instructional goals, instructional objectives, and assessments.

IN THIS CHAPTER

chapter 2

Assembling the Team and Collecting the Tools

IN CHAPTER 1, "INSTRUCTIONAL DESIGN 101," you learned about the ADDIE instructional process that guides the online learning application project. In this chapter, you'll explore the team roles of the people involved in the instructional process and the tools they use to accomplish their jobs. You'll also be introduced to working professionals in each of the team positions.

Assembling the teams and tools is an important step in making the design and development of your online learning application a smooth and successful process. Good job definitions at this point in the project will help all team members know what roles they play and what responsibilities they have. Your team needs to have (or get) the skills to successfully complete all assigned tasks.

Mark Steiner, an eLearning consultant with Mark Steiner, Inc., advises, "The most successful, well-run, least painful projects *are not luck*! One key to a successful project is a well-defined process, combined with the tools to support it." Use this chapter to formulate the choices that will ensure your project is well run and successful.

In this chapter, you will understand the following:

- The roles and responsibilities of team members on an online learning application development team

- The types of software and hardware tools you might need to create your online learning application

- Dreamweaver, Extension Manager, and CourseBuilder interface basics

Assembling the Team

Your team consists of members whose goal is to design, develop, and implement an online learning application. In the following sections, you'll find job descriptions for the various team members. Keep in mind that one person can play several roles during a project. For example, the instructional designer might also be the project manager, or a developer could also be skilled at graphic design.

Your team membership depends on which tools you select. If you decide to create an online learning application based on data from a database, you'll want to include a database developer in your team. You need to assemble team members who possess the required skills or can quickly get up to speed with training.

You might be the person who is shaking his or her head and saying, "Team? What team? I'm the team!" You might be a one-man or one-woman team, and that's okay, too. You must follow the same processes and create the same documents that a multi-member team creates. Why? Because you might need to hand the project off to someone later down the road. The instructional design process enables you to methodically step through the process, creating an effective and sound online learning application.

Team members become involved during various phases of the project. Obviously, a project manager needs to be involved throughout the entire project, shepherding the team through deadlines and roadblocks. The graphics designer, however, may join the team during the early development phase, creating all the graphics necessary for the project. After contributing to that single phase, the graphics designer probably will move on to another project.

Even though contributions from certain team members might not be required in early phases, it's a good idea to keep team members up to date on the project. Often, team members have important input on tools and techniques that can make later phases of the project go more smoothly. Team members given the opportunity to offer feedback early in the project pave the way for their own contributions farther down the road; they become invested in the project.

Introducing the Project Manager

The project manager is the glue that holds the entire project together. This person keeps track of deadlines and makes sure that all team members have the resources to get their jobs done. The project manager focuses on making sure all team members understand what is expected of them.

Power User Tip

Hiring professional contractors is an excellent way to work around a one-person team's weak points. Using a contract instructional designer, for example, helps ensure that you have a quality design. Consider budgeting for outside contractors in areas such as graphics and instructional design. Look in Appendix A, "Resources," for contracting resources.

Dana Joy is a curriculum manager with Gateway Training.

Dana lists communications skills, flexibility, and attention to detail as the three most important skills for her job. As a curriculum manager at Gateway, Dana manages the production of Gateway's online training, computer-based training, and instructor-led training products. Dana uses Microsoft Outlook, Word, and Project to facilitate communications and project tracking. Her main activities are completing product reviews, participating in conference calls, and completing project-specific forms.

Dana advises, "This is a fast-moving environment, so be sure to take the time to get organized right off the bat or multiple projects will snowball!" She also suggests documenting everything and backing up all the files.

Dana says, "In this industry, life changes on a daily basis. You have to stay positive, don't be afraid of change, and be able to laugh at yourself." She was previously an instructor with Gateway, and she believes that helps her understand the audience better.

The project manager keeps track of the project details and documents. He or she creates Gantt charts and other project documentation and may use project manager software, such as Microsoft Project, to track timelines and milestones. The project manager's essential personality traits are the ability to communicate well, good organization, and excelling at leadership, problem resolution, and diplomacy.

How many hours did the storyboarding process take? How much did the videographer charge for the video shoot? Which deadlines need to be adjusted? The project manager collects this and other information from team members. The information that the project manager collects throughout the project can be useful later when evaluating the project.

The project manager is also the keeper of the project timeline document, illustrated in Figure 2.1, as a Gantt chart. The team agrees on reasonable deadlines at the beginning of the project, and then strives to keep those deadlines to deliver the online learning application at the agreed-on date. The timeline contains milestones—pivotal dates for the project that the team members should be familiar with.

Introducing the Graphics Designer

An online learning project can have one or many graphics designers. You might even have a hierarchy within a graphics design team. For example, on your project, you might have a creative director who oversees an interface designer, an illustrator, and several graphics designers, or you might have one talented individual who will be producing graphics for the entire project. You might even share a graphics designer with other projects.

Power User Tip

If you are a one-man or one-woman team, you probably will have the most difficulty assuming this role. Graphics design requires a fair amount of innate talent and creativity. If you do not already have this talent, you might want to consider contracting this role to an experienced person. You could also consider acquiring rights to photos and other assets from companies that provide them for a licensing fee. See a list of some of these companies in Appendix A.

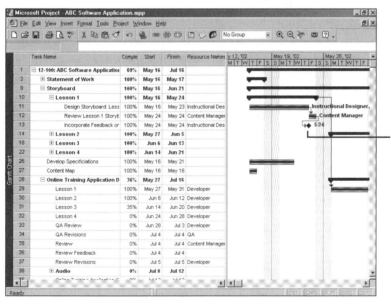

Figure 2.1
Many project managers use a Gantt chart, such as this one in Microsoft Project, to track project milestones.

Jennifer lists creativity, flexibility, and technical aptitude as the three most important skills for her job. As creative director for MediaPro, an instructional technology and services provider, Jennifer directs the interface design, graphics design, and image optimization for MediaPro training projects. Jennifer uses Adobe Photoshop and Macromedia Fireworks to create and optimize images. Her main activities are designing user interfaces, setting the graphic "tone" of projects, and creating graphics.

Jennifer advises, "Always be improving your skills and build a robust portfolio." She also suggests you should practice, practice, practice because the more design work you do, the better your designs will become. "Don't be afraid to experiment with styles," she says. Jennifer has always been a creative person and was fortunate to receive ample encouragement throughout her life. Courses in digital media helped her break into the field and learn to translate her creativity into digital graphics design.

Jennifer Henry is the creative director at MediaPro, Inc.

A graphics designer has an artistic eye, is very creative, and understands graphics file formats. To contribute to an online learning project, the graphics designer must be experienced at optimizing graphics for Web delivery and should be skilled at working with various graphics programs, such as Adobe Photoshop, Macromedia Fireworks, Adobe Illustrator, Macromedia Freehand, or Jasc Paint Shop Pro. Also, it's helpful if the graphics designer is familiar with Web development and can effectively communicate with development staff.

A graphics designer's most important skill is being able to create attractive and appropriate graphic images. He or she has the storyboard to follow, but sometimes must creatively interpret how to present the graphics indicated in the storyboard. The graphics designer must understand and adhere to the *look and feel*, including font and color choices, defined for the project.

In an online learning project, graphics designers need to be knowledgeable about Web optimization techniques and how to ascertain which file format is ideal for each graphic. Most likely, he or she will use the optimization capabilities of a software application such as Adobe Photoshop or Macromedia Fireworks, shown in Figure 2.2, to automate image optimization.

Introducing the Instructional Designer

The instructional designer is a key player on the team, especially during the design phase of the instructional process. This person creates the design documents, including the storyboard, that are used during development to create the online learning application. The instructional designer continues during the development phase as an important consultant, revising the storyboard as necessary and resolving questions about the content.

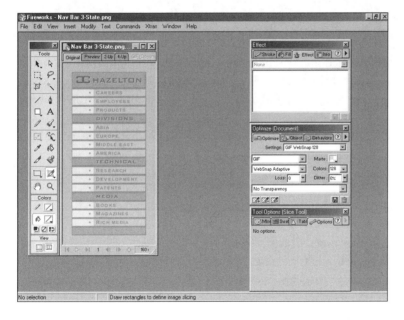

Figure 2.2

Graphics software, such as Macromedia Fireworks, enables the graphics designer to create image elements and optimize them for Web delivery.

Kathleen Peppers, MSgt. Retired USAF, is an instructional designer with the Boeing Company.

Kathleen lists personal energy, the ability to motivate, and good written and oral communication skills as the three most important skills for her job as an instructional designer for the Boeing Company. To make her more efficient at her job, Kathleen uses components of Mentergy Designer's Edge, but mostly uses original tools and documents developed for an individual project. Her main activities are meetings, motivating her team, and planning instructional projects.

Kathleen advises, "Find a seasoned instructional designer and stick to him or her for at least two years. And never be too shy to ask all the questions you can possibly ask." She says that her formal education helped instill the discipline to work a project full circle, but education isn't the only reason for her accomplishments. Kathleen cautions against using the same team members for design and development because it "will always elicit inferior results."

An instructional designer has experience developing instructionally sound online learning. He or she understands instructional methodologies, is creative, and can distill skills and concepts from multiple sources. The instructional designer produces logical and organized design documents. It's extremely important that this team member has good communication skills because they interact with all the other team members as well as the client and the SME (subject matter expert).

An instructional designer often has a graduate degree or certificate in instructional design, educational technology, technical communication, or adult learning. Some instructional designers gained their knowledge through extensive experience instead of academic studies. Either way, this member of the team must know how to design effective, interesting, and meaningful online learning applications and effectively communicate their ideas through the storyboard.

Introducing the Developer

The developer is the team member who gathers up all the assets and design documents and actually puts together the course. Like other team positions, this role can include multiple team members. The development staff might have a lead developer, course architect, and production or junior developers. You probably fulfill this role (or are interested in this role) if you are reading this book! The majority of this book covers the tasks that the developer accomplishes during an online learning application project.

A developer has excellent Web development skills and is an expert at Web-editing software, such as Dreamweaver. He or she can organize an efficient Web file structure and contribute to a meaningful specifications document (covered in Chapter 3, "Establishing the Course Specifications"). The developer is also able to communicate effectively with team members.

Interview with Brandon and Penny Carson: Developers

Brandon (left) and Penny (right) Carson are partners at CarsonMedia, Inc.

Brandon and Penny list flexibility, technical expertise, and time management as the three most important skills for their jobs as developers and partners in CarsonMedia, Inc. Because they own their business, they end up performing many of the roles on an instructional team. For their jobs as developers, they mostly use Flash, Dreamweaver, and database applications. To make them more efficient at their jobs, they also use Outlook, Project, and TimeTrax, a time-punch clock application. Their main activities are meetings, development, and QA (quality assurance).

Penny advises, "A sense of humor is a must!" and she adds, "You must be a jack of all trades and you can never know enough. Keep working with your tools to better yourself." Brandon agrees, "What seems important is gaining a specialized skill set that can be quickly applied in your day-to-day work." Both Carsons value their varied work experiences and often play multiple roles in the instructional process, from project manager to voice talent.

It's important that the developer understands all popular Web technologies, such as image formats, HTML, Dynamic HTML (DHTML), cascading style sheets (CSS), JavaScript, and others. He or she must also have knowledge of Web standards and browser inconsistencies. Developers usually have excellent attention to technical detail, and they need to pay attention to implementing the designs that others, such as the instructional and graphics designers, have created. It's helpful if the developer is proficient at troubleshooting technical issues, too.

Because the majority of this book is a guide for online learning developers, I won't say much more here about what a developer does. The developer does all the things that will be described in subsequent chapters! Online learning developers benefit from understanding instructional concepts, and they can offer invaluable technical input to the instructional designer during storyboard creation.

Introducing the Assets Specialist: Video, Audio, Animation

Adding rich-media assets, such as audio and animation, to online learning can increase the course's effectiveness and learners' retention. Hiring specialists who know how to efficiently create and deliver optimized assets is key to your online learning project appearing polished and professional. Often these professionals have special equipment, such as video cameras or a sound studio.

An assets specialist has experience producing specific asset types: video, audio, or animation. He or she is knowledgeable of best practices and the newest techniques in his or her field. The assets specialist understands and has access to the software and hardware needed to produce the specific assets. It's important that this team member understands how to optimize files for minimum bandwidth use over the Web.

As an audio engineer at Studio 5, Ruppi lists knowledge of audio recording and producing, ability to process digital audio files, and creating a good client relationship as the most important skills for an assets specialist. Ruppi uses WaveFrame and WaveLab along with professional microphones, mixing consoles, and sound-processing gear to create broadcast-quality narration for online learning applications. His main activities are recording and editing audio and mastering CDs.

Ruppi Barnickel is the Chief Engineer at Studio 5 Recording.

Ruppi gained his most practical experience in audio recording by being a studio musician. He also took college classes in audio production and practiced in his home studio. He advises, "Work accurately and be friendly with your customers. Have good ears for clean production, and keep up to date on software and equipment." Ruppi works closely with his clients, and he says it's important to make the client feel comfortable and create the best production atmosphere.

The skills and knowledge of an assets specialist vary, depending on what type of assets your project needs. Although these professionals are often expensive to hire (if you do not have the in-house capabilities), they usually work quickly and produce professional-quality assets that are worth the dent they make in the project budget.

Introducing the Training Champion

"Training champion" isn't an official job title, but I wanted to include this team member because he or she influences the amount of resources allocated for your online learning projects. If you have this person in your organization, you know that he or she is instrumental in guiding the organization's training effort. The training champion has enough influence in the organization to make sure that training is considered an important focus in the organization. This person could have many different titles, from president of the company to training manager to lead developer. It's not the title that matters, but the passion and commitment this individual brings to the company's training efforts.

Mark Moore, the Manager of Technical Education at AT&T Wireless, lists the abilities to communicate and prioritize as most important for his job. "The bottom line for us is that if we can't show how a project, task, or initiative supports the organization's goals and objectives, we don't expend our valuable resources on it." Mark's position also requires him to organize people and work to enable high productivity; he strives to balance cost, schedule, and training effectiveness. "If the learners don't learn, it doesn't matter how much money it saves, or how quickly it was delivered."

Mark Moore is Manager of Technical Education at AT&T Wireless.

Mark has performed virtually all of the instructional roles at one time or another in his career. He uses Microsoft Outlook, Office, and Project along with custom tools for his job. He also uses a PDA (portable digital assistant) and, of course, a wireless phone. Mark attributes his success to having the good fortune to work with very talented and enthusiastic people. He adds, "AT&T Wireless Services hires and develops the best people in the world. Check out our opportunities at http://jobsearch1.attws.com/jobs."

The training champion drives the company's investment in training because training increases competitiveness and profitability. He or she is also tenacious and dedicated, has clout in the organization, and has influence over budgets and other resources. The training champion has a passion for training, is friendly, and has a knack for bringing people together.

If you do not yet have a training champion, you should try to recruit someone or become one yourself. Do you really believe that training is important to the bottom line? Are you passionate and able to influence others in the organization? If so, you'd make a wonderful training champion.

If you are an online learning development company, you want to discover a company's training champion and make him or her your client! You won't have to convince this person how important training is to the organization. Instead, you can spend your time explaining to this person how you can fulfill his or her targeted needs. Again, if this person doesn't exist, try to groom and mentor someone to fulfill this important role.

Working Together

Did you notice that many of the roles require the ability to communicate well? When working in a team environment, good communication skills are always a valuable trait. Team members do not need to be best friends, but they do need to get along, act professionally, and always treat each other with respect.

Another valuable trait, or maybe we can call it a habit, is the ability to meet deadlines. You might be called on to finish a task before you think it's completed perfectly just to meet a deadline. Although leaving a task in a state that you believe is less than perfect is always hard, it might be necessary for you to move on to another task to complete the project on time. Remember that you can always improve the project later during the revision cycle.

Introducing Tools

Developing online learning applications requires appropriate software tools to get the job done efficiently. Talented developers using the best tools do not automatically make good training applications. However, developers working with an instructionally sound, creative design can make a robust training application. The lesson: Developers create a great training application from a great design.

You need to assemble the software and hardware tools necessary to produce the training application. You'll need Dreamweaver, as well as tools to produce course assets, such as sound, video, and graphics editing software. You might need to purchase server software or investigate a Web hosting service to house your final application.

This book presents development techniques for Dreamweaver MX—the most recent release of Dreamweaver. You'll supplement your developer's toolbox with various extensions that can be downloaded from the Internet. Most of the techniques in this book can be accomplished with Dreamweaver 4 or UltraDev 4 too.

Power User Tip

I've always found that candy, like M&Ms or little Snickers bars, helps build relationships with team members. If I call someone over to my desk to help me work through a problem, the atmosphere is always improved when chocolate is present.

Getting a Quick Look at Dreamweaver

Dreamweaver is arguably the best Web editor on the market. It excels at creating interactive Web pages using DHTML. Dreamweaver is a mature product that is considered a professional Web development tool, suitable for creating high-quality Web sites. Dreamweaver is the Web editing tool you will use to create and manage your online learning application. You'll use Dreamweaver to put together the user interface and create the templates you use during course production.

Power User Tip

Here's a shameless plug for another of my books! If you are a new Dreamweaver user, you might want to read my book *Sams Teach Yourself Macromedia Dreamweaver MX in 24 Hours*. This book covers all the fundamentals of Dreamweaver.

Macromedia sells Dreamweaver by itself or as part of a software suite. You can purchase Dreamweaver bundled with other Macromedia products, such as Flash, Authorware, Fireworks, or Freehand. Many of the Macromedia products have compatible file formats. For example, graphics created in Fireworks can be inserted automatically into a Web page created in Dreamweaver.

This book presents the workspace for Dreamweaver MX. If you chose the Dreamweaver 4 workspace option when you installed Dreamweaver MX, you might want to change to the Dreamweaver MX workspace. To change your workspace, select Dreamweaver Preferences (Edit, Preferences), select the General category, and click on the Change Workspace button. The Workspace Setup dialog box enables you to choose either the Dreamweaver MX or Dreamweaver 4 workspace.

You'll do most of your work in Dreamweaver in the *Document window*, shown in Figure 2.3. This visual Web editing environment is where you add text, assets, interactions, and everything that will make up your Web pages. Dreamweaver contains a number of *panels* that enable you to change the attributes of objects on the page. One special panel, the *Property inspector*, displays the attributes of any object you have selected in the Document window.

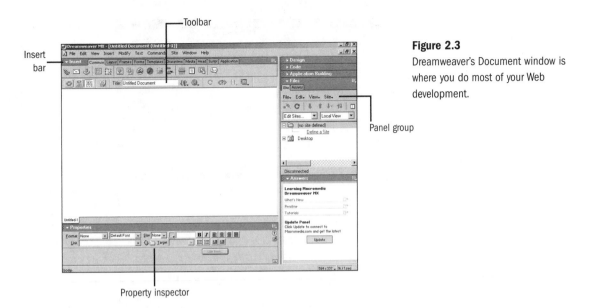

Toolbar

Insert
bar

Figure 2.3

Dreamweaver's Document window is
where you do most of your Web
development.

Panel group

Property inspector

Dreamweaver doesn't require you to write HTML, but it's helpful to
know some HTML to implement some of the advanced HTML necessary to create interactive Web pages. The tag selector in the status
bar of the Document window, shown in Figure 2.4, shows the tag
hierarchy of a selected object. The tag on the right is nested within
the tags listed to the left of it in the tag selector.

There are three ways you can view the Web page in the Document
window. By default, the Document window is in *Design view*.
Design view presents the Web page as it will appear in the Web
browser. Dreamweaver also enables you to easily view the HTML
code in *Code view*. The split *Code and Design view* displays both
Code view and Design view in the Document window, as shown in
Figure 2.5.

Power User Tip

Here are a few user interface tips
for users of previous Dreamweaver
versions: The Insert bar is what
used to be the Object panel; all
the panels are now docked on the
right side of the screen; and the
Property inspector is docked at
the bottom of the screen.

Figure 2.4

The tag selector shows the tag hierarchy for the object selected in the Document window (a table cell <td> in a table row <tr> in a table <table> in the body <body> of a Web page).

Tag selector

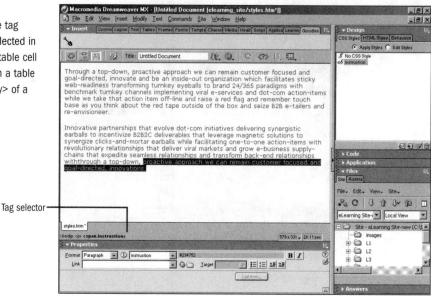

Figure 2.5

Dreamweaver's split Code and Design view displays both Code view and Design view in the Document window.

Show Code and Design view button

Show Design view button

Show Code view button

Code view

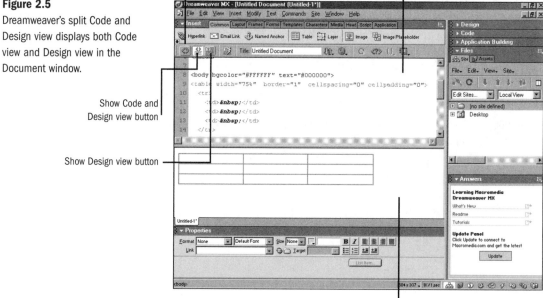

Design view

Regular and Dynamic Web Pages

Macromedia merged the functionality of the two previous Dreamweaver products, Dreamweaver and Dreamweaver UltraDev, into Dreamweaver MX. Dreamweaver UltraDev was an advanced version of Dreamweaver enabling you to create dynamic database-driven Web pages. Now there is a single version of Dreamweaver and the dynamic capabilities are part of Dreamweaver MX.

Regular Web pages are pages that do not contain server-side scripting that cause the page to change based on data in a database or on user input. The majority of the pages in this book will be regular Web pages. These regular Web pages end with the .html file extension. To create a regular Web page, select the New command (File, New) and select the Basic Page category. A regular Web page is created by selecting an HTML document, as shown in Figure 2.6.

Dreamweaver MX can also produce dynamic Web pages, pages that are modified by the Web server before sending the Web page to the learner's browser. You'll explore creating dynamic Web pages later in Chapter 13, "Creating and Tracking a Dynamic Web Site." Dynamic Web pages end with different file extensions depending on the type of server-side scripting that is used; examples include .jsp, .asp, .aspx, and .cfm.

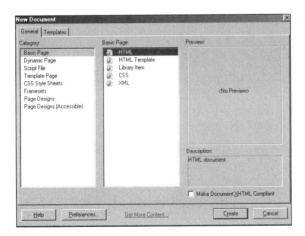

Figure 2.6

Create a regular Web page by selecting an HTML document from the Basic category.

Your decision to use regular or dynamic Web pages is based on the functionality required in your online learning application. You'll use dynamic Web pages if you need to generate Web pages that display data from a database. You can also use Dreamweaver MX to create Web pages that track users in your online learning application; you'll learn more about this feature in Part V, "Tracking the User."

To create dynamic pages, you select one of the choices from the Dynamic Page category of the New Document dialog box, shown in Figure 2.7. You select the dynamic format based on the application server and scripting language that your project will use (more about this in Chapter 13). To work with dynamic pages in Dreamweaver MX you also must set the application server and scripting language in the site definition. You'll define a site for regular Web pages in Chapter 4, "Creating a New Web Site Definition."

Dynamic pages are based on server-side processing technologies, so you will not be able to view the finished Web page without viewing the dynamic Web page from a server. Developers often install a personal or desktop version of Web server software to facilitate developing and testing dynamic Web pages. This makes creating Web pages and testing them a little more complicated.

Figure 2.7

Create a dynamic Web page by selecting one of the dynamic formats from the Dynamic category.

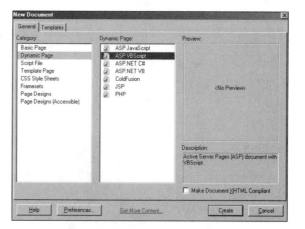

Dreamweaver enables you to view the actual dynamic data from the database right in the Document window. When you select Live Data view in a properly configured site, you will see the page displayed with real data. This feature makes it easier to design dynamic Web pages because you can see what your Web pages will look like and can be sure they are displayed attractively.

Macromedia Exchange

Macromedia hosts a Web site catalog of extensions to their popular software programs Dreamweaver, Flash, and Fireworks called the Macromedia Exchange. It's located on the Web at http://www.macromedia.com/exchange/dreamweaver/. After logging on to the site, you can search, download, and rate various extensions. Some of these extensions were created by Macromedia, but many were created by developers who want to share with others in the developer community.

Extensions are packaged in a special file format called an extension package file (with the .mxp file extension). You install extension package files into Dreamweaver with the Macromedia Extension Manager. The Extension Manager installs all the files contained in the package file into the proper Dreamweaver directories. It's a small software application installed automatically when you install Dreamweaver on your computer.

If you haven't already installed the CourseBuilder extension, now is the perfect time! You'll need CourseBuilder for Part IV of this book, "Using CourseBuilder." In your browser, open the Macromedia Exchange for Dreamweaver site. Create a username and password if you haven't already; you must log in to download extensions. Browse the Learning category by selecting it from the drop-down menu at the top of the main page, shown in Figure 2.8.

Power User Tip

Most of the extensions on the Macromedia Exchange site have traditionally been free, but some extension developers are now charging for their work. Supporting extension developer's work is important to ensure the public availability of these tools in the future. Often the price of the extension is small compared to the increase in efficiency.

Figure 2.8

Select the Learning extensions from
the drop-down menu at the top of
the main page of the Macromedia
Exchange site for Dreamweaver.

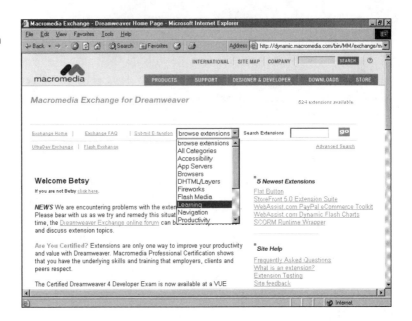

Select CourseBuilder for Dreamweaver from the list of learning
extensions. The CourseBuilder Web page describes the Course-
Builder extension and includes links to a discussion area, product
ratings, and extension download. Select the appropriate download
format (Windows or Macintosh extension package file) and save the
file to your local hard drive.

Open the Macromedia Extension Manager. This separate application is launched either from the Start menu or from the Commands
menu in Dreamweaver (Commands, Manager Extensions). Click the
Install button on the left side of the toolbar or choose the Install command from the File menu. The Extension Manager installs all the
CourseBuilder files into the correct directories in Dreamweaver.
Information about the extension, including how to access the commands, is listed in the bottom half of the Extension Manager, as
shown in Figure 2.9.

Install button

Figure 2.9
The Extension Manager facilitates installing extensions to Dreamweaver.

Installing the CourseBuilder extension into Dreamweaver creates a new tab in the Insert bar: the Learning tab. Select the Learning tab and you'll see the CourseBuilder Object. Follow the same procedure to download and install the Learning Site extension.

CourseBuilder

CourseBuilder, an extension to Dreamweaver, enables rapid development of interactions (multiple-choice, text-entry, drag-and-drop, and explore) and interactive elements (sliders, buttons, and timers). Macromedia created CourseBuilder and makes it available as a free download from the Macromedia Exchange site. Part IV covers how to use CourseBuilder to add interactive content and assessments to your online learning application.

After you've installed CourseBuilder into Dreamweaver, you'll be able to add CourseBuilder objects to your Web pages. In Course-Builder, you enter settings into a wizard interface to create interactions. A powerful customization tool, a part of CourseBuilder called the Action Manager, enables you to change the default settings and functionality. You can add a CourseBuilder interaction to both regular and dynamic Web pages.

To use CourseBuilder, you first create and save a Web page in Dreamweaver. You add a CourseBuilder object to the Web page by selecting the CourseBuilder object from the Learning tab on the Insert bar (or choose the CourseBuilder Interaction command from the Insert menu). The CourseBuilder Gallery, shown in Figure 2.10, enables you to insert one of the many different CourseBuilder interactions.

After you select one of the interaction types, you enter information about the interaction into several tabbed pages of the CourseBuilder wizard. The last tab in all the interactions, the Action Manager tab, is where you customize the way the interaction works.

You're going to use the CourseBuilder interactions later in this book. You also will do a lot of customization when you explore using the Action Manager in Chapter 11, "Conquering CourseBuilder's Action Manager." After you have customized an interaction, you can save it to the Gallery to use repeatedly and share the custom interaction with other members of your team.

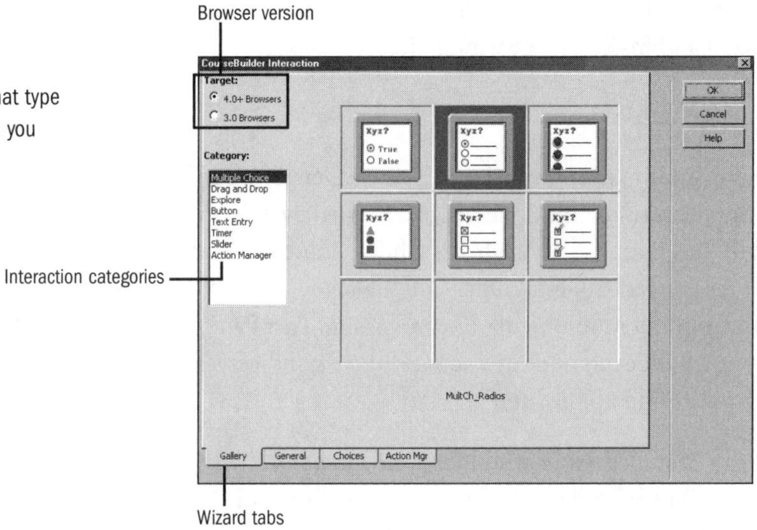

Figure 2.10

In the Gallery, you select what type of CourseBuilder interaction you insert in the Web page.

Summary

In this chapter, you learned about the responsibilities and skills of the team members involved in an online learning project. You also met some real-life individuals who perform those roles. You then were introduced to the tools you'll use to develop an online learning application in this book. You familiarized yourself with the Dreamweaver and CourseBuilder interfaces after installing the CourseBuilder extension to Dreamweaver using the Extension Manager. You also explored the Macromedia Exchange Web site.

IN THIS CHAPTER

chapter 3

Establishing the Course Specifications

THE COURSE SPECIFICATIONS DOCUMENT, usually simply called the "spec," details the technical requirements necessary to view a specific online learning application. It's best if you document all the course specifications. Often, during development, questions arise or team members have to solve a technical dilemma. The course specification document helps target development toward the audience identified during the analysis phase of the ADDIE process, answering questions and keeping the team on track.

The specifications document also can be given to learners so they can be sure they have the appropriate software and hardware to view your online learning application. Most courses either present a list of the minimum requirements necessary to run the course or test the learner's computer. It's important that the learner is told before beginning the course that they don't meet the requirements for the course so that they can address any problems. It's disruptive to learners to find out they don't have the correct browser type or a required player while they are in the middle of the course.

In Chapter 1, "Instructional Design 101," you explored planning the entire instructional project. Creating the course specifications comes during the planning stage of the development phase in the ADDIE process. What bandwidth does eLearning require? Does the storyboard call for rich media elements that require special players? You need to answer these as well as other questions before starting development.

The course specification document usually evolves throughout the project's prototyping phase. By the time you are into the full-fledged development of the course, the course specifications should be solid and well defined. Documenting the course specifications can also help get new members of the team quickly up to speed on the development of the online learning application.

In this chapter, you will understand the following:

- What to consider when creating course specifications
- How to specify browser types and versions
- How to open the online learning application in a new browser window
- What to consider when specifying the minimum computer requirements for the course

Creating a Specifications Document

There are many decisions to make on the course specifications. When "spec-ing out" the online learning application, you create a document that will evolve as your project evolves. This document might grow to include a style guide, a content naming guide, and a map of how the course is organized.

You will collect information about the audience for the online learning application, the technical environment where the learning application will be housed, and the types of content that the instructional designers have included in the course design. You'll use this information to guide the development of the online learning application. For example, if the course design specifies that audio narration will be included on each page, the template you develop will need to include a way of launching and controlling audio files. Or, you might be lucky enough to have a single browser type that is predominate among learners so you can develop with only a single browser in mind.

Figure 3.1 shows the eLearning Application Specifications Worksheet that I use to begin collecting course specifications. This worksheet covers eight major areas of technical specifications that need to be addressed before beginning development. Your project might not need all these areas, and you might need to address other areas unique to your project or your corporate environment.

Each of the eight major areas are covered in this chapter. They are Browsers, Players, Bandwidth, Applicable Web Standards, Target Browser Window Size, Operating Systems, Supporting Technologies, and Computer specifications. At the end of the chapter you'll see the specifications for the sample course that will be created in this book.

Specifying Browsers

Whether developing a regular Web site or an online learning application, most difficulties are caused by the major browsers having different implementations of Web technologies. Although the World Wide Web Consortium (W3C) provides HTML specifications, browser manufacturers either ignore the specifications or interpret them in different ways. You'll need to weigh the makeup of your target audience along with the technical requirements of your eLearning application when specifying the browser types and versions.

Figure 3.1

This eLearning Application Specifications Worksheet helps you document course specifications.

---

eLearning Application Specifications Worksheet

1. Browsers

	Browser Type	Version(s)	%
☐	Microsoft Internet Explorer	_____	____
☐	Netscape Navigator	_____	____
☐	AOL	_____	____
☐	WebTV	_____	____
☐	Opera	_____	____
☐	Other:_____	_____	____

2. Players

Content Type	Player Name	Plug-in	ActiveX
Audio			
Video	_____	☐	☐
Movies/Animation	_____	☐	☐
Other:	_____	☐	☐
Other:	_____	☐	☐
Other:	_____	☐	☐

3. Bandwidth

	Connection Speed	%
☐	T3	____
☐	T1	____
☐	ISDN	____
☐	Cable Modem	____
☐	DSL	____
☐	56 Kbps Modem	____
☐	28.8 Kbps Modem	____

4. Applicable Web Standards (Company or intranet)

Standard	Value
Maximum page size	_____
Default page name	_____
HTML Version	_____
Web Server Type	_____
CSS file	_____
	_____
	_____

5. Target Browser Window Size

Value
Screen Resolution   _____ x _____
Open New Window? ☐ Yes ☐ No
New window size   _____ x _____

6. Operating Systems

	Operating System	%
☐	Windows 95/98	____
☐	Windows Me	____
☐	Windows 2000	____
☐	Windows XP	____
☐	Mac OS9	____
☐	Mac OS10 (OSX)	____
☐	UNIX _____	____
☐	Others:_____	____

7. Supporting Technologies

	Technology	Version(s)
☐	Cookies	
☐	VBScript	_____
☐	JavaScript	_____
☐	ASP	_____
☐	JSP	_____
☐	CFML	_____
☐	ASP .NET	_____
☐	PHP	_____
☐		_____
☐		_____

8. Computer

	Hardware/Settings	Minimum
☐	Sound Card	
☐	CD-ROM Drive	
☐	DVD-ROM Drive	
☐	_____	
☐	_____	

Color Resolution ☐ 8 bit ☐ 16 bit ☐ 24 bit ☐ 32 bit
Processor Speed   _____
RAM   _____
Disk Space   _____

© 2002 Betsy Bruce eLearning

---

eLearning with Dreamweaver MX: Building Online Learning Applications

HTML 4 began being implemented in IE4 and Netscape 4. Browser versions have continued to increment, while HTML 4 (specifically HTML 4.01) remains the last HTML specification from the W3C. The version 4 browsers did not implement the entire HTML 4 specification and continue to catch up to the W3C recommendations. It is coincidence that the HTML specifications version is the same number as the browser versions.

Designing for version 4 browsers remains a common browser specification, targeting the fundamental DHTML capabilities of the first browser version to implement the HTML 4 specification. Many Web applications are created specifically for IE 5, IE 5.5, IE 6, and Netscape 6, and some teams will choose to specify new browser versions as they are released.

The advent of the W3C's HTML 4 specification, outlining the components of Dynamic Hypertext Markup Language (DHTML), made it possible to create interactive Web pages useful for learning applications. Although online learning applications could be created before HTML 4 arrived, this book will concentrate on the capabilities of more modern browsers. HTML 4 was mostly put into action in the version 4 browsers, such as Internet Explorer (IE) 4 and Navigator 4.

When you specify the browser type(s) (Internet Explorer, Netscape, and so on) for which your online learning application is created, you also must include the version number in the specification because browser manufacturers change the functionality from version to version. You'll build your online learning application to a certain current browser specification, but you should test your application on new browser versions as they are released. Be sure you update your learners on whether the application's functionality is supported by any new browser versions. For example, Netscape drastically changed its browser from version 4.7 to version 6, removing support for previously supported custom tags.

Examining Browser Statistics

You'll deliver the online learning application to a public or a private audience. If it's a public audience, you'll probably deliver over the Internet to an audience you have very little technical influence over. You'll need to conduct careful testing to verify that your application works on a variety of browsers and browser versions. If you are delivering your online training application via a CD-ROM, you can deliver the browser software along with the application on the CD (with permission from the browser creator, of course). You should build in a browser-detection feature to inform learners about changes they need to make to their browser or computer to run the online learning application.

More than 20 Web browsers are available, but these are the major ones:

- Microsoft Internet Explorer
- Netscape Navigator

Minor ones:

- Opera
- AOL Web Browser
- WebTV

Many developers build for the two major browsers—Internet Explorer and Netscape Navigator—and then regularly test on the other browsers. As of this writing, Internet Explorer has the majority of browser market share, with Netscape Navigator running a distant second. Other browser types have less than a couple of percentage points of market share. Unless your research shows a significant base of learners using one of the minor browser types, you can probably get by not supporting them for your online learning application. If your research shows that a large number of potential learners are AOL users, you probably will want to support the AOL browser.

If you have a Web site, your Web administrator can give you statistics on which browser versions are used to access the site. The browser statistics for my Web site are shown in Figure 3.2. Are these same viewers the audience for your online learning application? If so, these statistics are more useful than the general statistics available for the entire Internet population. You can find the current browser statistics for a sample Web site at www.thecounter.com/stats/.

You'll have the fewest compatibility issues when you deliver to a private audience, such as a group of employees on an intranet or in

Website Statistics Report for betsybruce.com

	Browser Type	Number of page requests	Number of page requests in the past seven days	Percentage of page requests in the past seven days
1.	**MSIE**	**6,344**	**1,108**	**88.42%**
	MSE/5	3,716	649	51.80%
	MSIE/6	2,542	439	35.3%
	MSIE/4	76	11	0.88%
2.	**Netscape**	**389**	**45**	**3.60%**
	Netscape/4	274	34	2.71%
	Netscape/3	45	6	0.48%
	Netscape/6	70	5	0.40%
3.	**Netscape (compatible)**	**246**	**25**	**1.100%**
4.	**Googlebot**	**115**	**24**	**1.91%**
	Googlebot/2	115	24	1.91%
5.	**Gulliver**	**13**	**13**	**1.3%**
	Gulliver/1	13	13	1.3%
6.	**FAST-WebCrawler**	**58**	**9**	**0.71%**
	FAST-WebCrawler/3	58	9	0.71%
7.	**Internet Ninja 6.0**	**12**	**8**	**0.63%**
8.	**Opera**	**48**	**5**	**0.40%**
	Opera/6	42	5	0.40%
9.	**BaiduSpider**	**8**	**4**	**0.31%**
10.	**Netscape**	**76**	**3**	**0.23%**
11.	**ia_archiver**	**8**	**2**	**0.17%**
12.	**Search.ch V1.4.2 (spiderman@search.ch; http://www)**	**2**	**2**	**0.17%**
	search.ch V1.4.2 (spiderman@search.ch; http://www)	2	2	0.17%
13.	**Microsoft URL Control- 6.00.8169**	**1**	**1**	**0.9%**
14.	**EmailSiphon**	**2**	**1**	**0.9%**
15.	**Java1.4.0**	**1**	**1**	**0.9%**
	[not llisted: 33]	63	2	0.17%

Figure 3.2

A browser statistics report lists the browser types and versions for the visitors to a Web site.

a controlled training room. Fortunately, many online learning applications are developed for this type of audience. Most companies specify a certain browser and browser version as their company standard. You can count on your audience having this software installed on their computer.

Newer browser versions add features that an experienced Web developer can use while developing an online learning application. Sometimes new features are superfluous, but at times, newer features can save a lot of development time. The time savings and added functionality may justify recommending browser upgrades to a large group of people (such as a browser upgrade for an entire company). Often, this type of change requires a lot of planning, so you should make your recommendations as early as possible.

Power User Tip

Just because a company standardizes on a specific browser doesn't mean a learner is using that browser. Sometimes employees download their own favorite browser instead of using the company standard browser. The good news is that these employees probably have the standard browser installed but aren't using it. You need to detect which browser they are using and direct them to use the correct browser if they aren't already.

Exploring Browser Differences

The more complicated you make your online learning application, the more likely you are to run into browser incompatibilities. This book introduces development techniques that degrade gracefully, meaning they will not cause huge problems for learners using incompatible browsers.

DHTML is an extension of HTML that enables greater control over page layout and positioning. DTHML also enables you to create learner interactions such as drag-and-drop questions, hotspots, and animations. Dynamic HTML is not an official term; it's an informal definition used by Web developers to mean the combination of HTML 4, JavaScript, and cascading style sheets (CSS).

You run into the majority of the incompatibilities between browsers when creating the following:

- **Dreamweaver layers:** Layers are implemented with the <div> tag. The attributes of this tag vary among browser types. You'll use layers to position elements on the Web page.

- **Table attributes:** Attributes, such as table borders, differ between various browser types. You'll use tables to position content in Web pages.

- **Browser events:** Events, such as a mouseover on a button or a click on an image, might or might not be available in the browser version the learner uses. You'll use events to capture learner input and interactions with the online learning application.

- **Cascading style sheets (CSS):** The CSS specification is interpreted differently among browser types. You'll use CSS to format text and position elements on the Web page.

For the project in this book, we'll specify that the application will work in Internet Explorer 4+ (IE 4, IE 5, IE 5.5, and IE 6) and Netscape Navigator 4. Figure 3.3 shows the Browsers section of the eLearning Application Specifications Worksheet with this

	Browser Type	Version(s)	%
☑	Microsoft Internet Explorer	4, 5, 5.5, 6	~80
☑	Netscape Navigator	4	~20
☐	AOL		
☐	WebTV		
☐	Opera		
☐	Other:_____		

Figure 3.3
The Browsers section of the eLearning Application Specifications Worksheet shows the specified browsers for the sample course in this book.

information filled in. This is a common specification for corporate training delivered to a mixed browser base. Many of my projects have specified an individual version of Internet Explorer (versions 4, 5, 5.5, or 6) because Internet Explorer is currently the dominant browser software and many corporations use it as their browser standard. It's never a good idea to develop separate applications for each of the major browser types, Internet Explorer and Netscape; this duplicate development is very time consuming. Instead, identify common capabilities and carefully test on each browser type.

If you are a beginning Web developer, you might not be familiar with the browser differences and incompatibilities. It's important that you test everything in all specified browser versions. The Check Target Browsers command (File, Check Page, Check Target Browsers) enables you to check whether the tags and tag attributes you've used in your online learning application are supported by different browsers. Dreamweaver contains definitions for all the major browser versions, shown in Figure 3.4, and you can download and install new definitions as new browsers are released. Run this report on your site often.

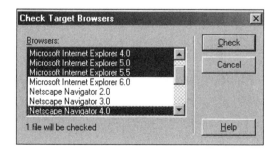

Figure 3.4
Dreamweaver enables you to select the browser types and versions to run the Check Target Browsers report.

Specifying a single browser and developing to that browser is the most efficient way of creating an online learning application. You need to test only to that browser, and you don't need to work around the browser incompatibilities you will inevitably encounter. If you have the freedom to specify a single browser—for example, your company's standard browser—you will have a faster and easier time developing online learning.

Some users might be inconvenienced, but creating learning applications is somewhat different from creating Web sites. Your learners will not surf to your learning application. They have usually paid for a course, or it's required for their job, or they are interested in the topic. Letting learners know what they are required to do for the best learning experience is preferable to having them encounter problems during the course.

Specifying Players

A *player* is a program that adds functionality to a Web browser. The Netscape browser began supporting plug-ins, applications installed so that non-native browser content can be viewed in the browser window. The plug-in functionality in Netscape Navigator is mirrored by ActiveX controls in Internet Explorer. I'll call the combination of plug-ins and ActiveX controls *players*. Popular players include Adobe Acrobat Reader, Macromedia Flash, Macromedia Shockwave, QuickTime, RealPlayer, and others.

Power User Tip

Dreamweaver automatically adds the code required for both plug-ins (the **<embed>** tag) and ActiveX controls (the **<object>** tag) when you use the Flash or Shockwave objects.

In versions of Internet Explorer prior to IE 6 (and some versions of IE 5.5), you could install plug-ins. In IE 6, Microsoft disabled IE's capability to use plug-ins to display non-native browser content in favor of exclusive use of Microsoft's own ActiveX technology. Most players are available as both an ActiveX control and Netscape plug-in. You should check that the type of player, plug-in or ActiveX control, is available for the browser versions you've specified.

Our Company Doesn't Support Players, but We Want to Use Flash in Our Course. Any Suggestions?

Many operating systems and browser installations include the Flash player. Of course, your IT department might have a custom installation that excludes the player. You can do an analysis of some target machines to determine whether the Flash player is installed. The easiest way to check this is to load the Test Macromedia Shockwave and Flash Players Web page at www.macromedia.com/shockwave/welcome/. You might find out that many users have the Flash player installed anyway.

Some companies are concerned about the security implications of some players and don't allow users to install these players from the Internet. You could allow users to install the players from your intranet instead, or you could ask your system administrators to install the player to users' machines during an upcoming software update.

The sample course in this book includes Macromedia Flash and Authorware content. To view the course, learners will need to have downloaded and installed the correct player for their browsers. Learners using Netscape will need to have the Flash and Authorware plug-ins installed, and learners using IE will need the ActiveX controls installed. Figure 3.5 shows the Players section of the eLearning Application Specifications Worksheet with this information filled in.

2. Players

Content Type	Player Name	Plug-in	ActiveX
Audio		☐	☐
Video		☐	☐
Movies/Animation	Flash MX	☑	☑
Other:	Authorware 6	☑	☑
Other:		☐	☐
Other:		☐	☐

Figure 3.5
The Players section of the eLearning Application Specifications Worksheet shows the specified players for the sample course in this book.

Specifying Bandwidth

You deliver an online learning application over the Internet or an intranet. The bandwidth available to learners is an important consideration for your online training application. *Bandwidth* is the amount of information that can be transferred over a certain amount of time. Think of bandwidth as the diameter of the pipe through which your online training application will be delivered; the bigger the pipe, the larger the size of the content you can deliver.

Bandwidth varies with the type of connection a learner has to the Internet. Bandwidth also varies from moment to moment, depending on network congestion. Common bandwidth measurements are as follows:

- **T3, T1:** Very high-speed connections usually available at commercial business sites

- **Integrated Services Digital Network (ISDN), cable modem, Digital Subscriber Line (DSL):** High-speed connections usually available at small businesses or homes

- **56Kbps modem:** Currently the highest speed modem connection

- **28.8Kbps modem:** Lower speed modem connection

To put bandwidth in perspective, remember that even a T1 connection to the Internet is only as fast as a single-speed CD-ROM drive.

In an online learning application, the majority of the content is text (HTML code), Flash animations, and graphics. The file size of the HTML code is usually small and quick to download on any type of connection. Flash animations are usually small if they use the native vector graphics drawing format in Flash. *Vector graphics* are created by using a mathematical language instead of mapping pixels in an image. Graphical image files can be large and must be optimized before they are referenced in a Web page. *Graphic optimization* is the process of comparing different graphics formats and graphics attributes, such as the number of colors or the amount of compression, to come up with the smallest file that is still attractive.

When learners encounter a single Web page in your online learning application, their browser downloads the HTML code associated with that page and then downloads all the graphics and other files associated with the Web page. These files are downloaded into the browser's *cache*, a directory on the learner's hard drive that is a temporary storage area for Web sites viewed in the browser. When you view a Web page, you are actually viewing on your hard drive, not the Internet. Because the files in the cache remain for a finite period (depending on what the user sets in browser preferences), users don't have to download the same files multiple times.

Your online learning application can also include audio or video, files that usually take a lot of bandwidth to play. Browsers don't play audio or video, so a browser player handles this type of content, or the browser launches an application to deal with the content. Audio files are usually narration, music, or sound effects. Popular compressed audio formats are MP3, QuickTime, Windows Media Player (WMP), RealAudio, and Flash audio-only movies. Video files usually demonstrate visual procedures. Popular compressed formats are QuickTime, Windows Media Player, and RealVideo.

You can calculate the minimum bandwidth that your course requires by examining a representative Web page. As you create Web pages in Dreamweaver, the status bar, shown in Figure 3.6, displays an estimate of the size of the Web page, including graphics and other files, and how long it will take to download.

Power User Tip

Unless video really adds information that cannot effectively be presented with any other method, I don't usually suggest using it, even if you already have the video and can inexpensively compress it for the Internet. The educational value of video often is not worth the amount of bandwidth it requires. Consider using audio along with a still photo, graphic, or animation. Video of "talking heads" should be avoided.

Total page size

Download time (at 56Kbps)

Figure 3.6

The status bar displays the size of the Web page and the time it will take to download at a specified connection speed.

This estimate is based on the Connection Speed setting in the Status Bar category of Dreamweaver preferences (Edit, Preferences). The Status Bar preferences, shown in Figure 3.7, enable you to set the connection speed that Dreamweaver used to calculate the download time displayed in the status bar. You can also run a report, described in Chapter 17, giving file download times for a group of Web pages.

Figure 3.7

The Status Bar preferences enables you to set the target bandwidth so Dreamweaver can calculate the estimated download time of the current page.

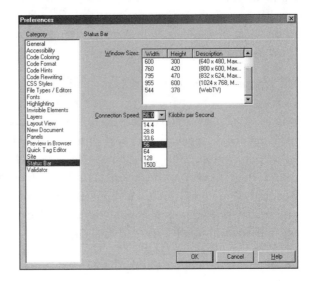

The sample learning application in this book is geared toward learners on an intranet (*not Internet*), so the bandwidth specification is T1 or T3 speeds. However, you'll also specify that some learners can access the online learning application from home or on the road at 56Kbps modem speed, so develop with a consideration for these learners, too. This is a common specification for corporate training applications, where the majority of learners are in the corporate environment with some learners—salespeople, for example—who are external. Figure 3.8 shows the Bandwidth section of the eLearning Application Specifications Worksheet with the bandwidth specifications filled in.

Figure 3.8

The Bandwidth section of the eLearning Application Specifications Worksheet shows the target bandwidth for the sample course in this book.

3. Bandwidth

	Connection Speed	%
☑	T3	~98
☐	T1	____
☐	ISDN	____
☐	Cable Modem	____
☐	DSL	____
☑	56 Kbps Modem	~2
☐	28.8 Kbps Modem	____

Specifying Applicable Web Standards

Before you embark on developing an online learning application, you'll want to check out any company standards that could affect your course specifications. You also might have to ask for special consideration from your Web administration team because online learning tends to be more media rich than regular Web sites.

The eLearning Application Specifications Worksheet, as seen in Figure 3.9, has some suggestions of Web standards to investigate:

- **Maximum page size:** The total of all the files involved in delivering a single Web page, including all graphics and other assets.

- **Default page name:** The Web server has a default page name that you can use so that you only need to reference the directory and the default page will load. It is usually index.html, index.htm, or default.htm.

- **HTML Version:** Specifies whether the eLearning application will support DHTML.

4. Applicable Web Standards (Company or intranet)	
Standard	**Value**
Maximum page size	75 kb
Default page name	index.html
HTML Version	HTML 4
Web Server Type	MS Windows 2000
CSS file	

Figure 3.9

The Applicable Web Standards section of the eLearning Application Specifications Worksheet shows the Web standards for the sample course in this book.

- **Web Server Type:** The Web Server software from which the final eLearning application will be served.

- **CSS file:** Some companies have a standard CSS file that can be referenced to get common styles. You'll learn more about CSS in Chapter 5, "Defining Cascading Style Sheets."

Some Web development groups specify the maximum size of each Web page. For example, they might limit the total size of all the files necessary to display a single Web page to 40KB. In the case of our sample course, we aren't deferring to any corporate standards. Considering there are some learners with 56Kbps modems, the course will adhere to individual Web pages totaling no more than 75KB.

This limit ensures that each Web page will take no more than 10 seconds or so to download under ideal connection conditions.

Specifying the Target Browser Window Size

The typical browser window is composed of the canvas, where you view a Web page, and the browser chrome. The browser *chrome*, shown in Figure 3.10, takes up a significant amount of space on the computer screen. The browser toolbars, status bar, personal bars, and menu bars all constitute browser chrome. The chrome shrinks the size of the canvas where you display your online learning application.

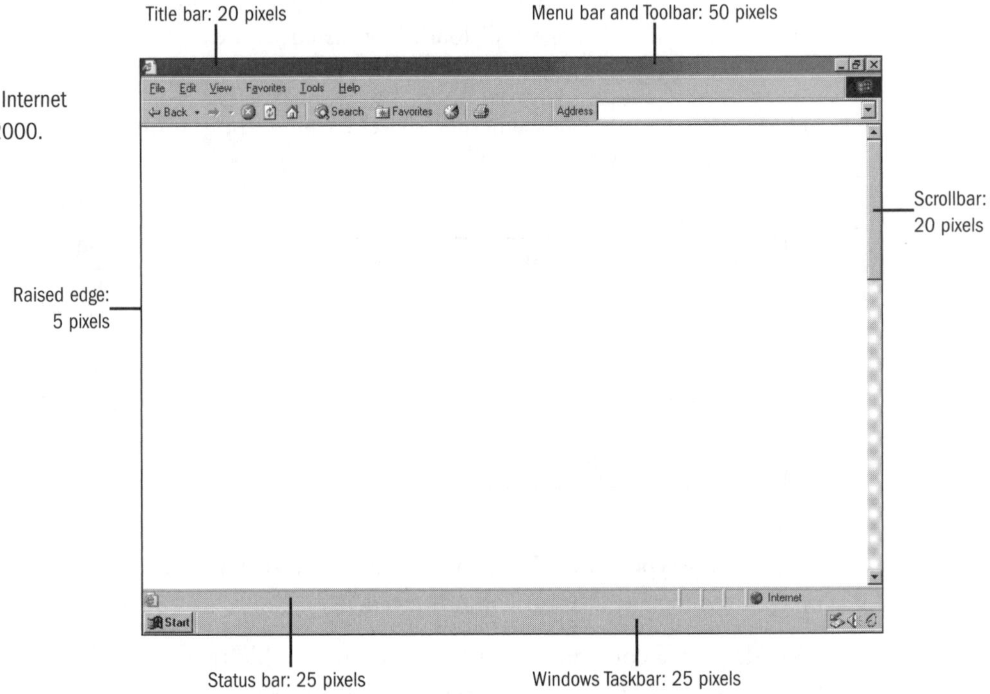
Title bar: 20 pixels
Menu bar and Toolbar: 50 pixels
Scrollbar: 20 pixels
Raised edge: 5 pixels
Status bar: 25 pixels
Windows Taskbar: 25 pixels
File Edit View Favorites Tools Help
Back
Search
Favorites
Address
Internet
Start

Figure 3.10
The browser chrome for Internet Explorer 6 in Windows 2000.

There are two ways to create online learning applications: a *scrolling design* or a *fixed design*. The scrolling design is presented in the normal browser window. If the Web page goes beyond the bottom of the screen, the learner can scroll to see the rest of the page. A fixed design opens the online learning application in a new fixed-size window that does not display the browser button bars, menu bars, or the status bar. The fixed design removes the browser chrome (everything but the title bar), making the maximum space available to present learning content. The sample course in this book uses a fixed design.

The online learning application is viewed within a browser window. Traditional computer-based training applications—those created with authoring tools such as Macromedia Authorware or Asymetrix Toolbook—are delivered in a window of a specific size. Keeping with that tradition and acknowledging a need to present single screens of interactive material, many online learning applications use a fixed design with a specific window size. Single screens of information help the learner more easily absorb the material and feel comfortable in the learning environment.

The first content that a person sees on a Web page makes the strongest impression; it's analogous to newspaper content that's "above the fold." Often Web users examine only the content they can see without scrolling; the content in the initial screen. To ensure that your online learning application is powerful and is viewed completely by all learners, it's best to present it in its own window, a window that doesn't require the learner to scroll to see any of the screen. In the sample course in this book, you'll open a new browser window so that you have more room to present learning content, as shown in Figure 3.11.

Power User Tip

Different operating systems (such as Mac), different browser types, and browser version, and different user configuration all affect the size of the browser controls. Therefore, you cannot depend on an absolute size, especially the height of a Web page.

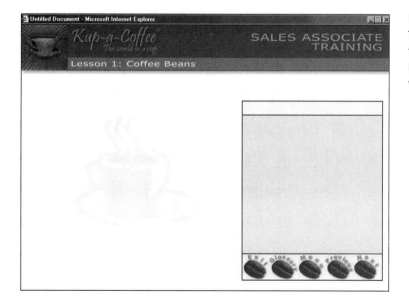

Figure 3.11
The sample course you'll create in this book is presented in a new browser window that is launched without chrome.

Do I Have to Launch the Learning Application in a New Browser Window?

No, but I believe it helps create a learning environment that looks different from the browser. It encourages the learner to stay within the learning application instead of surfing. It makes it easier to guide the user if navigation is included in the application. This is the only way to remove the browser chrome, giving you much more room to present learning content.

Power User Tip

When creating learning applications on computer software topics, you need to specify an online learning application window size of one resolution larger than the screen resolution you use to take screen captures. This makes it possible to present screen captures while leaving extra space on the screen for callouts and instructional text. It's not possible to successfully size down screen captures more than 10% or so. If you specify 800×600 pixels for the window size of the online learning application, you must take screen captures at the 640×480 screen resolution.

When specifying the target window size for the online learning application, you'll want to strike a balance between a window size that the majority of your learner audience can view without changing computer settings and a size that provides enough room to present all the course material. You may choose to detect (using JavaScript) the learner's screen resolution. You can redirect learners to another Web page if their computer is set to a screen resolution that's too small to view your online learning application. Currently, a common minimum screen resolution is 800×600 pixels and might increase to 1024×768 pixels on certain projects.

The learning application example in this book specifies that the learner's screen resolution should be set at a minimum of 800×600 pixels. The Target Browser Window Size specifications are shown in Figure 3.12. In the next section, you'll explore how to use Dreamweaver behaviors, Dreamweaver's method of inserting JavaScript in a Web page, to open a new browser window to display the online learning application.

Figure 3.12

The Target Browser Window Size section of the eLearning Application Specifications Worksheet shows the browser window size for the sample course in this book.

5. Target Browser Window Size	
	Value
Screen Resolution	800 x 600
Open New Window?	☑ Yes ☐ No
New window size	790 x 550

Opening Content in a New Window

Learning applications aren't usually the freeform browsing experience that simply surfing the Web is. Online learning applications control the learners' browsing experience, leading them through a learning application with navigation elements built in to the application. Many of the buttons and commands provided by the browser chrome are not necessary while viewing an online learning application.

The browser can have multiple windows open at the same time, each displaying a different Web page. You will use a Dreamweaver behavior, the Open Browser Window behavior, to open a new browser window. *Behaviors* are a way to insert JavaScript interactions into your Web pages. The interaction is triggered by a user event, such as a mouse click. Dreamweaver contains many behaviors, and you'll explore many more in Chapter 8, "Creating Interactivity with Behaviors and Animations."

You may eventually launch a course from a menu or from a learning management system, such as the one you'll explore in Chapter 15, "Using a Learning Management System." For now, you'll create a disposable Web page used simply to launch the course during development. Open a new Basic HTML page (File, New) in Dreamweaver as shown in Figure 3.13. Save this page (File, Save) as launch.html in a new directory called Example_Course. Type the text Launch Course on the page.

Power User Tip

You might have created a hyperlink that opens a new browser window by using the target **_blank**. This differs from using the Open Browser Window behavior because there is no way to control browser chrome by using a target.

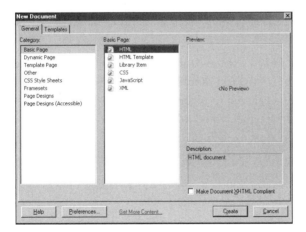

Figure 3.13
Open a new Basic HTML page using the New Document dialog box.

Power User Tip

Creating a null link with **Java-Script:void(0);** is much better than using the pound symbol (#). It used to be common to use the pound symbol as a null link, but that symbol actually jumps the browser window to the top of the Web page and can be distracting to the viewer.

Figure 3.14

Create a null link to capture an event to trigger the Open Browser Window behavior.

To trigger the behavior, you'll capture the user clicking on a link. Technically, this captures the onClick event on a hyperlink. A hyperlink usually loads a Web page into the same browser window. You want to launch a new browser window instead of loading a Web page in the browser window; you simply need a method to capture the onClick event. Instead of entering a URL to a Web page into the Link text box in the Property inspector, you'll create a *null link*. A null link is a hyperlink that doesn't load a new Web page. Select the text you just typed and enter JavaScript:void(0); into the Link text box in the Property inspector, as shown in Figure 3.14.

Null link

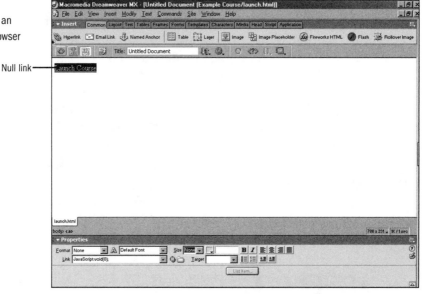

Select the linked text, expand the Design panel group, and click on the Behaviors tab. You should see <a> Actions at the top of the Behaviors panel, as shown in Figure 3.15. If you don't see <a> Actions at the top of the panel, you don't have the link selected and you should try to select the link again. The <a> stands for the anchor tag, the tag used to create a hyperlink. This is a visual clue that you indeed have the correct object selected on the page.

Actions menu (+) button

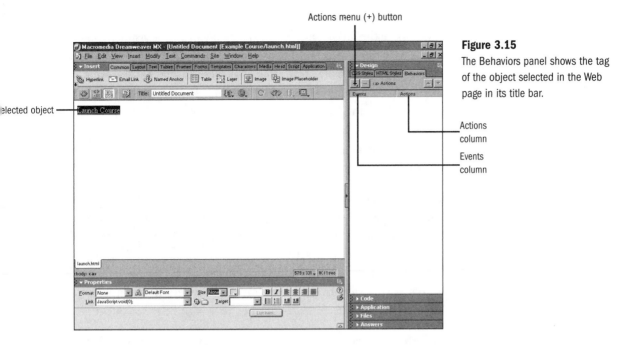

elected object

Figure 3.15
The Behaviors panel shows the tag of the object selected in the Web page in its title bar.

Actions column

Events column

Select the Actions menu by clicking on the plus (+) button in the upper-left corner of the Behaviors panel. Select Open Browser Window from the list. You'll open the first page of the online learning application in the new window. Enter index.html in the URL to Display text box, as shown in Figure 3.16. This is the first page of the online learning application but it hasn't been created yet. Enter 790 pixels as the window width and 550 pixels as the window height. Only check the Resize Handles check box. The other check boxes control the navigation bar and other chrome elements that you will not need. On some projects, you might want to turn on Scrollbars as Needed. Unfortunately, if you enable the scrollbars, you lose 20 pixels on the right border of the screen whether the scrollbars are necessary or not. Click the OK button to save the Open Browser Window settings.

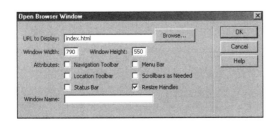

Figure 3.16
The Open Browser Window dialog box controls the URL and various browser chrome elements that will be active when the learner launches a new browser window with the behavior.

The Open Browser Window behavior is visible in the Behaviors panel while the link is selected. If the behavior is not visible, you do not have the link selected. Dreamweaver will select a default event, probably the onClick event in this case. Because the onClick event is the event you want, you do not have to make any changes. If onClick isn't visible in the Events column, you must highlight the behavior and select the Events menu button, the down arrow. This drops down the Events drop-down menu, shown in Figure 3.17, enabling you to choose a different event.

You've now added a behavior to your Web page, and Dreamweaver added all the necessary JavaScript for you. Preview the Web page in Internet Explorer by choosing the Preview in Browser command (File, Preview in Browser). Dreamweaver usually finds Internet Explorer on your computer during its install, so that browser should be available. You can set up additional browsers in Dreamweaver Preferences (Edit, Preferences) in the Preview in Browser category.

In the browser, you should see the Web page with the link in it. When you click on the link, a new browser window should open. It's okay that there is no content in the browser window because you haven't created the page index.html yet. Now you should have two browser windows open: the original page with the launch link on it and the new window without chrome.

Figure 3.17
The Events list enables you select the appropriate event to trigger the behavior.

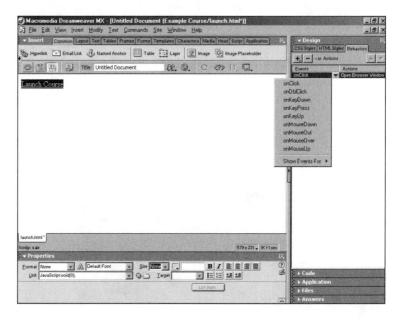

Specifying Operating Systems

Because you are using Dreamweaver to create online learning, it's a sure bet that you are using a computer running Windows or the MacOS because Dreamweaver is available on only those operating systems. However, Web browser software exists for every operating system. You need to analyze the audience for the online learning application and determine which operating systems they are using.

The following operating systems are the most popular (see Figure 3.18):

* Windows 95/98/NT/2000/Me/XP

* MacOS (including OS X)

* Unix (including Linux)

6. Operating Systems		
	Operating System	**%**
☑	Windows 95/98	40
☑	Windows Me	7
☑	Windows 2000	43
☑	Windows XP	7
☐	Mac OS9	___
☑	Mac OS10 (OSX)	3
☐	UNIX _____	___
☐	Others:_____	___

Figure 3.18
The Operating Systems section of the eLearning Application Specifications Worksheet shows the target operating systems for the sample course in this book.

The specified operating system(s) will help determine your specifications for players, scripting languages, and ActiveX controls because some technologies do not work on some operating systems. For example, ActiveX controls do not work on a Macintosh, nor does client-side VBScript. Many players are not available for UNIX Web browsers.

Specifying Supporting Technologies

The Supporting Technologies section of the eLearning Application Specifications Worksheet, shown in Figure 3.19, lists scripting languages and other technologies that may be included in the application. This is the section where you check the types of scripting you will use for a dynamic Web site (such as ASP, JSP, PHP, CFML). If you are using Dreamweaver behaviors to create interactions, you should check JavaScript.

Figure 3.19
The Supporting Technologies section of the eLearning Application Specifications Worksheet shows the supporting technologies for the sample course in this book.

7. Supporting Technologies

	Technology	Version(s)
☐	Cookies	
☑	VBScript	____________
☑	JavaScript	____________
☑	ASP	____________
☐	JSP	____________
☐	CFML	____________
☐	ASP .NET	____________
☐	PHP	____________
☐	____________	____________
☐	____________	____________

JavaScript, originally developed by Netscape, is the universal scripting language for Web browsers. JavaScript works on all browsers and is the language of Dreamweaver behaviors. VBScript is also a popular scripting language that mainly works on the Windows operating system. VBScript is easy to learn, popular among Active Server Pages (ASP) developers, and is one of the scripting languages you can choose in Dreamweaver to create ASP pages.

Power User Tip

JavaScript is not related in any way to the Java programming language. The two terms are not interchangeable, and they describe different technologies.

If your target learners are not all using Windows, you will need to use JavaScript as your client-side scripting language. This is usually only an issue only if you are using Dreamweaver to create ASP pages.

Some Web browsers have JavaScript disabled, so any interactivity you've added to an online learning application will not work. You can detect whether the user has JavaScript disabled by displaying a message with the <noscript> tag. If the user can see the message contained in the <noscript> tag, he or she has an old browser version or has JavaScript disabled. Your script would look something like this:

```
<noscript>You either have an older browser version or you have
  ➥JavaScript disabled. JavaScript is necessary to view this course and
  ➥you will need to enable scripting before you can proceed.</noscript>
```

A *cookie* is a nugget of information about you that is stored on your hard drive and retrieved later so that a Web site knows something about you. For example, a Web site can store your background color preferences, login name, or advertising preferences. When you return to the site, it reads the cookie that was stored previously and automatically logs you in or presents you with personalized content. Cookies are sometimes controversial, with some Web users feeling that their privacy is being invaded. In many cases, the use of cookies speeds up access to Web information.

It might be useful for you to use cookies in your online learning application. If your application isn't designed to store data on the server between learning sessions, writing a cookie to the learner's hard drive can be a useful way to store information between sessions. For example, you might want to store the last page learners viewed before they left your application and then allow them to return to that spot.

Like JavaScript, cookie storage can be disabled in the user's browser, so if you are using cookies, you'll need to detect whether they are enabled in the learner's browser.

Specifying Computer Requirements

After you've identified the players, browsers, and operating system needed to view the online learning application, you will examine the requirements of those software applications and come up with a minimum computer specification for the learner. You'll need to investigate the following (see Figure 3.20):

- Processor speed
- RAM
- Hard drive space

Figure 3.20

The Computer section of the eLearning Application Specifications Worksheet shows the hardware specifications for the sample course in this book.

8. Computer

	Hardware/Settings	Minimum
☐	Sound Card	
☐	CD–ROM Drive	
☐	DVD–ROM Drive	
☐	_____	
☐	_____	
	Color Resolution	☐ 8 bit ☑ 16 bit ☐ 24 bit ☐ 32 bit
	Processor Speed	Pentium/PowerPC G3
	RAM	32 MB
	Disk Space	~500 KB

For example, if your application requires one player that is 219KB and another that is 3.4MB, the learner needs approximately 3.6MB of hard drive space to install the two players. To install Internet Explorer 6, Microsoft recommends a Pentium processor and 32MB of RAM in Windows 2000.

You should specify the minimum color resolution needed for viewing the graphics in the online learning application. Although most computers now have the capability to view more than 256 colors (8-bit), some users do not enable higher color resolution. JPEG images are best viewed at high-color (16-bit) or true-color (24-bit) color resolution.

If your online learning application has an audio component, the learner needs to have a computer equipped with a sound card and speakers. If audio is included, you may suggest that learners have headphones so that they do not bother co-workers. Are you launching content from a CD? If so, the learner needs to have a computer with a CD drive. You dealt with bandwidth earlier in this chapter, but you might also want to specify that the user needs to have a modem or network card to connect to the Internet or an intranet.

Summary

In this chapter, you learned how to create specifications for an online learning application. You learned about the various browser types and versions. You learned about the bandwidth your learners need to be able to view your learning application and the screen resolution used to deliver it. You also explored additional requirements for the course, such as players, scripting languages, and cookies. You learned how to figure out the minimum computer requirements your learners need. You also saw an example of the specifications document you will use for the project in this book.

Part II

Creating a Prototype

IN THIS CHAPTER

chapter 4

Creating a New Web Site Definition

DEFINING YOUR SITE IN DREAMWEAVER is the first step to creating your online learning application. Properly defining your Web site enables Dreamweaver to offer features such as automatic link updates and enables you to view and organize all the files in a Web site. You create a Web site definition for each project you work on in Dreamweaver.

This chapter describes the definition of a local site, a group of Web pages stored on your hard drive. The local site is your private version of a Web site containing the Web pages you'll edit and create with Dreamweaver. Chapter 16, "Safely Collaborating and Sharing the eLearning Site," describes the definition of the remote site, the location where you share files with others. You don't need to create the remote site definition until you're ready to share files with team members or put your files out on the Internet for the public to view.

In this chapter, you will understand the following:

- How to set up a local site
- How to view and export the site map
- How to use design notes
- How to display data stored in design notes in the Site window

Defining Your eLearning Web Site

What is a Web site? A *Web site* is a group of related Web pages that includes a beginning page called the *home page*. You will call an entire online learning course one Web site and create a new site definition for each course you create. You can also divide an online learning course into several Web sites, each representing a logical division of the Web site (such as a lesson). A single Web site shares templates, images, scripts, and other files.

Your site definition describes an important location for your course: the *site root* directory. The site root is important because it's the home for all the files and subdirectories in the Web site. This location doesn't necessarily correspond with the site root on your Web server. For example, your server's site root might contain all your courses, with a separate directory for each course. You are working on a single course, which is in a directory under the courses directory, as shown in Figure 4.1. The directory called wwwroot (the default site root directory name for a Microsoft IIS server) is the site root, but you would define your local site as one of the directories in the courses directory under the site root.

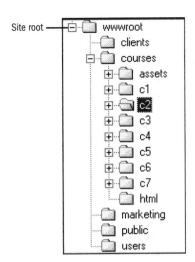

Site root

wwwroot
  clients
  courses
    assets
    c1
    c2
    c3
    c4
    c5
    c6
    c7
    html
  marketing
  public
  users

Figure 4.1

The site you are working on can be a directory in the site root of your Web server.

It can be difficult to decide the directory level to use as a local site definition. Some of the factors to consider include

- **Shared images**—You don't want too many duplicate images in multiple sites. Web sites that use many of the same images may be grouped into a single site.

- **Too many files**—Every time you modify a link or insert an image, Dreamweaver updates the *site cache*. This process can become very slow when there are too many files in a site.

- **Shared templates and library items**—You'll explore templates and library items in Chapter 7, "Building Reusable Templates and Library Items." Templates and library items are shared within a Web site in Dreamweaver, so you'll want to group lessons or courses that use the same ones. You might need to duplicate these files over several sites.

Creating Your Web Site with the Wizard

In preparation for the online learning application you'll build throughout this book, define a new Web site to house the files you will create. In this chapter, you'll define your *local site*. The local site contains your working files, the ones you are changing and editing. The local site is usually located on your local hard drive but may also reside on a network drive that holds your personal work.

Defining the Web site is always the first step in a new Dreamweaver project. You will define a site for each project you work on in Dreamweaver and make sure you've selected that site (more about that in a bit) before you change any Web pages within the site. Dreamweaver enables you to define many attributes of a Web site, such as the local site, the remote site, how you will transfer the local files to the remote site, and the application server language you will use (for dynamic Web sites). You don't need to define all these attributes at once, because you can always edit your site definition.

To begin defining your site, select the New Site command from the Site menu, shown in Figure 4.2. The Site Definition dialog box appears. In Dreamweaver MX, the Site Definition dialog box has two tabs at the top: Basic and Advanced. Select the Basic tab to use the Site Definition Wizard to set up your site. I'm not usually enthusiastic about wizards, but this wizard makes setting up a site quick and logical.

Power User Tip

Mac users will notice that they have many more commands in the Site menu than shown in Figure 4.2. There are some interface differences concerning site definitions between the Windows and the Mac versions of Dreamweaver MX. You'll learn more about this later in the chapter when you explore the Site window.

The Site Definition Wizard (the Basic tab of the Site Definition dialog box), shown in Figure 4.3, leads you through three sections, listed in the dark blue bar at the top of the dialog box: Editing Files, Testing Files, and Sharing Files. In this chapter, you'll fill in the Editing Files section. The Testing Files section is used when Dreamweaver MX will produce dynamic Web pages based on server languages such as ASP, JSP, PHP, or CFML. You'll learn how to set up a site to create dynamic Web pages in Chapter 13, "Creating and Tracking a Dynamic Web site." The final section of the wizard, the Sharing Files section, configures how you'll share and upload files to the remote site. This functionality is covered in Chapter 16.

Figure 4.2

Select the New Site command from the Site menu to open the Site Definition dialog box.

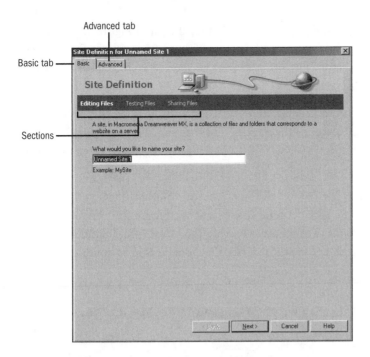

Advanced tab

Basic tab

Sections

Figure 4.3
The Basic tab of the Site Definition dialog box leads you through the three sections to create a site definition.

To create your Web site definition with the Site Definition Wizard, follow these steps:

1. On the first page of the Editing Files section, name your site **eLearning Site**. Dreamweaver uses this name to display the current site in a list of sites. Because this name is used only within Dreamweaver, you don't need to worry about using spaces or punctuation here. You'll want to use a site name that is short but meaningful, a name that enables you to select the proper site from a list that may contain many sites. Click the Next button.

2. The Editing Files, Part 2 page of the wizard asks if your site will use a server language. Select No because you will be creating regular Web pages in the first sections of this book. If you select Yes, you will have additional choices enabling Dreamweaver MX to set up a dynamic Web site. Click the Next button.

3. The Editing Files, Part 3 page of the wizard asks you to locate your local site. You can edit files either on your local machine or on a server. I strongly suggest you edit Web files on your local hard drive because it speeds up access and isn't subject to server problems. Select the top radio button next to Edit Copies on My Machine, Then Upload to Server when Ready (Recommended).

Enter the path to the local site, shown in Figure 4.4, by clicking the folder icon next to the Local Root Folder field. Create an empty directory on your hard drive as your local site. Click the Next button.

4. The Site Definition Wizard skips the Testing Files section and takes you to the Sharing Files section. You'll set up sharing in Chapter 16, so select None from the drop-down menu as shown in Figure 4.5. Click the Next button.

5. The last page of the Site Definition Wizard displays a summary of the site definition, as shown in Figure 4.6. Your summary should show that you set up the Local Info, including the site name and location. Click the Done button to complete the site definition process.

Figure 4.4

Enter the path of the location where you'll store your local copy of the site.

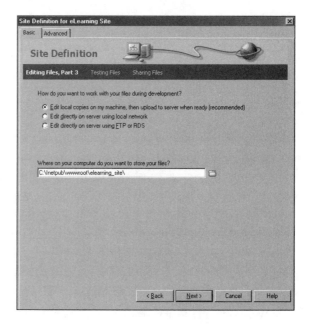

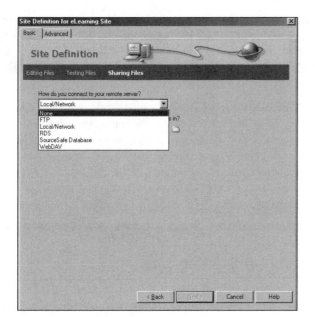

Figure 4.5

You can select None for the server connection, and then set up the transfer method you'll use later.

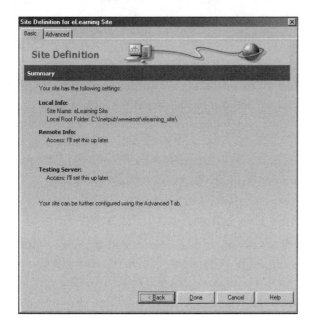

Figure 4.6

Double-check that the summary information for the site is correct.

Importing an Existing Site

Instead of creating a Web site from scratch, you might be updating an existing site in Dreamweaver. There isn't an actual import command in Dreamweaver because Dreamweaver edits and creates standard HTML files. To import a site into Dreamweaver, you simply create a site definition.

Begin importing an existing site by defining the local site with the same site definition procedure you just used. You should point to an empty directory on your hard drive as the local site. To transfer (or "import") the existing files, define the location of the existing files as the remote site and transfer them to your computer. In Chapter 16, you'll learn how to synchronize the local and remote site, moving all the files to your local drive so that you can edit them.

Modifying the Local Info in the Advanced Tab

While the Basic tab of the Site Definition dialog box enables you to quickly set up a site and offers additional settings to fine-tune your site definition, you might decide you prefer to define your sites using the Advanced tab. When you understand how Dreamweaver creates and manages Web sites, it might be quicker for you to use the Advanced tab to make changes to your site definition.

To modify your site definition, select the Edit Sites command from the Site menu. The Edit Sites dialog box, shown in Figure 4.7, lists all the Web sites you've defined in Dreamweaver. The buttons along the right side of the dialog box enable you to edit, duplicate, remove, export, or import the site definitions. Open the Site Definition dialog box again by selecting the name of your site and clicking the Edit button.

Figure 4.7
The Edit Sites dialog box displays all the sites you've defined in Dreamweaver.

Click the Advanced tab to display the advanced view of the site definition, as shown in Figure 4.8. Dreamweaver MX divides the site definition into seven categories, displayed on the left side of the Site Definition dialog box. The Local Info category is displayed by default. You should see the site name and location you entered earlier.

The additional attributes in the Local Info enable you to fine-tune your local site definition. Besides the Site Name and Local Root Folder settings, you can set the following:

- **Refresh Local File List Automatically**—Dreamweaver keeps the list of files up to date when this check box is selected. If you notice your computer pausing to refresh (indicating a slower computer system with insufficient memory), you can turn this option off.

- **Default Images Folder**—When you use an image that is outside your Web site, Dreamweaver prompts you to copy the image into the Web site. When you save the image, Dreamweaver automatically opens the default images folder defined here. Click the Folder icon and create a directory called images in your site root. Select this directory as the default images folder, as shown in Figure 4.9.

Figure 4.8

The Advanced tab displays all the attributes of your site definition.

Categories —

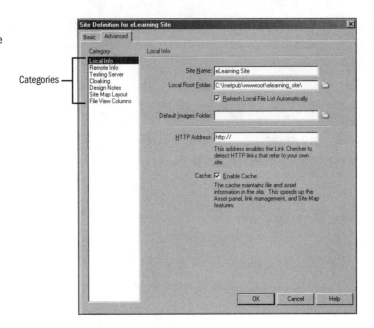

- **HTTP Address**—Specify the final URL of your site, if you know it. This helps Dreamweaver run the link-checking report (File, Check Links). If you don't know the final URL, just leave it blank.

Figure 4.9

Define a default images folder so Dreamweaver knows where to keep any images you import into your Web site.

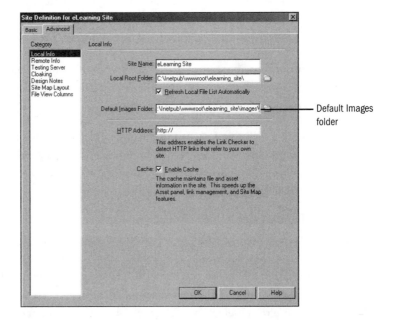

— Default Images folder

- **Cache**—You might have seen Dreamweaver quickly create a site cache after you defined your site. The site cache is turned on when this check box is selected. This command speeds up some of Dreamweaver's site resources and, most important, enables the Assets panel to work. If your computer is running very slowly, you can disable this option.

You'll explore some of the other categories in the Advanced tab of the Site Definition dialog box later in this chapter. Click the OK button to save your changes to the site definition, and click the Done button in the Edit Sites dialog box to close that dialog box.

Exploring the Site Panel and the Site Window

You can select a site, open files, run reports, and perform maintenance on an entire site in the Site panel and the Site window. The Site panel is part of Dreamweaver MX for Window's integrated interface. In Windows, the Site panel and the Assets panel are grouped together as the Files panel group, shown in Figure 4.10. The Site panel displays all the files in your site, making it easier to open files and manage your site.

Figure 4.10
The Site panel is grouped with the Assets panel. It displays all the files in your site.

Dreamweaver MX for the Mac has a floating panel interface. On the Mac, you view and launch files from the Site window, shown in Figure 4.11. Open the Site window by selecting the Site Files command from the Site menu. A separate window opens, displaying the remote site on the left side and the local site on the right. While working on the Mac, you'll want to keep this window open for quick and easy access to all of your files.

Figure 4.11

The Site window displays the local and remote site by default. On the Mac, the Site window is a separate window.

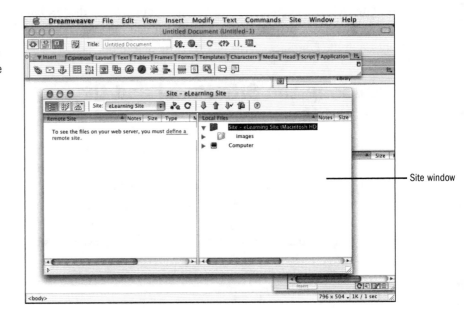

Site window

Power User Tip

There is a Site menu in the Document window, the Site panel, and the Site window. The Site menu in the Document window has fewer commands than the Site menu in the Site panel or the Site window.

To view the Site window in Dreamweaver MX for Windows, you can expand the Site panel by clicking the Expand/Collapse button, the button on the far right. This command doesn't open another window, as on the Mac, but expands the Site panel. To return to the Document window, click the Expand/Collapse button in the expanded Site window. You'll learn more about the various menu commands and buttons in the Site panel and the Site window in Chapter 16.

Changing the Current Working Web Site

Your Site window might already have a couple of sites defined. Dreamweaver might have created sample sites when it was installed or it could have imported sites defined in previous versions of Dreamweaver. If you have only the new site definition, don't worry; you'll be creating many sites after you get started with Dreamweaver.

Site definitions are easily accessible from the Site drop-down menu, shown in Figure 4.12. This menu lists all the sites you have defined and enables you to load different sites quickly and easily. If you are working on several projects at once, you can use the Site drop-down menu to change the site you are working on before modifying any site files.

Site drop-down menu —

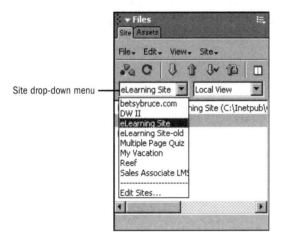

Figure 4.12
The Site drop-down menu enables you to select the site you are going to work on.

Creating a Quick Prototype and a Site Map

You can view the layout of your Web site in the Dreamweaver Site panel or Site window. It might be useful to create a mockup of the Web site structure to share with your team or include with a report.

You can do this in Dreamweaver without actually creating the files. You can quickly create and name new files, and then display a site map view of the site, showing the file and directory hierarchy. You can even create an image of the map to include in a report!

Creating Files and Folders in the Site

Before you can use the site map, you'll need to create some Web pages. You can do this quickly in the Site window. Right-click (Control-click on the Mac) on the top line in the local site; this line represents the site root. Select the New File command to create a Web page. Name the file index.htm, one of the standard names for a home page. Right-click (Control-click on the Mac) on index.htm, and choose the Set as Home Page command on the context menu. You must specify a home page for your site before you can create a site map.

In the Site window, switch between the Site Files view and the Site Map view by using the buttons on the left side of the Site window toolbar, shown in Figure 4.13. When you click the Site Map view button, you can choose Map Only or Map and Files. Select the Map and Files view so that you can see both the site map and the files in the local site.

Figure 4.13

The buttons in Dreamweaver's Site window toolbar enable you to switch between the Site Files view and the Site Map view.

Create several new directories, using the New Folder command in the pop-up context menu, representing lesson directories within the online learning application. Name the directories **L1, L2, L3,** and **quiz**. Be sure the directories are within the site root and not nested within each other or in the images directory. If you accidentally nest one of the directories, you can drag and drop it on the top line in the site to place it in the side root.

Create a new file in the L1 directory and name it 1_1.htm. Continue creating a single file in each directory, naming the files 2_1.htm (representing the lesson number and the page number), 3_1.htm, and q_1.htm. You can continue creating Web pages based on a storyboard or other plan for the online learning application.

Select index.htm in the Site Map view and you'll see the Point-to-File icon, the small circular icon to the right of the file. Click the Point-to-File icon and drag it over 1_1.htm in the site files, as shown in Figure 4.14. Dreamweaver creates a simple link in index.htm to the file, and it shows up as linked in the site map. You can continue to link files to each other, creating a mockup of the site navigation. You can use the Point-to-Files icon to link files or select a file and use the Link to Existing File (Site, Link to Existing File) or Link to New File (Site, Link to New File) commands. These commands are also available in the context menu.

Point-to-File icon

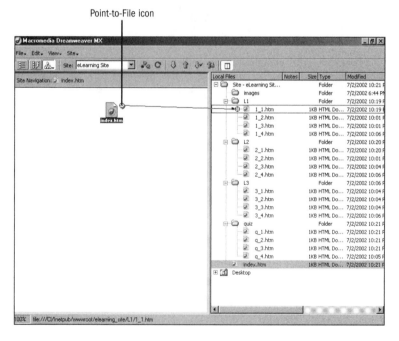

Figure 4.14
Drag the Point-to-File icon to another file to link the two together.

Modifying the Way the Site Map Appears

The Site Map Layout category of the Site Definition dialog box, shown in Figure 4.15, sets up the look of the site map. Open the Site Map Layout category by either editing the site definition, as described earlier in this chapter, or by selecting the Layout command (View, Layout). This category enables you to set the number of columns displayed in the site map and the width of the columns. You might need to modify these values to make your site map readable. For example, making the column width 150 pixels gives more room to display linked files.

Figure 4.15
You can change the width of each column and the number of columns displayed in the Site Map Layout category of your site definition.

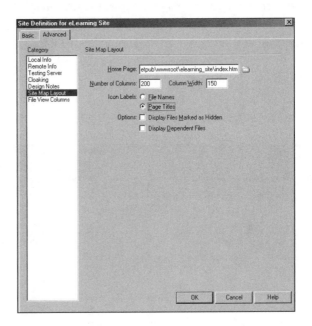

Icons in the site map can be labeled with the filename (the default view) or the page title of a Web page. When you view the files by the page titles, you can name the files right in the site map view by clicking on the title and entering a new one. You can also check Display Files Marked As Hidden (you can hide files in the site map with the Show/Hide Link command on the View menu) or check Display Dependent Files (shows images and other files along with the Web files). Because you don't have any hidden or dependent files in this site, you can leave both check boxes unchecked.

Saving the Site Map as an Image

One great Dreamweaver feature is the capability to export a picture of the site map as a BMP or PNG file. You can then import the image into proposals or use it to document your project. To accomplish this, choose the Save Site Map command from the File menu while in the Site Map view. Select either the PNG or BMP file format in the Save As Type drop-down list. You can import this image into a Word document, as shown in Figure 14.16, or insert a PNG into a Web page.

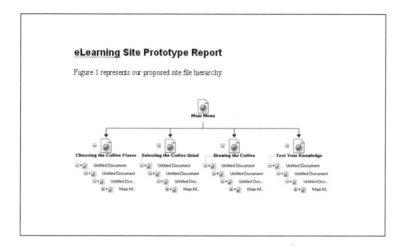

Figure 4.16
You can insert an image created from Dreamweaver's site map into documents or Web pages.

Adding Design Notes

Design notes enable you to attach notes visible only in Dreamweaver to individual files. You can also share the notes with your team members. These notes are useful for tracking the file's version, signaling bug fixes, and cataloging reference information. For example, attaching a design note to an image file listing the original Photoshop or Fireworks file is extremely useful when you need to find that original and make changes.

Design notes are visible only in Dreamweaver and are not visible to those who view your Web site. Dreamweaver creates a special _notes directory to hold all the design notes in your Web site. The _notes directory is not visible while you are in Dreamweaver, but you might see it if you browse through your site files outside Dreamweaver. Each design note is named for the file it's associated with and ends with the .mno extension.

Attaching Design Notes to Files

There are a couple of ways to attach a design note to a file. Attach a design note by right-clicking (Command+click on the Mac) on a file in the Site panel or Site window to bring up the context menu, as shown in Figure 4.17, and then choose the Design Notes command to open the Design Notes dialog box. You also can add a design note by using the Design Notes command on the File menu.

Figure 4.17
The context menu in Dreamweaver's Site panel or Site window has many commands, including a command to add a design note.

Creating a Basic Design Note

With the Design Notes dialog box open, as shown in Figure 4.18, add a simple design note to any file in your site. With the Basic Info tab selected (the default), drop down the Status list box and select Needs Attention in the list. Click the small calendar icon to add today's date to the Notes text box, and then type a note next to the date. Select the Show When File Is Opened check box at the bottom of the dialog box. Click the OK button when you are finished, to save the note. This design note will automatically open for the next person who opens the file. Double-click the file and try it!

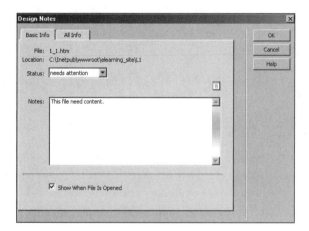

Figure 4.18
Set up a design note by selecting Status and adding a note. You can also select the Show When File Is Opened check box.

When a design note is attached to a file, you'll see a little yellow design note icon appear next to the filename in the Site window; the design note icon is not visible in the Site panel. Double-click the design note icon to open up the note to view, edit, or add additional information.

The Design Notes category in the Site Definition dialog box enables you to turn on design notes and share them with the rest of your team. To modify the way design notes are handled within your site, you edit your site definition, select the Advanced tab, and select the Design Notes category. In this category of the Site Definition dialog box, shown in Figure 4.19, you can choose to turn design notes on or off (the Maintain Design Notes check box) and choose to share design notes with others (the Upload Design Notes for Sharing check box). The Clean Up button deletes design notes that are attached to files that no longer exist in your site.

Power User Tip

When you import Fireworks files into Dreamweaver, Fireworks automatically adds design notes to the files. These design notes do not show up with design note icons next to the files, however. You can see these design notes if you peek at the **folder** or when you open up design notes on a file and see that notes already exist. These notes help Dreamweaver exchange information with Fireworks about the Fireworks source files, so it's a good idea to leave them.

Figure 4.19

Select both of the check boxes in
the Design Notes category to
enable design notes and share
them with others.

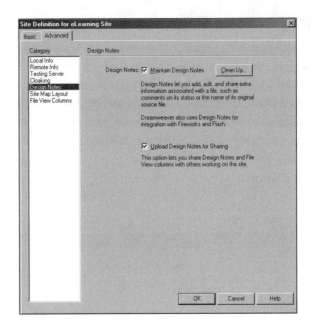

Creating a Custom Design Note

You just created a basic design note using one of the preloaded status notes available in the Basic Info tab. The All Info tab enables you
to create your own custom design notes categories. Add a design
note to the same file by opening the design note. This time, select the
All Info tab in the Design Notes dialog box to add a custom design
note. Note that there is already some data entered into the dialog box
from the prior note you created.

When you created a basic design note, Dreamweaver automatically
created a *name* and a *value* for your design note. Name is like a variable and value is the value that the variable holds. The name and
value pairs are listed in the All Info tab. You can create a custom
name and place a value into it.

Click the + button to create a new design note entry. Place your cursor in the Name text box and enter **Developer**. Move to the Value text
box and enter your name. Click the plus button to add more notes
or the minus button to remove notes. Your new design note appears
in the Info text box, as shown in Figure 4.20.

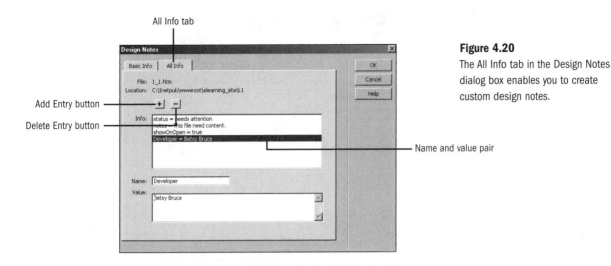

All Info tab

Add Entry button

Delete Entry button

Figure 4.20
The All Info tab in the Design Notes dialog box enables you to create custom design notes.

Name and value pair

Viewing Design Notes in the Site Window

Now you'll add a new column to the Site window displaying the value of the Developer design note you just created. To edit the columns, either edit your site and select the File View Columns category or select the File View Columns command (View, File View Columns).

Follow these steps to add a new column to the Site window:

1. You'll see a list of built-in columns that come with Dreamweaver. You can change the text alignment on all the columns by selecting a column and modifying its attributes in the dialog box. You also can hide all the columns except the Name column by deselecting the Show check box.

2. To add a new column, click the plus button above the column list. A new untitled column is created.

3. Enter **Developer** in the Column Name text box.

4. Enter **Developer** in the Associate with Design Note text box, as shown in Figure 4.21. You enter **Developer** because that's the name of the custom design note you created. You must type the entry into the text box instead of selecting one of the basic entries from the drop-down menu.

Figure 4.21

You can display a custom design note in a column in the Site window by creating a new column and linking it to the custom design note.

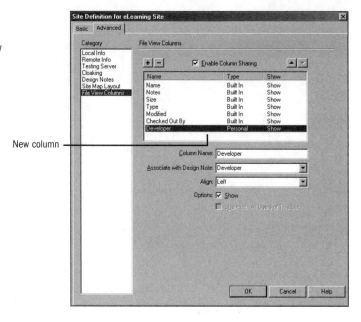

New column ——

Power User Tip

A quick way to edit the site you currently have open in the Site window is to double-click the site name in the Site window drop-down menu.

5. Select an alignment setting from the Align drop-down menu: left, right, or center.

6. Move your custom column by using the arrow buttons.

7. Select the Enable Column Sharing check box at the top of the dialog box. The dwSiteColumnsME.xml file in the _notes directory contains the custom column's definition. This file will be shared with others on your team so that you all have the same custom column definitions.

After you've saved your changes, note that a new column appears in the Site window. This column displays the contents of the Developer design note. Also, observe that the design note icon containing the Developer note is no longer visible beside the file. The design note icon doesn't appear if the note is already displayed in a column. However, if additional notes are attached to the file, the design note icon will appear.

Practice adding design notes to the files in your site. Add design notes using the various preloaded status notes in the Basic Info tab and more custom Developer notes in the All Info tab. Be sure your custom notes named **Developer** appear in the custom column you just created.

Summary

In this chapter, you defined your local site, where you will create and edit Web pages. You explored the Site panel and the Site window. You created a quick prototype and saved the site map as an image. You attached design notes to some files in your site and created a custom column in your Site window to display the contents of the design notes.

IN THIS CHAPTER

chapter 5

Defining Cascading Style Sheets

YOU'LL USE CASCADING STYLE SHEETS (CSS) to control the

appearance and placement of text and objects in your online

learning application. In this chapter, you'll create a single set of

CSS definitions that will globally affect every Web page in your

Web site. This makes it easy to maintain and update your entire

site by simply changing styles in a single location.

Defining positioning and appearance using CSS is the method approved by the W3C, the Web standards organization. CSS offers a powerful and flexible way to apply styles to blocks of text, headings, and any HTML tag. It can make your Web pages more streamlined and easier to read by describing lengthy definitions within CSS instead of at the tag level. CSS is part of an unofficial group of technologies called *Dynamic HTML*.

There is a movement in Web development toward separating content and presentation in Web pages. In an online learning application, the content will usually be text, HTML code, and other objects, such as images or Flash movies. CSS controls the presentation of the content. There are compelling reasons for separation of content and presentation, such as accessibility and delivery to multiple devices. Ideally, you can create an online learning application to deliver to learners at desktop computers, and then deliver the same content to learners connecting to the course using cellular telephones by simply swapping in a different set of styles.

When creating an online learning application, you'll gather a set of text styles and rules for positioning objects on the Web page and put them in a .css file. Each Web page in your online learning application will link to the external script files and have access to the functionality they define. You do not need to know how to write CSS to use Dreamweaver; Dreamweaver has tools that will write the code for you.

In this chapter, you will understand the following:

- What Dynamic HTML and CSS are
- How to create text styles (CSS)
- How to create positioning styles (CSS-P)

Using CSS Styles in Dreamweaver

Cascading style sheets are a component of *Dynamic HTML* (DHTML), an unofficial specification grouping three technologies:

- **Cascading style sheets (CSS)**—A collection of definitions formatting the appearance (such as fonts, colors, and spacing) of the content within Web pages. CSS enables you to define properties of Web page objects in a single location. CSS enables you to control formatting that cannot be controlled using HTML (such as specifying font size in points or ems).

- **Cascading style sheets-positioning (CSS-P)**—Styles that enable you to position elements exactly on a Web page. Dreamweaver calls these positioning elements *layers*. Using Dreamweaver layers is how you can position an object at a specific point on the screen, move objects, and even hide and show objects.

- **JavaScript**—A scripting language that can be embedded in a Web page and interpreted by the browser. JavaScript is added to your Web pages automatically by Dreamweaver behaviors. Dreamweaver adds *client-side* JavaScript, meaning that the script is interpreted by the browser and not by the server. Adding JavaScript to your Web pages enables you to create image rollovers, drag objects around the screen, pop-up message boxes, and add many different ways for the learner to interact with the online learning application.

Most of DHTML is detailed in the HTML 4.0 specification from the World Wide Web Consortium (W3C), the standards organization that guides Web technologies (the most recent version of HTML is HTML 4.01). The browser manufacturers use the W3C specification to determine the features that the browser will implement. The HTML 4.0 specification defining DHTML was implemented in the 4.0 version browsers, both Netscape Navigator and Internet Explorer. If your course specification stipulates that your course will provide learner interactivity and use CSS for formatting, then you will want to specify that the learner needs to have Internet Explorer or Netscape Navigator 4.0 or better to view the eLearning application.

Selecting a CSS Style Type and Storage Area

You'll use the Dreamweaver CSS Styles panel to create CSS styles to apply to your Web pages. You'll define CSS styles to format and position Web page elements on the page. The definition of CSS styles enables you to use the styles when constructing the interface for your online learning application (discussed in Chapter 6, "Constructing the Interface").

In this chapter, you'll experiment with different types of CSS styles while saving the styles for use later. Usually, the colors and fonts defined by CSS styles are part of your specification document, like the one described in Chapter 3, "Establishing the Course Specifications." You may also work closely with the graphics designer to implement his vision of the color and style for the online learning application.

First, create a new, blank Web page in Dreamweaver where you can experiment with styles. In this chapter, you're not creating a Web page in your Web site, but simply using a "dummy" page to create and test your CSS styles. Be sure the CSS Styles panel (Window, CSS Styles), shown in Figure 5.1, is open. This is where you'll define CSS styles. The panel is empty right now, but you'll have some styles listed there soon.

Figure 5.1

Add new CSS styles to your Web page in the CSS Styles panel.

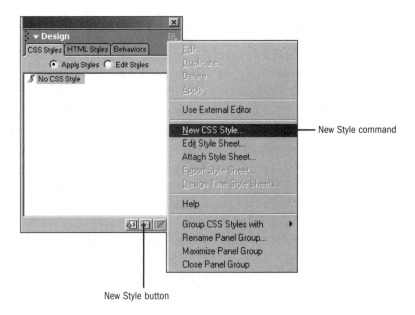

New Style command

New Style button

Click the New Style button in the lower-right corner of the CSS Styles panel (or choose the New Style command from the panel menu) to open the New Style dialog box. The New CSS Style dialog box, shown in Figure 5.2, enables you to select the type of style you are creating and where you'd like Dreamweaver to store the style. You'll create examples of each of the three different types of CSS styles.

There are three types of CSS styles: Redefine HTML Tag, Custom, and CSS Selector. You select the type of style by clicking one of the radio buttons next to your choice in the New CSS Style dialog box. The definitions of the three types of CSS styles are

- **Redefine HTML Tag**—These style definitions are reflected in every use of the specified tag in the page. For example, if you redefine the <p> tag (paragraph) as 10-point Verdana, then every word contained within <p> tags will be in that font and font size. You apply this type of style simply by applying HTML tags to objects on the page.

- **Custom (or class)**—Freeform styles that can be applied to any element on a Web page. You apply these styles by selecting an appropriate object on the Web page and applying the style from the list in the CSS Styles panel. For example, you can create a style called .highlight (all custom styles begin with a period) that highlights text in a light-yellow color (like a highlighter pen). When you select some text and click on the style in the CSS Styles panel, you'll see the text highlighted on the Web page.

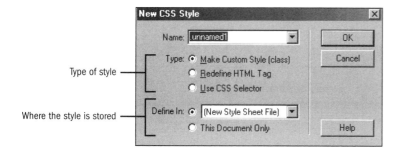

Type of style ——

Where the style is stored ——

Figure 5.2
The New CSS Style dialog box specifies the type of style and where it will be stored.

Custom styles might also be called *classes* because the class attribute is used to implement this type of style. For example, to apply a custom style to a paragraph, Dreamweaver would add the attribute like this: <p class=".maintext"> to add the custom style named .maintext.

- **CSS Selector**—Redefines specific HTML tags for an entire Web page; for example, all the paragraph tags within a table cell will affect only the paragraph tags in a table, not any other paragraph tags. These styles can also affect all tags containing a certain ID attribute. There are also some special styles called *pseudo-classes* available in this style category; you'll use them later in this chapter (see the "Using CSS Selector Pseudo-Classes" section) to change the way your hyperlinks appear.

To create your first style, select the Redefine HTML Tag radio button. The drop-down list above the style types enables you to select a specific tag. Drop down the list and select the <body> tag, as shown in Figure 5.3. The <body> tag contains attributes of the entire Web page, such as font, background color, link color, and others.

You've selected the type of CSS style that you want to create (Redefine HTML Tag) and now you need to decide where to store the style. CSS styles are stored in three locations:

- **External**—Styles are stored in an external file that is linked to a Web page. The external style sheet, which has the .css file extension, can be linked to multiple Web pages. These are also called *linked styles*.

Figure 5.3
You can select any HTML tag to redefine from the Tag drop-down list.

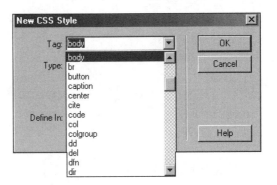

eLearning with Dreamweaver MX: Building Online Learning Applications

- **Internal**—Styles are stored in the <head> tag of the Web page, and the styles affect only the single page. These are also called *embedded styles*.

- **Inline**—Styles are stored in an attribute of the HTML tag.

I save the majority of CSS styles in external style sheets. This makes sense when your styles will be used in every Web page in the site. If a style is used on only a single page in a Web site, you can define this style as an internal style by selecting the radio button next to This Document Only in the New CSS Style dialog box, as shown in Figure 5.4. This setting saves the CSS style definition in the <head> section of the current Web page, and the style will affect only that Web page.

You may occasionally use an inline style to define a CSS style within an HTML tag. Although Dreamweaver automatically creates internal and external CSS styles, you will have to code inline styles by hand. The following example of an inline style defines a link so that it doesn't look like a link (no underline and no color):

<a href="main.htm" style="text-decoration:none; color:black">

This link will appear differently from all the other links on the page because of the added style attribute.

For your online learning application, you'll store style definitions in an external style sheet. In Chapter 7, "Building Reusable Templates and Library Items," you'll place a link to the style sheet in each template so that every page of the course will have the styles applied. The advantage of an external style sheet is that since all Web pages are linked to the styles in that one file, you can make a change to all the pages in the site simply by making a change to the external style sheet. This makes updates and changes quick and global.

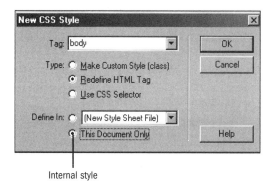

Internal style

Figure 5.4
Save a CSS style as an internal style, available only to the Web page in which it's contained, by selecting the This Document Only setting.

Did you wonder why cascading style sheets have the word "cascading" in the name? Cascading pertains to how style dominance flows, or cascades, through the document according to where a style is defined. You can follow this rule of thumb: A style defined closest to an element has dominance over styles applied to the element that are defined farther away. So, if two styles conflict (one defines text as red and one as blue), the style closest to the actual text is displayed. For example, an inline style for text color would be dominant over an internal style for text color, and both would be dominant over an external style for text color.

Save your style in an external style sheet by selecting the radio button next to the drop-down menu displaying New Style Sheet File in the New CSS Style dialog box. After you click OK, you're prompted to create the external style sheet. You have to do this step only the first time you add a CSS style to the external style sheet; the next time you want to add a style to the external style sheet, you simply select the name of the external style sheet file in the New CSS Style dialog box. To create a new external style sheet file:

1. Create a new directory called Scripts in the site root. Select the Create New Folder button, and create the scripts directory, as shown in Figure 5.5. This directory will also be used to store external JavaScript files that you create and that CourseBuilder adds to your site. You'll learn about this in Chapter 10, "Including CourseBuilder Interactions and Controls."

Figure 5.5
Create a Scripts directory and save the external style sheet.

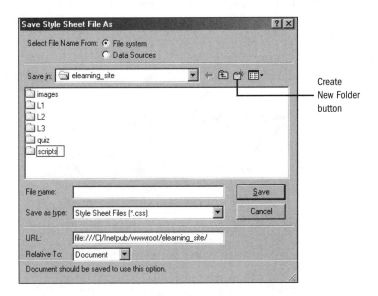

2. Double-click the new scripts directory to open it.

3. Name the external style sheet **learning.css** in the File Name text box.

4. Click the Save button.

Dreamweaver then opens the Style Definition dialog box, where you define the new style you're creating. The definition of this style will be stored in the learning.css file, the new external style sheet you just created. Dreamweaver added a link to the external style sheet file in the <head> of the Web page.

Redefining an HTML Tag: Background Color and Image

The Style Definition dialog box you just opened enables you to select style categories on the left. You'll explore these categories throughout this chapter. Right now, you're redefining the <body> tag, so you'll mostly set styles that pertain to body attributes. You'll set the background color and background image source of the <body>.

By redefining the attributes of the <body> tag, you'll affect every page that has the external style sheet linked in its <head> section. All the pages in your online learning application will have a similar look. The example course in this book has a design, shown in Figure 5.6, that employs a common background color (#FFFFE1), a background watermark image, and a common font family (Verdana, Arial, Helvetica, sans serif). Because every page has a <body> tag, you are adding this common appearance to every Web page by redefining the <body> tag.

Create a CSS style redefining the <body> tag attributes:

1. In the Type category, select Verdana, Arial, Helvetica, sans serif from the Font drop-down menu. All text in the eLearning application will appear as one of these font choices.

2. Select the Background category and enter a color value in the Background Color text box. The background color for the example course should be #FFFFE1. This is the same as entering the background color into the Dreamweaver Page Properties dialog box.

Figure 5.6

You take the value for the CSS styles from the design of the course interface.

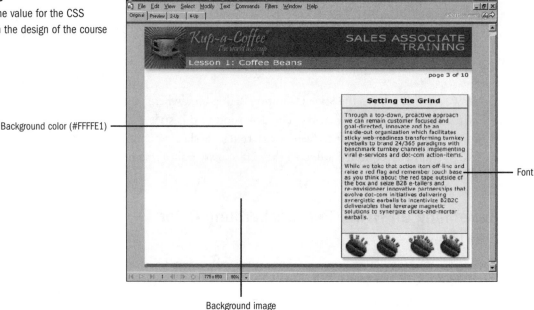

Background color (#FFFFFE1)

Font

Background image

3. Click the Browse button next to the Background Image text box and browse to the Images directory. Select watermark.jpg to use for a background image.

4. Select No-Repeat in the Repeat list box, shown in Figure 5.7, to stop the background image from repeating on the page.

5. Click the Apply button to see the background attributes applied to the current page. Select OK to save your changes.

In Dreamweaver, you can see the background color, but choose the Preview in Browser command (File, Preview in Browser) to view the background image. You also can set the background color and image in the Page Properties (Modify, Page Properties). Why create a style when you could simply add the background color and image in the Page Properties? You're planning ahead! What if the background image changes or you decide on a different background color? And what if you've already created 100 pages of content in your online learning application? Simply changing the style in a single external style sheet to update all the pages at once is much easier than modifying all the pages individually.

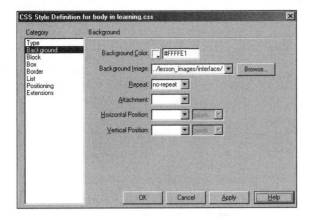

Figure 5.7
The Background category defines the background color and image attributes for elements of a Web page. You can also set the repeat attribute for the background image.

You've already encountered the idea that you can create a style in an external style sheet and propagate it over multiple pages, creating a quick way to update all the Web pages. Another reason to use style sheets is that many tag-based attributes, such as the background color in the Page Properties, have been *deprecated* by the W3C in the HTML specification, meaning they are tolerated but not recommended. Eventually, browsers might not support deprecated tags and attributes, although most support them today. Using CSS is the approved method of formatting elements on a Web page.

Exploring Style Definitions: The Background Category

You use Dreamweaver's Background category to set the background color, image, and repeat characteristics for the entire body of the Web page. Background settings aren't useful only for the body of a page; you can set the background color, for example, of a line of text or a table by using these settings. You define styles that are appropriate to the element you're applying the style to; for example, you wouldn't define a background color for an image because an image doesn't have any background color.

- **Background Color**—enables you to add a background color to elements, such as a table or the body of a Web page.

- **Background Image**—Enables you to add a background image to elements, such as a table or the body of a Web page.

- **Repeat**—Enables you to specify how a background image will repeat, or *tile*. Select No-Repeat in the Repeat list box to have the image appear only once. Select Repeat-X for the image to repeat only horizontally and Repeat-Y for the image to repeat only vertically. Select Repeat (the default) for the image to repeat both horizontally and vertically.

- **Attachment**—Works only in IE, enabling you to have an image scroll along with the page instead of being fixed.

- **Horizontal and Vertical Position**—Enable you to specify the position of a background image. Select Left, Center, or Right in the Horizontal Position list box, or enter a value and a measurement unit. For the vertical placement, select Top, Center, or Bottom in the Vertical Position list box, or enter a value and a measurement unit.

Use the CSS Reference

To find out more about CSS settings and attributes, you can consult the CSS reference, shown in Figure 5.8, available in the Reference panel (Window, Reference); select the CSS Reference in the Book list box. To understand more about the background color attribute, select Background-Color in the Style list box.

Power User Tip

If you feel as though your eyes are straining to read the Reference panel, you can select a larger display font in the panel menu in the upper-right area of the panel.

In the upper-right corner of the description, you see which browsers support this style and whether it's inherited, meaning that all objects enclosed within the tag containing the style will have the style applied. The background color attribute is not inherited, which is good; otherwise, all your text, tables, and other elements would have the same background color as the body of the page.

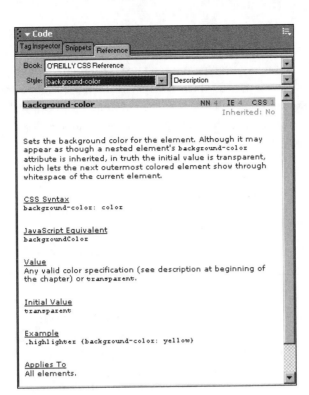

Figure 5.8

Dreamweaver's Reference panel includes a CSS reference.

Defining Text Styles

Although you can define both the appearance and the position of objects in an HTML page, the majority of CSS styles you create will affect the appearance of text in your Web site. HTML does not give developers much control over text attributes such as font face, font size, and line height. Using CSS styles enables you to have better control over the way text appears on the page.

Defining Text Styles by Redefining HTML Tags

All the body text in the online learning application is contained within paragraph tags (<p>). You can create a CSS style to redefine the <p> tag to format all the body text in the course. In this style, you'll set the font size and font color of any text contained in a paragraph. The text inside <p> tags will use the font face you defined earlier in the <body> tag redefinition style, as will all the text on the page.

Add some text to the Web page that you have open. Because you'll be redefining <p> tags, this text should be a paragraph. An HTML paragraph is text within paragraph tags; the paragraph tags are considered a container in which the text resides. Redefining the container tags affects all the text in the container. You can follow this same technique for other containers, such as table cells (<td>) and layers (<div>).

First, be sure the text on the Web page is contained within a paragraph. You apply paragraph tags to a block of text by selecting Paragraph in the Property inspector's Format list box, as shown in Figure 5.9. If the text is contained within <p> tags, Paragraph will already be selected. In HTML, individual paragraphs have a blank line (two carriage returns) between them.

Power User Tip

One of my favorite extensions is the Insert Corporate MumboJumbo extension available at the Macromedia exchange (in the Text category). It's useful for creating blocks of placeholder text and for getting a few laughs too. I used it in Figure 5.9.

Be sure your cursor is positioned in a paragraph before you create the next style. When you redefine an HTML tag, Dreamweaver picks up the current tag you're using in the Web page and automatically selects it in the Tag list box. To redefine the <p> tag, follow these steps:

1. Click the New Style button in the CSS Styles panel to open the New Style dialog box. Be sure the radio button next to Redefine HTML Tag is selected. The paragraph tag should be automatically selected for you. If it isn't, select p from the drop-down menu.

2. Again, you'll define this style in the external style sheet you named learning.css. Be sure this external style sheet is selected in the New CSS Styles dialog box.

3. Click the OK button to open the Style Definition dialog box. In the Type category, select 10 from the Size drop-down menu and select points as the measurement unit.

4. Set the text color by entering a hexadecimal color value, **#5D3B3A** for the example course, in the Color text box.

5. Tighten the distance between the lines in the paragraph by entering **14** in the Line Height text box and selecting Points in the Measurement Units list box, as shown in Figure 5.10. Selecting Normal in the list box allows the browser to calculate the line height. This setting is traditionally called *leading* (pronounced like "lead" in a pencil).

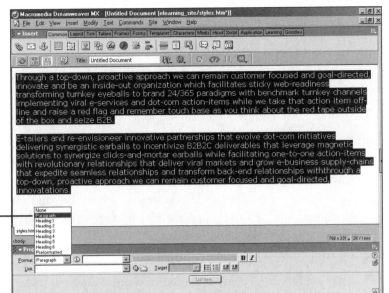

Figure 5.9
You apply **<p>** tags to text in the Property inspector.

agraph format

6. You don't need to save your changes to see their effect. Click the Apply button at the bottom of the Style Definition dialog box to apply the style changes to your Web page. You should see your paragraph text change. This enables you to fine-tune the style without opening and saving it multiple times.

7. Click the OK button to save the redefined paragraph tag style.

You just formatted text on the Web page by redefining the look of an HTML tag that had been applied to the text. How would you apply this style to any new text you added to the page? If you answered, "Apply the paragraph format using the Property inspector," you would be right. Next, you'll define a custom style that's applied to a block of text instead of to an entire container, such as a paragraph.

Exploring Style Definitions: The Type Category

Other Type category settings enable you to further define the way text will look when the style is applied. You'll use the settings in the Type category often.

■ **Weight**—Sets text bolding; although there are several settings, from 100 (very light) to 900 (very bold), most browsers can't

Power User Tip

Macromedia Exchange includes an extension created by Massimo Foti that loads a style sheet based on whether the learner views the Web page with a Mac or a PC. This helps diminish the differences between font sizes in the Mac and PC. The extension is called the CSS on Platform Extension and can be found in the Scripting category.

display all the weights. A weight setting of 700 is the standard bold formatting, or you can simply select Bold in the Weight list box to apply the standard bold.

- **Variant**—Enables you to set text to display as small caps, which works only in IE. With this setting, the first letter in a sentence is a slightly larger capital letter than the subsequent letters, which are also capitalized.

- **Case**—Enables you to set different letter cases for the text. The Capitalize option capitalizes the first letter of every word; the Lowercase option displays all the text in lowercase; and the Uppercase option displays all the text in uppercase. This setting works in both IE and Netscape.

- **Style**—Enables you to set the text as italic or oblique. Italic fonts are fonts that contain slanted versions of the letters. Most fonts do not contain italic versions, so the browser (and other applications) simply slants the regular font. If you know a font you are using actually has an italic version, you may specify Italic in the Style setting because it will look better than the slanted version of the regular font.

Figure 5.10
Set the Line Height, or leading, in the Type category.

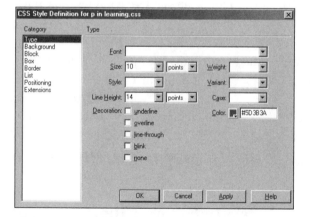

- **Decoration**—Enables you to control underlines, overlines, linethroughs (often called strikethrough), and even blinking text. All the decorations are visible in both Netscape and IE except for the blink setting, which is visible only in Netscape. The None setting is useful for turning off the hyperlink underlines.

Understanding Style Measurement Units

Dreamweaver offers several different measurement units. What's the difference between them, and when should you use each one?

Table 5.1 lists absolute measurement units. Picas, points, inches, millimeters, and centimeters are technically constant, although there are variations in the way different browsers display the size of these supposed constants.

Table 5.1   Absolute Measurement Units

Name	Description	Example
picas (pc)	Traditional measurement unit for type describing font size; 1 pica equals 12 points.	1pc
points (pt)	Traditional measurement unit for type describing font size.	12pt
inches (in)	Standard measurement.	.25in
millimeters (mm)	Standard measurement; 10 millimeters equals 1 centimeter.	25mm
centimeters (cm)	Standard measurement.	.25cm

Table 5.2 lists measurement values that are relative to other values.

Table 5.2   Relative Measurement Units

Name	Description	Example
em	The em measurement equals the em dash (—), which represents the width of the uppercase letter *M* for the selected font; 1.5em specifies 1.5 times the size of the default font, so if the default font is 12-point, 1.5em equals 18-point.	2em
ex	The ex measurement equals the height of the lowercase letter *x* for the selected font and works the same way em does.	4ex

continues

Table 5.2 Continued

Name	Description	Example
pixel (px)	Pixel value is based on the viewer's monitor resolution, which varies but is usually 96dpi or 72dpi.	14px
percentage (%)	Percentage behaves differently depending on the attribute, but it generally varies the size in relation to whatever the default is (100%).	25%
multiple	The multiple setting represents double-spacing if set to 2, triple-spacing if set to 3, and so on.	2

Editing CSS Styles

The CSS Styles panel in Dreamweaver MX has two different views: Apply Styles and Edit Styles. You select the view by clicking one of the radio buttons at the top of the CSS Styles panel. In the Edit Styles view, shown in Figure 5.11, Dreamweaver displays the CSS styles in the left column and their definitions in the right column.

Figure 5.11

The CSS Styles panel displays all the CSS styles and the style definitions in the Edit Styles view.

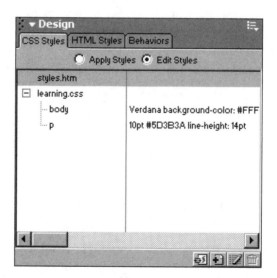

| **eLearning with Dreamweaver MX:** Building Online Learning Applications

Styles contained in an external style sheet appear nested beneath the style sheet name. Styles that are internal to the current Web page appear nested beneath the Web page file name. To edit a style, simply double-click it while in the Edit Styles view. The CSS Style Definition dialog box opens and you can make changes to the style.

Defining Custom Text Styles

You might need to highlight some text to set it off from other text. For the example online learning application in this book, you need to create two custom text styles: a style to set off instruction text giving directives to the learner and a style for glossary words. You'll define custom styles in Dreamweaver that enable you to set instruction and glossary text off from the regular paragraph text.

First, you'll define a custom style that can be applied to any text that directs the learner to interact with the online learning application. For example, an instruction such as "Click on the File menu" appears in the text in a different color so that it stands out and is easy to find.

Follow these steps to create a custom style defining the instruction text:

1. Click the New Style button in the CSS Styles panel to open the New Style dialog box.

2. Select Make Custom Style (Class) as the type of style.

3. Dreamweaver inserts the placeholder name .unnamed in the Name text box. Replace this placeholder with **.instruction**, as shown in Figure 5.12. Custom style names always begin with a period, but if you forget it, Dreamweaver adds it for you.

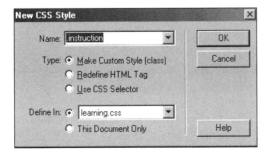

Figure 5.12
Custom style names always begin with a period.

4. Be sure the style will be saved to the external style sheet. Click OK to open the Style Definition dialog box.

5. In the Type category, simply enter the hexadecimal value for a color, for the example course enter **#294752,** in the Color text box.

6. Click the OK button to save the style. You'll see the style listed in the Apply Styles view of the CSS Styles panel, as shown in Figure 5.13. The external style sheet icon, the small link icon next to the style name, signifies that the style is stored in an external style sheet.

Figure 5.13

Custom styles are listed in the CSS Styles panel.

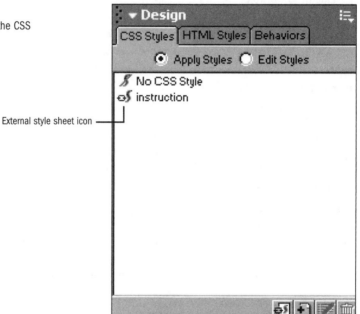

To apply the custom style, select some instruction text on your Web page and click the style name in the CSS Styles panel. Dreamweaver applies the style by surrounding the text in <span> tags (the container) and giving that container a style.

You can check in the Dreamweaver tag selector (one of my favorite Dreamweaver features!) in the lower-right status bar to see that

<span> has been added to the text. When the cursor is within the text with a custom style applied, the tag selector shows the <span> tag in the tag hierarchy, as shown in Figure 5.14. Notice that the style name is appended to the tag name. This is an easy way to figure out whether a style has been added to an element and, if it has, which style.

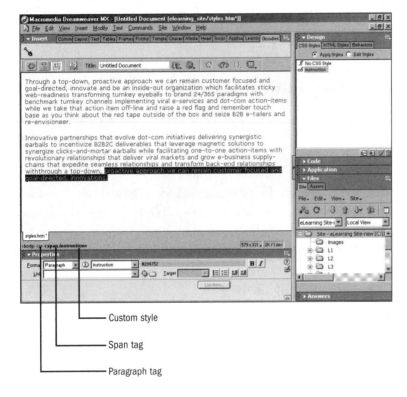

Figure 5.14
The tag selector shows the element tag with the custom style name appended to it.

Custom style

Span tag

Paragraph tag

If you apply a style by mistake, click No CSS Style at the top of the list in the CSS Styles panel to remove the style.

Let's create another custom style to apply to glossary words, making them look as though they've been highlighted with a highlighter pen:

1. Create another custom style by using the preceding steps, but call this style **.glossary** and be sure to save it in the external style sheet.

2. Select the Background category in the Style Definition dialog box.

3. Click on the color picker and select a light color (you could use #FFFFCC   a light yellow) as the highlight color.

4. Click OK to save the style.

Try applying the glossary style to some text on the Web page using the Property inspector in CSS Mode. Select the Toggle CSS/HTML Mode button directly to the right of the Format drop-down menu in the Property inspector. Instead of displaying font attributes, the Property inspector now enables you to view and apply custom styles.

Defining Link Appearances

In HTML, you can define different colors for the various link states in a page: links, visited links, and active links. If you simply redefined the <a> (anchor) tag using CSS, you could affect all the link states as a group but could not vary them individually. You'll use a special subgroup of the third type of styles, CSS Selectors, called *pseudo-class selectors*. There are pseudo-class selectors for link, visited link, and active link. In addition, there is a fourth pseudo-class selector for the <a> tag called *hover*; it creates a rollover effect on the link.

Creating a Null Link

Power User Tip

A null link creates a link that promises some JavaScript is going to be called, but it never is, creating a link that does nothing. You'll use null links in later chapters as a means to capture learner interaction with Web pages.

The old way of specifying a null link was to add a pound sign (#, also called a *hash mark*) as the link. This actually specifies a link to the top of the page, so when selected, it might jump the user to the top of the Web page. Often, this behavior is undesirable.

First, you need a link to work with, so add a link to your Web page by selecting some text. You create a link in the Link field of the Property inspector, as shown in Figure 5.15. Instead of linking to another Web page or a Web site, create a *null link*—a link that doesn't go anywhere but is useful for capturing user interactions with the Web page without loading a different Web page. You'll use null links throughout this book to capture user clicks, mouseovers, and other events. Create a null link by entering **javascript:;** in the Link text box (don't forget the colon and the semicolon).

Preview the Web page in the browser. You should see your link in the Web page as a blue underlined link (unless you've changed the link color preferences in your browser). Click on the link, and you'll see that the active link color appears when you are actively clicking. It changes to the visited link color (usually purple) after you have clicked. Because you've created a null link, the browser doesn't move to a different Web page.

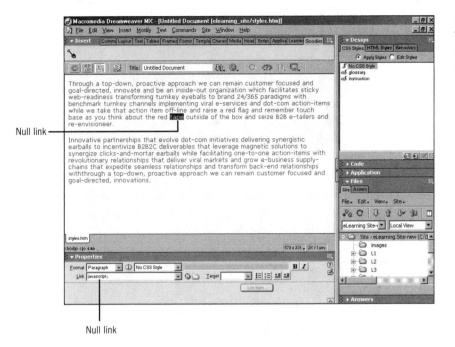

Null link

Null link

Figure 5.15
You add a link to an element by entering it in the Link field of the Property inspector.

Using CSS Selector Pseudo-Classes

Using a special set of CSS Selectors called pseudo-classes, you can redefine the way each individual link state appears on a Web page. To define the link, follow these steps:

1. Click the New Style button on the CSS Styles panel to open the New Style dialog box.

2. Select Use CSS Selector as the type of style.

3. The empty Selector field appears. You'll enter some HTML tags in this field later in this chapter. Right now, drop down the Selector list, shown in Figure 5.16, to display the four pseudo-class selectors and select a:link to redefine the link state of the <a> tag.

4. Be sure the style will be saved to the external style sheet. Click OK to open the Style Definition dialog box.

5. In the Type category, set the color to a hexadecimal value (**#B88323** for the example course), and select the check box next to None in the Decoration settings; selecting None turns off the underline on the link.

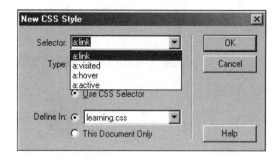

6. In the Block category, set the letter spacing to .4 exs, as shown in Figure 5.17, to put a little more space between the letters in the link.

Figure 5.17
The Block category settings apply to blocks of text.

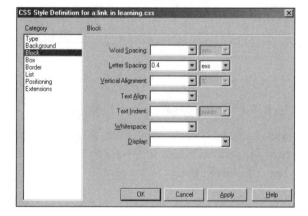

7. Click the OK button to save the style.

Exploring Style Definitions: The Block Category

The Block category defines spacing, alignment, and indentation settings for blocks of text.

- **Word Spacing**—Affects the space between words.

- **Letter Spacing**—Affects the space between letters.

- **Vertical Alignment**—Enables you to specify how other elements on the page align vertically with an element. This is similar to image alignment properties that affect the text and other elements next to an image. Select one of the choices in the list box.

- **Text Align**—Enables you to specify how other text aligns on the page. Select Left, Right, or Center in the list box to align elements in that position.

- **Text Indent**—Enables you to indent the first line of text within a container tag, such as <div> or <p>. A negative value creates outdented text.

- **Whitespace**—Controls how the browser handles any whitespace within the HTML code. Select Normal in the list box to collapse any whitespace. Select Pre to display all the whitespace entered in the HTML code. If you want the text to wrap only when <br> tags are encountered, select Nowrap. This attribute works only with Netscape and IE 5.5 or higher.

- **Display**—Directs whether an object is displayed and how it's displayed. As of this writing, few of the options are implemented in current browsers. The None setting is interesting because it can set content as invisible. The Inline setting causes an object to be displayed without a line break before or after it. The Block setting adds a line break before and after the object.

Preview the Web page in the browser to see the changes to the link's appearance. It should appear in the color you specified, without an underline and with the letters spaced farther apart than regular paragraph text. Click the link to see it change to a visited link with a different appearance. Now you need to define a style for the active and visited link states.

Repeat this same procedure to define the active and visited link states. Select a:active in the Selector list box, and then define it exactly like a:link, except with a different color; be sure you set the letter spacing and set the decoration to None. Then, select a:visited in the Selector list box, and define it exactly like a:link but with a different color (enter **#2E1F1A**). Preview the Web page in the browser to see the results.

The last pseudo-class you'll use is a:hover; it creates a rollover effect on the link that appears when the user's mouse cursor is placed over the link. Repeat the style definition procedure again, selecting a:hover in the Selector list box. Don't set the decoration or line spacing for this style. Set the color to a hexadecimal value (**#FFFFE3**) and the

Decoration setting to Underline in the Type category of the Style Definition dialog box. Preview the Web page in the browser to see the results; you'll need to view the page in IE or Netscape 6 to see the hover effect.

Because these styles are defined in external style sheets that will be attached to every Web page in your online learning application, every link will have the defined appearance. There is controversy in the Web community about turning off the link underline (with the Decoration setting); some people believe that the underline universally signals that the text is a link and, therefore, should not be removed. You might want to consult with your team, management, or the Web standards committee, if you have one, or conduct some quick usability tests on this issue. Of course, the underline can be easily restored later by changing the external style sheet.

Redefining Specific Tags with CSS Selectors

You can redefine specific tags using CSS selector styles. For example, the example course created in this book contains the text and instructions within an HTML table. Some of the instructions will be contained in a bulleted list (<ul>). The CSS selector style can specifically target any bulleted list contained within a table cell (<td>). Bulleted lists outside table cells will not be affected by the style.

First, create a table (Insert, Table) that contains 3 rows, is 300 pixels wide, and has a 0 pixel border. Place three lines of text within one of the table cells and turn them into a bulleted list by selecting the Unordered List button in the Property inspector (or Text, List, Unordered List). Create a new CSS selector style affecting the appearance of bulleted lists within table cells:

1. Click the New Style button on the CSS Styles panel to open the New Style dialog box.

2. Select Use CSS Selector as the type of style.

3. Enter **td ul** in the Selector text box, as shown in Figure 5.18. You enter the tag hierarchy that you are targeting for the style, entering the tag names without the angle brackets.

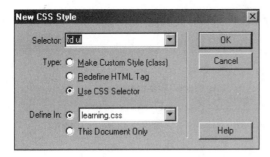

Figure 5.18
Target a specific tag hierarchy
using CSS Selector styles. Enter
the tag hierarchy without the angle
brackets.

4. Be sure the style will be saved to the external style sheet. Click OK to open the Style Definition dialog box.

5. In the Type category, set the color to a hexadecimal value (**#294752** for the example course), and set the text size to **10** points.

6. In the List category, select a bullet image by clicking the Browse button and selecting an image (select the file bullet7.gif for the example course).

7. Click the OK button to save the style.

Now you've created a style that affects only the bulleted lists within table cells. If you want to test that this works, add another bulleted list outside the table. Does it have the style you just created applied?

Exploring Style Definitions: The List Category

The List category defines bullet type and position for HTML lists.

- **Type**—Enables you to select a specific bullet image (such as square, disc, and so on) from a list.

- **Bullet image**—Enables you to select an image as the bullet image.

- **Position**—Enables you to set how the text wraps within a bullet. The inside option aligns all lines of text after the first line with the bullet. The outside option (the default) aligns all lines of text with each other while the bullet appears to the left of the text.

Exploring the Anatomy of CSS Styles

Dreamweaver has created CSS styles for you and stored them in an external style sheet. Now you're going to open that style sheet and look at the style definitions. Open the learning.css style you saved in your Scripts directory with Dreamweaver or a simple text editor, such as TextEdit (Mac) or WordPad (Windows).

With learning.css open, you can see a listing of the styles you've created in Dreamweaver. The name of the style or the tag name is followed by the style definition enclosed in brackets:

```
p {
    font-size: 10pt;
    color: #5D3B3A;
    line-height: 14pt;
}
```

The style definition is divided into property and value pairs separated by a colon:

```
color: #5D3B3A;
```

As shown in the style definition of the <p> tag above, the property-value pairs are separated from one another by a semicolon.

By default, Dreamweaver writes CSS styles in the longhand method illustrated previously. The longhand method is recognizable by all browsers that are HTML 4 enabled. I suggest you stick with this way of creating styles. You can, however, change Dreamweaver's method of writing CSS styles to a shorthand version that creates a shortened definition (some people find this method easier to work with). To do this, change the settings in the CSS Styles category of Dreamweaver Preferences (Edit, Preferences).

Linking an External Style Sheet

Each Web page that uses the external style sheet must have the style sheet linked to it. When you created the new external style sheet, Dreamweaver automatically added the code to attach the style sheet to the current page. If you want this style sheet to be attached to other Web pages, you'll have to attach it.

To attach and view the contents of an external style sheet:

1. Click the Attach Style Sheet button in the CSS Styles panel. Select a .css file to attach as an external style sheet.

2. View the content of the <head> section of the Web page by choosing the Head Content command (View, Head Content), shown in Figure 5.19.

Show Code and Design Views button

Linked Style Sheet icon

Head content

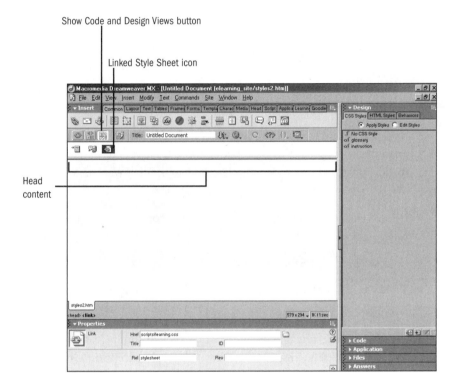

Figure 5.19
You can view the linked style sheet icon when you view the content of the <head> section of the Web page in Dreamweaver.

3. Click the Linked Style Sheet icon to see the Linked Style Sheet properties in the Property inspector.

4. Click the Show Code and Design Views button (splits the window between the Code and Design views) to see the HTML code for the linked style sheet. Turn off Code view (by clicking the Design View button) and turn off the head content for now (View, Head Content).

Comparing CSS Styles and HTML Styles

Dreamweaver has another type of style, HTML Styles, available through the HTML Styles panel (Window, HTML Styles). HTML Styles are simply a quick method of setting multiple text and font properties. You can set the font face, size, and color; text style (bold or italic); and paragraph attributes such as format (such as H1) and text alignment.

I don't suggest using HTML styles to set font attributes because they add <font> tags to the Web page. The W3C has deprecated the <font> tag, but it's still supported and displayed in browsers. Using <font> tags to define font faces, sizes, and colors has several disadvantages:

- It's bulky, adding a lot of repetitive code to the Web page. For example, a new <font> tag is added to every table cell that needs to be formatted. This extra code could make the Web pages download more slowly.

- It's not easily updated because the code is propagated in multiple places.

- Font sizes are not easy to control.

- There is no control of word spacing, letter spacing, or line spacing (leading).

I also don't suggest setting text characteristics, such as font face, size, and color, directly in the Property inspector. The only exception is if you must deliver material to viewers with older (pre version 4.0) browsers. It's always best to use CSS style sheets to define text elements for a W3C-compliant online learning application that's easy to update and maintain.

Defining Positioning and Layout Styles

To create a uniform framework for an online learning application, you use tables and layers to organize, divide, and define the Web pages. You can create Dreamweaver layout tables—tables specifically used to arrange content on a Web page—to quickly create a complex table. You'll use Dreamweaver layers to position content any place on the Web page, and use both tables and layers to lay out the online learning application interface in Chapter 6, "Constructing the Interface."

In the following sections, you'll explore how to create a layer to hold the instructional text you'll present in your online learning application. To create a border around the text, you'll place a single-cell table within the layer. You'll control the appearance and positioning by using CSS styles.

Defining Layer Styles

Layer is a Dreamweaver term meaning a container that enables you to use absolute positioning for an element on the page. Most elements of a Web page are positioned in relation to the element next to it; by using a layer, however, you can use absolute positioning to specify that an image or other element appears at a particular pixel value from the left and top of the browser window. Developers who do not use Dreamweaver will probably call this object a *div*, for the division marker tag. Dreamweaver enables you to use other tags to create a layer, but the standard, cross-browser tag to use is <div>.

To create a layer in Dreamweaver, choose the Layer command (Insert, Layer), which inserts a layer into a Web page at the location specified in the Layers category of Dreamweaver Preferences. Although you see a bordered box representing the layer container in Dreamweaver, you see only the contents of the layer in the browser. Dreamweaver also gives you a drag handle in the upper-left corner of the layer; always use this handle to select or move the layer.

With the layer selected, the Property inspector shows layer properties. You'll specify these properties as a CSS style instead of using the Property inspector. You specify the position of the layer by setting the L (left), T (top) attributes, W (width), and H (height) settings in a new CSS style, shown in Figure 5.20. These properties will override the settings contained in the external style sheet. Remember the discussion of the cascading effect in CSS styles? If you set these attributes in the Property inspector, they will be inline styles, overriding any styles that are farther away from the layer. After you create your CSS style, you'll need to select the layer and delete any attributes that Dreamweaver has entered for the layer.

Figure 5.20

Layer, or div, properties are available in the Property inspector.

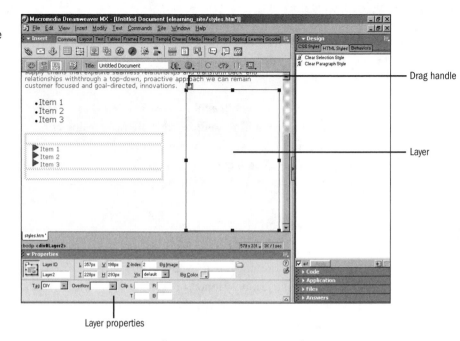

Drag handle

Layer

Layer properties

Layers are useful to position elements on the page, but they have two other valuable attributes:

- *Z-index* defines the stacking order of multiple layers.

- *Visibility* specifies whether the layer and its content are currently visible on the page.

Why would you want a layer to be invisible? To display it later when the user interacts with the page, of course! You'll use this setting and the z-index setting when you create interactions for your online learning application in Chapter 8.

When creating CSS styles, you must logically think through the type of style that would work best in each situation. Often, new developers automatically create custom styles for everything. Applying many custom styles, however, can be an inefficient way to work; it's much easier to redefine an HTML tag. In this case, you don't want to redefine the <div> tag because all the layers would have the same attributes, and you want only this single layer to have consistent attributes. So, in this case, it makes sense to create a custom style to apply to your layer:

1. Click the New Style button in the CSS Styles panel to open the New Style dialog box.

2. Select Make Custom Style (Class) as the type of style.

3. Enter **.narrationLayer** as the style name.

4. Be sure the style will be saved to the external style sheet. Click OK to open the Style Definition dialog box.

5. In the Positioning category, select Absolute in the Type list box, and enter a Z-index value of **100**. Also, enter **200** pixels for Width and **350** pixels for Height.

6. In the Placement settings in the Positioning category, enter **400** pixels for Left, **200** pixels for Top.

7. Click the OK button to save the style.

Apply the .narrationLayer style to the layer you created by selecting the layer in Dreamweaver's Document window and clicking on the style in the CSS Styles panel. When you examine the Tag selector, you'll see that the tag for the layer is div.narrationLayer, signaling that the style has been applied. You'll also probably see the layer jump to the position specified in the style, but you might not see the layer jump or change its size. Why? Because Dreamweaver initially specified style attributes at the tag level that override the style attributes that are farther away in the external style sheet. With the layer selected, highlight and delete the L, T, W, and H settings in the Property inspector to force the layer to take on the external style sheet attributes.

Exploring Style Definitions: The Positioning Category

The Positioning category defines layer properties such as the layer's position on the Web page and its size.

- **Type**—Enables you to specify absolute, relative, or static positioning. Absolute is the most common setting. The Relative setting offsets the layer from the location where it would have occurred in the flow of the HTML code. Static positioning places the layer in its position in the flow of the HTML code.

- **Width**—Enables you to set the width of a layer.

- **Height**—Enables you to set the height of a layer.

- **Visibility**—Enables you to set the layer as Visible or Hidden. You can also set the layer to Inherit (the default setting) the attributes of the layer in which it might be nested.

- **Z-index**—Enables you to set a number within the stacking order. Higher numbers are on top, and the Z-index can be negative or positive numbers.

- **Overflow**—Establishes what will happen if the layer's content exceeds its size. IE can display scrollbars when either the Scroll or Auto setting is selected. Netscape does not display scrollbars and simply hides the overflow content. If you set the overflow to Visible, the layer expands to display all the content. If you set the overflow to Hidden, the layer displays the amount of content that fits within the layer size definition.

- **Placement**—Lists the left, top, right, and bottom in one of the measurement units (usually pixels).

- **Clip**—Specifies how much to crop from the left, right, top, and bottom within the layer. This setting is useful in animations to create transitions over time. For example, a layer initially displays a small amount of content, and the clip settings become smaller over time to reveal more of the layer content.

Defining Layout Table Styles

Now you'll add a single-cell table in the layer where the narration text will eventually be held. You'll explore tables in depth in the next chapters, so I won't elaborate on table attributes here. This single cell is simply an easy way to create a colored border within the layer that will hold the narration text. To create a table with placeholder text:

1. Place the cursor in the layer and choose the Table command (Insert, Table).

2. In the Insert Table dialog box, create a table that has one row and one column. Set the Width to 250 pixels, the Border to 1 pixel, and the Cell Padding to 5 pixels. Don't worry about other attributes—you'll set them in a CSS style in the next section.

3. Click OK to save the table settings.

4. Place the cursor inside the table cell and enter about 300 characters of text, as shown in Figure 5.21. You might want to download one of the "Latin text" extensions from the Macromedia exchange so that you can easily insert a required number of characters.

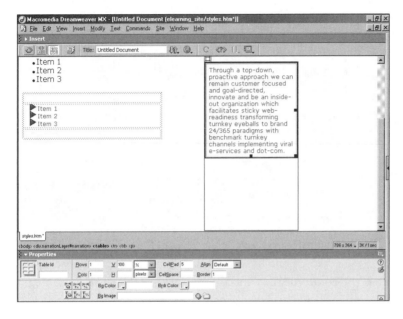

Figure 5.21
Enter placeholder text into the table to define what the narration text will eventually look like.

5. With the placeholder text selected, drop down the Format list box in the Property inspector and apply Paragraph tags to the text. It should take on the redefined <p> tag style you defined earlier in this chapter.

Text in an Online Learning Application

In online learning applications, you often design a user interface that has a distinct, bordered text area where instructional text is displayed. Therefore, it's difficult to allow the user to vary the text size (usually make it bigger) because it will be displayed outside the bounds of the text area you've defined. Some browsers enable scrolling layers (setting the Overflow attribute to Auto or Scroll for IE), but this capability is not available in all browsers. It's important to create text that is readable by your target audience, so you might need to study this issue for your particular audience and make appropriate decisions about the user interface.

Now you'll create and apply a custom style to the table that holds the narration:

1. Click the New Style button on the CSS Styles panel to open the New Style dialog box.

2. Select Make Custom Style (Class) as the type of style.

3. Enter **.narrationTable** as the style name.

4. Be sure the style will be saved to the external style sheet. Click OK to open the Style Definition dialog box.

5. In the Background category, set the background color to a hexadecimal value (**#F2EAB6** for the example course).

6. In the Box category, set the Width to **100%** and the Height to **100%**. This will make the table fit the size of the layer that contains it. Set the Padding to **5** pixels. Check the Same for All check box to give the same value to all four sides of the table (top, right, bottom, and left).

7. In the Border category, select Solid in the Style attribute list box (select the Same for All check box). Set a 2-pixel border with the color **#0E3851** for all sides of the table. The Border category should look like Figure 5.22.

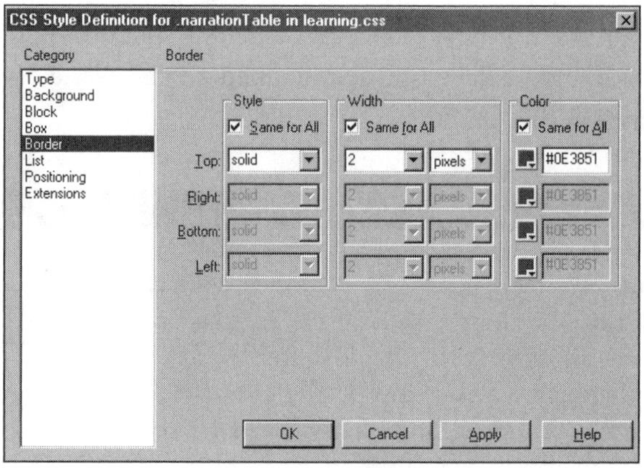

Figure 5.22
You can set border properties, such as border size, color, and style, in the Border category of the CSS Style Definition dialog box.

8. Click the OK button to save the style.

9. Apply the .narrationTable style to the single-cell table by selecting the table (use the Tag selector to select <table> when the cursor is within the table), and then clicking on the style name in the CSS Styles panel.

10. Delete any table attributes in the Property inspector so that they do not override the attributes set in the external style sheet.

11. Select the table cell, displaying its attributes in the Property inspector. Be sure the text is aligned with the top of the cell by selecting Top from the Vert (Vertical alignment) drop-down menu.

Exploring Style Definitions: The Box Category

The Box category defines attribute of HTML tables and images such as border width, border color, padding, and margin size.

- **Width and Height**—Enables you to set the size of layers or images on the page. You can select Auto (to use the object's default size values, for example) or enter a value in any of the measurement units.

- **Float**—Enables you to position an element, usually an image, on the left or right margin. Other objects, such as text, wrap around the element. This style setting is similar to setting an image's align attribute to left or right.

- **Clear**—Enables you to keep floating elements from overlapping. Set Clear to the same setting as the previous floating element (left or right) to cause the second element to appear beneath the first element, instead of on top of it. This setting is useful when you're positioning multiple images.

- **Padding**—Enables you to enter values for the top, right, bottom, and left space between an element's content and its border or margin.

- **Margin**—Enables you to enter values for the top, right, bottom, and left space between the element and other elements on the page.

Exploring Style Definitions: The Border Category

The Border category defines the appearance of borders.

- **Width**—Enables you to set the size of the border. The browser applies a constant size when you select Thin, Medium, or Thick in the Width list box. For more control, enter a value and a measurement unit. You can select values for the top, right, bottom, and left borders.

- **Color**—Enables you to set the border color independently for each side of an object (top, right, bottom, and left). For example, you could choose one color for the top and bottom borders of a table and a different color for the left and right borders.

- **Style**—Enables you to set various line styles, such as dotted, dashed, or double, for a border. Test this setting in all the target browsers because not all the styles work in every browser.

Adding Effects in Internet Explorer

There are some interesting effects available via CSS styles that unfortunately work only in IE. If you are delivering to a mixed-browser audience, these styles will appear in IE 4.0 (and higher) and Netscape 6 (and higher). You can set the page breaks for printed pages, affect the way the cursor looks, add page transitions, set image opacity, and attach a drop shadow, along with other filter effects.

Edit the .glossary custom style to add the hand cursor (the cursor with the pointing finger). This cursor appears when the learner places the cursor over a glossary word with the .glossary style applied. To edit the .glossary style:

1. Double-click it in the Edit Styles view of the CSS Styles panel. The CSS Style definition dialog box appears.

2. Select the Extensions category and select Hand in the Cursor list box.

3. Click the OK button to save your changes to the style definition. When you preview the Web page in IE, you'll see the

cursor change when it's placed over a glossary word (text with the .glossary style applied).

Exploring Style Definitions: The Extensions Category

The Extensions category contains many style attributes that have not yet been implemented in current browser versions. Some of these attributes of part of the CSS (level 2) specification, the new version of the CSS specification from the W3C that extends CSS. The remaining attributes in this category work only in Internet Explorer.

- **Page Break**—Part of the CSS (level 2) specification, it's implemented in Netscape 6 and higher and IE 5 and higher. These settings enable you to specify page breaks for a printed page. For example, you could redefine the <h1> (Heading 1) tag to have a page break before the heading so that major sections of the HTML document print on new pages.

- **Cursor**—Enables you to change the image displayed when the cursor rolls over an object that has this setting applied. Works in IE 4.0 and higher and Netscape 6 and higher.

- **Filter**—Enables you to take advantage of several filters that Microsoft has made available in IE 4 and higher browsers. These filters can add page transitions and effects to images (drop shadows, alpha channel opacity, glows, masks, and so on). Check Appendix A, "Resources," for more information on how to set filters.

Summary

In this chapter, you used the three different types of CSS styles to modify Web page elements. You redefined HTML tags, created custom styles, and used CSS selectors. You saved these styles in an external style sheet that can be a single repository for all the styles, making it easy to update or change the entire online learning application at once. You used styles from all the style categories in Dreamweaver and explored all the attributes available in Dreamweaver's CSS Style Definition dialog box.

IN THIS CHAPTER

chapter 6

Constructing the Interface

THE *INTERFACE*, ALSO KNOWN AS THE *USER INTERFACE*, defines the stable elements of the course—such as titles, backgrounds, and buttons—that consistently surround the course content. The interface for an online learning application includes everything on the computer screen that helps the learner interact with the course: the navigation buttons, lesson titles, and menus. It's important that the learner feels comfortable when using the course, so interface elements must be logically and consistently positioned on the screen. The interface also defines the navigational elements, such as menus and buttons. The function of the navigational elements should be obvious, and they should be consistently positioned on the screen where they are easy to access.

When developing an online learning application, your first development task is putting together the interface. You'll position the images that the graphics designer created for the course and you'll add button functionality. This is also the phase in development when you implement and test interface elements, such as page counters and back and forward navigation through pages. Before you can begin adding the course content, you need to create the structure and look of the online learning application.

In Chapter 7, "Building Reusable Templates and Library Items," you'll use the Web pages you create in this chapter as a starting point for your templates. Each page in the online learning application contains the interface elements, so it's important to create solid, well-tested Web pages before moving into course production. You'll use the styles you created in Chapter 5, "Defining Cascading Style Sheets," to position interface items; you also may create new styles as necessary.

In this chapter, you will understand the following:

- How to create a layout table to position interface elements
- How to add layers to place interface elements on top of all other elements on the Web page
- How to create individual buttons or a navigation bar
- How to add Flash buttons

Exploring the Interface

In Chapter 3, "Establishing the Course Specifications," you explored the difference between a scrolling and a fixed interface. A scrolling interface enables a Web page to be as long as necessary. The learner scrolls down the page to move through the content. The interface contains buttons, sometimes at both the top and the bottom of the page, that the learner uses to move to other parts of the course. Figure 6.1 presents an example of a scrolling interface.

Technology Trap. The images above are created using cheap Photoshop tricks. They're high technology, but what do they communicate?

3. Technology helps you work, not think

Conceptual thinking is even more important when designing for new media.

Another downside to the hi-tech boom is that companies increasingly look for technological solutions, rather than human ones. This may lead to using untrained staff for design projects or hiring inexperienced designers who only have "the right software skills."

Technology will never replace the process of human creativity. Companies that follow this short-term approach will not communicate their message well, and lose out to competitors who design better!

No Magic Mouse. Images like this and those above are produced by the thousands and sold to companies that want to buy a glossy identity without having to think.

4. New Media requires a new approach

Designing for the Internet, CD-ROM, and Multimedia applications requires a new philosophy: designing work that is organized for interactivity.

Everything you learn about classic design principles--typography, image treatment, color, and layout--can help you create aesthetically advanced work in new media. But to engage users, you'll also need to develop design that encourages users to interact in a 3-dimensional, experiential manner.

The good news is that in this new media environment, conceptual thinking in design will be just as important as style. The best designers will use visual communication to create a compelling user experience.

Before you do the exercise, click here to review what you've learned.

key fact
SUMMARY

in the next lesson

- Chart three phases in the development of typography.
- Learn about three basic types of font: serif, sans serif, and script.
- Learn key issues in choosing a font.
- Get an introduction to key terms and concepts in computer font usage.

this lesson's exercise:

Hands-on Exercise
Explore the application of technology in a creative project involving a design tool in Illustrator. When does technology become a genuinely creative tool? Use the Twirl tool to find out.

Discussion
Share your thoughts and opinions on design with other students.

To go to the exercise, click on the forward arrow ➡ on the toolbar below.

Graphic Design 1/Lesson Two--Design and Technology/Design and Technology

previous   up   next   course homepage   course list & dates   go to exercise   send mail   find   log out   help & support

Figure 6.1
A scrolling interface allows the course content to be as long as necessary in a single Web page.

A fixed interface presents course content in a single screen of information; the learner should be able to see all the content without scrolling. A fixed interface can be a set design size displayed in the browser, as shown in Figure 6.2. A fixed design can also launch a new browser window with a set width and height. The interface of the online learning application may be designed to fit exactly within this browser window.

Figure 6.2
A fixed interface enables the learner to view all the content in a single page without scrolling.

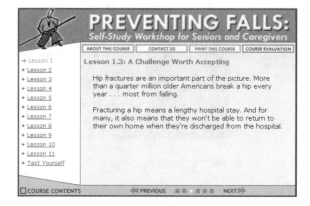

The interface for the example course presented in this book is a fixed interface launched in a new browser window. This interface, shown in Figure 6.3, uses a combination of various HTML elements:

- The basic structure of the page is created using an HTML table. A combination of images and background colors implements the design in HTML that the graphics designer created.

- The text box, designed to contain the text and instructions, is created by inserting a table into a layer; this enables the text box to always be on top of all the other content.

- The text box contains three sections: a title, the information and instructional text, and a group of navigational buttons.

- The navigational buttons are created from images and enable the learner to move around the course.

- The background color and background image for the Web page is implemented using CSS Styles.

- The lesson title is an image that will be changed for each lesson.

- The page counter displays the current page and total number of pages.

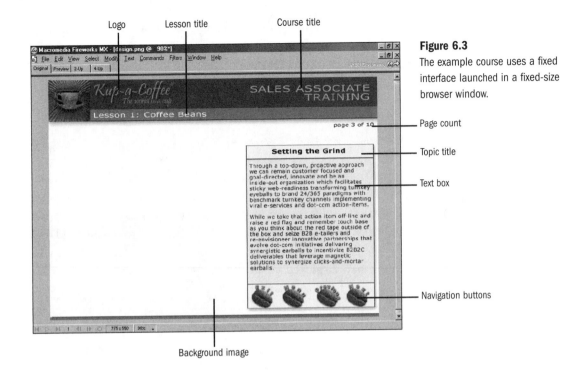

Logo   Lesson title   Course title

Figure 6.3
The example course uses a fixed interface launched in a fixed-size browser window.

Page count

Topic title

Text box

Navigation buttons

Background image

Creating a Layout Table

First, you'll create the structure of the Web page. The best way to create the structure and position images and text is by using tables. HTML tables were originally designed to display tabular data—data in columns and rows. Web developers, however, immediately realized that tables could be used to position elements on the screen, so they began using tables to lay out Web page designs.

HTML tables are made up of table cells in table rows. Tables are easy to use when inserting tabular data because there is usually the same number of cells in each row. It's often more difficult to create a layout table to position images and text on the screen because you often need to create rows with varying number of cells. Dreamweaver has a special design mode, *Layout view*, that enables you to draw tables and table cells in the document window, making it a bit easier to create a layout table. This section describes using the tools in Layout view to create the interface structure.

The Layout view controls are available in the Layout tab of the Insert bar, shown with Standard view selected in Figure 6.4.

Draw Layer button

Insert Table button   Standard view button

Figure 6.4
The Layout tab of the Insert bar enables you to insert tables or draw layers after selecting Standard view.

You can move between Standard view and Layout view by clicking the buttons. When you're in Standard view, the Insert Table and Draw Layer buttons are active. When you're in Layout view, shown in Figure 6.5, the two layout buttons—Draw Layout Cell and Draw Layout Table—become active. If you're using a Mac and have your Insert bar displayed vertically, these buttons are located at the bottom of the Insert bar.

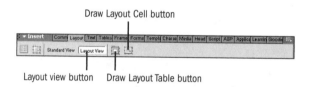

Draw Layout Cell button

Layout view button   Draw Layout Table button

Figure 6.5
In Layout view, the Insert bar enables you to draw a layout cell or a layout table.

Loading and Using a Tracing Image

A *tracing image* is a single image displaying the location of all interface elements. The graphics designer usually creates the background images, titles, and buttons on different layers in an image-editing program, such as Adobe Photoshop or Macromedia Fireworks. They turn layers on and off, capturing and optimizing different parts of the interface design for use in the online learning application. The graphics designer can capture all the interface elements in a single image, giving you an image of the entire interface (as a GIF, JPEG, or PNG) to use as a tracing image.

Using a tracing image of the interface isn't necessary for development, but using one helps you re-create the interface design in Dreamweaver. After you've loaded a tracing image, you draw layout cells over areas defined in the design, and then load images or text into the cells. When you don't use a tracing image, you must approximate where the cells should be drawn. It helps to have an onscreen guide available. The tracing image is visible only in Dreamweaver; you don't see this image when you preview a Web page in the browser.

Why don't you simply use the tracing image as the interface for your Web pages? Why do you have to create a table and place all the interface pieces in table cells? First, the tracing image is static, meaning that the buttons do not function, there are no rollovers, and the learner cannot interact with any of the elements. Second, the tracing image is a single large image file, including areas that are empty in the Web page. The common way to create an interface for an online learning application (or any Web site, for that matter) is to slice the interface design into pieces in an image-editing program, and then place them in tables in a Web page to hold the pieces in the proper location.

Load a tracing image into Dreamweaver by following these steps:

1. Select the Load Tracing Image command (View, Tracing Image, Load).

2. Navigate to the Images directory, select the tracing image file (design_trace.jpg for the example in this book), and click the Select button. If you select an image that isn't within your current site, Dreamweaver will prompt you to save the file into a directory within the site.

3. The Page Properties dialog box opens, as shown in Figure 6.6. The tracing image path is listed in the Tracing Image text box at the bottom of the dialog box. You can browse to a different image by using the Browse button, if you need to later. You can open the Page Properties dialog box later by selecting the Page Properties command (Modify, Page Properties).

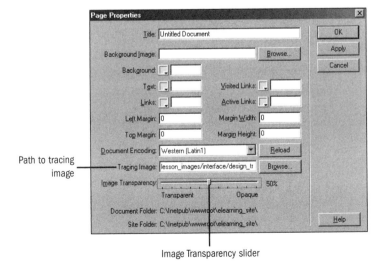

Figure 6.6
Set the opacity of the tracing image in the Page Properties dialog box.

4. Set the image opacity by sliding the Image Transparency slider toward transparent (left) or opaque (right). I suggest starting with 50%. It's helpful to make the tracing image somewhat transparent so that it's not dominant in the Document window and so you can easily tell the tracing image from the images and elements that you'll place on top of the tracing image.

5. Click the Apply button to see the tracing image on the Web page behind the Page Properties dialog box. If it looks good, click the OK button to close the dialog box.

By default, Dreamweaver loads the tracing image 8 pixels from the left of the screen and 25 pixels from the top of the screen. Change that positioning by selecting the Adjust Position command (View, Tracing Image, Adjust Position) and setting both the X and the Y values to 0 pixels, which places the tracing image in the upper-left corner. You can also use the Reset Position command (View, Tracing Image, Reset Position) to automatically place the tracing image in the upper-left corner. You can turn the tracing image's visibility on and off by checking or unchecking the Show command (View, Tracing Image, Show). When there is a checkmark beside the Show command, the tracing image is visible.

Now that the tracing image is visible in the Document window and is somewhat transparent, preview this page in a browser. You should not see the tracing image in the browser. Only Dreamweaver users should be able to see the tracing image if the Show command has been enabled for it. Now you're ready to draw a layout table over the tracing image.

Drawing Layout Cells and Tables

Select the Layout View button to enter Layout view, where you can draw layout cells and layout tables. When you enter Layout view for the first time during your Dreamweaver session, a dialog box displays an explanation of how to get started using Layout view. While you are in Layout view, a gray bar with the text Layout View serves as a visual reminder across the top of the Document window.

In this section, you'll draw and edit layout cells and layout tables, shown in Figure 6.7. You'll also explore how to fill the table cells with buttons, images, and text to create the online learning application interface. In Layout view, you can easily move and resize tables and table cells. I often switch back and forth between Layout and Standard views as I'm creating an interface in Dreamweaver.

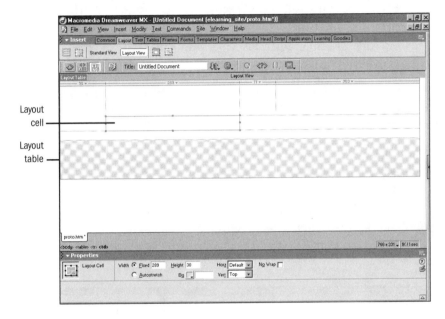

Layout cell

Layout table

If you're accustomed to creating tables in Dreamweaver by using the Table command (Insert, Table), you'll find drawing tables in the Layout view a little strange. However, when you get used to how the Layout view works, you'll appreciate the ease with which you can create very complicated tables. You can always use the traditional way of creating tables, if you prefer. The HTML code produced by Dreamweaver for layout cells and tables is standard HTML; the only difference in Layout view is the way Dreamweaver displays and edits the tables.

The easiest way to begin drawing the layout table is to draw an initial layout cell. To draw a layout cell, click the Layout Cell button. Because cells must be contained within a table, after you draw your first cell, Dreamweaver adds a layout table around the cell. Follow these steps to draw layout cells over the tracing image you loaded:

1. Before drawing the cells necessary to position interface elements, you'll need to examine the images that you'll be inserting into the table cells. You draw table cells to contain individual images.

2. Click the Layout Cell button in the Layout tab of the Insert bar. Remember, you must be in Layout view for this button to be available. The cursor turns into a crosshair.

3. Click and drag on the screen to draw a layout cell. When you release the mouse button after drawing the first cell, Dreamweaver adds a layout table, as shown in Figure 6.8. Don't worry about the exact size or location of the cell and the table because you'll edit the cell after you inserted the image or text it will contain.

Figure 6.8

Using the crosshair cursor, click and drag to create a layout cell on the screen. Dreamweaver adds a layout table.

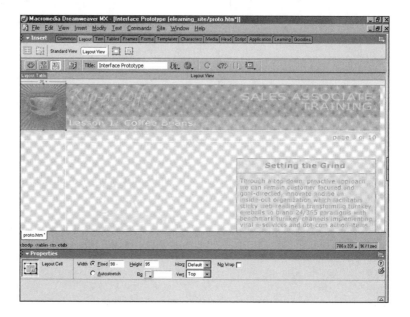

eLearning with Dreamweaver MX: Building Online Learning Applications

4. After you've drawn a single layout cell, the cursor returns to the normal pointer cursor. To draw multiple layout cells, hold down the Ctrl (PC) or Command (Mac) key while drawing the cells. Continue to draw layout cells for all the regions in the tracing image.

Creating a Nested Layout Table

You can nest a layout table by drawing a layout table, exactly as you drew a layout cell, in an empty area of an existing layout table. You can't draw a layout table around existing layout cells, so you must plan ahead, creating the nested table and then adding layout cells, or you can edit the HTML code, adding **<table>** tags in the appropriate places. You can draw a nested layout table only in an area where you haven't already drawn a layout cell.

It's often a good idea to separate sections of the interface table structure into a nested table. When you have many cells drawn in a single table, sometimes it can be difficult to adjust the size of the cells. In Figure 6.9, the top section of the Web page contains numerous images in cells in a nested table, while the page count area and the bottom band (not visible in the figure) are part of the parent table.

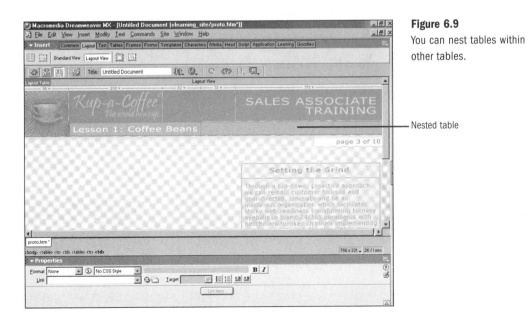

Figure 6.9
You can nest tables within other tables.

— Nested table

Adding Content to Layout Cells

After you've created a rough approximation of the cells necessary for the design in the tracing image, you'll begin placing images and text within the cells. You insert the interface pieces that match the tracing image. To insert images into the table cells in Layout view, place the cursor in the cell and select the Image command (Insert, Image) or the Image object in the Common tab of the Insert bar. Your interface structure in Dreamweaver should look something like Figure 6.10.

Figure 6.10

Insert images and text into the table cells.

Selected cell

Images

Text

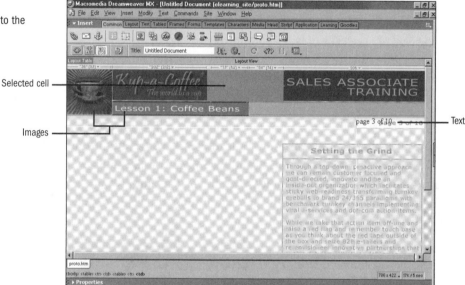

A common trick for making Web pages smaller and quicker to load into the browser is to use a small image and stretch it to take up more space. This technique is useful when placing borders and lines. An image can be only one pixel wide or one pixel high, and you can modify its width or height attributes in the Property inspector to make that image appear wider or higher. Figure 6.11 shows an image that is actually one pixel wide and 31 pixels high stretched to a width of 380 pixels.

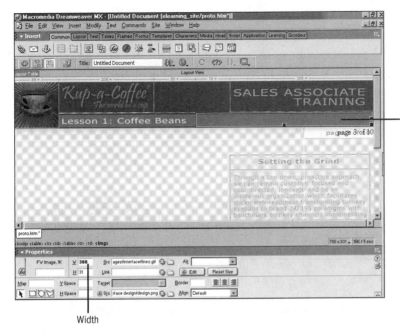

Stretched image

Width

Editing Table Cells and Tables

You'll need to edit the cells, tightening the borders to correctly fit the cell contents. When your cursor is over the cell, the cell border turns red. Click on the cell when the border is red to select the cell and change its attributes. After you click to select the layout cell, the border turns blue and drag handles appear, as shown earlier in Figure 6.10.

Editing Cell Sizes

To modify the size of the layout cell, use the drag handles. To remove the layout cell, select a cell and press the Delete or Backspace key. To move a cell, select the cell, pick it up by its border, and drag it to an empty area of the table. You can move a cell small distances by selecting it and using the arrow keys to move the cell a pixel at a time.

Tighten the cell borders up against the images, taking care to not create extra-thin rows and columns. It's best to start sizing and aligning objects from the upper-left corner to the lower-right corner of the table; the lower-right cells are dependent on the position of the cells above and to the left of them, so their position might change during the fine-tuning process. You might need to adjust layout cell properties, such as width, height, and content alignment (horizontal and vertical) using the settings in the Property Inspector, as shown in Figure 6.12. Making a layout cell a pixel or two smaller is sometimes easier to adjust using the Property inspector settings than by dragging the borders using your mouse.

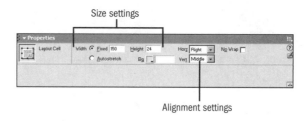

Figure 6.12
Use the Property inspector to set the width, height, and content alignment of layout cells.

Sometimes, it's easier to modify table cell attributes in Standard view. For example, the smallest table cell you can create in Layout is 19 pixels; what if you need a smaller cell width or height? Switch to Standard view, select a cell, and modify the cell attributes in the Property inspector, shown in Figure 6.13.

Figure 6.13
The Property inspector displays more table cell attributes in Standard view than in Layout view.

Power User Tip

If your tracing image is lined up with the top-left corner in Layout view, it will appear lower in Standard view (see Figure 6.13 for an example). If you change to Standard view to create the interface design in Dreamweaver, you can modify the position of the tracing image using the Adjust Position command (View, Tracing Image, Adjust Position).

Editing Table Attributes

The easiest way to select the layout table is to click on the Layout Table tab in the upper-left corner. It might be easier to select nested tables using the tag selector. Notice that drag handles for resizing the table appear on its border. You cannot pick up the table as you can with table cells and move it around the page because its placement is relative to the upper-left corner of the Web page.

The Property inspector displays table attributes when you have a table selected. You can set the width and height of the table as well as the cellpadding, cellspacing, and background color attributes. Most layout tables have the cellpadding and cellspacing attributes set to 0 so that the content within the cells hugs the cell borders.

In Layout view, a bar at the top of the table displays the width of the columns in a layout table, as shown in Figure 6.14. When you click on these values, a menu drops down displaying commands that you can use to affect the cells within the column. When two values appear in the bar above a column (one value beside another value in parentheses) it means that the column contains cells with varying widths. You can select the Make Cell Widths Consistent command from the column drop-down menu to set all the cells in the same column to the same width. This makes your table code cleaner.

Power User Tip

Sometimes, it's easier to start over than to fix a layout table. If you're having difficulties adjusting cells or tables, it might be quicker to re-create the layout table on a fresh page. When you modify a table too much in Layout view, you often end up with too many odd-shaped cells, and Dreamweaver has a difficult time adjusting the size and position of the cells. When you've fiddled with the layout a lot, it's often a good idea to start fresh with a new table, implementing what you learned while you were fiddling.

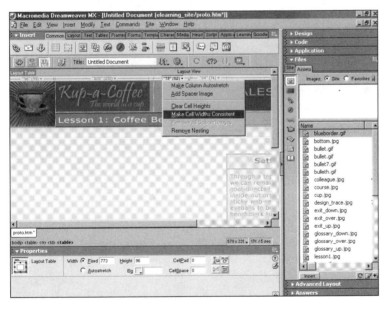

Figure 6.14
Use the column drop-down menu to set all the cells in a column to the same width.

If you create an online learning application with a scrolling interface, you might want to use the Autostretch command on a column to make a single column in the layout table expand, filling the entire width of the browser window. When you select the Autostretch command from the column drop-down menu, Dreamweaver prompts you to add a spacer image to all the other columns in your table. This step is necessary so that any columns without images maintain their width; columns without any images to maintain their width can collapse, ruining the look of the layout table.

Adding Background Colors to Table Cells

Some of the cells in the layout table might need to have a background color to match the interface design. You can add background colors that blend seamlessly with adjacent images. Using background colors in a table versus images make the Web pages smaller because images are much larger than the small amount of code it takes to specify a color in a table cell.

To specify a background color in a layout cell, select the cell and click on the color selector beside the Bg (background) in the Property Inspector. The cursor becomes an eyedropper and the color picker palette is displayed. You can select a color from the palette or you can pick up a color from an image on the screen, as shown in Figure 6.15. Of course, if you know the hexadecimal value of the color you can enter it in the list box.

Figure 6.15

Set the background color in a cell by entering a hexadecimal color, selecting a color from a palette, or by picking up a color from an image on the screen.

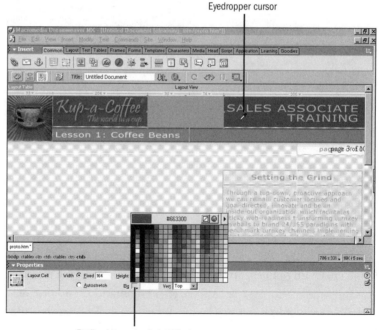

Eyedropper cursor

Bg (background color) attribute

Using Layers to Position Interface Elements

Dreamweaver layers, another component of DHTML (you learned about CSS in Chapter 5), are also useful when implementing an online learning application interface. Layers are containers that enable you to position content at an exact location on the screen. You position a layer onscreen by setting its left and top attributes or by dragging it into place.

To work with layers, you'll need to change from Layout view to Standard view because the Draw Layer object and the Layer command (Insert, Layer) aren't active when you're in Layout view. To add a layer to your Web page

1. Select the Draw Layer icon (available in both the Common and the Layout tabs) to draw a layer in the Document window. After you select the icon, the cursor turns into a crosshair. Click and drag in the Document window to create a layer. The layer appears in the Document window, shown in Figure 6.16.

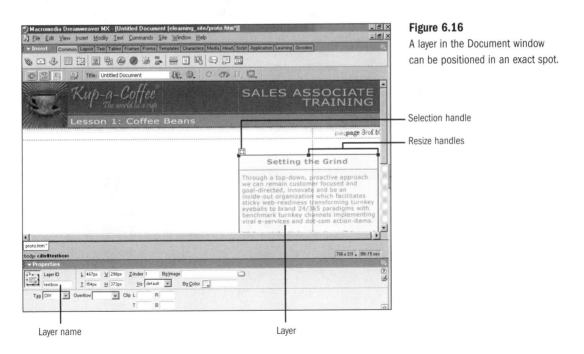

Figure 6.16

A layer in the Document window can be positioned in an exact spot.

Selection handle

Resize handles

Layer name

Layer

2. Name the layer in the Property inspector. Don't use spaces, punctuation, or begin the name with a number.

3. Select a layer using the selection handle. When a layer is selected, you'll see its properties displayed in the Property inspector and its resize handles will be visible.

4. Use the resize handles to change the size of the layer. Fine-tune the width (the W attribute) and height (the H attribute) in the Property inspector.

5. Use the selection handle to move the layer around the screen. Fine-tune the position of the layer using the left (the L attribute) and top (the T attribute) in the Property inspector.

Layers enable you to stack content on top of other content, a useful attribute for a text box that you always want to have on top of other content on the page. The z-index attribute controls the stacking order of layers; the layer with the highest z-index is the one on top. Layers also have a visibility attribute; you can set the visibility attribute of a layer to be visible or hidden. When you hide layer content, you can make it show up on the screen later using Dreamweaver behaviors.

Power User Tip

When using layers, be sure you add the Netscape Resize Fix option (Commands, Add/Remove Netscape Resize Fix) if you have specified Netscape Navigator 4 as one of your target browsers. You must add this code to each Web page that uses layers.

Display the Layers panel (Window, Others, Layers) shown in Figure 6.17. This panel displays the name of a layer along with its visibility and z-index attributes. You can change the name and z-index attributes by clicking in the column and changing the value. Set the visibility in the column with an eye at the top. The closed-eye icon means the layer is hidden, and the lack of an eye icon indicates that the visibility is set to the default (visible).

Figure 6.17
The Layers panel displays the name, visibility, and z-index values of all the layers in a Web page.

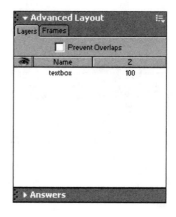

To finish creating a text box to display instructional text to the learner, you'll want to place a table in the layer. You should set the table to the same height as the layer. The text box for the example course in this book uses a table with three rows, shown in Figure 6.18. The table has its border set to 2 pixels with a border color. Each cell in the table has a subtle background color.

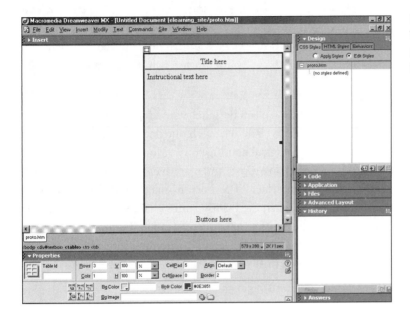

Figure 6.18
You can insert a table in a layer to create a border and individual cells for different kinds of content.

The bottom cell in the table in Figure 6.18 will hold the navigational buttons that you'll create in the next section. The top and middle cells hold the subject of the current page and the instructional text that will be presented to the learner (along with images, movies, and other media). Don't forget to attach any external style sheets to this page by selecting the Attach Style Sheet button in the CSS Styles panel. You'll need the styles you've defined to complete the design of the interface (the background image for the Web page, for example).

Adding Buttons for Navigation

Computer users are familiar with buttons and button functionality. Most online learning applications have buttons enabling the learner to navigate through the course. Buttons are an important element of the interface, facilitating the learner's progression through the pages in the online learning application. You'll create button functionality from images or add Flash movies to create buttons.

Understanding Button States

Buttons usually have shadowed edges, consistent shading, and different representations for the various button states, such as down, up, and over. A button can have five different states: up, down, over, over while down, and disabled. An image is required for each state used for the button. Initially, the button is in the up state.

The most common button states are the up state, the down state, and the over state. The graphics designer who creates the button images for the interface needs to deliver each button state image in the *exact same size* and use a logical naming convention for button states (such as exit_up.jpg, exit_down.jpg, and exit_over.jpg) so that it's easier to put together the interface. The button images must be exactly the same size because when the button states changes to a different button state, it changes only the src (source) attribute, and the rest of the image attributes stay the same, including width and height. An image tag looks like this:

```
<img src="exit_up.jpg" width="55" height="35">
```

If one of the button state images is 60 pixels wide, instead of the 55 specified in the image tag's attributes, the browser will shrink the image and it will look bad.

Adding a Navigation Bar

You can quickly add a group of buttons by using a *navigation bar*. This Dreamweaver object enables you to add buttons arranged horizontally or vertically. In Chapter 8, "Creating Interactivity with

Behaviors and Animations," you'll explore the JavaScript behind buttons. When you add a navigation bar, Dreamweaver automatically inserts all the JavaScript necessary to make the buttons work. To add a navigation bar to your Web page:

1. Place the cursor where you'd like to insert the navigation bar in the Web page. Select the Navigation Bar command (Insert, Interactive Images, Navigation Bar).

2. The Insert Navigation Bar dialog box, shown in Figure 6.19, enables you to set up the individual buttons in the top portion of the dialog box. The Nav Bar Elements text box will contain a list of all the buttons in the navigation bar after you have finished setting it up.

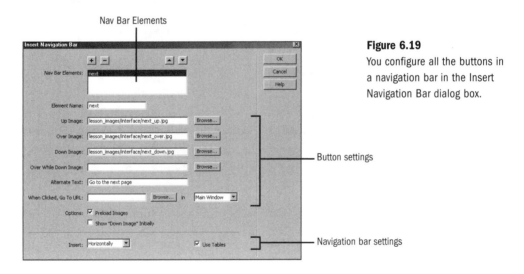

Figure 6.19
You configure all the buttons in a navigation bar in the Insert Navigation Bar dialog box.

3. Name the first button **Next** in the Element Name text box. When you press the Tab key or click in another field, you'll see the Next text appear in the Nav Bar Elements text box.

4. Click the Browse button next to the Up Image text box and load next_up.jpg. Repeat this step to load the over image and the down image with next_over.jpg and next_down.jpg. You can leave unused button states blank, such as the over while down state. Enter **Go to the next page** in the Alternate Text text box. Leave the When Clicked, Go To URL text box blank for now.

5. Click the + button above to add additional buttons to the navigation bar. For the example in this book, you create menu, previous, and exit buttons in addition to the next button.

6. Name each button (exit, menu, and previous) and load its button states. Add appropriate alternative text and leave each URL blank. Use the arrow buttons to arrange the buttons.

7. Select the Preload Images check box to be sure all the images are downloaded into the browser cache so that there is no delay in button functionality.

8. In the bottom portion of the dialog box, you determine whether the navigation bar is displayed horizontally or vertically (select horizontally for the example course). You can also choose to place each element in the navigation bar in individual table cells by checking the Use Tables checkbox. Carefully choose both of these options because you cannot edit them after you've clicked the OK button.

9. Click the OK button to save your navigation bar settings.

You can insert one navigation bar per Web page. To edit the navigation bar, use the Navigation Bar command (Modify, Navigation Bar). You can add or delete buttons, or load different image files.

You can add hyperlinks to the buttons by selecting them individually and adding a link in the Link text box of the Property inspector. You can enter **menu.htm** into the link text box for the menu button (even if you haven't created that page yet). You'll add the Next and Previous button links individually on each page (because they'll link to different pages on each Web page). Add the following JavaScript code in the Link text box of the Exit button to close the window (shown in Figure 6.20):

javascript:window.close();

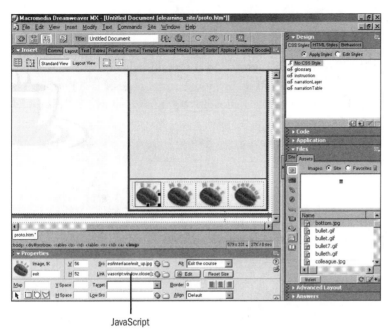

Figure 6.20
Add JavaScript in the Link text box
of the Property inspector.

JavaScript

When you preview the Web page in the browser and click the Exit button, a Confirm Alert box appears, asking whether you want to close the window. This alert box does not appear when you launch a page from the menu, as you will do later. The alert appears only when you attempt to close a browser window that hasn't been opened using JavaScript. If you use Dreamweaver's Open Browser Window behavior to open the online learning application window, this alert box will not appear.

Adding Flash Buttons

The online learning application sample course that you are developing with this book does not include any Flash buttons, but because you might want to use them in future projects, I've included information on them. Dreamweaver includes some fun Flash button templates, and you can download even more from the Macromedia Exchange. Flash buttons can include animations and interaction that are not possible using HTML and JavaScript.

Open a new, blank Web page on which to experiment. You can create Flash buttons—actually, individual Flash movies that contain buttons—to place in your online learning applications. You do not need Macromedia Flash to use the Flash button templates. To add a Flash button in Dreamweaver:

1. Click the Flash Button icon in the Object panel or select the Flash Button command (Insert, Interactive Images, Flash Button). The Insert Flash Button dialog box appears, as shown in Figure 6.21.

Figure 6.21

You can add Flash movies of buttons in Dreamweaver.

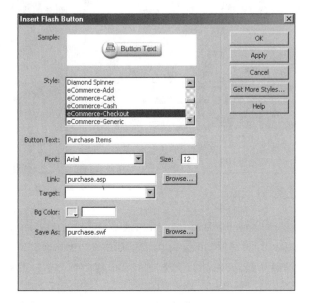

2. Choose a style from the Style list box in the Insert Flash Button dialog box. Note that the sample shown at the top is interactive and functions as the finished button will function, including animation and mouseover effects.

3. If the button style you've selected shows Button Text on the sample, you can customize the text in the Button Text text box. Select a font and a font size for the button. The button template does not grow to accommodate extra text, so your button text must fit the existing button size.

4. You can also specify a link—either to an external Web site or to a Web page in your online learning application—that a button click triggers. You can specify a target for the button, such as _blank to open a new browser window. Some of the buttons have an irregular shape, so you might need to specify a background color to make the button blend with the Web page's background instead of having white edges.

5. The Save As text box in the Insert Flash Button dialog box enables you to specify a filename for the button. Note that the file is saved as an .swf file, a packaged Flash movie.

6. Click the OK button to save the Flash Button settings.

To use this button again, you do need to create a new Flash button. You've already created a Flash movie, so you'll use the Flash command (Insert, Media, Flash) to insert another instance of the button in your Web site. With the Flash button selected, notice the Flash movie attributes in the Property inspector, shown in Figure 6.22. You can change some of the button's attributes in the Property Inspector, or you can click the Edit button to open the Insert Flash Button dialog box to change other attributes. You'll learn more about Flash movies in Chapter 9, "Adding Rich Media Content."

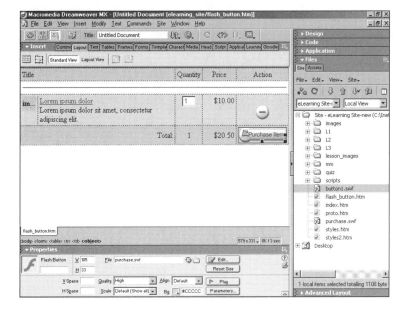

Figure 6.22
When you select a Flash button in the Document window, you see Flash movie attributes in the Property inspector.

Summary

In this chapter, you used Dreamweaver's Layout view to design a complicated table by tracing over an image of the artist's rendering of the interface design. You then loaded the images into the table cells. You used layers to add interface elements that need to be on top of other interface elements, and you added a navigation bar with buttons.

Part III

Inserting Content

IN THIS CHAPTER

chapter 7

Building Reusable Templates and Library Items

USING REUSABLE CONTENT, VIA DREAMWEAVER templates and

library items, offers several advantages. You save time by not re-

creating similar content, and you can maintain consistency

throughout the pages in the eLearning application. Also, Web pages

based on templates or containing library items maintain a connec-

tion to the parent template or library item, so to update multiple

pages, you simply change the parent template or library item.

Library items are one way you can reuse content in Dreamweaver. *Library items* are objects or groups of objects that can be placed within a Web page. In this chapter, you'll create library items for commonly used objects.

You'll also create templates as a base for all the Web pages in the online learning application. So far, you've added cascading style sheet (CSS) styles, links to external scripts, and interface elements to a regular Web page. In this chapter, you'll turn that Web page into a Dreamweaver template, a special type of Web page.

In this chapter, you will understand the following:

- Using and organizing assets in the Assets panel

- How to create and use Dreamweaver templates

- How to use XML with Dreamweaver templates

- How to create and use Dreamweaver library items

Using the Assets Panel

The Assets panel catalogs and organizes the images, colors, links, movies, scripts, templates, and library items in your Web site. This panel is divided by categories, which are accessed by clicking the category buttons. The Assets panel helps you organize and use the media assets, such as images, colors, and movies, in your online learning application. Dreamweaver uses the site cache, initially created when the site is defined, to catalog the site assets.

The assets in all the categories, except the Template and Library categories, can be displayed in two ways: a Site list and a Favorites list. The radio buttons at the top of the Assets panel, shown in Figure 7.1, control the display of these two lists. When the Site list radio button is selected, the Site list displays all of a particular type of asset (such as images) in the current site.

The Template and Library categories are different from the other categories. You'll explore these categories later in the chapter. Most of the categories catalog assets that are already in the site, but the Template and Library categories can be used to create new templates and library items.

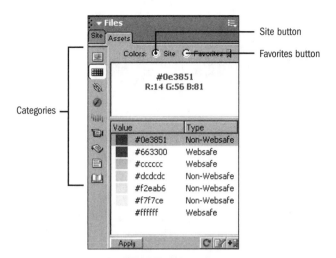

Categories

Site button

Favorites button

Figure 7.1
Many of the Assets panel's cate-gories can be displayed as a Site list or a Favorites list.

Cataloging Images, Colors, and Links

The Images category of the Assets panel lists the name, file size, type of image, and path to the image. Selecting an image displays it in the upper half of the Assets panel. To change the order for the list of images in the site, click on the Name, Size, Type, or Path column headings. You might want to order the list of images by file size, for example, to identify which images in the site are very large.

To use images from the Assets panel in a Web page, you either drag and drop the image, or click the Insert button at the bottom of the Assets panel to insert the selected image at the insertion point. If you have recently saved an image in your site, you might need to refresh the list by clicking the Refresh Site List button (the blue rounded arrow), shown in Figure 7.2. You can edit an image in whatever image-editing application is specified in the File Types/Editors cate-gory in Dreamweaver Preferences (Edit, Preferences). Click the Edit button to edit the selected image in the external application.

The Colors category lists the hexadecimal value and the type, Web-safe or Non-Websafe, of every color used in the site. Selecting a color in the list displays the hexadecimal and RGB values of the selected color in the upper half of the Assets panel. When displaying the col-ors in a Favorites list, you can create new colors; the Site list displays those colors already used in the site.

Figure 7.2

The Image category of the Assets panel has buttons in the lower-right corner to insert or edit an image and refresh the assets list.

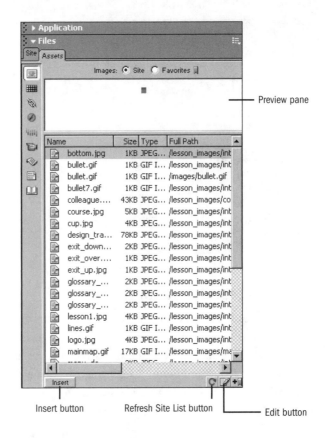

Preview pane

Insert button   Refresh Site List button   Edit button

The Colors category is most useful as a reference to the colors your site uses. I've been successful at applying colors to only selected text within a Web page. To use the colors in table cells, body background colors, or other color boxes, type the hexadecimal value that you see in the Assets panel into a color attribute text box in the Property inspector.

The Links category lists the URL value and the type of link (for example, http for a Web page or mailto for an email link) for every link in the site. Selecting a link in the list displays the URL in the upper half of the Assets panel. When you select an object, such as an image or some text, in the Document window, you select a link and click the Apply button to apply the link to the object.

Managing Flash, Shockwave, and Movies

Three categories organize the movie formats you use in your online learning application. There are special categories for Macromedia Flash (.swf) or Macromedia Shockwave movies (.dcr or .dir). The third movie category lists QuickTime (.mov) or MPEG movies. You'll be using only Flash movies in the online learning application you're creating in this book. When you select a movie from the list, a play button appears in the upper half of the Asset panel; click the play button to preview the movie. Previewing movies in Dreamweaver will be covered in Chapter 9, "Adding Rich Media Content."

Organizing External Scripts

The scripts category lists the name, file size, type, and path of the external JavaScript (.js) or VBScript (.vbs) scripts in the site. When you select a script, the code contained in that script is displayed in the upper half of the Assets panel. You can quickly add a link to an external script in the head of a Web page by first displaying the content within the <head> tags (View, Head Content). Drag and drop a script from the Assets panel into the head section of the page, as shown in Figure 7.3.

Head section   Dragging script

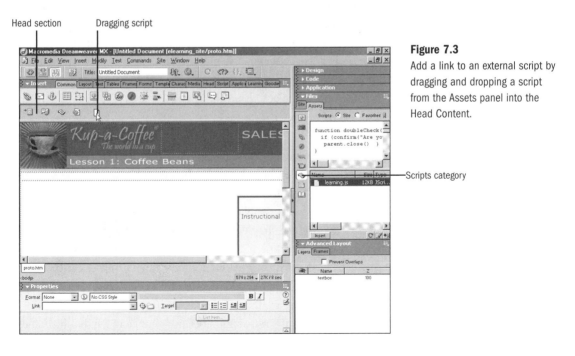

Figure 7.3
Add a link to an external script by dragging and dropping a script from the Assets panel into the Head Content.

Scripts category

Organizing the Favorites List

So far, you've explored the assets categories that enable creating a Favorites list (all but Templates and Library). Why would you want to create a list of favorites? In a very large site, it's difficult to find the exact asset you need simply by scrolling through a list of file-names. It isn't easy to uniquely name large numbers of asset files—image files, for example—in a way that makes it easy to quickly identify the image file to use. Of course, you have your storyboard as a guide, but again, it slows down development to have to match up asset names to what's in the storyboard.

A Favorites list gives you two ways of better organizing assets: creating virtual folders and giving assets nicknames. Before you can organize assets in the Favorites list, you need to tag the assets as favorites. To add assets to the Favorites list, select a group of assets in the Site list of the Assets panel, right-click (Control-click on the Mac) to bring up the context menu, and select the Add to Favorites command, as shown in Figure 7.4. You use this same method to tag images, colors, or URLs as favorites.

When you add files from the Site list to the Favorites list, they still appear in the Site list. The Favorites list is a subset of the Site list. If you select the Favorites radio button at the top of the Assets panel, you should see the files that you just added in the Favorites list. If you've added a file to the Favorites list by accident, you can remove it by clicking the Remove from Favorites button in the lower-left corner of the Assets panel (the button looks like a ribbon with a minus sign next to it).

Adding a Nickname

Power User Tip

You can also edit nicknames by "soft-clicking" on the nickname. Select the list entry, and then single-click on the nickname. It should become editable. Be careful not to double-click the name when editing an image's nickname because you might launch an editing program, such as Fireworks.

By default, the name listed in the Favorites list is the name of the file (for an image or a movie), hexadecimal value (color), or a URL (link). The filename 104581.gif, for example, is meaningless. Notice that the File-name column becomes the Nickname column when you view the Images category Favorites list. To give an item in the Favorites list a more meaningful name, add a nickname. To rename a favorite, right-click (Control-click on the Mac) to bring up the context menu and select the Edit Nickname command. The filename becomes editable so that you can give this item a more meaningful name, such as "rightborder" or "cof-fee_guide." Editing the nickname does not change the actual filename; the nickname information is available only in Dreamweaver.

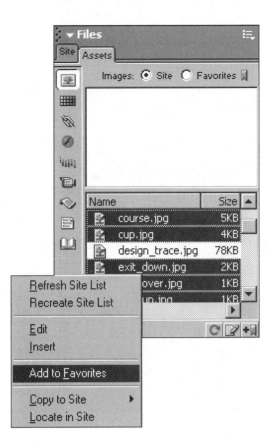

Figure 7.4
Use the Add to Favorites command
to add assets to the Favorites list.

Creating Favorites Folders

When organizing the file structure of a Web site containing many images, there is always a dilemma. It's just too difficult to place all the assets into a single directory. Do you place the assets into groups according to which lesson they occur in? For example, you could have one main directory named images containing directories named lesson1, lesson2, lesson3, and so on. Inevitably, however, an image will be used in lesson2 and lesson4, for example. What do you do then? If you place the file in both directories, the browser will not recognize the asset as the same file because it has a different URL, so the assets will be downloaded again instead of using the file in the browser's cache.

Using virtual favorites folders in the Assets panel helps solve organization problems, enabling you to classify images and other assets in a logical way without duplicating the files. Creating virtual folders does not create an actual folder in the Dreamweaver site structure. To create a virtual folder, click the New Favorites Folder icon in the lower-left corner of the Assets panel. A new folder appears in the Favorites list, as shown in Figure 7.5, with the folder title in editable mode. You can then name the new virtual folder.

Figure 7.5

Create a virtual folder in the Favorites list to organize assets.

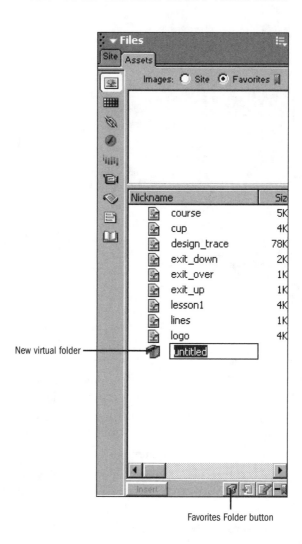

To add asset favorites to the virtual folder, you simply drag and drop the files into the folder. When the favorites folder has files in it, a little + symbol appears next to the folder name; click the + to expand the folder and see the files it contains. If you'd like to add a file to two separate folders—for example, if an image is used in two separate lessons—simply add the image to the Favorites list twice. Place one of the instances of the file into one favorites folder and the other instance into the other favorites folder.

Exporting Your Site Definition

After the online learning application assets are organized into the Favorites list, you might want to share this organization with team members. You can export your site definition, including the organization of the Assets panel Favorites list. You can share the exported site with others on your team so that everyone has their sites defined in a similar way and everyone has access to the same Favorites list.

To export the site definition, open the Edit Sites dialog box (Site, Edit Sites), shown in Figure 7.6. This dialog box displays all the sites currently defined in Dreamweaver. Select the site definition that you want to export, and click the Export button. A dialog box appears, prompting you to save the .ste file. This site definition file is what you share with others.

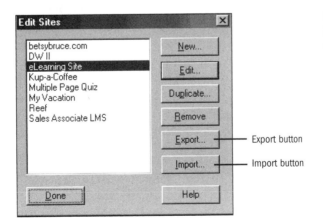

Figure 7.6
Export your site definition to share with other people.

Your team members will need to open up the Edit Sites dialog box and click the Import button to import the site definition you created. They will then have all the settings that you have in your site definition plus the Favorites list that you created.

Creating Dreamweaver Templates

You've created what could generically be called a *template*, the Web page on which all the other Web pages will be based. You've implemented the interface, added links to shared scripts and style sheets, and left room for the individual content that will be added for each page of the online learning application. Now you will turn this Web page into a Dreamweaver template.

Dreamweaver templates have two advantages: You can update all the Web pages based on the template at once, and you can lock down content so that it doesn't accidentally get changed. Dreamweaver implements this functionality through some custom Dreamweaver tags that are added to the Web page; these tags are readable only by Dreamweaver and are ignored by browsers or other Web page editors. Templates are stored in the templates directory in the root of the site, a directory that Dreamweaver automatically creates if it doesn't already exist.

Open the file that you created in Chapter 6, "Constructing the Interface." To make this file a Dreamweaver template, select the Save As Template command (File, Save As Template). The Save As Template dialog box appears, as shown in Figure 7.7; enter the name (**content** for the example course) in the Save As text box at the bottom of the dialog box, and then click the Save button. Notice that "<<Template>>" appears in Dreamweaver's title bar, signaling that you are editing a template.

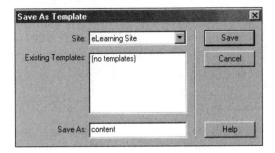

Figure 7.7
Save a regular Web page as a template by naming it in the Save As Template dialog box.

The columns in the Templates category of the Assets panel list the name, file size, and path to the template. A preview of the template is visible in the upper half of the Assets panel. All templates are saved to a directory named Templates in the site root with the .dwt file extension. To edit a template, you can either open the template from the Templates directory or click the Edit button in the lower-left corner of the Assets panel.

After you've finished creating your template, you can open a Web page based on the template to create each Web page in the eLearning course. By default, all objects in the template are locked, so they cannot be changed. You mark areas in the page as editable so that you can place unique content in each page. In the following section, you'll create and name editable regions in the template.

Making Template Regions Editable

In this section, you explore creating a template then using the template to create Web pages. When you create a Web page based on a template, everything on the page is locked to editing except for areas specified as editable. You need to add editable regions to the template so that content can be added to Web pages. Areas of the template not marked as editable can be changed by a developer using the template.

Power User Tip

You should delete the tracing image before creating templates. Tracing images are useful when creating the interface design, but aren't necessary during production after the design has been implemented. The tracing image can be distracting when you are inserting content into the online learning application.

Select an object or region in the template to set as an editable region. In the example course, for example, the image displaying the lesson title for lesson one will need to be changed in other lessons. With an object selected, select the New Editable Region command (Insert, Template Objects, New Editable Region). Or, right-click (Control-click on the Mac) to display the context menu; select the Templates submenu to find the New Editable Region command, as shown in Figure 7.8. The New Editable Region dialog box appears; enter the name **lesson_title** in the Name text box, and then click the OK button.

Figure 7.8
Select the New Editable Region command to mark an object as editable in the template.

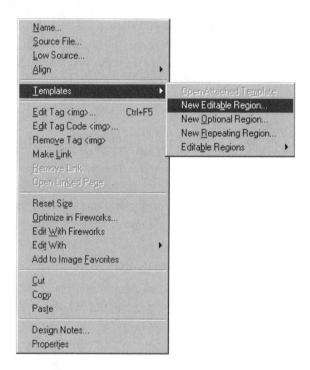

Power User Tip

Adding editable regions to the template might seem to throw off the interface design you worked so hard on in the previous chapter. These changes probably appear only in Dreamweaver, however. Check the template by previewing in the browser to make sure the design is intact. There are markers for the editable regions in a template that can be turned off by disabling the option for invisible element visibility (View, Visual Aids, Invisible Elements).

Next, you'll mark a block of text as editable. Select some text in the template, mark it as editable, and call it **text**. Because you've marked only the text as editable—not any table cells or other objects—you will not be able to change the size, color, or any table attribute when you use the template to create a Web page. You'll be able to change only the text.

To easily select or view the list of editable regions, choose the Modify, Templates menu command. When you select one of the editable regions from the menu, it is selected in the Document window. Notice that there is an additional editable region, one you did not create, called "doctitle." Dreamweaver automatically adds an editable region around the Web page title in the head of the document so that you can change the title in each page created from the template.

Adding Editable Tag Attributes

Because you'll need to change the links for the Next and Previous buttons on each page, you also need to mark them as editable. You do not need to mark the other buttons as editable because they will not change from page to page.

When creating pages based on the template, the developer will not have to change anything about the button except for the link URL. Instead of marking the entire image as editable, you can simply mark the href attribute, the attribute that holds the URL, as editable. The href attribute is actually an attribute of the anchor tag, <a>, that surrounds the button image.

To mark a tag attribute as editable, select the object in the Document window or the tag in the tag selector. If you are making the href attribute editable, you'll need to select the <a> tag in the tag selector. To set an attribute as editable:

1. Select the Make Attribute Editable command (Modify, Templates, Make Attribute Editable) and the Editable Tag Attributes dialog box displays all the attributes of the currently selected tag, as shown in Figure 7.9.

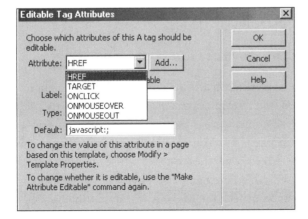

Figure 7.9

When you select a tag or object and select Make Attribute Editable, you can select an attribute from the list.

2. In the Editable Tag Attributes dialog box, select the attribute to mark as editable from the Attribute drop-down list. Click the Add button to add an attribute that isn't available on the list (but that you know is valid).

3. Select the Make Attribute Editable check box.

4. The developer using this template will set the attribute in the Template Properties dialog box (you'll explore this later in this section). You need to label this attribute with a meaningful name. For the example course, the href attribute label is Next Page, as shown in Figure 7.10.

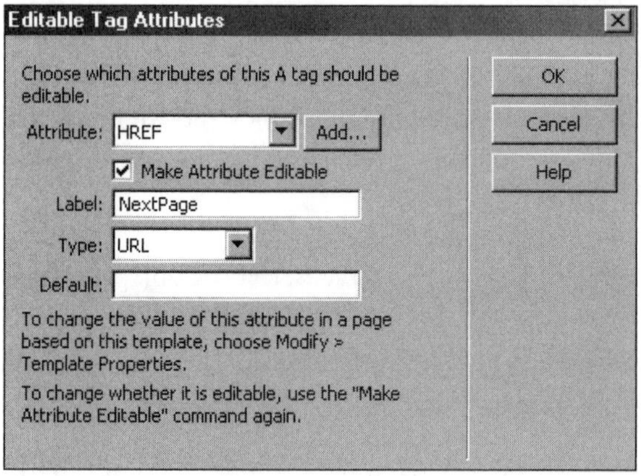

Figure 7.10

Enter a name for the editable attribute so the developer knows what to enter into the Template Properties dialog box.

5. Select the type of data that the developer enters for the attribute: text, URL, color, true/false, or number. In the example course, you would choose URL.

6. Enter a default value for the attribute value. You can leave this blank if you'd like.

7. Click the OK button to save your changes.

After you've marked an attribute as editable, you might notice some "funny" code in Dreamweaver. Dreamweaver adds specific code into the template implementing the editable region that you created, as shown in Figure 7.11. You shouldn't delete or change this code. If you want to remove the editable attribute, reselect the Make Attribute Editable command (Modify, Templates, Make Attribute Editable) and uncheck the Make Attribute Editable check box.

Editable attribute code

Figure 7.11
Dreamweaver adds code to implement the editable attribute.

When you create a Web page based on a template with editable attributes, you select the Template Properties command (Modify, Template Properties) to display the attributes and set the values. You select an attribute label name, as shown in Figure 7.12, enabling you to set the attribute value. Enter values for all the attributes, and then click the OK button to save your changes.

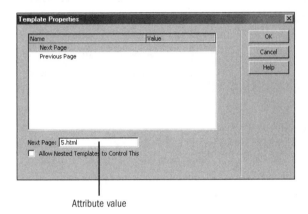

Attribute value

Figure 7.12
You enter the attribute values in the Template Properties dialog box.

Creating a Nested Template

You can create a base template, and then use that template to create other templates. In an online learning application, it's useful to create a base template containing most of the interface elements, and then create templates nested within the base template for individual interaction types, quiz questions, or different types of content. All the editable regions in the base template are passed onto the nested template.

To create a nested template, right-click (Control-click on the Mac) a template from the Templates category of the Assets panel and select the New from Template command. You've just created a template-based Web page. Instead of saving this file as a Web page, save it as a template (File, Save As Template) to create a nested template. Essentially, a nested template is a template that's created from a template. You can now add new editable regions within the available editable regions.

Power User Tip

Template syntax was changed and template functionality greatly expanded from Dreamweaver 4. You can use Dreamweaver 4 templates in Dreamweaver MX, but after you've added new editable regions in Dreamweaver MX, you will not be able to use the templates again in Dreamweaver 4.

In a nested template, you can add editable regions only to regions that are editable in the base template. In the example course, a single editable layer created in the base template holds any images, movies, or other assets added in the nested templates. Insert a layer (Insert, Layer) into the base template that covers most of the blank space on the left of the page. If you have a layer on the page that is functioning as a text box, as in the example course, you'll need to give this layer a lower z-index value; I'd suggest a z-index value of 1.

Because the entire page may be a table, you might accidentally insert a layer into a table cell. Because of Netscape's difficulties with layers in table cells, it's never a good idea to place layers there. Double-check that the layer you inserted is not in a table cell by examining the Tag Selector; if the <div> tag appears inside a <td> (table cell) tag, you should either start over or go into the code and move the entire tag outside the table. An easy way to insert a layer outside a table is to first select the <body> tag in the tag selector before inserting the layer.

Enlarge the layer so that it fills the entire blank area of the screen, as shown in Figure 7.13. Select the layer and make it editable; you'll need to use the Modify, New Editable Region command because the layer context menu does not contain the New Editable Region command. You can name the editable region **content**. It's important that you mark the layer (not just the inside of the layer) as editable because you might need to change layer attributes, such as width, height, or position, during development.

When creating a nested template from a template that has editable attributes, you need to set up the editable attributes so they'll continue to be editable in the new template. Set the editable attribute properties by selecting the Template Properties command (Modify, Template Properties). Because you might not want to set this attribute now—you may set it during development—you can select the Allow Nested Template to Control This check box to pass on the control of the attribute to the nested template. Notice that Dreamweaver makes the attribute to "pass through" to the nested template, as shown in Figure 7.14.

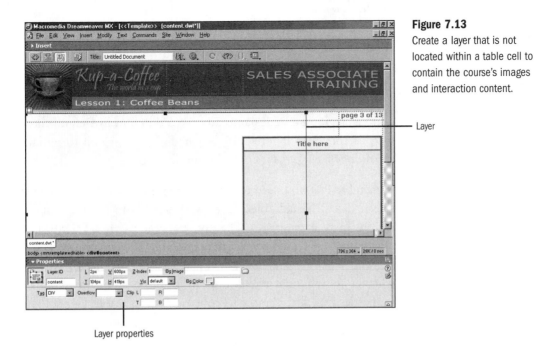

Figure 7.13
Create a layer that is not located within a table cell to contain the course's images and interaction content.

Layer

Layer properties

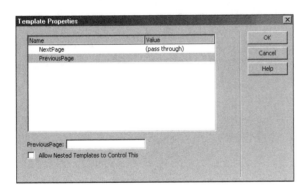

Figure 7.14
Set editable attributes to pass through to the nested template in the Template Properties dialog box.

Adding an Optional Region

Dreamweaver MX enables you to place an editable region within a template that might or might not be used when creating the template-based Web page. For example, you can add an optional region called "picture" into a template. If the page doesn't require a picture, the developer of the page can simply turn off the optional region in the template properties.

To create an optional region, select an area on the Web page and select the Optional Region command (Insert, Template Objects, Optional Region). Dreamweaver prompts you to enter a name for the optional region and set whether it shows up by default when a developer creates a Web page based on this template. Give the optional region a unique name, and check the Show by Default check box, as shown in Figure 7.15, if you'd like the region to initially show up when a page is created from this template.

Remember that you need to have invisible elements showing on the screen (View, Visual Aids, Invisible Elements) to see the editable regions in your templates. The optional regions are labeled beginning with "if," signifying that the region might or might not be displayed. When you create a template-based Web page, you set whether the optional region appears in the page in the Template Properties (Modify, Template Properties), as shown in Figure 7.16. Turn the optional region on or off by selecting it in Template Properties and setting the Show *regionname* check box.

Figure 7.15
Name an optional editable region and specify whether it is shown by default in the New Optional Region dialog box.

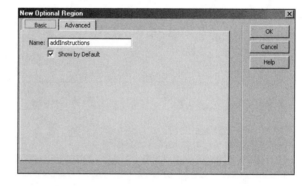

Figure 7.16
Turn the optional region on and off in a template-based Web page using the Template Properties dialog box.

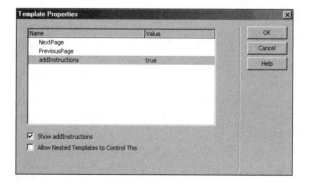

Adding a Repeating Region

You can set a region in your template to repeat and, in the template-based Web page, Dreamweaver displays a small + button, enabling a developer to create additional instances of the region. This feature is usually used to repeat table rows, but you can use it on other objects in a Web page if necessary.

To create a repeating region, select the region of the template you'd like to repeat, apply the Repeating Region command (Insert, Template Objects, Repeating Region), and name the region. You can also use the Template tab of the Insert bar, shown in Figure 7.17, to create regions in templates.

When you mark a region as repeating, it sets the content of the region as editable. You need to add editable regions to the content if you want to be able to edit it in the template-based Web page. It's common, for example, to create a repeating table row containing multiple table cells. All the table cells might not need to be editable, so apply Editable Region (Insert, Template Objects, Editable Region) to the cells that do need to be editable.

When you create a template-based Web page from a template with editable regions, Dreamweaver displays the repeating region controls, as shown in Figure 7.18. Use the plus (+) and minus (–) buttons to add or delete regions. Use the arrow keys to arrange the regions within the list. None of these controls appear in the browser.

Figure 7.17
You can use the Template tab of the Insert bar to create regions in a template.

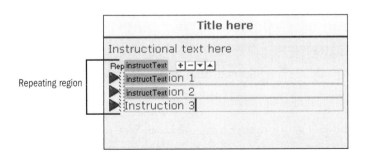

Figure 7.18
You can add regions to a repeating region list in a template-based Web page using the region controls.

Creating a Template-Based Web Page

Power User Tip

Be careful not to leave your template file open while you're working. It's easy to accidentally make changes to that file when you intended to make changes to a Web page based on the template that is also open.

To create a template-based Web page, choose the New command (File, New) to create a new Web page. The New Document dialog box appears, displaying the General and Templates tabs at the top of the dialog box. Select the Templates tab to choose a template on which to base your Web page. By default, your current site is selected in the left column and all the templates defined in that site are displayed in the middle column, as shown in Figure 7.19. A preview of the template is displayed on the right side of the dialog box. Select a template from the list and click the Create button to make a new Web page.

Figure 7.19

Use the Templates tab of the New Document dialog box to select a template on which to base your Web page.

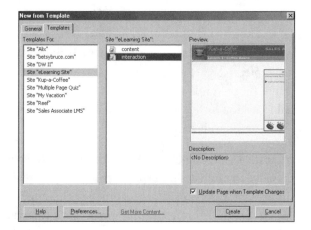

As you move your cursor over the page, you'll be able to see whether the area is editable. You can select and edit only the areas of the page that are within editable regions. You'll see the editable regions highlighted when you have invisible elements showing (View, Visual Aids, Invisible Elements).

Understanding Behaviors, Styles, and Timelines in Templates

Dreamweaver adds two additional editable regions every time you create a template. Both editable regions are in the <head> section of the template. The first is wrapped around the <title> tag so that you can add an individual title to each template-based Web page. The second editable region is called "head." This editable region is available to receive JavaScript and CSS definitions that need to be kept in the <head> section of the document when you add Dreamweaver behaviors or CSS styles to a template-based Web page.

You cannot add a timeline to a template-based Web page. Although you can create a template that includes a timeline and then edit the existing template when you create a Web page based on the template. This is difficult and enables you to to create only very simple timelines. Instead, it's best to use the Detach from Template command (Modify, Templates, Detach from Template) to separate a Web page based on the template from the original template file. That means you won't be able to automatically update template content, but it gives you a lot more flexibility to modify the page.

Importing and Exporting XML

One of the reasons you named each editable region instead of simply marking them as editable is that Dreamweaver can import or export content to or from the regions. Exported content can be used in another application or stored in a database. Probably more important, though, is Dreamweaver's capability to import content formatted in XML into Web pages based on templates.

XML is a markup language similar to HTML that is used to describe data. In HTML, there are predefined tags, such as <img> for an image and <a href> for a link. In XML, you can make up your own tag depending on your needs. If you are creating an XML file describing students in a class, you could create the <student> tag to describe the entire student record and have multiple <coursename> tags describing each course a student is currently enrolled in. It might look something like this:

```
<student>
<firstname>Susie</firstname>
<lastname>Smith</lastname>
<empID>12345</empID>
<courses>
<coursename>Introduction to Computers</coursename>
<section>Q3</section>
<coursename>Intermediate C#</coursename>
<section>Q2</section>
</courses>
</student>
```

The beauty of XML is that you can separate your content from the presentation. When you separate your content from the styles that format its presentation, you can reuse the content for multiple purposes. For example, you can use the same content imported into a Flash movie or formatted, using CSS or *eXtensible Stylesheet Language (XSL)*, and displayed as a Web page. You could also format the content in *Wireless Markup Language (WML)*, a type of XML, so that it can be viewed on wireless devices, such as cellular phones.

The easiest way to see what format to use for importing your data into a Dreamweaver template is to first export the content from a Dreamweaver template. Using a template-based page, export the editable region content by choosing the Export Data as XML command (File, Export, Export Data as XML). An Export Template Data as XML dialog box appears, asking whether to export the XML in the standard Dreamweaver format or use the editable region names as the XML tag names. You can use the latter choice only if you have just simple editable regions in your template-based Web page; if you have repeating regions or editable attributes, the choice will not be active. Click the OK button to save the XML file.

Open the XML file in Dreamweaver, and it displays the XML code in Code view. Note that the content of each editable region is contained within tags with the editable region's name. The content is surrounded by a content tag that names the type of template. Dreamweaver places the content from each editable region into a *CDATA* section, which protects the content from processing. This protection is important because blocks of text often contain characters that are considered special characters in XML, such as < and &, and they would be misinterpreted if processing occurred.

You can create XML files based on the example you exported for each page, and then import the XML into Dreamweaver to create Web pages. The content, including text and HTML, would be held in an XML file specifying the correct template. The easiest way to do this is to create a database entry form so that your data gets stored in a database. Then, export the data from the database formatted to fit into your template's editable regions.

Unfortunately, you can import only a single XML file into a single Web page in Dreamweaver. This functionality would be much more useful if you could import a single large XML file, which would create multiple Web pages in Dreamweaver. In theory, you could create the bulk of your eLearning course in a single import! Macromedia, are you listening?

Updating Web Pages Based on Templates

One of the major advantages of using templates to create Web pages is that you can change something in the original template, and that change flows to all the Web pages based on the template. You can easily update your entire site simply by changing one page! Dreamweaver updates only objects in locked regions of the template because you, of course, wouldn't want to replace content you've added to editable regions.

Open a template from either the Site window or the template category of the Assets panel. You're going to change the template so that you can practice updating the template-based files. You can then update all the files based on the template reflecting this addition. To change a template and automatically update Web pages with your changes, follow these steps:

1. Change any object in a locked region in the template.

2. Test your code before you spread it throughout the course! Preview the template in the browser, click the Exit button, and be sure the window closes.

3. Close the template file and save your changes.

4. The Update Template Files dialog box appears, showing a list of Web pages based on the template you just changed. Simply clicking the Update button updates all the files, or you can pick certain files from the list and click Update.

5. The Update Pages dialog box, shown in Figure 7.20, displays a progress bar and information about the update process. It's important to confirm that all the files you expected to be updated were actually updated. Examine the section of the log showing how many files were updated and how many files could not be updated.

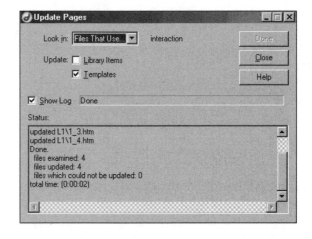

After you've updated all the Web pages based on the edited template and confirmed that the update was successful, you can be confidant that your edits were placed in each Web page. In what instance might a Web page not be successfully updated? The usual cause is that you do not have the Web pages checked out. You'll learn more about Dreamweaver's check in/out system in Chapter 16. The update also might not work if you currently have the Web page open in Dreamweaver.

Creating Library Items

You've created a template and used it as a base for entire Web pages, but what if you want to reuse just a group of objects instead of a whole Web page? Dreamweaver enables you to create *library items*, which are a group of objects, stored in the library, that you can drag and drop onto any Web page. Library items contain groups of objects, formatted exactly as you wish, that you can add to Web pages. Like templates, they can be automatically updated by editing the original library items and updating all the instances of the item within your site.

Library items are stored in the Library category of the Assets panel. When you create the initial library item, Dreamweaver automatically creates a Library directory in the root of your site. Library items are actually snippets of HTML code that can be added to a Web page once or many times. Dreamweaver wraps library item tags around the item, so you'll see <mm:libitem> in the Tag Selector when you select a library item in the Document window.

Creating a Library Item

You create a library item from an object or group of objects. After you've turned them into a library item, you can no longer edit the objects in the library item in the Document window. You will need to open the library item, edit it, and update the instances of the library item, just as you did with templates.

The easiest way to create a library item is to pick up an object or a group of objects and drop them into the Library category of the Assets panel. You name the library item in the panel. When you double-click a library item in the Library category of the Assets panel, Dreamweaver opens the library item in the Document window. Notice that this window displays "<<Library Item>>" in the menu bar. When you create a library item, you are creating a snippet of HTML code, not an entire Web page.

To add a library item to a Web page, simply drag and drop it from the Assets panel onto a blank section of the Web page. When you select the library item in the Document window, you can't edit it. The Property inspector displays the library item properties, not the properties of the objects in the library item. Library items, like templates, belong to the site in which you are currently working. This is based on which templates and library items are located in the Library and Template directories in the root of the site.

The Property inspector, shown in Figure 7.21, displays library item properties. You can detach the library item from the parent library item by clicking the Detach from Original button. If you lose the original library item file, you can re-create it by clicking the Recreate button.

You can also use the library as a holding area for objects, breaking the link between the objects and the library item. If you drag an item from the library onto a Web page while holding down the Ctrl key (Windows) or Command key (Mac), you detach it from the library. This is a handy way to add an object or group of objects to multiple pages and still be able to edit the object.

Editing and Updating Library Items

You might decide to change the content of a library item. For example, if you've created a library item of multiple buttons and you need an additional button added to every page, you can edit the library item and update all the instances in the Web site.

To edit a library item, select a library item in the Assets panel and click the Edit button in the lower-right corner of the Assets panel, or simply double-click the item. Select the image and add alt text in the Property inspector. Close and save the library item. In the Update Library Items dialog box that opens, click the Update button.

Summary

In this chapter, you learned how to organize your course assets by using the Assets panel. You also learned how to create, modify, and update a Dreamweaver template and how to import and export XML into a template. You also learned how to create, modify, and update a library item. All of these functions of Dreamweaver enable you to organize and reuse content in your online learning site.

chapter 8

Creating Interactivity with Behaviors and Animations

ONE OF THE EXCITING BENEFITS OF BEING AN ONLINE learning

application developer is the opportunity to create interactive Web

sites. Interactions simulate activities for learners so that they

can practice procedures, and they engage learners by calling on

them to perform some activity. Although learning applications

can vary in interactive levels and complexity, all learning applica-

tions should have some interactivity.

Implementing interactivity in Web pages is often challenging. However, Dreamweaver stands out from the HTML editor pack in this area. Macromedia has loaded up Dreamweaver with many useful *behaviors*, cross-browser JavaScript functions that enable you to perform interactions such as opening a new browser window, popping up an alert box, or controlling a Flash movie.

Many people do not realize that Dreamweaver is capable of simple animations. Well, Dreamweaver is! And animations can be fun as well as informative for the learner.

In this chapter, you will understand the following:

- How to use and edit Dreamweaver behaviors
- How to use the Show-Hide Layers, Set Text of Layer, and Drag Layer behaviors to change layer attributes
- How to swap multiple images at one time
- How to create and link an external JavaScript file
- How to create animations by using Dreamweaver's Timelines panel

Exploring Dreamweaver Behaviors

Behavior is a Dreamweaver term that describes a combination of JavaScript triggered by a browser event. If you talk to HTML hand-coders about behaviors, they won't know what you mean! The JavaScript portion of a behavior is called an *action*, an appropriate name for an object that enables interaction in a learning application. The second part of a behavior is an *event*. Events are fired by the browser when something happens, such as the user clicking on a link or button in the Web page. Many people use the terms *behavior* and *action* interchangeably.

Dreamweaver behaviors are another component of DHTML, the collection of technologies enabling you to make Web pages more interactive. Adding interactivity to online learning applications helps engage the learner, keeping his attention and increasing the value of the learning activity. Instead of listing the steps that the learner must remember to complete a task, you create an interactive simulation of that task using Dreamweaver. You use behaviors to create interactivity in Dreamweaver.

You'll use Dreamweaver's Behaviors panel to apply and modify behaviors. The panel, shown in Figure 8.1, has two columns displaying the two parts of the behavior: the Events column on the left and the Actions column on the right. You use the + button to add behaviors and the – button to remove behaviors. The up and down arrow buttons are for changing the order in which behaviors are triggered.

You apply behaviors by first selecting the object on the Web page that will trigger the behavior. For example, if you were going to use the Swap Image behavior to swap an image when users roll their mouse over it, you would select that image to apply the behavior. If you want to pop up a new browser window after the user leaves the current Web page (don't you hate when people do that?), you would select the current page's <body> tag because it contains the onUnload event that's triggered when you leave the Web page.

When you select an object on the Web page, the tag for that object is displayed in the Behaviors panel. This enables you to double-check

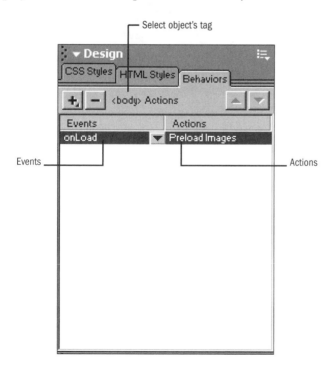

Figure 8.1
The Behaviors panel displays a behavior's actions and events in columns.

that you have the correct object selected. Behaviors must be applied to the appropriate object on the page. Objects have various events associated with them. To complicate matters further, different browser types recognize different events.

Dreamweaver comes with many behaviors, and you can download even more from the Macromedia Exchange. There are probably a few of the behaviors that you will use repeatedly in your online learning application. You'll use Dreamweaver layers to position and control content in your learning application Web pages, so you'll use the Drag Layer, Show-Hide Layers, and Change Property behaviors to manipulate layers. You've already used the Swap Image behavior when you set up the navigation bar in Chapter 6, "Constructing the Interface"; the Swap Image behavior is popular, and you'll use it in a different way in this chapter. You'll also use the Popup Message behavior often. Figure 8.2 displays the Behaviors drop-down menu, and Table 8.1 describes all the behaviors that come with Dreamweaver.

Figure 8.2
The Behaviors drop-down menu enables you to choose different behaviors depending on what's selected in the Document window.

Table 8.1 Dreamweaver Actions

Action	Description
Call JavaScript	Adds a custom line of JavaScript code to an object.
Change Property	Changes objects' properties, such as the background color of a layer.
Check Browser	Redirects the browser to different Web pages based on the browser type or version.
Check Plugin	Redirects the browser to different Web pages based on whether they have a plug-in installed. This works only with plug-ins and not ActiveX controls (more about this in Chapter 9, "Adding Rich Media Content.")
Control Shockwave or Flash	Controls playing, stopping, rewinding, or going to a specific frame in a Shockwave or Flash movie.
Drag Layer	Makes a layer able to be dragged by the user.
Go to URL	Opens a new URL in the browser window.
Hide Pop-Up Menu	Hides a pop-up menu.
Jump Menu	Transforms a menu form object into a menu of hyperlinks.
Jump Menu Go	Enables a button to trigger a jump menu's hyperlinks.
Open Browser Window	Opens a URL in a new browser window and enables you to specify window properties such as size and browser window attributes.
Play Sound	Plays a sound.
Popup Message	Presents a JavaScript alert message. This pops up a noneditable alert box with an OK button.
Preload Images	Loads specified images into the browser cache in the background.
Set Nav Bar Image	Adds an image to a navigation bar or adds advanced functionality to existing navigation bar images.

continues

Table 8.1 Continued

Action	Description
Set Text of Frame	Inserts HTML into a frame.
Set Text of Layer	Inserts text, including HTML formatting, into a specific layer.
Set Text of Status Bar	Inserts text in the status bar located in the lower left of the browser window.
Set Text of Text Field	Inserts text into a text field of a form.
Show Pop-Up Menu	Displays a pop-up menu consisting of multiple menu commands with nested menus. The pop-up menu can be either horizontal or vertical.
Show-Hide Layers	Sets a layer or group of layers as visible or hidden.
Swap Image	Changes the source of an image.
Swap Image Restore	Changes the source of an image back to the original source.
Go to Timeline Frame	Places timeline playback at a specific frame.
Play Timeline	Plays a timeline.
Stop Timeline	Stops a timeline.
Validate Form	Tests the content of form text fields to prevent empty or incorrect information from being submitted to the server.

Power User Tip

Dreamweaver grays out inactive behaviors in the Behaviors drop-down list box. For example, if you don't have any layers in your Web page, Dreamweaver grays out the Show-Hide Layers behavior.

Exploring Browser Events

One half of a Dreamweaver behavior is the action, or the activity that you want to happen. The other half of the behavior is the event, or what triggers the action to happen. When you add a behavior and then select the behavior in the Behaviors panel, an arrow appears next to the event name. Click on this arrow to drop down the Events list box, as shown in Figure 8.3.

The last listing in the Events drop-down menu enables you to specify the target browser, which has a huge effect on the number of available events. You need to select the browser version appropriate for your training application specifications. In Figure 8.3, 4.0 and Later Browsers was selected from the browser version list. If the events list is too lengthy for your screen, there are small arrows that act as scroll buttons.

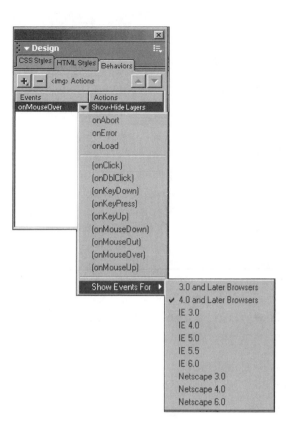

Understanding Dreamweaver Layers

In Chapter 5, you were introduced to Dreamweaver layers, the containers that you'll use to hold much of the content in the learning application's pages. Layers possess attributes that make them useful in creating user interactions. The three main layer attributes for learning interactions are as follows:

- **Absolute positioning**—You can manipulate a layer's L (left) and T (top) attributes to change its position on the screen.

- **Visibility**—Layers can be visible or hidden from view. When layers are hidden, they still exist on the page but the viewer cannot see them. You can switch a layer's visibility from hidden to visible so that the viewer can then see the layer content.

Power User Tip

Some of the events are enclosed in parentheses. These are events that require another tag, usually an **<a>** for creating a hyperlink, to be wrapped around the current object. The event is captured on the hyperlink instead of on the currently selected object. This is a common workaround for attempting to capture a user's click on an image because Netscape cannot capture click events on an image, but it can capture a click on a hyperlink.

- **Z-index**—The layer's z-index indicates its position in the stacking order. Because layers can be stacked on top of one another, the z-index attribute specifies which layer is on top of another layer. The higher the number, the more on top the layer is.

Whatever content you place in a layer is controlled by the layer attributes. If you set a layer's visibility attribute to hidden, the content within the layer is also hidden. If you change the L (left) attribute, which specifies the number of pixels from the left side of the browser window, the layer's content will appear to move horizontally. Placing content in layers is the only way to have this type of control over the content.

You'll use the Layers panel, shown in Figure 8.4, to modify and name your layers. The Layers panel displays three columns of information: the visibility (the eye icon), the layer name, and the z-index. You can pick up a layer and move it above another layer in the list to place it higher in the stacking order.

Layers should be implemented using the <div> tag, which is the tag that is cross-browser compatible. The <layer> tag is a Netscape 4 container tag that can also be used to create layers; however, Internet Explorer does not support this nonstandard tag, nor does Netscape 6. Dreamweaver defaults to the <div> tag, so you'll be fine as long as you don't change the tag in either the Property inspector or in the Layers category of Dreamweaver preferences.

Figure 8.4

The Layers panel enables you to set layer attributes and view the layers you have on the current Web page.

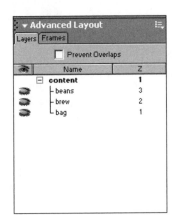

Stacking Layers

Layers can be stacked one on top of another, and the *z-index* value determines where the layer is located in the stacking order. You can easily see your layers' stacking order by examining the column on the right in the Layers panel. The higher the z-index value, the farther on top the layer is. A z-index can be a positive or negative value. Think of the z-index as the third-dimensional axis attached to an x-axis and y-axis. The z-index is coming out of the screen toward you, as shown in Figure 8.5.

Although multiple layers can have the same z-index (they stack according to their position in the HTML code), Dreamweaver prefers to place each layer with its own z-index value. The stacking order arranges the layers in relation to each other, so the starting number doesn't really matter.

If you want to be sure a certain layer is on top no matter how many layers are added to a Web page, you can set its z-index to a much higher number. Set the z-index by clicking in the z-index column of the Layers panel or by setting the value in the Z-Index text box in the Property inspector. Dreamweaver then displays this layer at the top of the list in the Layers panel.

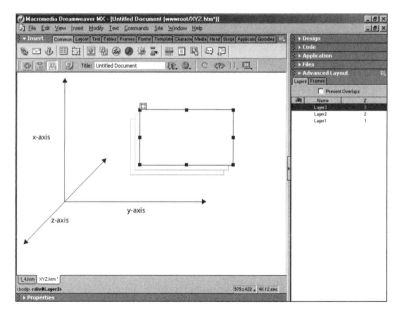

Figure 8.5
The z-index represents the third dimension and controls the stacking order of layers.

Nesting Layers

If you drag a layer on top of another layer in the Layers panel while holding down the Ctrl or Command key, you will nest the layer. The nested layer is now positioned in relation to the parent layer instead of the Web page; that means if its L attribute is 100 pixels, it will be positioned 100 pixels from the left side of the parent layer. Nested layers are indented under the parent layer name in the Layers panel, as shown in Figure 8.4.

To unnest a layer, drag the layer name and drop it above the parent layer name. Nesting layers is helpful when you want to control a group of layers with a single command, but be careful because nested layers can sometimes cause mysterious JavaScript errors. Although nested layers are displayed in Netscape 4, most behaviors will not work on these nested layers.

The default visibility setting for nested layers is to inherit the visibility of the parent layer. You can also set the visibility to inherit in the Property inspector. Sometimes, you can set the visibility of nested layers to a different value than the visibility settings for the parent.

Netscape Resize Fix

Be sure you add the Netscape Resize Fix option (Commands, Add/Remove Netscape Resize Fix) to any Web page that contains layers if Netscape is listed in your course specifications as a target browser for your learning application. The fix adds JavaScript to the top of the page, so you'll need to add this to your template or your external JavaScript file. This code is necessary to maintain the position of layers in the Netscape 4 browser. Netscape fixed this problem in version 6 of the Netscape Navigator.

By default, Dreamweaver adds the Netscape Resize Fix code to a Web page the first time you insert a layer in the page. This code causes the Web page to refresh when the browser window is resized. If you are not targeting Netscape 4 as a delivery browser, you should turn this option off in Dreamweaver preferences (Edit, Preferences) in the Layers category.

Using the Show-Hide Layers Behavior

You use the Show-Hide Layers behavior to manipulate the visibility attribute of a single layer or multiple layers on a page. Using this behavior enables you to capture user input and react to it by hiding or showing layers on the screen. The user does not need to leave the current Web page to have the view of the page change.

Showing and hiding layers is useful when simulating tasks; for example, leading the learner through a series of steps to save a file in a software program. When the user clicks on an image of a menu, you can load a new Web page displaying a save file dialog box. Or, you could hide an image of the save file dialog box in a layer on the same screen, showing the layer and hiding the menu layer instead of loading a new Web page.

For the learner, remaining on the same Web page more closely resembles what the real software application is like. They don't see a new Web page being loaded as they go to the next step. This technique enables you to logically group a set of tasks into a single Web page. The content in the hidden layers loads into the browser cache even though it is not visible on the screen. Figure 8.6 displays a page where the learner places the cursor over three different images. When the mouse is over the images, one of the three hidden layers appears, displaying a picture of that phase of a process.

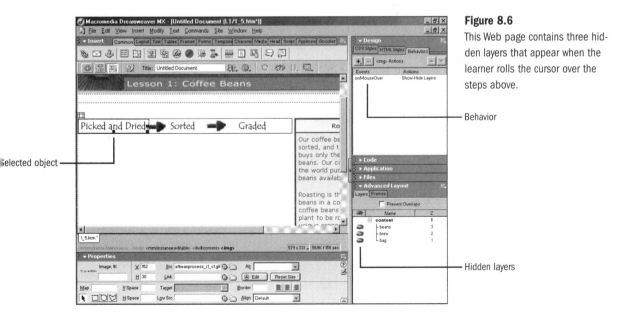

Figure 8.6
This Web page contains three hidden layers that appear when the learner rolls the cursor over the steps above.

I also like to use the show/hide technique to present digestible blocks of text to learners. Instead of presenting multiple paragraphs of text on a single page, you can give learners a single paragraph of text or a single idea, allow them to read it, and then present more text when they click the Next button. In this case, the Next button would show another layer instead of taking the user to a new Web page.

Creating Rollovers Using the Show-Hide Layers Behavior

Let's try creating a Web page with multiple layers and then using the Show-Hide Layers behavior to walk through multiple steps in the learning application. This interaction requires users to click on an arrow to go to the next step in the process. Follow these steps to set up the screen for the interaction:

1. Create a new Web page from the Content template (File, New from Template).

2. Insert new layers into the Web page. You use either the Draw Layer button on the Insert bar (both the Common and the Layout tabs) or use the Layer command (Insert, Layer).

3. Name each layer either in the Property inspector, as shown in Figure 8.7, or in the Layers panel.

4. Load images into each layer by placing the cursor within the layer, and then choosing the Insert Images command (Insert, Image).

5. Arrange the layers, moving them onscreen by picking them up by the selection handle in the upper-left corner. You can fine-tune the layer position by selecting the layer and using the arrow keys.

Now you have all the layers set up and ready to control with behaviors. First, hide the layers that will be hidden initially when the learner enters the Web page. You can either click within the "eye" column, the column in the Layers panel that has a picture of an eye as its heading, next to the layer name. Or, you can change the visibility using the Vis drop-down menu in the Property inspector, shown in Figure 8.8. The Layers panel displays the closed-eye icon next to hidden layers.

---

eLearning with Dreamweaver MX: Building Online Learning Applications

Selection handle

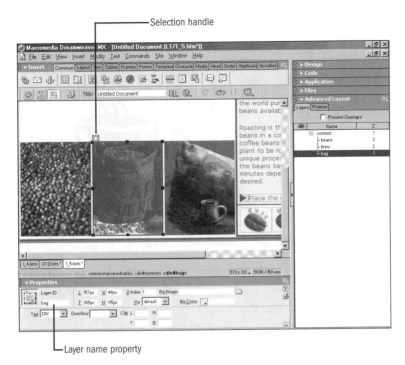

Layer name property

Figure 8.7
Name the layers in the Property inspector.

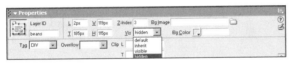

Figure 8.8
Use the Vis drop-down menu in the Property inspector to set a layer's visibility property.

You need to add objects to the Web page to trigger the layers changing from hidden to visible. Usually, you'll add an image or a hyperlink that the learner needs to click on to see the layer content. To add the Show-Hide Layers behavior to an image, first select the image and confirm that <img> appears in the Behaviors panel. Click the + button and select the Show-Hide Layers behavior from the behaviors drop-down. The Show-Hide Layers dialog box appears, as shown in Figure 8.9, with a list of all the layers in the Web page.

Figure 8.9
The Show-Hide Layers dialog box lists all the layers in a Web page, enabling you to set the visibility to show or hide.

You change the visibility attribute of layers by selecting them from the list in the Show-Hide Layers dialog box, and then clicking the Show or Hide button. Select a layer and click the Show button; the dialog box indicates that the layer is set to be visible by displaying (show) next to the layer name. Click the OK button to save your settings.

You've set up the action half of the behavior, but you need to make sure the correct event is set in the Behaviors panel. Dreamweaver adds a default event, but you need to verify that it's the event you want to capture. If you are creating a rollover effect, you'll select onMouseOver from the Events drop-down menu. If you are capturing the learner clicking on the object, you'll select onClick as the event. You could also capture onMouseDown or onMouseUp to capture the learner clicking on an object.

At this point, you should preview your Web page in the browser and check the functionality. When you click on the object to which you attached the behavior, the layer content should appear on the screen. Fun, isn't it? You'll need to repeat this process for each show-hide interaction on the Web page. If you wanted to hide the layer, you would repeat this process selecting the Hide button and the onMouse-Out event.

You should attach the Show-Hide Layers behaviors to images instead of the layers in which the images are contained. Netscape 4 cannot capture events on the <div> tag, the tag used to implement Dreamweaver layers (Netscape 6 and IE 4+ can). If you are creating a learning application targeted to Internet Explorer, you could attach these behaviors to a layer instead of an image, if you wanted.

Showing and Hiding an Information Box

It's common in eLearning applications to provide the learner with more information by clicking on a link (either hyperlinked text or an image). You can present this additional information in a layer, which is hidden when the learner enters the page. After the learner has displayed the information by clicking on the link, they might want to hide it so that they can look at the content on the Web page that resides behind the additional information. An example of this type of information in a layer appears in Figure 8.10.

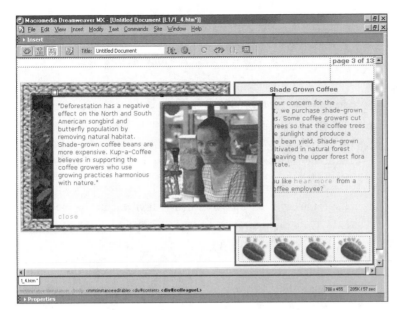

Figure 8.10

This Web page shows an information box that is initially hidden when the user enters the Web page. They can click on a link to show the information box.

For this interaction, you need to add a link to the page to show the layer and a link within the layer to hide itself. You'll add these two behaviors to two different objects, and they'll work together to toggle the information on and off. It's important to set a high value for the z-index of this type of layer so that it appears above everything else on the Web page.

The information box displayed in Figure 8.10 consists of a single-cell bordered table within a layer. Inside the table is an image and some text aligned to the left of the image. Remember to name your layer (so you can pick it from the list in the Show-Hide Layers dialog box) and to set its visibility to hidden. To show and hide an information box, do the following:

1. Select the object on the screen that will trigger the layer containing the information box to show. This will probably be an image or some text.

2. Click the + button and select the Show-Hide Layers behavior from the Behaviors drop-down menu. In the Show-Hide Layers dialog box, select a layer and click the Show button. Click the OK button to save your settings. You've now added one of the two behaviors necessary to toggle the layer on and off.

3. Select the correct event from the Events drop-down menu. You'll want to select the onClick event if the learner is required to click an object to view the information box.

4. Select the object within the layer that will trigger the layer to hide. To view the hidden layer within Dreamweaver's Document window, you can simply select it in the Layers panel. You don't need to set its visibility to visible; you'll be able to see even hidden layers when they are selected in the Layers panel.

5. Click the + button, and then select the Show-Hide Layers behavior from the Behaviors drop-down menu. In the Show-Hide Layers dialog box, select a layer, and click the Show button. Click the OK button to save your settings.

6. Select the correct event from the Events drop-down menu. You'll want to select the onClick event if the learner is required to click an object to view the information box.

7. Preview the Web page in the browser and check the functionality.

Hopefully, it works perfectly. If not, retrace your steps to see what went wrong. Be sure you are capturing the expected event and that the behaviors are attached to the correct objects on the Web page. When you select an object on the page, all behaviors attached to that object are listed in the Behaviors panel. Double-click the behavior to edit its attributes.

Dragging a Layer

You can use the Drag Layer behavior to enable users to move a layer onscreen. This behavior is useful for creating puzzles and sliders. You are not going to specify a target for the dragging layer in this chapter, but specifying a target opens the possibility for drag-and-drop interactions. In Chapter 10, "Including CourseBuilder Interactions and Controls," you'll explore using the Drag and Drop CourseBuilder interaction.

You'll make the information box draggable so that the user can move it around on the screen. Oddly, you do not attach this behavior to the actual layer object. You attach the behavior to an object that can trigger an event at the appropriate time to enable the layer to be draggable. Usually, you attach this behavior to the <body> tag and trigger the behavior's action when the onLoad event happens (when the Web page is loaded into the browser). When you are working with templates, however, you do not have access to the <body> tag because it isn't in an editable region. Fortunately, there's a workaround!

Images also have an onLoad event. You can attach the Drag Layer behavior to an image and have the layer become draggable when the image's onLoad event happens (when the image is loaded into the browser). Using the onLoad event of an image instead of the <body> tag is useful when you are working with template-based Web pages where the <body> tag cannot be selected or edited. To add the Drag Layer behavior, do the following:

1. Select an image in the information box layer. Remember that you can display a hidden layer by selecting it in the Layers panel.

2. Click the + button in the Behaviors panel and select the Drag Layer behavior from the Behaviors drop-down menu. The Drag Layer dialog box, shown in Figure 8.11, appears.

3. From the Layer drop-down menu, select the appropriate layer. You can leave all the other attributes alone. Click the OK button to save your changes.

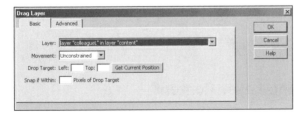

Figure 8.11
The Drag Layer dialog box has two tabs: Basic and Advanced.

4. Change the event to onLoad, as shown in Figure 8.12.

5. Preview the Web page in the browser to test the functionality.

When the information box becomes visible, you should be able to drag it around the screen. You can double-click the behavior in the Behaviors panel and edit it if you'd like to experiment. You can constrain the movement within a certain area, as shown in Figure 8.13. In the Movement drop-down list box, select Constrained. Enter pixel values into the four boxes to limit where the layer can be dragged.

Figure 8.12
Select the onLoad event from the Events list box in the Behaviors panel.

Figure 8.13
Constrain the area within which the layer can be moved by editing the Drag Layer behavior.

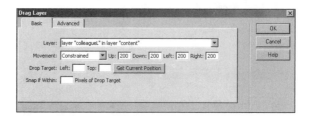

Changing Layer Content

Next, you'll create a page with an interaction designed to load feedback into a single layer. As the learner clicks on various images on the page, information about the image is displayed in the feedback layer. When the learner clicks a new image, the previous information is replaced by information about the newly clicked image. You'll use the Set Text of Layer behavior to facilitate this functionality.

The Set Text item in the Behaviors drop-down list contains four behaviors. Along with setting the text of a layer, you can also set the text for a frame, a text field, and the status bar. You're not using frames in this book, but they enable you to seamlessly load multiple Web pages into a single browser screen. The Set Text of Frame behavior enables you to send text to a particular frame (a portion of the screen). This behavior is useful, for example, to present a quiz question in one frame and the question feedback in a different frame. You use the Set Text of Status Bar behavior to change the text in the status bar along the bottom of the browser window. The Set Text of Text Field behavior enables you to set the text within the form element known as a text field.

Create a new Web page from a template as you did earlier in this chapter. Save this Web page, add layers to it, and load images into each layer. Add an additional layer and name it **Feedback**; this layer will display information about each item in the layers. Position the layers on the Web page using the selection handle; an example is shown in Figure 8.14.

Now you'll capture the user's clicks on each image to trigger setting the text of the Feedback layer. Repeat this process for each image:

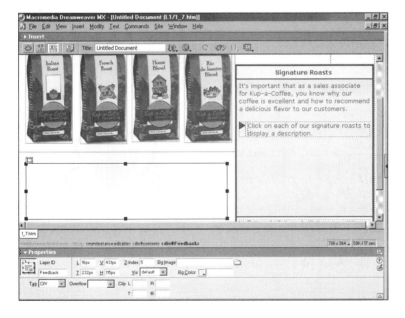

Figure 8.14
Arrange content in several layers and add an additional empty layer to display information about each item.

1. Select one of the images within a layer. You must select the image and not the layer (<div> tag) if you are targeting Netscape 4 for your Web page. If your layer doesn't contain an image, you should create another layer over it with a clear spacer GIF in it stretched to the proper size to create a hotspot.

2. Click the + button in the Behaviors panel and select the Set Text of Layer behavior. The Set Text of Layer dialog box appears, as shown in Figure 8.15.

Figure 8.15

The Set Text of Layer dialog box enables you to enter HTML that will be loaded into the target layer.

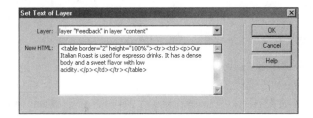

3. Select the Feedback layer from the Layers drop-down list box. You'll replace the content of whatever layer you select here, so if you select the wrong layer, one of your images will be replaced with text.

4. Type or copy and paste text from the storyboard into the New HTML text box. Notice that the text box is called "New HTML," not "New Text." Does that give you a hint that you can do more than simply put text here? I like to contain the content sent to a layer in a one-cell table so that it has a border. You'll have to type in the HTML code or copy and paste it from Dreamweaver's code view.

5. Click the OK button to save your changes.

6. Change the onClick as the event.

After you've set up all five images, preview the page in the browser, and click on each image to see the text appear in the Feedback layer. If you place initial text in the Feedback layer, it will be replaced the first time you click one of the coffee bag images.

Changing Property with Behaviors

You can use the Change Property behavior to change layer properties, such as background color, background image, fonts, and even the HTML within the layer. You attach a behavior to an object on the page, such as an image, that will capture an event. Selecting the Change Property behavior in the Behaviors panel opens the Change Property dialog box, shown in Figure 8.16.

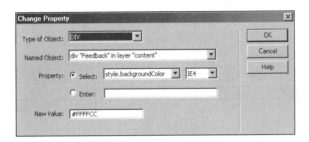

Figure 8.16

The Change Property behavior enables you to change the attributes of numerous types of objects on the Web page.

You are actually working with <div> tags when working with Dreamweaver layers. Don't get that confused with the <layer> tag, the Netscape-specific tag that is similar to <div>. The <div> tag is the standard tag for implementing layers and DHTML, so select it from the Type of Object list box at the top of the Change Properties dialog box. Note that you can change the properties for a variety of objects by using this behavior.

From the Named Object list box, select the layer that will have its properties changed with this behavior. If you need to change the properties of multiple layers, you need to add the behavior multiple times. Next, select the target browser from the browser list box; you can select IE3 (Internet Explorer 3), NS3 (Netscape 3), IE4, or NS4. The various browsers enable you to change different properties, so you must be careful that the properties you'd like to change are available after you set the browser type and version.

To add a property, you can select one from the Select list box, or you can type a known property name in the Enter text box. For example, if you've selected IE4 as the browser version, you can select style.backgroundColor from the Select list box. After you've selected the property to change, you must enter a valid value in the New

Value text box at the bottom of the dialog box. For example, you could change the backgroundColor property to #FFFFCC. Click the OK button to save your changes.

Swapping Images

Sometimes you might want to trigger the Swap Image behavior when the user interacts with one image, but actually change to a different image. You can do this more complicated swap with the Swap Image behavior. You will create a Web page that displays an image. When the user clicks on areas of the image, a different image will be swapped.

How does an image swap work? The actual image object isn't being swapped; the src (source) attribute, which contains the URL of the image source file, changes. When you place an image object on the page, you can swap the src attribute as many times as you please. All other attributes of the image, such as width, height, alt, border, h (horizontal) space, and so on, will stay the same. Because all the other attributes of the image stay the same, it's important to swap only images that are the same size; otherwise, the browser will stretch or shrink the image to be the size of the original image.

Add three layers to a Web page and name the layers. You can add the letter *L* to the layer name to signify that it's a layer. Because you are using the Swap Image behavior, you must give the images names in this page. If layers and images have the same names, sometimes JavaScript can get confused and you will get errors. Be sure that you give your images and your layers different names. The final setup for this group of interactions can look like Figure 8.17.

Load an image into one of the layers to serve as a map; this image doesn't require a name because you are not going to add a Swap Image behavior to it. This image will be the image that the user clicks to load information into the other layers. Load an initial image into the layer where the swap will take place. Name the image in the Property inspector.

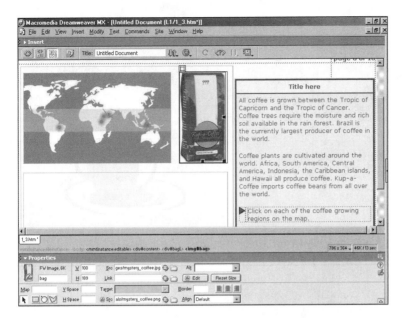

Figure 8.17

When you click on an area in the map layer, the image src attribute of the coffee bag is swapped and information appears in the bottom layer.

Next, you'll create an image map from an image. An *image map* is an image with multiple clickable areas, or *hotspots*. Select an image, and you'll see the map tools in the lower-left corner of the expanded Property inspector, shown in Figure 8.18.

Image map tools

Figure 8.18

The tools to create an image map appear in the lower-left corner of the Property inspector when an image is selected.

There are four tools: the pointer, the rectangular hotspot tool, the oval hotspot tool, and the polygon hotspot tool. The rectangular and oval hotspot tools are used to make regularly shaped hotspots on an image. The polygon hotspot tool is used to make irregular hotspots on an image. The pointer is used to reposition or resize the hotspots.

First, name the image map in the empty text box beside the word *Map* in the Property inspector. Select the rectangular hotspot tool, and draw five rectangles over five regions on the map. If you need to resize or reposition one of the rectangles, select the pointer tool and drag one of the resize handles on the hotspot, or pick the hotspot up and move it.

Each hotspot will be a null link, and you'll attach the Swap Image behavior to each hotspot. Select each hotspot with the pointer tool, and enter **javascript:;** in the Link text box of the Property inspector, as shown in Figure 8.19. Be sure you also add alternative text in the Alt text box in the Property inspector; in most browsers, this text appears as a tool tip over the hotspot.

Figure 8.19
Image map hotspot properties enable you to add a link, a null link in this example, to a specific region of an image.

Start by selecting one of the hotspots, and then set up the Swap Image behavior:

1. Click the + button in the Behaviors panel, and then select the Swap Image behavior from the Behaviors drop-down list box.

2. Select settings for the two check boxes, Preload Images and Restore Images onMouseOut, at the bottom of the Swap Image dialog box. Because you'll use the onClick event to trigger this behavior, you'll want to uncheck the Restore Images onMouse-Out check box. You can leave the Preload Images check box selected to get better performance from the interaction.

3. From the list of images at the top of the Swap Images dialog box, select the image you want to swap. Don't select the image where you set up your hotspots. Click the Browse button, and select the new image to load into that image. Notice the asterisk beside the image name in the list, as shown in Figure 8.20; the asterisk indicates that this image will be swapped in this behavior. If you swapped multiple images with this event, multiple images would display asterisks in this box.

4. Click the OK button to save your changes.

5. In the Events list box, select the onClick event.

When you preview the Web page in the browser, click on the hotspot, and notice that the image source changes. You'll need to complete this interaction by repeating the preceding steps for the other hotspots.

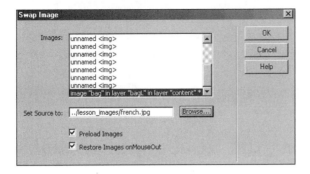

Figure 8.20

An asterisk displayed beside an image name indicates that the image will be swapped in the behavior.

Popping Up Messages

I'm not a big fan of using JavaScript alert boxes, which is what the Popup Message behavior uses, but there are times when it can be useful. You'll add a pop-up message stating that the user is exiting the course when he or she clicks the Exit button you created in Chapter 6. To add a pop-up message to the Exit button, follow these steps:

1. Open the template where you added the Exit button.

2. Select the Exit button image.

3. In the Behaviors panel, multiple behaviors are already attached to this image. Add a new behavior by clicking the + button and selecting the Popup Message behavior from the Behaviors list box.

4. Type **You are exiting the course.** in the Message text box.

5. Click the OK button to save your changes.

6. Select the onClick event from the Events list box.

Because two onClick events are attached to this object, you can arrange them with the arrow buttons in the Behaviors panel. If you place the Popup Message behavior above the Set Nav Bar Image behavior in the list, the button image will not change until after the user has closed the pop-up message. That would look a little strange to the user. When you have multiple behaviors triggered by a single event, you need to consider the order in which the behaviors must occur.

Because you've just made a change to a template, when you save your changes, Dreamweaver will prompt you to update all the pages that contain the template. So, go ahead and update the pages in your course, and then open one, preview it in the browser, and test the Exit button functionality.

Moving the JavaScript Functions to an External Script

When creating an online learning application, Dreamweaver uses JavaScript to accomplish much of the interactivity. It's best to store all the JavaScript for your site in a single location. This enables you to update the JavaScript in a single place and saves download time by not requiring the learner to continually download the same JavaScript code contained in multiple pages. You'll gather the JavaScript that Dreamweaver produces and put it in a .js script file.

Dreamweaver adds JavaScript *functions*, a group of code statements that perform a task such as swapping an image or playing a Flash movie, to the <head> tag of your Web page. You usually end up using the same behaviors repeatedly, so it makes sense to collect these functions and save them in an external JavaScript file.

An external JavaScript file is referenced at the top of each page using the <script> tag with a SRC (source) attribute pointing to the file's location. JavaScript files end with the .js file extension. You'll move all the JavaScript out of the templates and any pages you have created and save the file as an external JavaScript file. You'll then add a reference to each Web page in the online learning application by adding it to the templates.

Open each Web page and examine the <head> section of the page in Code view. All the JavaScript is contained between <script language="JavaScript"></script> tags, and the Macromedia JavaScript functions used to implement behaviors all begin with MM_. For

example, the Swap Image behavior starts function MM_swapImage().
Paste a single copy of each function you've used into Code view of a
new Web page (use the Other category in the New File dialog box
and select a JavaScript file) in Dreamweaver. Save this file as **learn-
ing.js** in the Scripts directory of your site. You can delete any extra
<script> tags from the original files; you also do not want to add
<script> tags to the .js file.

View the <head> content (View, Head Content) of the page so that
you can edit the <script> tag to point to the external JavaScript file.
Add a link to the external JavaScript file. Insert a <script> tag by
choosing the Script command (Insert, Script Objects, Script). Leave
the Script field blank and click the OK button. Click the Script icon
in the <head> content, as shown in Figure 8.21. With the Script icon
selected, you can use the Property inspector to select the external
JavaScript file as the source. Click the folder icon beside the Source
field to navigate to learning.js.

Script icon

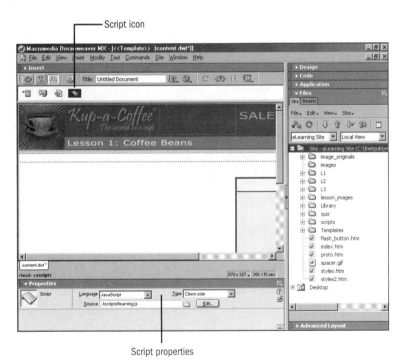

Script properties

Figure 8.21
The <head> content shows icon
representations of the elements
contained in the head of the Web
page.

The external JavaScript file will be downloaded into the browser cache the first time the learner downloads a page referencing it. Subsequent Web pages referencing the external file will simply use the file that has already been downloaded. Also, if you need to change or fine-tune the code, it's contained in only one place in the online learning application. You can add a JavaScript function into the external JavaScript file and have it available to every page in the eLearning application.

Understanding Dreamweaver Animation

Dreamweaver can create simple animations that add interest and instructional depth to your learning application. You use the Timelines panel, shown in Figure 8.22, to implement animations. If you are familiar with time-based animation programs, such as Macromedia Flash or Director, the Timelines panel will look familiar.

Figure 8.22

The Timelines panel enables you to create simple animations in Dreamweaver.

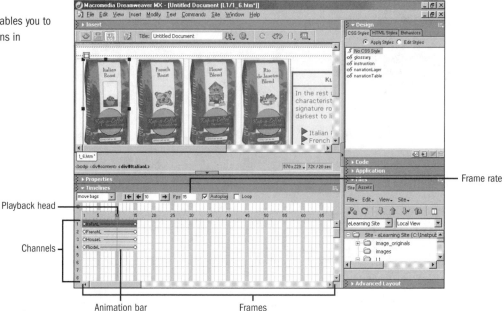

In Dreamweaver, you can animate two types of objects in the Timelines panel: layers and images. The most common type of animation involves changing layer attributes over time. For example, you can change the L value of a layer over time to make the layer move horizontally across the screen, or you can change a layer's T value over time to make it move vertically. The JavaScript that Dreamweaver adds to the Web page interpolates the position so that the layer moves smoothly between positions.

You can also use the Timelines panel to change the src attribute of an image over time. If you want to move the image around the screen, you'll need to place the image in a layer and animate the layer by using the Timelines panel.

In the rest of this chapter, you'll create three different animations using three techniques. The first animation will manipulate layer attributes over time, the second animation will use Dreamweaver's capability to record movement of an object, and the third animation will use behaviors in a timeline.

Using the Timelines Panel

You cannot add a timeline animation to a Web page linked to a template because the timeline animation needs to write JavaScript to the page's <head> tag. So, you'll need to detach this page from the parent template (Modify, Templates, Detach from Template). Now this page will not be automatically updated if you update the template, so it's a good idea to note that somewhere.

Make a Web page with several layers that you'd like to move around the screen. Name the layers and add content to them. To create an animation, follow these steps:

1. Open the Timelines panel and drag each layer into a separate channel. You should see the name layer listed in the animation bar. If you see the name of an image instead, you must delete the animation bar and start over. Be careful to drag the layer, not the image contained in the layer.

Power User Tip

If you have design notes enabled in your Web site, add a design note to record that this page is detached from the template (File, Design Notes). Type **Page is detached from template** in the Notes field, and then click OK. You'll see a notes icon next to this page in the Site window.

2. By default, the animation bar has two keyframes: one keyframe at the beginning and one keyframe at the end. Layer properties can change only at keyframes. You'll learn how to add additional keyframes later.

3. Select the first keyframe on the animation bar. Click in frame 1, channel 1 to select this keyframe. If you look at the Property inspector, you'll see the layer attributes at this keyframe. Move the layer to its position at the beginning of the animation.

4. Select the last keyframe on the animation bar. Pick up the layer by its selection handle in the upper-left corner and drag it. An animation path appears as a thin line in the Document window.

5. Select the Autoplay check box in the Timelines panel to make the animation play when the Web page is loaded. This adds the Play Timeline behavior, triggered by the onLoad event, to the <body> tag.

6. Preview the Web page in the browser, and check that the animation occurs. You can click the Reload button in your browser if you'd like to view the animation again.

To make an animation path more complicated, you can add additional keyframes. When you hold down the Ctrl or the Command keys, the cursor turns into a keyframe. Click on frame to add a keyframe in that frame. Select the new keyframe and move the layer to change the animation path.

Recording a Timeline Animation

You just set up an animation by hand, but Dreamweaver also enables you to record an animation while you move a layer around on the screen. To record a timeline animation, follow these steps:

1. Add a layer to Web page and insert an image into it.

2. Select the layer and choose the Record Path of Layer command (Modify, Timeline, Record Path of Layer).

3. You don't want to make the animation complicated, so simply pick the layer up by its drag handle and move it around the screen a bit. As you drag the layer, you'll see a dotted animation path that turns to a solid path when you release the layer.

4. The new layer's animation appears in the Timelines panel. You can shorten the animation bar by dragging the last keyframe. Notice that the keyframes automatically arrange themselves.

Preview the Web page in the browser, and check that the animation works.

Adding Behaviors to a Timeline Animation

So far, you've added layers to the Timelines panel and changed layer attributes (L and T) at the keyframes. You can also create an animation by using a special channel called the *B channel* (B stands for "behavior"). The B channel is located above the other channels, directly above the frame numbers. When you click in one of the frames in the B channel, you can add a Dreamweaver behavior that will happen at that frame in the animation.

Add a Dreamweaver behavior to the B channel by following these steps:

1. Double-click a frame in the Timelines panel's B channel. This opens the Behaviors panel.

2. Click the + button to drop down the Behaviors list box, and select a behavior.

3. Set up the specific behavior, and then click OK to save the changes.

4. Notice that Dreamweaver adds onFrame15 as the event because this behavior will be triggered when the timeline encounters frame 15. The frame number used depends on which frame you clicked in the B channel, as shown in Figure 8.23.

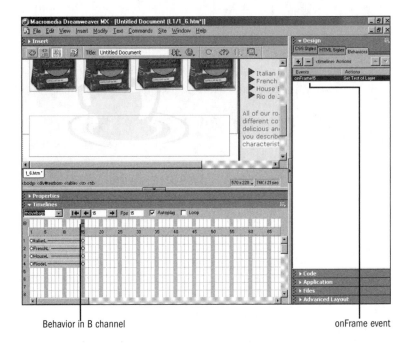

Behavior in B channel   onFrame event

5. To slow down the animation, change the frame rate from the default of 15fps (frames per second) to 5fps. Now the animation will run three times slower.

Preview the Web page in the browser, and test your animation!

Summary

In this chapter, you learned that an action and an event make a Dreamweaver behavior. You explored layers and many of the behaviors you can apply to behaviors, including the Show-Hide Layer and Set Text of Layer behaviors. You use the Swap Image and the Popup Message behaviors to create interactivity. You also created different types of animations using Dreamweaver Timelines panel.

IN THIS CHAPTER

chapter 9

Adding Rich Media Content

AT TIMES, YOU'LL WANT TO ADD *rich media content* to your Web

pages. Rich media content includes animation, audio, video, or

other content that uses advanced technology (such as stream-

ing video) and increased bandwidth, and might interact with the

learner. Viewing rich media content requires the viewer to have a

player installed in the browser. *Players* are programs that add

functionality to Web browsers, enabling you to include rich media

content that couldn't be viewed in a plain ol' browser. Adding rich

media content, such as Flash movies, to your learning applica-

tions can complicate delivery but also increase the application's

instructional value.

Rich media content enables you to add complex animation, interaction, and sound to Web pages—types of content that just can't be created in HTML code. This content is created in an authoring program, such as Flash or Authorware. The files produced by the authoring programs are linked to a Web page. When the learner loads the Web page, the Web browser handles the HTML code and JavaScript, and the appropriate player handles the rich media content.

Playing rich media content requires that learners have successfully installed the appropriate player applications to their browsers. It's best if your learning application is set up to detect whether the appropriate player is installed on learners' systems so that you're assured they can view all the content. Dreamweaver enables you to use the Check Plugin behavior to direct learners to a site for downloading players if they don't already have them installed.

In Chapter 3, "Establishing the Course Specifications," you specified which players and media types would be included in an online learning application. You also need to consider the specified browsers. The two major browsers, Netscape Navigator and Microsoft Internet Explorer, use two different types of players. Netscape uses *plug-ins* and IE uses *ActiveX controls* to play rich media content. These players are available as a free download, usually from the software company that creates the authoring program.

In this chapter, you will understand the following:

- How to insert and control Flash content in your Web pages
- How to insert Authorware programs
- How to insert streaming media formats, such as RealMedia
- How to detect player installation

Understanding Flash Content

Macromedia Flash is an extremely popular software program that creates vector-based animations. As of December 2001, Macromedia statistics show that almost all browsers on the Web—98%, to be exact—have the Flash player installed. Before including Flash content in your learning application, you might want to do a survey of your targeted users. Some corporate audiences have a custom software installation that strips many of the common browser player applications from company workstations, so you might need to consult with the IT department to orchestrate the installation of a required player.

When you create a Flash movie (check out Appendix A, "Resources," for books on that topic), you save it as a .swf file (pronounced "swiff" file). Flash enables you to create a Web page along with your Flash movie, but because you are using a prepared Dreamweaver template to create your learning application, you simply need the Flash movie file, the .swf. You can create a directory in your Web site called "movies" to hold any Flash movies.

The reason Flash is so popular is its capability to create small files that can quickly be loaded into a viewer's browser. If you use Flash's internal drawing tools to create a Flash movie, your movie can be extremely small, even smaller than a GIF or JPEG image! If you import bitmap images into Flash, however, the movie size includes the bitmap's size and could become quite large. Of course, if you need to include photographs and other types of images that exist as bitmaps, you'll have to add bitmaps to your Flash movies.

Besides the small file size, another advantage of Flash movies is the capability to scale Flash vector graphics without any degradation or distortion of the movie. This capability does not work as well if the Flash movie contains bitmap images. One of the advantages of vector graphics—graphics created from mathematical formulas—is scalability.

Inserting Flash Movies

First, create a new Web page where you'll insert a Flash movie (File, New), save it, and give it a name. To insert a Flash movie into this page, follow these steps:

1. Place the cursor in the Web page.

2. Insert a Flash movie (Insert, Media, Flash or click the Flash object in the Object panel). The Flash movie object appears in the Web page, and the movie attributes are displayed in the Property inspector, as shown in Figure 9.1.

3. Name the movie in the Name text box in the upper-left corner of the Property inspector.

4. The Play button enables you to preview the Flash movie right in Dreamweaver, without previewing the Web page in the browser. Click the Play button to watch the movie. After you click the button, it becomes a Stop button that you can use to stop playing the movie.

   Dreamweaver can play player content via Netscape plug-ins directly in the Document window. You cannot directly play content via ActiveX controls in Dreamweaver. Dreamweaver comes with the Flash plug-in installed in the configuration/plugins directory. You'll explore ActiveX and plug-ins in "Understanding ActiveX and Plug-Ins," later in this chapter. To find out more about the configuration directory, look at Chapter 18, "Creating Custom Objects and Commands."

5. Deselect the Loop check box. Leave Autoplay selected; you'll uncheck it later when you add controls to the movie. The Autoplay feature causes the movie to play when the Web page loads in the browser.

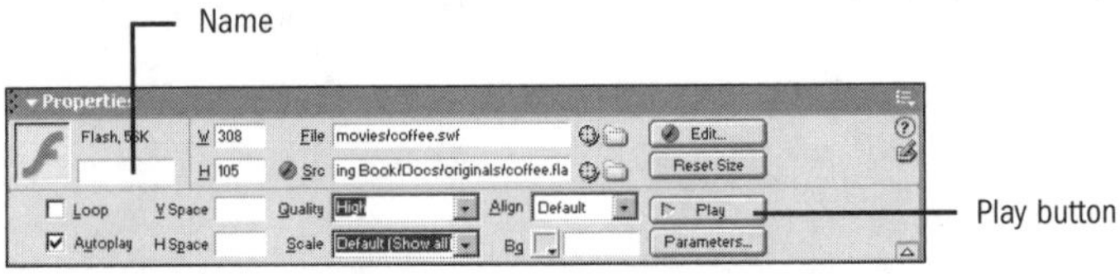

Figure 9.1

The Flash movie properties are displayed in the Property inspector.

6. In the Quality drop-down list, select Auto Low. This setting enables the movie to load quickly, potentially sacrificing some of the visual quality. After the movie is loaded, the visual quality will improve.

Preview the Web page in the browser to view the Flash movie. You must have the Flash player installed in your browser for this to work. The movie should play automatically a single time. If the movie doesn't play, double-check that you've selected the Autoplay check box.

Controlling Flash Movies

If you want to give the user some control over viewing the Flash movie, you can use Dreamweaver's Control Shockwave or Flash behavior to enable the user to play, stop, rewind, or go to a particular frame of a movie. You attach these behaviors to a button or hyperlink on the Web page. To add some controls to your Flash movie, follow these steps:

1. Add hyperlinks underneath the movie to act as movie controls. Type the words **Play, Stop**, and **Rewind**. If you like, separate each word by entering a pipe symbol (|), usually located above the backslash on your keyboard.

2. Make each of these words into null links by selecting each word individually and entering **javascript:;** in the Link text box of the Property inspector.

3. Select the Play link and click the + button in the Behaviors panel to drop down the Behaviors list box. Select the Control Shockwave or Flash behavior.

4. The Control Shockwave or Flash dialog box appears, as shown in Figure 9.2. Be sure your movie is selected in the Movie drop-down list box.

Figure 9.2

In the Control Shockwave or Flash dialog box, you enable users of your learning application to play, stop, rewind, or go to a specific frame of a Shockwave or Flash movie.

5. Select the Play radio button, and click OK to save your changes.

6. Confirm that the onClick event is listed in the Events column of the Behaviors panel.

7. Select the Flash movie, and deselect the Autoplay check box.

Preview the Web page in the browser. This time, the movie shouldn't play immediately when the Web page loads. When you click the Play hyperlink, the Flash movie should play.

Unfortunately, this behavior does not work in some browsers. A Macromedia technote states that the Control Shockwave and Flash behavior won't work in Internet Explorer on the Mac and Netscape 6. As a learning application developer, you will get used to this type of incompatibility among browsers and versions, if you aren't all ready used to it! Fortunately, there are workarounds.

Using Flash Extensions

One workaround is to create movie controls in Flash. This would have to be done before the Flash movie is exported as a .swf file. An alternative to using the behaviors initially installed with Dreamweaver is using an extension to Dreamweaver that you can download from the Macromedia Exchange. This extension, called the JavaScript Integration Kit for Flash 5, installs a number of behaviors that can control Flash movies. Download and install this extension to use the behaviors you will explore next.

The JavaScript Integration Kit for Flash 5 installs several additional behaviors, shown in Figure 9.3, that specifically control Flash movies. If you like, you can replace the previous behavior you attached to the Play hyperlink by selecting that text, selecting the Control Shockwave or Flash behavior in the Behaviors panel, and clicking the – button to delete the behavior. Now you can attach the new Flash behavior that you installed.

1. Select the word *Play*, and then click the + button in the Behaviors panel. Select the Play Flash behavior from the MM Flash Player Controls submenu of the Behaviors drop-down list box.

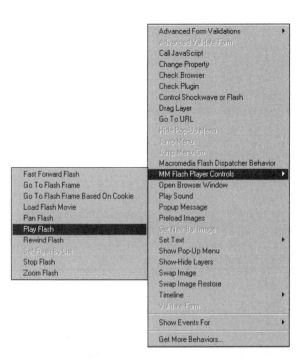

Figure 9.3
The JavaScript Integration Kit
installs additional behaviors to
control Flash movies.

2. Select the correct movie from the Movie drop-down list.

3. Click OK to save your changes. If you get an alert message stating that you might need to give the Flash movie an ID, click
OK to have Dreamweaver add an ID. The same name that you
gave your movie will be placed in the ID attribute.

Test the behavior's functionality by previewing the Web page in the
browser and clicking on the Play hyperlink. Repeat these steps to add
the Stop Flash behavior to the Stop hyperlink and the Rewind Flash
behavior to the Rewind hyperlink.

Understanding ActiveX and Plug-Ins

When you insert a Flash object into the Web page, Dreamweaver
automatically adds both the <object> tag, necessary for the ActiveX
control version of the Flash player, and the <embed> tag, necessary
for the plug-in version of the Flash player. If your learning application targets only one browser version, you might not need both these

tags. For example, if you are targeting only IE, you do not need the <embed> tag, but it will not hurt anything to leave that HTML code in the page. Here's the code that Dreamweaver adds:

```
<object classid="clsid:D27CDB6E-AE6D-11cf-96B8-444553540000"
codebase="http://download.macromedia.com/pub/shockwave/cabs/
flash/swflash.cab#version=5,0,0,0" width="305" height="108"
name="coffee" id="coffee">
        <param name=movie value="../movies/coffee.swf">
        <param name=quality value=autolow>
        <param name="LOOP" value="false">
        <param name="PLAY" value="false">
        <embed src="../movies/coffee.swf" quality=autolow
pluginspage="http://www.macromedia.com/shockwave/download/
index.cgi?P1_Prod_Version=ShockwaveFlash"
type="application/x-shockwave-flash" width="525" height="351"
loop="false" name="coffee" swliveconnect="true" play="false">
        </embed>
    </object>
```

Understanding Authorware Content

Authorware is Macromedia's premiere authoring tool for creating instructional content. Authorware has many built-in capabilities, such as score tracking and a visual flowline, that make it a powerful program for creating training applications. Unfortunately, many Authorware training applications are too large to deliver over the Internet.

You can easily package individual Authorware interactions for use in your online learning application. As with Flash, you can create complex interactions in Authorware that you just cannot create in pure HTML code. Also like Flash, Authorware requires that a player be installed in the user's browser to view Authorware content.

When you publish an Authorware program, you can select the Publish For Web check box to create files that can be viewed via a Web browser. There are a number of factors to consider when authoring for the Web in Authorware. For example, you probably want to make your Authorware piece as small as possible in screen size; this will make the files smaller. You also want to use small graphics without gradients. When you export your Authorware piece, you need to refer to your course specifications and target the appropriate bandwidth speed.

When you publish an Authorware program for the Web, Authorware divides the program into segments with the .aas file extension. The segments are sized according to the target Internet connection speed. For example, if the target is 56Kbps, the segments will be smaller than for a T1 connection.

During the publishing process, Authorware also creates a *map file* with the .aam file extension, shown in Figure 9.4. This map file lists all the individual segments and acts as a map for the Authorware player, directing the player to download the appropriate segments and files in the correct order. The map file is the file you point to when you insert an Authorware object into a Web page.

When you view an Authorware piece over the Web, the Authorware player displays a Security dialog box, shown in Figure 9.5.

Power User Tip

Authorware comes with an optional server component, Advanced Streamer, that collects information about which segments users are downloading and when they're being downloaded. The streamer uses this information to intelligently push segments to users, anticipating the section of the program they will most likely need next. The streamer can speed up downloading Authorware pieces over the Web.

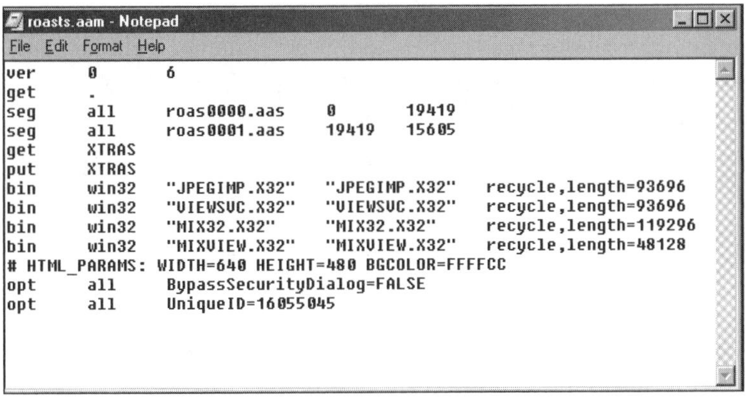

roasts.aam - Notepad

File Edit Format Help

```
ver     0       6
get     .
seg     all     roas0000.aas    0          19419
seg     all     roas0001.aas    19419      15605
get     XTRAS
put     XTRAS
bin     win32   "JPEGIMP.X32"   "JPEGIMP.X32"   recycle,length=93696
bin     win32   "VIEWSVC.X32"   "VIEWSVC.X32"   recycle,length=93696
bin     win32   "MIX32.X32"     "MIX32.X32"     recycle,length=119296
bin     win32   "MIXVIEW.X32"   "MIXVIEW.X32"   recycle,length=48128
# HTML_PARAMS: WIDTH=640 HEIGHT=480 BGCOLOR=FFFFCC
opt     all     BypassSecurityDialog=FALSE
opt     all     UniqueID=16055045
```

Figure 9.4

An Authorware map file lists the segments and directs the player to download the appropriate files.

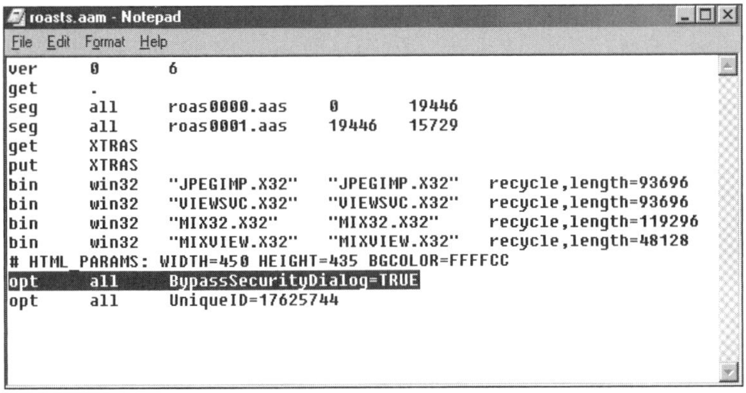

roasts.aam - Notepad

File Edit Format Help

```
ver     0       6
get     .
seg     all     roas0000.aas    0          19446
seg     all     roas0001.aas    19446      15729
get     XTRAS
put     XTRAS
bin     win32   "JPEGIMP.X32"   "JPEGIMP.X32"   recycle,length=93696
bin     win32   "VIEWSVC.X32"   "VIEWSVC.X32"   recycle,length=93696
bin     win32   "MIX32.X32"     "MIX32.X32"     recycle,length=119296
bin     win32   "MIXVIEW.X32"   "MIXVIEW.X32"   recycle,length=48128
# HTML_PARAMS: WIDTH=450 HEIGHT=435 BGCOLOR=FFFFCC
opt     all     BypassSecurityDialog=TRUE
opt     all     UniqueID=17625744
```

Figure 9.5

You can place code into your Authorware program to bypass the Security dialog box.

Authorware has two modes of running over the Web: trusting and non-trusting modes. When viewing Authorware over an intranet, the Security dialog box is unnecessary and confusing to some users. You can place code into the Authorware program that bypasses this dialog box from certain URLs.

Inserting Authorware into a Web Page

Unlike Flash, an Authorware object is not part of the standard Dreamweaver installation. If you are going to be adding several Authorware objects to a learning application, you might want to download the Authorware object from the Macromedia exchange. You'll insert the Authorware piece without using the Authorware object that you can install into the Dreamweaver Insert bar. First, you'll insert the movie by hand, and then you'll explore using the Authorware object to set up Authorware in a Web page.

Create a new Web, save the file, and give it a name. Like the Flash movie, you will insert the Authorware program into a layer. Be sure the Authorware .aam file, all the segment files, and other necessary files are located in a directory in your site. To add Authorware to this Web page, follow these steps:

1. Place the cursor within the content layer. Insert an ActiveX object (Insert, Media, ActiveX).

2. Select the ActiveX object in the Document window, set both the W (width) and the H (height) in the Property inspector.

3. Enter **CLSID:15B782AF-55D8-11D1-B477-006097098764** in the ClassID text box in the Property inspector. This is the universal class identifier for the Authorware Web Player ActiveX control.

4. In the Base text box in the Property inspector, enter the URL where users can download the ActiveX control if they do not have it. Enter **http://download.macromedia.com/pub/ shockwave/cabs/authorware/awswaxf.cab#version=6,0,0,63**. This is the location for the Authorware 6 player download. If you need a different version of the player, you'll need to look up its location on the Macromedia Web site.

5. Add the code to support a Netscape plug-in player by selecting the Embed check box in the Property inspector.

Dreamweaver adds the <embed> tag inside the <object> tag for the ActiveX control.

6. Load the Authorware map file in the <embed> tag by clicking the Browse Folder icon next to the Src text box in the Property inspector, as shown in Figure 9.6. You might need to select Shockwave for Authorware as the file type in the Files of Type drop-down menu. Select .aam from the directory in your Web site. This attribute is not used to set the source for the <object> tag and the ActiveX control.

7. To give the ActiveX control the correct URL for the Authorware map file, you must add a parameter. First, copy the URL to the Authorware map file in the Src text field in the Property inspector. Click the Parameters button in the Property inspector, and type **SRC** into the first line in the Parameters dialog box. Enter **URL** into the Value column, as shown in Figure 9.7.

8. When you add parameters in the Parameters dialog box, Dreamweaver adds individual <param> tags for the ActiveX control and adds attributes with the parameters to the <embed> tag. Authorware has three other parameters you can add: palette, window, and bgcolor (background color). You'll explore these parameters in the next section when you use the Authorware object.

9. You can preview the Authorware program right in the Document window by clicking the Play button in the Property inspector.

Figure 9.6
Enter the Authorware map file URL into the Src text box in the Property inspector.

Figure 9.7
You need to add the src attribute to the ActiveX control so the control knows where the Authorware map file is located.

The previous exercise demonstrated some of the differences between the two types of players and the HTML code necessary for each. It's much easier to download the free Authorware object from the Macromedia Exchange and use it to set up an Authorware program in your Web page. Installing the Authorware 6 object adds the Authorware object to the Learning tab in the Insert bar and adds an Authorware command to the Media submenu in the Insert menu. Here's how to use it to insert an Authorware program into your Web page:

1. Delete the object created by the previous exercise.

2. Insert an Authorware 6 object (Insert, Media, Authorware 6). The Insert Authorware 6 dialog box appears, as shown in Figure 9.8.

3. Select the Web Player version to download if the user does not have it installed. You can select the complete player, which includes only the Authorware 6 Web player plus standard Xtras.

4. Click the Browse button, and select the drag.aam file in the Authorware directory in the Web site.

5. Set the Width and Height. The Authorware object should automatically pick this up from the map file.

Figure 9.8

You set up the Authorware object's properties in the Insert Authorware 6 dialog box.

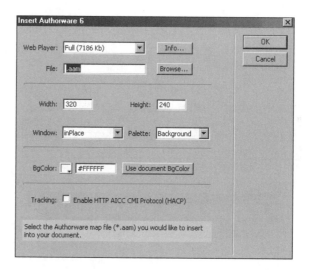

6. In the Window drop-down list box, select the type of window for displaying the Authorware program. Select the inPlace setting to display the Authorware piece right in the browser window. If you want the Authorware program to appear in a window of its own, select onTop. If you want the browser window to be minimized after launching an Authorware program on top of it, select onTopMinimize.

7. Select Background in the Palette drop-down list box. This choice instructs the Authorware program to use the system palette. If the Authorware program had its own custom palette, you would select Foreground from the list.

8. The BgColor field holds the hexadecimal color of the rectangle that appears on the Web page before the Authorware program loads. You can leave it at white, #FFFFFF.

9. Don't enable HTTP AICC CMI Protocol (HACP). This feature is used if you are launching the learning application from an AICC-compliant Learning Management System (LMS). You'll explore LMS standards and procedures in Chapter 15, "Using a Learning Management System."

10. Click OK to save your changes.

You can preview the Web page in the browser to check functionality. It's much quicker to use the Authorware object to set up an Authorware program in your Web page.

Using RealMedia

You can add sound or video to your Web pages. Because of the size of these types of files, however, you must carefully consider the file format you want to use. Sound and video files are handled differently and unpredictably by various browsers. This section explores ways to include these media files with predictable results.

The easiest way to include sound in a Web page is to create sound-only Flash files. (There's an extension on the Macromedia Exchange that can do this right in Dreamweaver.) Flash can compress audio very well, and because the Flash player is so universal, most users can quickly hear the audio. Flash compresses audio into the MP3 format and can even create streaming audio that begins to play before the browser downloads the entire file.

To embed a Flash audio-only movie into your Web page, you would follow the steps you used earlier in this chapter. Controls for the audio and for the Play, Stop, and Pause buttons could be built into the Flash movie or created by using Dreamweaver behaviors, as you did in the movie example earlier.

RealAudio compresses files even smaller than Flash and can stream audio files via RealServer or a Web server. Users must install RealPlayer, including the ActiveX control (IE) or plug-in (Netscape), for RealAudio to work in their browsers. You can configure the RealAudio files to launch the external RealPlayer application or to use controls embedded into the Web page.

The way you reference the RealMedia files depends on how you will serve and store the files. If you have purchased the RealServer application to serve RealMedia files, you would reference that server address when playing the audio. If you are serving the RealMedia files from a special spot on a Web server, you would need to use that address. Or, the example this book shows is simple: You will link to a RealMedia file stored in the media directory of your Web site.

RealAudio files come in a couple of different formats:

- **.ra or .rm**—A compressed RealAudio file made from a sound file.

- **.ram**—A RealAudio metafile containing the URL to a RealAudio file. You need to create and link to .ram files to use streaming. The .ram file contains the URL in the formal pnm://real.domain.com/audio.ra (older protocol) or rtsp://real.domain.com/audio.rm. You'll need to consult your administrator to find the correct format for your server.

In this example, you will not need a metafile to reference the RealMedia audio file. You will simply link to the file in your Web site. You need a metafile only when referencing a streaming RealMedia file. To set up a RealMedia file in a Web page, follow these steps:

1. Open a Web page to add the audio.

2. Insert an ActiveX object (Insert, Media, ActiveX).

3. In the Property inspector, enter **200** for the W (width) attribute and **30** for the H (height) attribute. That's a nice size to display the RealMedia control panel.

4. Enter the universal class identifier for RealPlayer into the ClassID attribute: **CLSID:CFCDAA03-8BE4-11cf-B84B-0020AFBBCCFA**. This ClassID should be available when you drop down the ClassID list box in the Property inspector. That's much easier than typing this number!

5. Select the Embed check box, click the Browse Folder icon next to the Src text box, and browse to the intro.ra file in the media directory of your Web site. You might need to drop down the Files of Type list box and select All Files to be able to locate the .ra file.

6. Click the Parameters button to enter the ActiveX control parameters. Enter the URL just entered in the Src text box into a parameter called SRC. Enter another parameter called Controls with the value controlpanel. The Controls parameter manages the appearance of the embedded RealMedia controls. The parameters should look like Figure 9.9.

Preview the file in the browser, and you should see a small, embedded RealMedia player in your page if you have it installed in your browser. Click the Play button to play the audio file.

You can use these same steps to play Windows Media Player or QuickTime audio. The file formats are different, and they require different software to compress, but the idea is the same. You can use this technique to add controls for any type of media files that require players. The most difficult part is tracking down the parameters that the individual players recognize.

Figure 9.9

The SRC and Controls parameters tell the RealMedia ActiveX controls which audio file to play and what the embedded controls should look like.

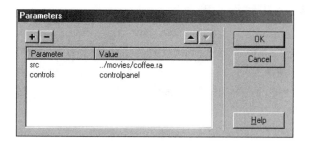

You can also use these steps to play compressed video. Unless all your students have consistent broadband (DSL, cable modem, or T1 connections), you probably do not want to include video in your learning application. Even intranets on a local network can become congested with video files. There should be an overwhelming advantage to requiring video in your online learning application to justify its use. If there is such a justification, you follow steps similar to the audio steps to embed video in the page.

You can also have live broadcasts by using RealAudio, Windows Media Player, and QuickTime. Sometimes, distance learning courses have a *webcast* component, where learners get together on a regular basis to listen to a broadcast from the instructor. Usually, these broadcasts are accompanied by an online chat with other learners. You set these audio links up according to the URL provided by your administrator. The link works only during the broadcast.

Checking for Players

Dreamweaver enables you to check for a player in the user's browser before the Web page is even loaded. This makes it easy to guide the user to the correct download. Although you can provide a URL that takes users directly to the download page for the appropriate plug-in automatically, this can be confusing for the user. It's best to detect this yourself and add user-friendly instructions for the download.

The Check Plugin behavior enables your Web page to detect whether a certain plug-in is present, and then redirects the user to a download page. You can detect plug-ins at the beginning of an online learning application, or you can do the detection at a certain page of content. It's helpful for users to create a page to detect all the necessary players right at the beginning of the learning application. However, if you have bookmarks allowing users to jump to their last spots in the course, and they log into the course on a different computer, they could bypass the detection routine.

The following steps usually work only with Netscape. Most ActiveX players cannot be detected; therefore, player installation in Internet Explorer cannot usually be checked by the behavior. It's best to display a small movie on a detection page and have users check whether they can see the movie.

In this example, add the Check Plugin behavior to the page containing some media that requires a player:

1. If your Web page is not attached to a template, select the <body> tag in the tag selector; otherwise, select one of the editable button images in the lower-right area of the Web page. The onLoad event will trigger the detection of the Flash player.

2. Click the + button in the Behaviors panel, and select Check Plugin from the Behaviors drop-down list box. The Check Plugin dialog box appears, as shown in Figure 9.10.

3. Select Flash from the Plugin drop-down list box.

4. Leave the If Found, Go to URL text box blank. If the Flash player is found, you want the user to stay on the current page. You could enter a URL here if you wanted to redirect the user after successful detection of the Flash player.

5. Enter **../needflash.html** into the Otherwise, Go To URL text box. You need to create this Web page in the site root, explaining to users that they need to download and install the Flash player to successfully view the content. You should include the URL to the Flash download page on the Macromedia Web site.

6. Click the OK button to save your changes.

7. Be sure the onLoad event is listed in the Events column of the Behaviors panel.

Figure 9.10
The Check Plugin behavior enables you to check whether users have a particular plug-in installed.

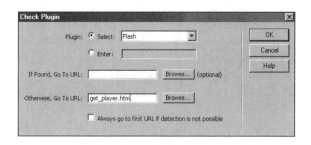

Unfortunately, it's difficult to test this functionality when you actually have the player installed in your browser. If you have the player installed and nothing happens when you load the page, you know that this part of the functionality works correctly.

It was easy to detect the Flash player with the Check Plugin behavior because it was listed in the Plugin drop-down list box. What if a player you need to detect isn't listed? You will need to look up the player's exact name. The easiest way to do this is to make sure the plug-in is installed in Netscape, and then select the About Plug-ins command from Netscape's Help menu. A Web page appears with the names of all the installed plug-ins. The player name is listed directly beneath the filename. For example, the exact name I get in Netscape for the installed Authorware plug-in is "Macromedia Authorware Web Player Netscape plug-in, version 6.0 F1."

Summary

In this chapter, you inserted various media types that require players to be installed in the browser. You inserted and configured Macromedia Flash and Authorware movies. You also inserted a RealMedia file and set its parameters to display a control panel. You then checked the user's browser to see whether a required player was installed using the Check Plugin behavior.

Power User Tip

If you installed the JavaScript Integration Kit for Flash 5, you have access to a behavior specifically designed to detect the Flash player. It's called Macromedia Flash Dispatcher behavior, and it's available in the Behaviors drop-down list box.

Part IV

Using CourseBuilder

IN THIS CHAPTER

chapter 10

Including CourseBuilder Interactions and Controls

THE COURSEBUILDER EXTENSION FOR DREAMWEAVER is a "must have" for learning application developers. This extension began as a software package, called Attain Objects for Dreamweaver, that was available for purchase. Now Macromedia generously gives this extension away on the Macromedia Exchange. Course-Builder enables you to quickly and easily add learning interactions to your Web pages. CourseBuilder creates multiple choice, text entry, drag and drop, and other types of assessment interactions using a wizard interface. This extension enables you to create interactions that would take hours or days to do by hand in Dreamweaver alone with HTML and JavaScript.

Another advantage of using CourseBuilder is it enables your team to have consistent code. Reusing proven CourseBuilder interactions is better than having individual team members create interactions by using many different methods. Having consistent code makes it easier to troubleshoot problems you might run into when implementing your learning application.

This chapter covers the basics of inserting and editing CourseBuilder interactions and controls. Chapter 11, "Conquering CourseBuilder's Action Manager," goes into more depth on customizing interactions to work in unique ways. Chapter 12, "Scoring an Assessment and Hiding the Answers," explores gathering scores from CourseBuilder interactions and scoring a quiz.

In this chapter, you will understand the following:

- How to insert and edit CourseBuilder interactions and controls

- How to configure the General tab of a CourseBuilder interaction

- How to configure Multiple Choice, Drag and Drop, Explore, and Text Entry interactions

- How to configure Button, Timer, and Slider controls

Exploring CourseBuilder

Installing the CourseBuilder extension in Dreamweaver adds the CourseBuilder object to the Learning tab of the Insert bar. If you didn't install CourseBuilder in Chapter 2, "Assembling the Team and Collecting the Tools," you'll want to return to the Manage Extensions section of that chapter and install CourseBuilder now.

After you install the CourseBuilder extension, you're ready to create new Web pages and insert the interactions. Installing the Course-Builder extension adds three major commands to Dreamweaver:

- **A new Insert bar category**—The Learning tab enables insertion of a CourseBuilder object into a Web page. You can use the Course-Builder object from the Learning tab of the Insert bar or select the CourseBuilder Interaction command from the Insert menu.

- **The CourseBuilder submenu**—Added to Dreamweaver's Modify menu, shown in Figure 10.1, this submenu contains commands to control CourseBuilder interactions.

- **The Using CourseBuilder command**—Available under the Help menu, this command gives you access to the extensive CourseBuilder help that's available.

CourseBuilder's strength is the JavaScript functions that control interactions.

Figure 10.1
The CourseBuilder submenu in the Modify menu gives you access to CourseBuilder commands.

When you insert a CourseBuilder object into a Web page, you are presented with the CourseBuilder Gallery, shown in Figure 10.2. In the upper-left corner, you can select interactions that will work in 3.0 or 4.0+ browser versions. If you select 3.0 browsers, you can add only simple Multiple Choice and Text Entry interactions. For the examples in this chapter, select the 4.0+ Browsers radio button.

Figure 10.2

The CourseBuilder Gallery displays CourseBuilder interactions that work in 3.0 or 4.0+ browsers.

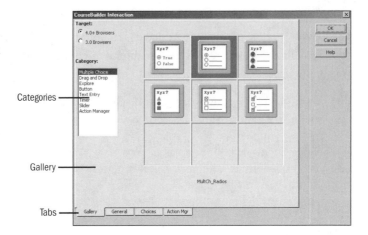

With the 4.0+ Browsers option selected, the CourseBuilder Gallery has eight categories: Multiple Choice, Drag and Drop, Explore, Button, Text Entry, Timer, Slider, and Action Manager. When you select one of the categories listed on the left side of the Gallery, the interactions available in that category appear on the right, represented by icons. When you select an interaction, the tabs to set up the interaction appear at the bottom beside the Gallery tab. The tabs vary according to the function of the interaction you select.

CourseBuilder objects are divided into two groups: interactions and controls. In the interactions group are the Multiple Choice, Drag and Drop, Explore, Text Entry, and Action Manager categories. These objects are useful in online learning applications as assessment questions and knowledge checks.

In the controls group are the Button, Timer, and Slider categories. These objects are useful as navigation controls, switches, and time-monitoring devices. This type of CourseBuilder interaction is more like a "gadget" that you add to your Web page.

Copying Support Files

Before you insert a CourseBuilder interaction, you must save the Web page so that CourseBuilder can insert the correct hyperlinks. The first time you insert a CourseBuilder interaction into a Web page in your site, CourseBuilder prompts you to copy support files. The Copy Support Files dialog box is shown in Figure 10.3. The support files consist of a scripts directory, containing the external JavaScript files that make the CourseBuilder interactions function, and a directory of images, including placeholder graphics and images used for buttons and timers.

By default, CourseBuilder inserts the support file directories into the same directory where the current Web page is saved. That means if you add CourseBuilder interactions to multiple directories, the support file directories are added to each directory. Because you already have a scripts and an images directory in the root of your Web site, it's more efficient to use those same directories instead of creating new ones.

In an online learning application project, you can modify the Course-Builder preferences file, Preferences.txt, so that CourseBuilder looks for the support file directories in a single, standard location. The Preferences.txt file is stored in the Dreamweaver\CourseBuilder\Config directory.

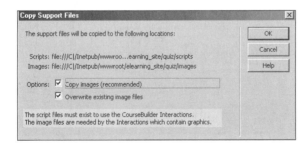

Figure 10.3

The Copy Support Files dialog box prompts you to copy the external JavaScript files and images necessary for CourseBuilder interactions to work.

To edit Preferences.txt, you can open the file in a text editor or in Dreamweaver, but it's best to use Dreamweaver, shown in Figure 10.4, because the formatting is easier to read. Dreamweaver uses this file to set various CourseBuilder preferences, and you might want to explore this file further after you are more experienced with CourseBuilder. For now, simply modify the first two preference variables in the file: PREF_scriptsUrl and PREF_imagesUrl.

The online learning application site you are creating is designed to contain all the content Web pages in lesson directories under the root directory. The PREF_scriptsUrl and the PREF_imagesURL variables are relative to the location where you save the Web pages containing the interactions. To link to the images directory and the scripts directory, the URLs will be ../scripts and ../images. The ../ means to go up one directory level and points to the site root when used in one of the lesson directories. Change PREF_scriptsUrl to ../scripts and change PREF_imagesURL to ../images. Then CourseBuilder creates a new directory within your existing images directory to store all the images it adds. Save your changes to the Preferences.txt file and restart Dreamweaver.

Figure 10.4

Modify CourseBuilder preferences by editing the Preferences.txt file in Dreamweaver.

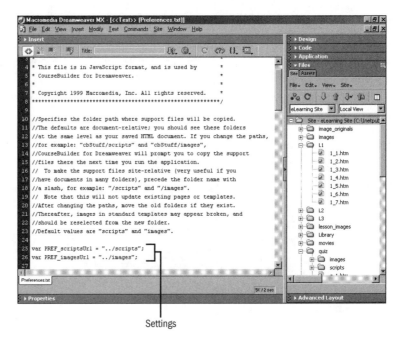

Settings

eLearning with Dreamweaver MX: Building Online Learning Applications

Every time you insert a CourseBuilder interaction, CourseBuilder checks to see whether the support file directories exist. Instead of waiting for CourseBuilder to prompt you, however, you'll create these directories now by using the Copy Support Files command:

1. Create a new Web page, save the file, and name it. If you changed your Preferences.txt, you'll need to place your Web page in a directory beneath the site root (maybe a directory called quiz). Now that you have established the location of the current Web page, CourseBuilder will know where to place the support files relative to this file.

2. Create the support file directories with the Copy Support Files command (Modify, CourseBuilder, Copy Support Files).

3. The Copy Support Files dialog box appears, as shown in Figure 10.5. The URL should point to directories in the site root if you've modified the Preferences.txt file correctly. Click the OK button to copy the scripts and images to Course-Builder. You can leave the Overwrite Existing Images check box unchecked.

4. Examine the scripts and images directories in the Site panel or Site window. The new files should be present.

Now you have added single copies of the files necessary for Course-Builder to work. You should not have to add these files again while developing this site, as long as any files containing a CourseBuilder interaction are saved in the subdirectories (lesson1, lesson2, quiz, and so on) off the site root.

Power User Tip

In the first paragraph, the Preferences.txt file states that you can make your directories site-root relative. A *site-root relative directory* begins with a slash and indicates that instead of being relative to the current page, the URL is relative to the site root. Site-root relative addressing is useful when working on large projects, but for the URLs to work, you must always view Web pages through a Web server. I find it easier to preview the Web sites I create on my computer instead of through the server (either local to My Computer or somewhere else).

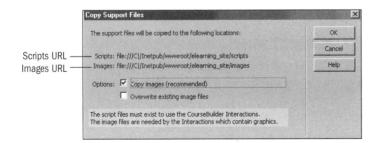

Scripts URL
Images URL

Figure 10.5
Check that the Copy Support Files dialog box lists the correct URLs for the common scripts and images directories.

Adding the Template Fix

When you insert a CourseBuilder interaction into a Web page, Course-Builder adds a JavaScript function call to the <body> tag. The JavaScript code calls the MM_initInteractions() function, which sets up the CourseBuilder interactions on the page. The problem appears when you add a CourseBuilder interaction to a Web page based on a template; you cannot edit the <body> tag in these pages. CourseBuilder solves this problem by installing the Add Template Fix command.

You need to create a template that includes the template fix code for use with CourseBuilder interactions. Open one of your templates, select the Add Template Fix command (Modify, CourseBuilder, Add Template Fix), and then save the template with another name. The Add Template Fix dialog box appears, as shown in Figure 10.6.

Click the Add button to add the initialization code to both the current page and the parent template file. From now on, all pages using this template will have the initialization code in the <body> tag. The code looks like this:

```
<body bgcolor="#FFFFFF" text="#000000" leftmargin="0" topmargin="0"
marginwidth="0" marginheight="0" onLoad="MM_initInteractions>
```

Examining Browser Compatibility

Macromedia engineers have invested their talents in making CourseBuilder functionality as cross-browser compatible as possible. You should be aware of functionality issues of the interactions you insert into your learning application. Table 10.1 lists compatibility issues with the two major browsers, Netscape Navigator and Microsoft Internet Explorer.

Figure 10.6

Add necessary JavaScript code to the template by using the Add Template Fix command.

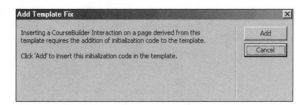

Table 10.1 CourseBuilder Interaction Compatibility with Different Browsers

CourseBuilder Interaction	Netscape 4	Netscape 6	Internet Explorer 4+
Multiple choice with form elements	OK, but Reset button does not reset radio buttons, and disabling interaction does not prohibit the user from selecting radio buttons or check boxes.	OK	OK
Multiple choice with graphic elements	OK	OK	OK
Drag and drop	OK, but do not insert in layer.	Does not work.	OK
Explore	OK, but do not insert in layer.	Does not work.	OK
Button	OK	OK	OK
Text entry	OK, but disabling interaction does not prohibit the user from entering text.	OK	OK
Timer	OK, but limited to one per page.	OK	OK

continues

Table 10.1   Continued

CourseBuilder Interaction	Netscape 4	Netscape 6	Internet Explorer 4+
Slider	OK, but limited to one per page. Do not set a background color in the slider layer.	Does not work.	OK
Action Manager	OK	OK	OK

Inserting a Multiple Choice Interaction

The first interaction you'll try is in the Multiple Choice category. There are six different types of multiple-choice questions listed in Table 10.2.

Table 10.2   Multiple Choice Category Interactions

Icon	Interaction Name	Description
Xyz? ⊙ True ○ False	True/False	Two radio buttons enabling the learner to select true or false as an answer.
Xyz? ⊙— ○— ○—	Radio buttons	Multiple radio buttons enabling the learner to select a single answer.
Xyz? ●— ●— ●—	Image radio buttons	Multiple button images that act like radio buttons, enabling the learner to select a single answer.
Xyz? ▲ ● ■	Image buttons	Multiple button images enabling the learner to select multiple correct answers.
Xyz? ☒— ☐— ☐—	Check box buttons	Multiple check boxes enabling the learner to select multiple correct answers.
Xyz? ☑— ☐— ☑—	Image check box buttons	Multiple button images that act like check boxes, enabling the learner to select multiple correct answers.

The Multiple Choice interaction can be sorted into two groups: answer selections that act like radio buttons and answer selections that act like check boxes. These two common form elements function in slightly different ways. Radio buttons act as a group, presenting mutually exclusive values. You should use radio buttons when a question has a single answer. Check boxes function independently, with each check box toggling an answer value on and off. You should use check boxes when a question has multiple answers.

Follow these steps to insert a CourseBuilder interaction into the Web page you created earlier, 1.html in the Quiz directory:

1. Place the cursor in the Content layer on the left side of the Document window.

2. Click the CourseBuilder object in the Learning tab of the Insert bar, or use the CourseBuilder interaction command (Insert, CourseBuilder Interaction). The CourseBuilder Gallery appears.

3. Be sure 4.0+ Browsers is selected as the Target.

4. Select the Image Radio Buttons multiple choice interaction.

After you select the interaction in the Gallery, the General, Choices, and Action Manager tabs appear along the bottom of the Course-Builder Interaction dialog box. You can also see the question inserted into the Document window behind the CourseBuilder Interaction dialog box (you might have to move the dialog box out of the way). Usually, you can see the updates you make in the CourseBuilder Interaction dialog box as you set up the interaction.

Note

The name of the icon appears when you place the cursor over the interaction icon in the Gallery.

Using the General Tab

All CourseBuilder interactions have a General tab where you set the question stem, when the interaction will be judged, when the answer is correct, and whether you want to limit the time or tries for the question. The General tab also has an option to turn on Knowledge Track, the automatic tracking on the interaction to a learning management system (LMS). You'll learn more about this option in Chapter 15, "Using a Learning Management System."

Select the General tab in the CourseBuilder Interaction dialog box to display the General tab options, shown in Figure 10.7.

To configure the General tab for this multiple-choice question, follow these steps:

1. Leave the default name in the Interaction Name text box. This name is used only by CourseBuilder.

2. Enter the text for the question in the Question Text text box.

3. In this interaction, select the When the User Clicks a Button Labeled radio button, and enter **Check Answer** as the button label. The other settings in the Judge Interaction radio buttons enable you to judge the question when the user clicks a button, immediately when the user clicks a choice, or on some other event. The other event might be after an animation finishes or when the user places the cursor in a certain area of the screen.

4. The Correct When drop-down list box enables you to specify whether the user must select all the correct answers when there are multiple correct answers. For example, if you asked the question "What regions of the world grow coffee?" you could have the following possible answers: Africa, Antarctica, Greenland, and Indonesia. Both Africa and Indonesia are correct answers. Will you require the learner to select both answers or just one to have the question marked as correct?

For this interaction, you have only a single correct answer, so you can select either choice from the Correct When drop-down list

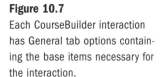

Figure 10.7

Each CourseBuilder interaction has General tab options containing the base items necessary for the interaction.

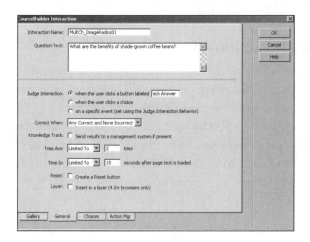

box. Both All Correct and None Incorrect or Any Correct and None Incorrect will cause the interaction to be scored correctly.

5. You can skip the Knowledge Track check box for now. You'll deal with this in Chapter 15.

6. In the Tries Are list box, select Limited To, and type **2** in the Tries text box. In the Time Is list box, select Limited To, and type **15** into the Time text box.

7. Select the check box next to Reset to add a reset button to the interaction. This button resets the interaction to its original state.

8. Leave the Layer check box unchecked. This interaction is already contained in a layer. If it was not, however, it's good to choose this setting so that you can easily position the interaction. Be sure you always consult the compatibility guidelines in Table 10.1, as some interactions do not work when placed in layers.

Don't click the OK button yet! You will go on and set up the next two tabs before exiting the CourseBuilder Interaction dialog box and testing the interaction.

Using the Choices Tab

The Choices tab enables you to set up the answer choices, consisting of the correct answer or answers and the incorrect answers (*distractors*). This tab, shown in Figure 10.8, is divided into an upper and a lower half. The upper half is a list of all the available choices. The lower half displays the attributes (choice options) of the choice selected in the upper half.

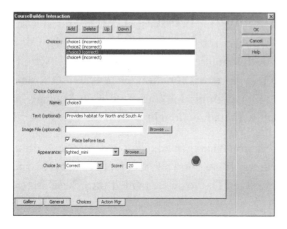

Figure 10.8

The Choices tab enables you to set up the attributes of the correct and incorrect answer choices.

If you receive an error message warning you that CourseBuilder can't find button images, it's because you moved the location of the CourseBuilder images from their default spot. You'll be able to browse for the image files when you are setting up the choices.

Follow these steps to configure the Choices tab for this multiple-choice question:

1. CourseBuilder displays four choices. Click the Add button to add additional answer choices, and click the Delete button to delete extra choices. You can also rearrange the choice with the Up and Down button.

2. Select the first choice, choice1. The Choice options appear in the lower half of the dialog box. You can leave the default name in the Name text box as choice1.

3. You can have text or an image as an answer choice, or you can have both. Enter the answer text in the Text text box and enter the path to an image (if available) in the Image File text box.

4. Select the type of button in the Appearance drop-down list box. Selecting one of the button images displays a sample of the button to the right of the drop-down list.

5. Set whether the current answer choice is correct or incorrect in the Choice Is drop-down list box. Set the score for this answer in the Score text box.

6. Repeat these steps for each of the other three choices. All the choices should have the same button appearance.

Using the Action Manager Tab

The Action Manager tab contains the "brain" of the CourseBuilder interaction. In this chapter, you do not modify the Action Manager because you'll explore that function extensively in the next chapter. In this section, you simply look at the Action Manager and familiarize yourself with its functionality.

Click on the Action Manager tab. The logic of the Action Manager, shown in Figure 10.9, controls the functionality of the Course-Builder interaction. The logic is divided into three sections, called *segments*, in this type of interaction. The Check Time segment controls the time limit functionality, the Check Tries segment controls the tries limit functionality, and the Correctness segment directs what happens if the question is answered correctly or incorrectly.

If a segment is collapsed, you see a plus sign beside the segment name. To see the logic contained in the segment, select the segment name and click the + button. The lines of code in the Action Manager are written in something close to real language—statements that can be understood.

You can see that the default feedback for a correct or incorrect answer is a pop-up message. The pop-up message used in the Action Manager is the same Popup Message behavior you used in Chapter 8, "Creating Interactivity with Behaviors and Animations." Also, notice that when the Check Tries or Check Time segments are triggered, CourseBuilder disables the interaction. Again, you'll learn about editing and inserting this type of functionality into Action Manager in Chapter 11.

Click the OK button to save the CourseBuilder interaction. Preview the Web page in a browser and check the page's functionality. Check that the buttons appear and work the way you expected (only one can be selected at a time). Also, check the Time limit and Tries limit functionality. Be sure you check that the correct answer works and the incorrect answers behave as expected. In the next section, you'll change the generic feedback that CourseBuilder inserts.

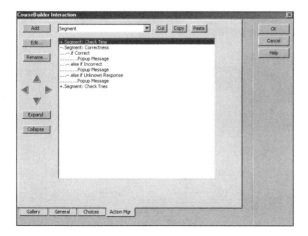

Figure 10.9
The Action Manager tab controls the logic behind the CourseBuilder interaction.

Editing an Interaction

When you insert a CourseBuilder interaction into a Web page, the CourseBuilder icon appears if you have invisible elements set as visible (View, Visual Aids, Invisible Elements). You can select this icon to edit an existing CourseBuilder interaction. Sometimes, because of where the CourseBuilder icon is located in the Document window, you cannot see the icon even if invisible elements are showing. You'll learn two additional methods to edit an interaction when that is the case.

When you select the CourseBuilder icon, the Property inspector displays the CourseBuilder interaction attributes, shown in Figure 10.10. Click the Edit button in the Property inspector to display the CourseBuilder Interaction dialog box, where you edit settings for the interaction.

Dreamweaver uses the <interaction> tag to identify CourseBuilder interactions. You can see this tag in the tag selector when you place the cursor anywhere within the CourseBuilder Interaction elements in the Web page. This tag is Dreamweaver specific, is not recognized by the browser, and is simply ignored when the Web page is displayed in the browser. To use the second editing method, select the <interaction> tag in the tag selector to display the CourseBuilder Interaction Edit button in the Property inspector.

Power User Tip

Until you close and save the interaction settings during the initial setup, you can always go back to the Gallery and change the type of CourseBuilder interaction you want to use. After you've closed the CourseBuilder dialog box, you can no longer change the type of interaction because the Gallery tab no longer appears in the CourseBuilder dialog box.

Figure 10.10
When the CourseBuilder interaction is selected, the Property inspector displays interaction attributes.

CourseBuilder icon —

Interaction tag —

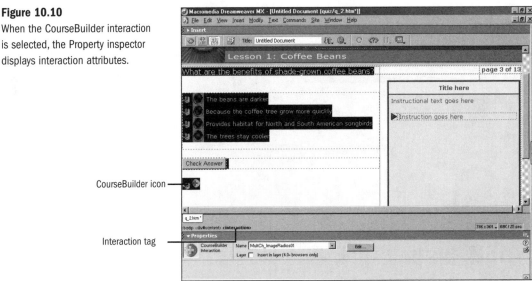

| **eLearning with Dreamweaver MX:** Building Online Learning Applications

The third editing method is to again place the cursor anywhere within the interaction elements. Select the Edit Interaction command (Modify, CourseBuilder, Edit Interaction) to open the CourseBuilder Interaction dialog box. This technique can be tricky when there is more than one interaction in a Web page.

You haven't yet created a Web page with multiple CourseBuilder interactions, but when you do, you can select and edit a specific interaction in the Name drop-down list in the Property inspector, as shown in Figure 10.11.

Figure 10.11
The Name drop-down list enables you to pick a CourseBuilder interaction to edit when there are multiple interactions in a Web page.

Modifying the Feedback in the Action Manager

You are not stuck with the default functionality of a CourseBuilder interaction because you can change the code in the Action Manager. Each CourseBuilder Interaction can be changed to respond to learner inputs differently, display different feedback, and to trigger any of the behaviors installed in Dreamweaver. All this is accomplished in the Action Manager.

Open the CourseBuilder Interaction dialog box, using one of the three methods listed previously. To edit the Action Manager of an interaction, follow these steps:

1. Select the General tab. Turn off the Tries limit and the Time limit by selecting Unlimited from the drop-down lists.

2. Select the Action Manager tab. Because you removed the Tries limit and the Time limit, you can remove that code from the Action Manager. Although this step isn't required, it helps keep the Action Manager lean and easy to understand. Select the Segment: Check Time line, as shown in Figure 10.12, and click the Cut button at the top of the dialog box. Select the Segment: Check Tries line and again click the Cut button. Be sure you've selected the correct line because there is no undo command!

Warning

CourseBuilder gives each interaction a unique identifier by using the object attribute of the **<interaction>** tag. The identifiers appear as G01, G02, G03, and so on. Many of the elements involved with the interaction, such as layers and images, are named using the identifier. Never rename these objects or modify any Course-Builder JavaScript code by hand because you will probably impair the interaction's functionality.

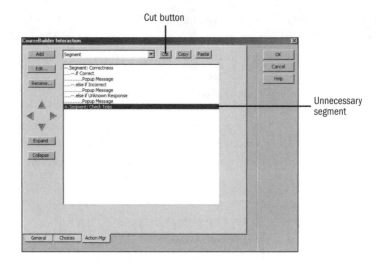

Figure 10.12

Delete segments of unnecessary code from the Action Manager using the Cut button. Careful! There is no undo command.

Cut button

Unnecessary segment

3. In the Correctness segment, there are three expressions. The first expression is triggered if a correct answer is selected; the second expression, if an incorrect answer is selected; and the third expression, if an unknown response is selected. Because you defined all the potential responses, you will have no unknown responses, so you can select the --else if Unknown Response line and click the Cut button.

4. Now you're left with the fundamental code that judges the correctness of the multiple-choice question. The default feedback for a correct or incorrect answer is a pop-up message.

   Select the Popup Message line under if Correct, click the Edit button on the left side of the dialog box, and enter a friendlier message as shown in Figure 10.13. Repeat for the Popup Message line under the else if Incorrect line.

5. Click the OK button to save your settings, and test the Web page in the browser. You should get the new text in the pop-up messages.

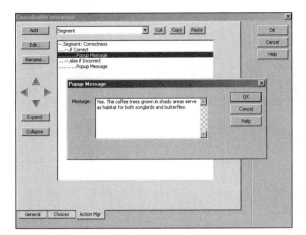

Figure 10.13
You can edit the default Popup Message behavior in the Action Manager.

Inserting a Drag and Drop Interaction

Many learners find Drag and Drop interactions fun. Because these interactions engage learners by allowing them to manipulate objects onscreen, they also can be educational. The Drag and Drop CourseBuilder interaction can judge pairings of objects as correct or incorrect and make objects snap back to their original positions if they are incorrect.

In this section, you'll add a Drag and Drop interaction to a page, setting up the relationships between the pairs of drag objects and target objects. In Chapter 11, you'll add advanced functionality, including feedback particular to individual drag/target pairings. There are seven different Drag and Drop interactions, listed in Table 10.3.

Table 10.3 Drag and Drop Category Interactions

Icon	Interaction Name	Description
	One-way many-to-many	A multiple drag and multiple target interaction, enabling the learner to drag the drag elements to the target elements.
	Two-way many-to-many	A multiple drag and multiple target interaction, enabling the learner to drag the drag elements to the target elements or drag the target elements to the drag elements.

continues

Table 10.3   Continued

Icon	Interaction Name	Description
	One-way one-to-many	A single drag and multiple target interaction, enabling the learner to drag the drag element to the target elements.
	Two-way one-to-many	A single drag and multiple target interaction, enabling the learner to drag the drag element to the target elements or drag the target elements to the drag element.
	Two-way one-to-one	A single drag and single target interaction, meant as a starting point for creating a custom Drag and Drop interaction.
	Two steps in order	A single drag and multiple target interaction, requiring the learner to drag the drag element to the target elements in a certain order.
	Two steps in order with distractor	A single drag and multiple target interaction, requiring the learner to drag the drag element to the target elements in the proper order when a distractor is present.

The Drag and Drop interactions can be sorted into three groups: the one-direction interactions, the two-direction interactions, and the ordered interactions. You select the interaction type according to the functionality specified in the storyboard.

Using the General Tab

Insert a CourseBuilder Interaction (Insert, CourseBuilder Interaction) into a Web page. Select the one-way many-to-many Drag and Drop interaction. The Drag and Drop interactions have General and Action Manager tabs, like the Multiple Choice interactions, but they also have an Elements tab, where you set up the drag and target elements, and the Pairs tab, where you set up the relationships between the drag and target elements.

Set up the General tab as shown in Figure 10.14. Leave the default name and judge the interaction when the user clicks the Check Answer button. Leave the Tries and Time limits as Unlimited. Be sure the Reset check box and the Snap Back If Not Dropped on Target check boxes are selected. Leave the Snap Back If Incorrect check box deselected because this interaction enables the learner to make incorrect pairings that are judged when the Check Answer button is clicked.

Using the Elements Tab

The Elements tab, shown in Figure 10.15, presents a list of elements at the top of the CourseBuilder Interaction dialog box and the individual element options at the bottom. Elements can be defined as drag or target elements. The interaction comes with a default number of three drag elements and three target elements. You can add as many elements as you need for your interaction.

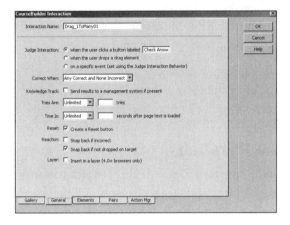

Figure 10.14
The General tab in a Drag and Drop interaction enables you to configure the basic settings.

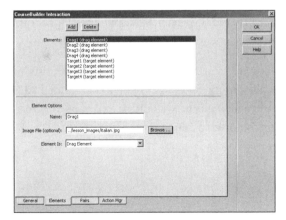

Figure 10.15
The Elements tab enables you to set up each drag and target element, loading images and naming the elements.

To configure the Elements tab for a Drag and Drop interaction, follow these steps:

1. Add an additional drag element by first selecting the element named Drag3. You'll add the new drag element under Drag3. Click the Add button to add it to the list. Because elements are added directly below the selected element, you select Drag3 first so that the drag elements stay in order.

2. Set up the new element's options in the lower half of the dialog box, and enter **Drag4** in the Name text box. Ignore the Image File text field for now. Be sure that Drag Element is selected in the Element Is drop-down list.

3. Add a target element by first selecting the element named Target3. Click the Add button to add it to the list.

4. Set up the new element's options in the lower half of the dialog box. Enter **Target4** in the Name text box. Again, ignore the Image File text field. Make sure that Target Element is selected in the Element Is drop-down list.

5. Load the drag and target images for each element. Select Drag1, click the Browse button, and select an image. Repeat this step for each element, loading all the images.

Using the Pairs Tab

The Pairs tab, shown in Figure 10.16, enables you to set up all the possible pairs of drag and target elements as either correct or incorrect. CourseBuilder automatically added the nine possible pairs for the three default drag elements and the three default target elements, so you'll need to add the seven additional pairings. You must define all possible pairs as either correct or incorrect pairings.

The drop-down list at the top of the dialog box lists pairings that aren't yet added to the Pairs list. If you hadn't added additional drag and target elements, this box would say all pairs are created. All nine pairings for the original three drag elements and the original three target elements have already been added to the Pairs list, so you need to add the pairs created by the additional drag and target elements (Drag4 and Target4). To define the additional pairs:

1. It's easier to understand the pairs if you keep them in a logical order. So, add the pairs in the most logical location by selecting the line above where you want the pair located, and then clicking the Add button. For the first pair in the drop-down list, Drag1:Target4, select Drag1:Target3, and then click the Add button. The pair Drag1:Target4 is added under Drag1:Target3.

2. Repeat this procedure for Drag2:Target4 and Drag3:Target4. Select the last line in the Pairs list and add the new Drag4 pairs at the end of the list.

3. For this drag-and-drop question, here are the correct answers: Drag1:Target1, Drag2:Target2, Drag3:Target3, Drag4:Target4. Select each pairing in the Pairs list and set whether they are correct or incorrect in the Choice Is drop-down list.

4. In the Score text box, give each correct pairing a score of 5.

5. Each pairing also has a Snap If Within and a Snap To setting. Leave the default 75 pixels as the Snap If Within setting and leave the Snap To setting as Center. You can edit these settings and fine-tune them later if you need to.

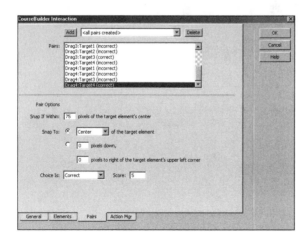

Figure 10.16

Configure the pairings in this Drag and Drop interaction in the Pairs tab.

Using the Action Manager Tab

You can leave the default settings in the Action Manager tab. Right now, the code in the Action Manager judges the correctness of all the Drag and Drop pairings, but you'll edit that setting in Chapter 11. Click the OK button to save your settings for the CourseBuilder interaction.

In the Document window, you arrange the drag and target elements, mixing them up so that they aren't immediately obvious to the learner. You can delete the directions that the interactions placed on the Web page, leaving the Check Answer and Reset button in a form. Click on one of the buttons, and then select the <form> tag in the Tag Selector. Cut and paste the form and buttons into the Content layer. Resize the layer and move it to the bottom of the Document window. The finished Drag and Drop interaction should look something like Figure 10.17. Preview the Web page in a browser and check the interaction's functionality.

Figure 10.17

The drag and target elements must be arranged onscreen.

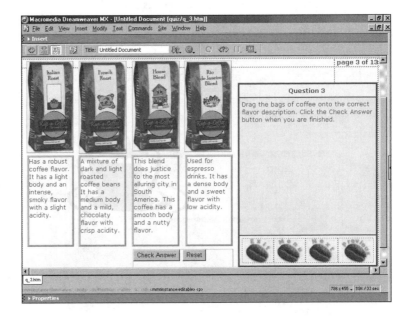

Inserting an Explore Interaction

Explore interactions usually are not used for quiz questions, but they enable the learner to explore information by clicking onscreen elements. An interaction where the learner clicks on the various objects on the page and gets information on them is a perfect example of an Explore interaction. You'll create an Explore interaction with CourseBuilder and see how quickly an Explore interaction can be created. There are three different types of Explore interactions, listed in Table 10.4.

Table 10.4   Explore Category Interactions

Icon	Interaction Name	Description
	Explore with transparent hotspots	The hotspots that the learner clicks on are transparent GIFs in layers set over areas of the background image.
	Explore with images as hotspots	The hotspots contain the individual images that the learner clicks.
	Explore in order	The hotspots contain individual images that must be clicked in a certain order.

The Explore interactions differ depending on whether the hotspots hold the actual images that learners click on to trigger the feedback. If you have a single image over which you need to create hotspots, similar to an image map, you use the first Explore interaction with the transparent hotspots. CourseBuilder places layers containing a transparent GIF; these layers act as hotspots when placed over a region of the background graphic. You must resize the transparent

GIF in the Property inspector, as shown in Figure 10.18. Although Internet Explorer captures the onClick event on a layer (<div> tag), Netscape cannot. Therefore, CourseBuilder places the transparent GIF within the layer because both browsers can capture the onClick event on an image.

Open a new Web page, save the page, and name it. Add a Course-Builder interaction to the Web page (Insert, CourseBuilder Interaction), and select the Explore category. Select the interaction called Explore_Transparent.

Using the General Tab

The Explore interactions have the standard General and Action Manager tabs plus a Hot Areas tab, where you set up the content of the hotspots. Set up the General tab as shown in Figure 10.19. Leave the Judge Interaction setting when the user clicks a hot area. Leave the Correct When setting alone; this interaction will not be judged. Set the Tries Are text box to 2. Leave all the other settings at the default value, but either change the Backdrop Image or remove the URL; interactions do not have to have a backdrop image.

Figure 10.18

When you select the Explore inter-action using transparent hotspots, you need to resize the transparent GIFs that CourseBuilder inserts into the layer hotspots.

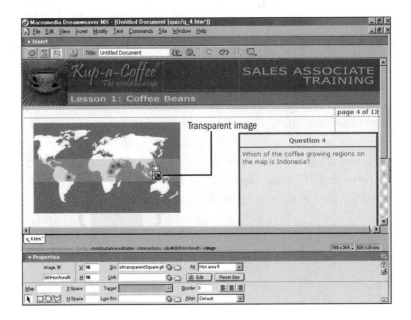

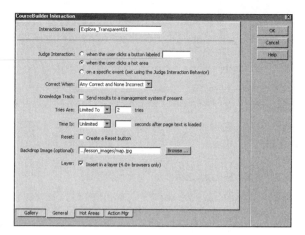

Figure 10.19
The General tab of the Explore interaction contains the basic interaction settings.

Using the Hot Areas Tab

Select the Hot Areas tab to set up the individual hotspots. By default, CourseBuilder creates five hotspots. If that's not how many you need for the interaction, click the Add or Delete buttons. You can accept the default hotspot names in the Name text box and leave the Text text boxes empty. Each hotspot contains a transparent GIF image.

Using the Action Manager Tab

Select the Action Manager tab to investigate the code behind this interaction. Because you are not using the Check Time segment, you can delete it by selecting the segment and clicking the Cut button. That leaves seven segments: one segment for each hotspot, a segment judging correctness, and a segment checking the tries.

Each of the remaining hotspot segments establishes whether the learner clicks on one of the hotspots and then opens a pop-up message specific to that hotspot. You can edit the pop-up message by selecting it in the Action Manager, clicking the Edit button, and modifying the text in the Message text box. In Chapter 11, you'll modify this interaction to set the text of a layer.

Click the OK button to save the CourseBuilder interaction settings. Arrange the layers and stretch the transparent GIFs by selecting them and dragging the drag handles to cover the hotspot area. Remember, you need to capture a click on the image and not the layer, to be cross-browser compatible. Preview the Web page in a browser and check the interaction's functionality.

Inserting a Text Entry Interaction

Now you'll insert another quiz question by using the Text Entry CourseBuilder interaction. Text Entry interactions are best for single-word answers. CourseBuilder enables you to look for certain words as answers, either correct or incorrect, and even gives you control over judging capitalization. Table 10.5 lists the two types of Text Entry interactions.

Table 10.5   Text Entry Category Interactions

Icon	Interaction Name	Description
	Single-line text entry	Learner enters answer text into a single-line text area.
	Multiple-line text entry	Learner enters answer text into a multiline text area.

The two Text Entry interactions differ simply in the size of the text area available for the learner to enter the answer.

Using the General Tab

Create a new Web page, save the page, and name it. Place the cursor in the Content layer and insert a CourseBuilder interaction (Insert, CourseBuilder Interaction). Select the Text Entry category and click on the single-line Text Entry interaction, the one on the left.

When you insert the Text Entry CourseBuilder interaction, it places the question stem text on the Web page. You don't set up the question stem within the CourseBuilder Interaction dialog box. After you set up this interaction, you'll save your changes and then add the question text.

Set up the General tab as shown in Figure 10.20. You can use the default interaction name. The text you enter in the Initial Text text box appears in the text area where learners answer the question and requires that they select and delete the text before entering their answers; for now, leave this text box blank. Judge the interaction when the learner clicks the Check Answer button. Leave the Correct When drop-down list as Any Correct and None Incorrect. Leave the Time and Tries limit as Unlimited. The Reset check box should be selected, and the Layer check box should be selected.

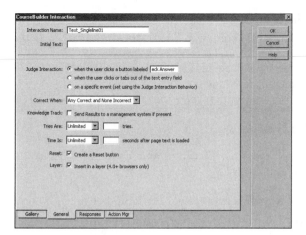

Figure 10.20
The General tab of the Text Entry interaction contains the basic interaction settings.

Using the Responses Tab

The Responses tab enables you to specify the correct and incorrect responses. All other responses are considered unknown by Course-Builder and trigger the Unknown Response code in Action Manager. The Responses tab has three sections. The top section is a list of possible responses, both correct and incorrect. The middle section enables you to set up the possible responses. The lower section is where you specify what to do with any other responses to the question.

To create one correct response and one incorrect response, follow these steps:

1. Select the third response in the Possible Responses list and click the Delete button.

2. Select Response1 at the top of the dialog box. Leave the default name in the Name text box.

3. In the Must Contain text box, enter the text of the correct answer.

4. Leave the Case Sensitive check box deselected because you won't need specific capitalization for this answer.

5. Leave the Exact Match Required check box deselected so that the learner can enter answers such as "arabica beans" or "*coffea arabica*," the botanical term for coffee, and still be correct when the correct answer is set as "arabica."

6. The Match Is drop-down list should be set to Correct. The Score setting should be 20.

7. The Any Other Response Is drop-down list should be set to Incorrect, as shown in Figure 10.21.

8. Select Response2 at the top of the dialog box. Leave the default name in the Name text box.

9. In the Must Contain text box, enter the text of an anticipated incorrect answer.

10. Leave the Case Sensitive and Exact Match Required check boxes deselected.

11. The Match Is drop-down list should be set to Incorrect with a score of 0.

Using the Action Manager Tab

The Action Manager, by default, contains the Check Time, Check Tries, and Correctness segments. Because you have only a single correct and a single incorrect answer, you essentially have specific feedback for both answers as well as a generic feedback message, contained in the else if Unknown Response statement. You can delete the Check Time and Check Tries segments and edit the pop-up messages.

Click the OK button to save your CourseBuilder interaction settings. Preview the Web page in a browser to test the functionality. Try entering the correct answer, and then try entering phrases, including the correct answer. Are these answers judged as correct? Try entering the incorrect answer. Also, try entering other answers to get the unknown response feedback.

Figure 10.21
The Responses tab enables you to set up the correct and incorrect responses to a Text Entry question. Any other responses are unknown.

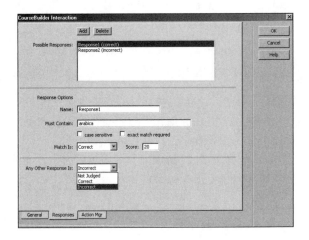

Inserting a Button

You can use a Button control interaction to create complex simulations or to control other objects onscreen. In this example, you'll modify the page where you placed the Flash controls in Chapter 9, "Adding Rich Media Content." There are two different types of Button control interactions, listed in Table 10.6.

Table 10.6   Button Category Interactions

Icon	Interaction Name	Description
	Toggle button	Remains in a certain state when clicked by the learner.
	Push button	Returns to its original state after being clicked by the learner.

Open the Web page you created in Chapter 9 with a Flash movie, save, and name the file. To insert three CourseBuilder Button controls, do the following:

1. Place the cursor before the hyperlinked word Play and insert a new table. The table should have two rows and three columns and be 350 pixels wide. You can set the other attributes to 0.

2. Drag the word Play into the second row, first column. Drag the word Stop into the second row, second column. Drag the word Rewind into the second row, third column. Place the cursor in the first row, first column cell. This is where you'll insert the first button, the button that plays the Flash movie.

3. Insert a CourseBuilder interaction, and select the Button category. Click on the push button.

4. Select the General tab. Leave the default name in the Interaction Name text box. In the Appearance drop-down list, select Emboss. In the Type drop-down list, make sure that Push is selected. The Highlight on Mouse Over check box should be selected.

5. The Initial State drop-down list should be set to Deselected and select Enabled in the drop-down list box next to that setting. The General tab of the Button control should look like Figure 10.22.

6. Judge the interaction when the user clicks the button.

7. Set the interaction as Not Judged. The Tries and Time limits should be set to Unlimited.

8. The Button control should not be placed in a layer.

9. Click OK. You'll set up the Action Manager later in this section.

10. The interaction places some text in the table cell that you need to delete.

11. Place your cursor close to the new button until you see the <interaction> tag in the tag Selector. Select the <interaction> tag in the tag Selector, and copy the interaction by using the Copy command (Edit, Copy on the menu, Ctrl+C for Windows, or Command+C for Macintosh). Place your cursor in the cell in the first row, second column and paste the interaction by using the Paste command (Edit, Paste on the menu, Ctrl+V for Windows, or Command+V for Macintosh). Also, paste the interaction in the cell in the first row, third column.

Figure 10.22

You set up most of the Button control settings in the General tab.

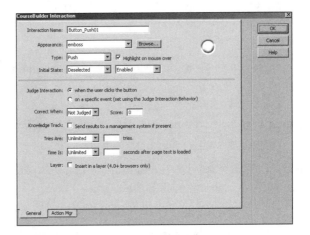

You now have three different Button controls for the CourseBuilder interaction in this Web page. When you select one of the Course-Builder interactions, you can drop down the Name list box and select which one you will edit when you click the Edit button. Before you proceed, preview the Web page in a browser. When you click each Button control, you should see a pop-up message.

Now you'll go into the Action Mgr tab and change the feedback for the buttons:

1. Select one of the interactions. Next, select the first Button interaction, Button_Push01, in the Name list box, and click the Edit button.

2. Select the Action Mgr tab. You can delete the Check Time and Check Tries segments.

3. The remaining segment, Button Feedback, contains a single behavior: Popup Message. Select the Popup Message line and delete it by clicking the Cut button.

4. Add a new action to the Button Feedback segment by selecting one of the actions from the drop-down list at the top of the dialog box, shown in Figure 10.23.

5. Toward the end of the list, you should find the Play_Flash command that you loaded with the JavaScript Integration Kit for Flash 5 extension. With that action displayed in the drop-down list, click the Add button. Or, you can use the Control Shockwave or Flash action.

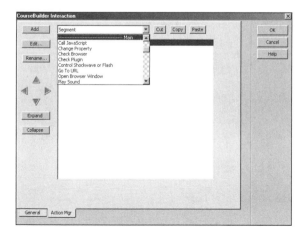

Figure 10.23
The drop-down list at the top of the Action Mgr tab lists the types of new expressions, including actions, that you can add in Action Manager.

6. The Play Flash dialog box appears. Select the coffee movie and click the OK button.

7. A Play_Flash action is added to Action Manager, so clicking the Button_Push01 button now triggers this action.

8. Click OK to save your settings. Preview the Web page in a browser and check that the Play button does indeed play the Flash movie as expected.

9. Repeat these steps, selecting the second button, Button_Push02, and adding the Stop_Flash action. Then select the third button, Button_Push03, and add the Rewind_Flash action.

Inserting a Timer

CourseBuilder enables you to insert Timer controls into Web pages. Many different timer graphics that are quite clever are available. You can choose from a director's clapboard, an hourglass, various rising bars, and other graphics. A Timer control is usually placed in a Web page that already contains a CourseBuilder interaction and is especially useful in certification situations where the learner is limited to a certain period for a specific question.

In this example, you open one of the questions you've already created and add a Timer control. In the next chapter, you'll modify the Timer interaction so that it disables the CourseBuilder interaction question after the time is up. Table 10.7 lists the two different types of Timer control interactions.

Table 10.7   Timer Control Interactions

Icon	Interaction Name	Description
	Single-trigger timer	Has a single trigger time for giving the learner feedback.
	Two-trigger timer	Has two trigger times for giving the learner feedback.

The Timer control interactions enable you to add *trigger times*, points in time at which some sort of feedback is given to the learner. You can add as many of these triggers as you want.

To add a Timer control to a Web page, follow these steps:

1. Open a Web page with an existing CourseBuilder Interaction.

2. Insert a CourseBuilder interaction. Select the Timer category and click on the two-trigger timer, the second icon from the left.

Using the General Tab

You set up the look and functionality of the Timer control in the General tab of the CourseBuilder Interaction dialog box:

1. Click the General tab. Leave the default interaction name in the Name text box.

2. Select Small_Rising_Bars (or any of the timer choices) in the Appearance drop-down list. You'll see a preview of what the timer looks like, as shown in Figure 10.24.

3. Set the timer duration to 30 seconds in the Duration text box.

4. Judge the interaction when any trigger condition is met.

5. Correctness does not matter, as this interaction will not be judged.

6. Tries are unlimited.

7. Leave the Reset button unchecked but select the Layer check box.

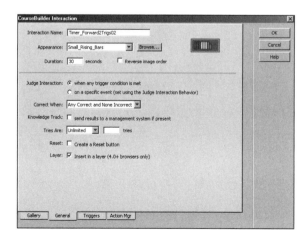

Figure 10.24

You can select various timer graphics in the General tab of the Timer control interaction.

Using the Triggers Tab

The Triggers tab enables you to set up single or multiple triggers that occur during the duration of the timer. In this interaction, you give the user a warning 10 seconds before the timer ends. You can always add triggers in this tab if you need more than the default number. To set up Trigger1 and Trigger2, follow these steps:

1. Select Trigger1 in the Triggers list box. You can leave the default name in the Name text box.

2. Enter 20 seconds in the Trigger Once After text box. This is a warning message to the user 10 seconds before the second and final trigger at 30 seconds.

3. Leave both the trigger and the interaction as Not Judged in the Interaction Is drop-down list. You might want to add judging or a score to a Timer interaction if the learner is supposed to get extra points for completing the question before the timer is up. The Triggers tab looks like Figure 10.25.

4. Repeat the preceding steps for Trigger2, making sure the Trigger Once After text box is set to 30 seconds.

Figure 10.25
Set up the individual triggers to occur at a set time.

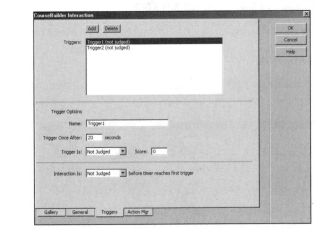

Using the Action Manager Tab

The Timer control interaction's Action Manager tab has two segments, one for each of the triggers. Edit the Popup Message behaviors to warn learners that they have only 10 seconds left in the Trigger1 pop-up message, and tell them they are out of time in the Trigger2 pop-up message. A disadvantage of using the Popup Message behavior here is that the timing continues while the message box is onscreen, and learners are required to click the OK button in the message box before they can proceed, thus losing valuable time.

Click the OK button to save your CourseBuilder interaction settings. Preview the Web page in a browser and make sure the Timer control works. In Chapter 11, you'll cause it to disable the test question when time runs out.

Inserting a Slider

The Slider control interaction enables you to add a draggable slider to your Web page and judge where the learner leaves the slider. You'll add a question to the quiz that uses a Slider interaction so that learners can set how many seconds coffee beans should be ground. You could also use a Slider control as a navigational control, taking the learner to different pages in a Web site, for instance. There are two different types of Slider control interactions, listed in Table 10.8.

Power User Tip

The timer graphics work by doing a swap image over time, similar to adding the Swap Image behavior to the B channel of a Dreamweaver timeline. You can also add your own custom timer graphics to CourseBuilder.

Table 10.8   Slider Control Interactions

Icon	Interaction Name	Description
	Single-range slider	Has a single range that triggers feedback for the learner.
	Two-range slider	Has two ranges that trigger feedback for the learner.

Using the General Tab

Open a new Web page, save the page, and name it. The Slider control will not work in Netscape if you insert the interaction into the Content layer. Click beneath the layer at the bottom of the Document window and insert a CourseBuilder interaction (Insert, CourseBuilder Interaction).

Select the Slider category in the CourseBuilder Interaction dialog box and click on the two ranges slider, the first one on the left. To set up the attributes of the Slider control, follow these steps:

1. Click the General tab. Leave the default name in the Interaction Name text box.

2. Select the slider's look in the Appearance drop-down list. Select the first slider, Black_h_Penta. You'll see a preview of the slider in the dialog box, as shown in Figure 10.26.

3. Set the Range values to begin with 5 and end with 22. Set the Initial Value to 5.

4. Judge the interaction when the user clicks the Check Answer button.

5. Set the interaction in the Correct When drop-down list to Any Correct and None Incorrect.

6. Leave the Tries and Time limits as Unlimited.

7. Leave the Reset check box selected and the Layer check box deselected.

Figure 10.26

The General tab settings enable you to select the appearance of the Slider control and determine how the Slider interaction will be judged.

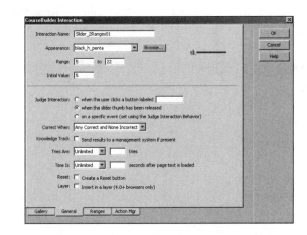

| **eLearning with Dreamweaver MX:** Building Online Learning Applications

Using the Ranges Tab

Select the Ranges tab to set up the ranges for the interaction. To set up the ranges, follow these steps:

1. Add three additional ranges by clicking the Add button at the top of the dialog box.

2. Select the first range. In the Range Options section, enter a name in the Name text box.

3. Give it the range 5 to 9 seconds.

4. This is the correct answer, so mark it as Correct in the Range Is drop-down list and give it a score of 10.

5. Select each of the other ranges, name them for the grind, enter the range, and mark them as Incorrect. The finished Ranges tab should look like Figure 10.27.

Using the Action Manager Tab

Select the Action Mgr tab to edit the pop-up messages for each slider range. The ranges you added do not have default Popup Message behaviors, so you need to select the conditional lines (if medium selected, if fine selected, and so on), load the Popup Message behavior in the drop-down list at the top of the dialog box, and click the Add button. You can set up each message to give learners feedback about the type of grind they will get if they grind the coffee for that length of time. You can delete the Check Tries and Check Time segments, if you like.

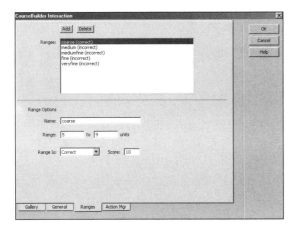

Figure 10.27
The Ranges tab presents the options for the ranges that are judged in your Slider control.

Click the OK button to save your CourseBuilder interaction settings. Select the question stem text and the two buttons, and either drag or copy and paste them into the Content layer. Enter the question **How long should you grind coffee beans in a hand grinder for a coarse grind to be used in a French press?** Add some extra room under the question text, and move the slider between the question text and the buttons. Be sure the slider layers are not overlaying the buttons because that could make it impossible for learners to click the buttons.

Preview the Web page in a browser and check the Slider control's functionality. It should move only within the confines of the slider graphic. Check both the correct and the incorrect answers.

Summary

In this chapter, you explored all the CourseBuilder interactions and created Web pages including examples of each. You selected various interactions from the Gallery and opened and edited existing interactions. And, you modified some of the code in the Action Manager.

IN THIS CHAPTER

chapter 11

Conquering CourseBuilder's Action Manager

IN CHAPTER 10, "INCLUDING COURSEBUILDER Interactions and Controls," you added several different CourseBuilder interactions to Web pages and were introduced to the Action Manager tab. This chapter expands on what you did in the previous chapter, introducing you to the power of using the Action Manager to create custom interactions that process learner feedback and produce the exact results that you would like from the interaction. In the Action Manager, you really get what you pay for the CourseBuilder extension . . . Oh, wait—it's free! What a great deal—thanks, Macromedia.

When you add a CourseBuilder interaction to a Web page, the interaction has some default Action Manager segments. In most interactions, there are a Check Time segment, a Check Tries segment, and a Correctness segment; some of the interactions vary from these three. What if the default segments don't provide the functionality you want? You can add various types of logic and functionality by adding your own custom segments, conditionals, and actions. Some people mistakenly believe that CourseBuilder is limited because they haven't adequately explored these capabilities.

In this chapter, you will understand the following:

- How to add segments and conditions to the Action Manager
- How to edit and rename lines in the Action Manager
- How to disable an interaction
- How to save a custom interaction to the Gallery

Working with the Action Manager Interface

Let's take a little time to explore the Action Manager interface in depth. You might be amazed to learn that the CourseBuilder interface (and the entire Dreamweaver interface) is programmed in HTML and JavaScript! Because the interface is created with these commonly used scripting languages, extending Dreamweaver's functionality by creating extensions is easy. You've explored a number of extensions in this book, and Chapter 18, "Creating Custom Objects and Commands," gives you an opportunity to create your own extensions to the Dreamweaver interface.

The disadvantage of creating the CourseBuilder interface in HTML and JavaScript is that some of the shortcuts you are used to in the Windows and Mac operating systems don't work. For example, you can't copy with the Ctrl+C or Command+C shortcut keys, and you can't double-click a collapsed segment to expand it. You'll need to use the buttons in the Action Manager tab to control these activities.

Copying, Cutting, Pasting, and Editing

You can copy, cut, paste, and edit by using the Copy, Cut, Paste, and Edit buttons. The Copy, Cut, and Paste buttons are located at the top of the CourseBuilder Interaction dialog box, and the Edit button is on the left side of the dialog box, beneath the Add button. These buttons work on whatever line you have selected. When you perform the Copy or Cut commands on a segment or condition that has other lines grouped under it, the commands copy or cut the entire group.

As I mentioned in Chapter 10, there is no undo command, so if you accidentally cut a segment unintentionally, you should click the Cancel button, closing the CourseBuilder Interaction dialog box and discarding any changes you made. Open the interaction again to edit it. When making extensive changes to a CourseBuilder interaction, it's a good idea to follow this procedure after every few changes so that if you do make a mistake, you don't lose all your work. There is no way to save your work while in the CourseBuilder Interaction dialog box. You must close the dialog box, save your changes in Dreamweaver, and then open the interaction to continue to edit it.

After you've inserted a segment, condition, or action into the Action Manager and set it up just as you want it, you can copy and paste that particular action. After you've pasted the action, you can edit it by clicking the Edit button, modifying it to work the way you want. Often, setting up a segment, condition, or action, copying and pasting it, and then editing it takes less time than setting up each line individually.

Moving Segments

When you paste in the Action Manager, the line or lines are pasted beneath the line that is currently selected. If you need to paste something at the top of the list of commands, you should paste below the first line, and then click the up arrow button to move the line or lines to the top of the list. The up and down arrow buttons, shown in Figure 11.1, can move an individual line or a group of lines to a different location in the list of actions. When you select a line in the Action Manager that has other lines indented beneath it, you move the entire section.

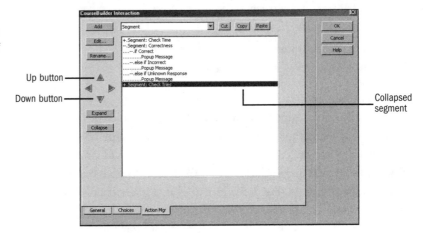

Up button

Down button

Collapsed segment

Adding Actions

A variety of actions is available in the Actions drop-down list box at the top of the Action Manager tab, shown in Figure 11.2. You use this list to select the action you want to add to the Action Manager list. After selecting the action, you select the line directly above where you'd like the action to be added. Then, click the Add button to add the action to the list.

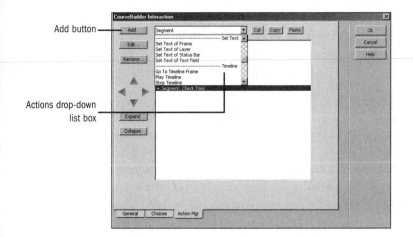

Add button

Actions drop-down list box

The actions are divided into the following groups:

- **Built-in actions**—Contains the basic Segment, Condition, Else, and Stop actions.

- **CourseBuilder actions**—Contains the Judge Interaction, Reset Interaction, and Set Interaction Properties actions.

- **Dreamweaver actions**—Contains most of the actions that ship with Dreamweaver, the same ones you find listed in the Behaviors panel drop-down list box (such as Show-Hide Layers, Popup Message, and so on).

- **Set Text actions**—Contains the actions that send text or HTML to objects on the screen, including Set Text of Frame, Set Text of Layer, Set Text of Status Field, and Set Text of Text Field. These are the same actions you'll find in the Set Text submenu of the Behaviors panel drop-down list.

- **Timeline actions**—Contains actions to control timelines: Go to Timeline Frame, Play Timeline, and Stop Timeline. These are the same actions you'll find in the Timeline submenu of the Behaviors panel drop-down list.

- **Knowledge Track actions**—Contains actions controlling Knowledge Track functionality, including Send Interaction Info, Send Lesson Status, Send Lesson Time, Send Objective Info, and Send Score. You'll learn more about these actions in Chapter 15, "Using a Learning Management System."

- **Other actions**—Contains actions that you've added to Dreamweaver via extensions.

Power User Tip

The Action Manager drop-down menu is loaded from ActionMenu.htm, which is in the CourseBuilder\Config directory. If you'd like to reorganize the Action Manager drop-down menu, you can modify this HTML file in Dreamweaver. The built-in items at the top of the menu—Segment, Condition, Else, and Stop—are not editable and do not appear in this file. You will need to make a backup copy of the Web page first!

The rest of this chapter walks you through adding actions from the Built-in and CourseBuilder action groups. The Dreamweaver, Set Text, Timeline, and Other action groups are the same actions, with the same functionality, as Dreamweaver behaviors. If you need more information on using them, you should consult a basic Dreamweaver book (see Appendix A). You'll add some of them in this chapter, too, simply because they contain useful functionality for offering feedback (the Popup Message or the Set Text of Layer actions) or remediation (the Go To URL action). As noted previously, the Knowledge Track actions are covered in Chapter 15.

When you add an action to the Action Manager, the action's dialog box opens, enabling you set up the attributes of whichever action you've added. You can always change an action's attributes by clicking the Edit button with a specific line in the Action Manager selected. You'll explore adding various actions and setting their attributes in the rest of this chapter.

Adding Built-in Actions: Segment, Condition, Else, and Stop

You'll use two of the built-in actions, Segment and Condition, often when doing custom coding in the Action Manager. You'll probably use Else frequently and the Stop action once in a while. Because all Action Manager code must be contained in a segment, you'll need to add a new segment for every logical division of the code and a condition every time you need CourseBuilder to make some sort of decision.

Often, you'll be modifying the default code that the CourseBuilder interaction inserts for you. In this case, the default segments are already present, and you can modify the actions nested within the segments. To do this, you simply delete the unwanted action and add the replacement. For example, you can delete a Popup Message action and replace it with the Set Text of Layer action.

Sometimes, you need an interaction that works completely differently from any of the default CourseBuilder interactions. In this case, start with an empty Action Manager, adding the segments, conditions, and other actions that will implement the necessary logic. You should plan the logical flow of the Action Manager code on a piece of paper before you start coding. You can use *pseudocode*, a real-language way of expressing computer code, or you can create a traditional code flowchart.

Edit an existing drag-and-drop CourseBuilder interaction, or create a new one. Delete all the code from the Action Manager by selecting each segment and clicking the Cut button. The empty Action Manager looks like Figure 11.3. Now you are ready to create custom Action Manager code.

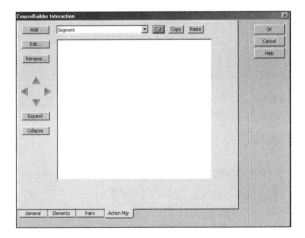

Figure 11.3

Cut all the segments from the Action Manager to ready the interaction for custom code.

Adding a Segment

To hold a section of code in CourseBuilder's Action Manager, you add a segment. In most of the interactions you created in Chapter 10, the Action Manager contained three common segments: Check Time, Check Tries, and Correctness. Each segment contained the logic implementing the functionality implied by the segment titles.

The CourseBuilder default segments all begin with the word "Segment:" and then a description of the segment functionality. When I'm working in the Action Manager, I find it helpful to maintain this naming scheme so that I can easily identify the logical divisions of code in the Action Manager. I prefer to expand the segments I'm working on and collapse the rest, so I can focus on a single segment's functionality. Using a naming convention, such as always beginning a segment name with "Segment:," helps me quickly expand and collapse the appropriate segments.

To add a new segment to the Action Manager, select the line above where you'd like the segment to appear. Select Segment from the Action Manager drop-down menu, and then click the Add button to open the Segment Editor dialog box. If you select a line in the middle of another segment, CourseBuilder inserts the segment underneath the code contained in that segment; you cannot nest segments.

Setting the Segment Evaluation

The Segment Editor dialog box, shown in Figure 11.4, enables you to set the name of the segment and specify how the segment will be evaluated. After you've added a new segment you must name the segment uniquely.

Figure 11.4

Set the segment's name and evaluation properties in the Segment Editor dialog box.

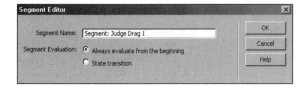

You can evaluate the conditions in a segment in two ways: Always Evaluate from the Beginning and State Transition. You used Course-Builder interactions with both types of segments in Chapter 10. Most interactions use the Always Evaluate from the Beginning setting. You added one interaction that uses the State Transition setting—the Timer interaction.

So, how does the Action Manager evaluate the lines of code it contains? Here's a description of the two methods:

- **Always Evaluate from the Beginning**—The segment is processed line by line from the beginning every time the interaction is judged. When a true condition is encountered, the actions under the condition are processed. When a false condition is encountered, the processing moves on to the next action. The segment always responds the same way.

- **State Transition**—The segment is processed line by line from the beginning until a true condition is encountered. Course-Builder processes the action contained in the condition, and then stops. If the interaction is judged again, the condition that was previously true is skipped and the remaining conditions are evaluated. It's as though CourseBuilder checks that condition off and skips it for subsequent tries.

The multiple-choice question you added in Chapter 10 contains segments that are all set to Always Evaluate from the Beginning. If you open up the Multiple Choice CourseBuilder interaction you created in Chapter 10 and select the Action Manager tab, you can select the Segment: Correctness line and click the Edit button to see the segment's evaluation setting. You'll see that the segment's evaluation setting is Always Evaluate from the Beginning. All the conditions under this segment will be evaluated every time the interaction is judged.

The Timer interaction you created in Chapter 10 has two segments in the Action Manager. When you select one of the segments and click the Edit button, note that Segment: Trigger1 Feedback and Segment Trigger2 Feedback are marked with the State Transition setting, as shown in Figure 11.5. When a segment's State Transition radio button is selected in the Segment Editor dialog box, CourseBuilder adds the label (State Transition) beside the segment name.

The trigger segments in the Timer interaction must be state transitions because when the learner encounters a trigger, you don't want them to encounter it again. If you didn't mark trigger1 as a state transition, you would need to add extra code to judge whether the learner has previously seen the trigger. Why add the extra code when you can simply make the segment a state transition? Using the State Transition setting is useful when you have conditions that should be encountered only once per page.

Now you'll add a new segment to the Drag and Drop interaction you created in Chapter 10. You'll modify the interaction to give learners individual feedback depending on their answer. By default, feedback built in to the interaction gives feedback if they get the interaction correct or incorrect. If you want to explain to learners why their answer is not correct, you need to add individual segments judging the learner's answers.

Figure 11.5

The trigger segments in the Timer interaction are set to State Transition so that they appear only once per interaction.

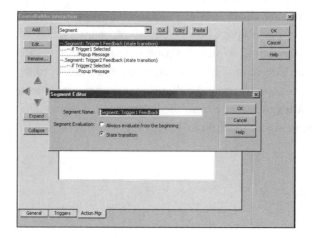

First, edit the Drag and Drop interaction. Cut all the existing segments from the Action Manager tab. To add a segment, follow these steps:

1. Be sure that Segment is showing in the Action Manager drop-down list box. Click the Add button.

2. The Segment Editor dialog box opens. Name this segment **Segment: Judge Drag 1**.

3. Set the segment evaluation to Always Evaluate from the Beginning.

4. Click the OK button to save the settings. The segment appears in the Action Manager list.

Add an additional segment for each drag object, setting the segment to Always Evaluate from the Beginning.

Renaming Segments

If you change the functionality of a segment, or if you come up with your own naming scheme, you can rename any segment by clicking the Rename button. Actually, you can rename any action that you add to the Action Manager by using this button. Select the line you want to rename, click the Rename button, and the Name Editor dialog box opens, as shown in Figure 11.6.

Figure 11.6
Click the Rename button to rename any action in the Name Editor dialog box.

Adding a Condition

Within a segment, you can insert other actions. If you want to control when actions are triggered, you insert a condition that judges the interaction's current state. Conditions are like if-then-else statements in other programming and scripting languages. If x is true, then y happens, or else if x is false, then z happens.

When you add a condition to the Action Manager, the Condition Editor dialog box opens, as shown in Figure 11.7. Name the condition in the Condition Name text box. This name appears in the Action Manager code listing, and you should name it logically according to the condition's function.

Using the text boxes and drop-down lists in the Condition Editor, you build the expressions displayed in the Expressions list at the top of the dialog box. As you change the values of the text boxes and drop-down lists, you'll see the expression change. The expression compares two objects and returns a value of True or False for the comparison. For example, you can create an expression in a Drag and Drop interaction comparing when the drag1 element is paired with the target1 element.

You build an expression by comparing two objects. The Type drop-down list in the middle of the Condition Editor specifies the first object in the comparison. The Equals/Does Not Equal drop-down list specifies the relationship. The Type drop-down list at the bottom of the Condition Editor specifies the second object in the comparison. You can also select True/False from this Type drop-down list.

Figure 11.7

The Condition Editor enables you to build an expression that will be evaluated by CourseBuilder.

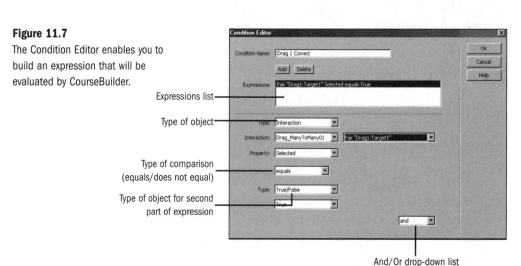

Expressions list

Type of object

Type of comparison (equals/does not equal)

Type of object for second part of expression

And/Or drop-down list

Creating Multiline Expressions

A condition might need multiple lines in the Expressions list. For example, in the Drag and Drop interaction, maybe you'd like to add different feedback depending on the learner's browser version. You can add multiple lines to the expression, connecting them by selecting And or Or in the And/Or drop-down list in the lower right of the Condition Editor. Select And if both connected expressions must be true; select Or if either connected expression can be true. A multiline expression looks like Figure 11.8.

To begin building an expression in the Condition Editor, select the type of object being compared. CourseBuilder's Condition Editor enables you to choose four types of objects in the Type drop-down list: Interaction, Action Manager, Document Tag, or JavaScript. The following sections discuss each object.

Comparing Interaction Objects in an Expression

Select Interaction from the Type drop-down list to compare elements of a CourseBuilder interaction in an expression. This setting enables you to use the entire interaction in your comparison (such as "Is the multiple-choice question's correct answer selected?") or an element in the interaction (such as "Is button1 in the multiple-choice question selected?"). You can select any interaction on the page; you aren't limited to the properties and elements of the interaction you are currently editing.

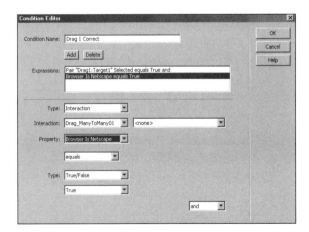

Figure 11.8
Create a multiline expression by connecting the expressions with an And or Or connection.

You must add a condition that judges whether a certain pairing of a drag object and a target object has occurred. Follow these steps to add a condition below the segment you created in the Drag and Drop interaction earlier in this chapter:

1. Select Condition from the Action Manager drop-down list, and click the Add button to open the Condition Editor.

2. Name the condition **Drag1 Correct**. CourseBuilder displays the word "if" at the beginning of the condition name in the Action Manager.

3. Select Interaction from the Type drop-down list. Because there is only one CourseBuilder interaction on this Web page, it will be the only entry in the Interaction drop-down list.

4. By default, no elements are selected in the drop-down list to the right of the Interaction drop-down list, so the expression applies to the entire interaction. In this segment, you are testing whether the pairing of the drag1 and target1 objects is selected (the correct pairing). In the Elements drop-down list, shown in Figure 11.9, select Pair Drag1:Target1.

5. The Property drop-down list automatically defaults to the Selected property. You'll explore other available properties later in this section. The Selected property is the correct setting because you are comparing whether the pair is selected.

Figure 11.9

Use the Elements drop-down list to specify individual elements or pairs of elements to be used in the expression.

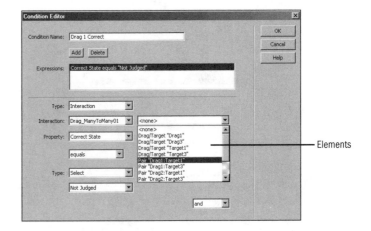

6. In the Equals/Does Not Equal drop-down list, Equals should be displayed.

7. In the Type drop-down list for the second half of the comparison, select True/False.

8. In the True/False drop-down list, select True.

9. The completed Condition Editor should look like Figure 11.10. Click the OK button to save your settings.

The Condition Editor usually displays the options that are appropriate to the object you choose. However, the Condition Editor isn't intuitive, so as you are experimenting with the settings, keep an eye on the expression you are building. Does it seem to logically express what you are trying to accomplish? If not, experiment with other settings. In the preceding steps, you built this expression: Pair "Drag1:Target1" Selected equals True. When the learner matches the object Drag1 with the object Target1, the action nested below this condition will be triggered. You'll add that action in the next section.

Using Other Object Types in Expressions

The most common type of object used in expressions built in the Condition Editor is the Interaction object you used previously, which gives you access to interactions and interaction elements.

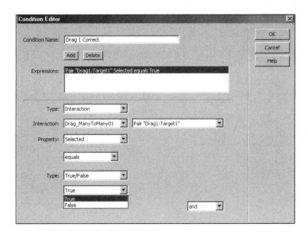

Figure 11.10
The Condition Editor's settings enable you to build the required expression.

The second most common type of object used in expressions is the JavaScript object. You'll use this object in Chapter 12, "Scoring an Assessment and Hiding the Answers," when you are building a quiz. The JavaScript object enables you to write JavaScript directly as an expression. If you know JavaScript, this task is very easy for you. Some of the fundamental JavaScript statements that you might want to use with CourseBuilder are covered in Chapter 12.

The Action Manager object type is infrequently used in expressions. This object type enables you to select entire segments from a drop-down list displaying all the segments in the interaction. You can build an expression that evaluates how that segment compares to a second type of object.

The final type of object that can be used in expressions is the Document Tag. It can be used to build an expression that judges an HTML object or its attributes. For example, you can trigger feedback based on whether a layer is visible. To do this, you create an expression, as shown in Figure 11.11, that judges whether the layer's visibility attribute is set to visible.

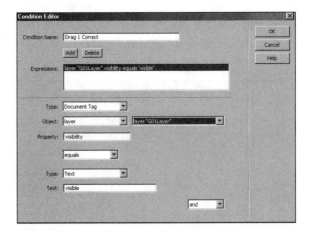

Adding an Else Condition and Promoting or Demoting Conditions

When you have two states—correct and incorrect, for example—you can add a condition for the true state and an Else action for the false state. Figure 11.12 illustrates using Else to trigger an action if the condition above the Else is not true. In this case, if the question is correct, the learner gets the first pop-up message; if the question is incorrect, the learner gets the second pop-up message.

For each condition, there can be only a single Else statement. However, you can add multiple else if statements. CourseBuilder automatically adds else if when you add multiple conditions. You use the left and right arrow buttons to promote or demote the statements. You'll copy and paste the drag-and-drop pair condition that you just added to the Action Manager to create a list of else if statements.

First, add a Popup Message behavior under the if Drag1 Correct condition. For now, just enter the generic feedback of some placeholder text as the message; you can go into the Popup Message behavior and edit it with the appropriate feedback later.

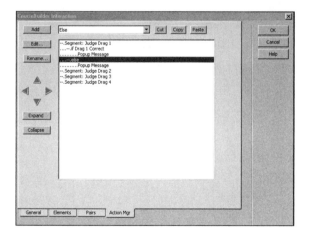

Figure 11.12
The Else action is useful for capturing the false state and displaying feedback.

To copy, paste, and edit conditions, follow these steps:

1. Select the condition line if Drag1 Correct in the Action Manager.

2. Click the Copy button. When you select and copy the condition, CourseBuilder also copies the actions beneath it. In this case, there is just a single action, the Popup Message, but if there were multiple actions beneath the condition, they would all be copied.

3. Leaving the same line selected, click the Paste button. Course-Builder adds a copy of the condition below the original line and names it else if Drag1 Correct, as shown in Figure 11.13.

4. If you had selected the Popup Message line instead of the condition line, CourseBuilder would have nested the if statement. If you did this, as shown in Figure 11.14, you can simply select the nested condition statement and click the left arrow button to promote the statement.

5. The newly pasted else if line should be selected. Click Paste again to add another copy of the condition. Continue to paste until you have the three incorrect conditions.

Figure 11.13

Adding a condition below another condition makes an **else if** statement.

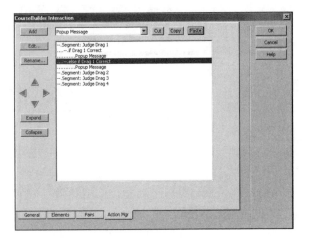

eLearning with Dreamweaver MX: Building Online Learning Applications

6. Edit each new condition by selecting it and clicking the Edit button. First, rename the condition, reflecting the next pair in the sequence (Drag1:Target2, Drag1:Target3, Drag1:Target4). Select the correct pairing from the Elements drop-down list, as shown in Figure 11.15. Save your changes in the Condition Editor.

7. Edit each new Popup Message behavior, reflecting feedback for the current condition.

8. Click OK to save your changes to the CourseBuilder interaction. Preview the Drag and Drop interaction in your browser to check the functionality. You should see unique feedback for every drag and target combination.

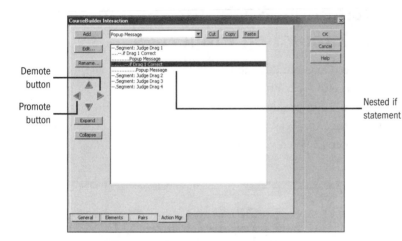

Demote button

Promote button

Nested if statement

Figure 11.14
If you nest an **if** statement accidentally, use the promote (left arrow) button to unnest the statement.

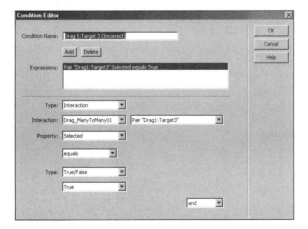

Figure 11.15
Edit the conditions, changing the name and the selecting pair in the Elements drop-down list box.

Adding a Stop Action

The final member of the Built-in actions in the Action Manager drop-down list is the Stop action. When you want to stop processing the Action Manager code, you use the Stop action. For example, because the learner can drag and drop only one element at a time, you can add a Stop action after each Popup Message behavior in the Drag and Drop interaction you've been working on, as shown in Figure 11.16. This saves a little processing power by stopping the processing of the code when the Stop action is encountered.

Adding CourseBuilder Actions: Judge Interaction, Reset Interaction, and Set Interaction Properties

The three CourseBuilder actions in the Action Manager drop-down list are useful for controlling CourseBuilder interactions. In this section, you'll explore the functionality of the Judge Interaction, Reset Interaction, and Set Interaction Properties actions. You'll use them in Chapter 12 when you create a quiz.

Figure 11.16
The Stop action stops the processing of the Action Manager code.

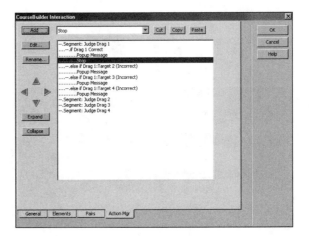

Adding Judge Interaction

The Judge Interaction action is similar to clicking the Check Answer button that you added to several CourseBuilder interactions in Chapter 10. The action initiates the processing of the Action Manager code. Because the action is actually contained in the Action Manager code, it's used to judge another interaction on the Web page, not the interaction that contains the action.

Adding Reset Interaction

The Reset Interaction action returns the interaction to the original state when the Web page was loaded. This action clears any answers that the learner has made, resets any state transition segments that have been encountered, and puts all page elements back in their original positions. Reset Interaction acts similarly to the Reset button that you can add to an interaction in the General tab.

Adding Set Interaction Properties

The Set Interaction Properties action resets most of the properties that you have set in the CourseBuilder Interaction dialog box. You're going to use this action to disable the multiple-choice question when the timer runs out. You'll also use this action to disable the timer when the learner answers the multiple-choice question correctly.

The Set Interaction Properties action has three types of objects: Interaction, Action Manager, and JavaScript. Notice the similarity with the object types in the Condition Editor. You'll use the Interaction object in this section. The Action Manager object is useful when setting properties for all segments of the interaction, and the JavaScript object is useful for entering custom JavaScript.

To add a Set Interaction Properties action, follow these steps:

1. Open the Timer interaction and edit it. Select the Action Manager tab.

2. You must disable the multiple-choice question after the second trigger, so select the last line in the Action Manager, the second Popup Message behavior.

3. Select Set Interaction Properties from the drop-down list, and click the Add button to open the Set Interaction Properties dialog box.

4. Select Interaction from the Set drop-down list.

5. Select MultCh_ImageRadios01 from the Interaction drop-down list. Do not select any individual elements of the interaction. You want to disable the entire interaction, not just a single button.

6. Select Disabled from the Property drop-down list. Notice that the properties you can set are similar to the properties you can compare in the Condition Editor.

7. In the Equal To section of the Set Interaction Properties dialog box, select True/False from the Type drop-down list. You can also select JavaScript if you want to use JavaScript variables.

8. Because you need to set the Disabled property to True, select True from the True/False drop-down list, as shown in Figure 11.17. Click OK to save your settings. Close the CourseBuilder Interaction dialog box by clicking OK.

Figure 11.17
The Set Interaction Properties action builds an assignment that changes the properties or element of an interaction.

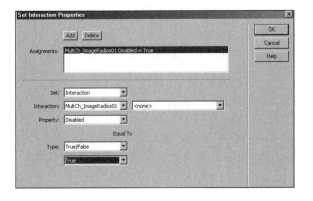

Now you've modified the timer so that it disables the multiple-choice question if the learner has taken too much time. Preview the question in the browser and let the timer run out. You should be unable to select any buttons after the time limit. Carefully check for browser compatibility because disabling doesn't work in all browsers.

What if the learner answers the question before the timer runs out? The timer is still going! You'll also need to disable the timer by adding a Set Interaction Properties action to both the correct and the incorrect sections of the Action Manager code, as shown in Figure 11.18. Make these changes to the Multiple Choice interaction, and then preview in the browser to check the functionality.

Power User Tip

If you are interested in the JavaScript that CourseBuilder is writing, set up a Condition or Set Interaction Properties action, and then change the type to JavaScript. CourseBuilder will display the JavaScript for what you just set up.

Saving a Custom CourseBuilder Interaction to the Gallery

After you've created a custom CourseBuilder interaction, you don't want to have to repeat your work. You can save any interaction to the CourseBuilder Gallery, ready to add it to other Web pages. You can also share the Gallery with members of your team.

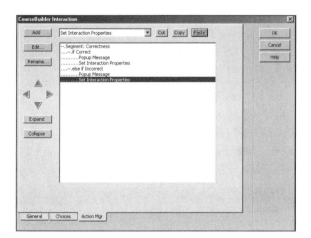

Figure 11.18
You must add a Set Interaction Properties action to disable the timer at any terminal spot in the interaction. Here it is added after both the correct and the incorrect responses.

After creating a CourseBuilder interaction that you want to add to the Gallery:

1. Select the interaction (by the CourseBuilder icon or the <interaction> tag).

2. Select the Add Interaction to Gallery command (Modify, CourseBuilder, Add Interaction to Gallery) to open the Add Interaction to Gallery dialog box, shown in Figure 11.19.

3. You can select an existing gallery category or create your own. Dropping down the Existing Category list displays the current categories in the gallery. Select one of these categories if you'd like to save your new interaction to it. To create your own gallery category, select the New radio button and type in a name for the category. I like to create separate galleries for different projects I'm working on.

4. Select the target browser for your new interaction. If you aren't sure, you should select the 4.0+ Browsers option.

5. Give your interaction a name in the Template Name section of the Add Interaction to Gallery dialog box. If you chose to save your interaction in one of the existing categories, you can replace an existing interaction by selecting one of the existing interaction names. Please be very careful when doing this. Most often, you should select the New radio button and enter a name for your interaction. You cannot use spaces or punctuation in the name.

6. You can also add a custom icon for your custom interaction. Create an 80 × 80-pixel GIF in your favorite image-editing program. CourseBuilder resizes the image to 80 × 80 pixels if it's a different size. Click the Select Icon button and load the GIF image.

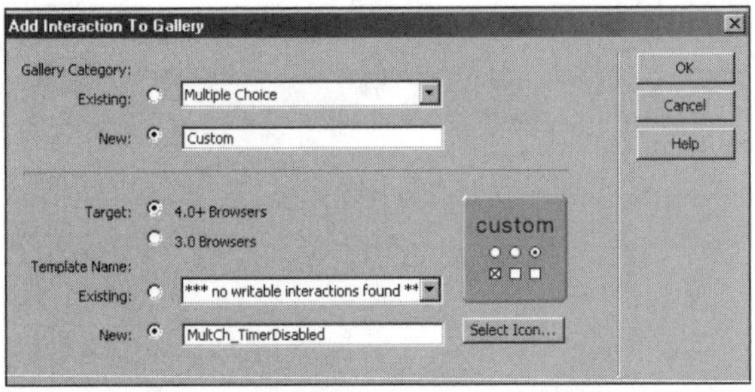

Figure 11.19

The Add Interaction to Gallery dialog box enables you to set up the name and location of the new custom interaction you're adding to the Gallery.

eLearning with Dreamweaver MX: Building Online Learning Applications

7. Click the OK button to save your settings. Now, when you insert a new CourseBuilder interaction into a page, you'll see the new custom interaction listed in the CourseBuilder Gallery.

Sharing the CourseBuilder Gallery

In Chapter 10, you explored a bit of the CourseBuilder directory when you modified the Preferences.txt file. The CourseBuilder directory, under the Dreamweaver directory, contains the files that control CourseBuilder as well as the Gallery directory, shown in Figure 11.20. It controls the Gallery category structure and contains all the interaction files.

Notice that the directories within the Gallery directory have the same names as the gallery categories. CourseBuilder builds the gallery based on the directories contained here. Stored inside each category directory are two files for each CourseBuilder interaction: an .agt file and a .gif file. The .gif file is the interaction icon and the .agt file controls how the interaction works.

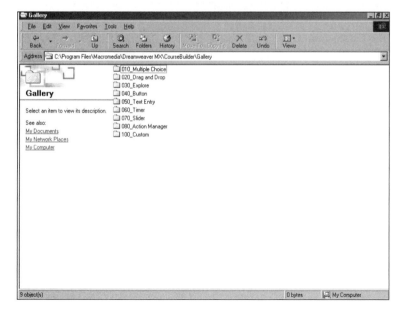

Figure 11.20
The Dreamweaver\CourseBuilder\ Gallery directory controls the structure of the CourseBuilder Gallery.

To share the custom interactions with team members, simply copy the appropriate files from this directory into the same directory on another computer. The next time your team member runs Course-Builder, he or she will see the new additions to the CourseBuilder Gallery. When you intend to share CourseBuilder interactions with others, it's easiest to keep them in separate gallery categories so that they are easier to share. Always remember to back up any files you are replacing so that you don't accidentally overwrite a file you wanted to keep.

Summary

In this chapter, you explored the power of the CourseBuilder Action Manager. You created new segments and populated them with conditions judging parts of the interaction. You also added actions, the same actions available in the Behaviors panel, to the Action Manager. You rearranged the statements in the Action Manager and edited their names. You also saved a custom interaction to the Gallery and learned how to share those files with others on your team.

IN THIS CHAPTER

chapter 12

Scoring an Assessment and Hiding the Answers

ONLINE LEARNING APPLICATIONS OFTEN have an assessment section—a quiz or a test for evaluating the learner's understanding and immediate retention of the material. Levels of assessment vary. An assessment could be a simple "knowledge check," in which learners are evaluated and given feedback on their performance that only they can see, or it could be an important certification exam, where the results must be securely tracked and transmitted.

This chapter covers informal quizzes and knowledge checks, the type of assessments that aren't required to be securely transmitted for certification. This is the most common type of assessment used in eLearning applications. The assessment is designed to challenge learners and confirm to them that they understand a procedure, principle, or fact about the topic.

This type of informal assessment offers another opportunity for learning. *Remediation*, directing learners to the original content when they answer a question incorrectly, gives them another chance to understand the information. You can provide links to portions of the course or even take learners there automatically when they get a question wrong.

In this chapter, you'll explore scoring a quiz. In Chapter 14, "Tracking with Learning Site," and Chapter 15, "Using a Learning Management System," you'll cover tracking the learner's progress and recording their scores. Tracking is much more involved than simply scoring a quiz; it requires learners to log in to the server and requires communication of scores between the browser and the server. Scoring a quiz is more informal and is not recorded permanently. The score is used to help learners assess how well they understand the course objectives.

In this chapter, you will understand the following:

- How to use the Action Manager CourseBuilder interaction
- How to create a single-page quiz
- How to create a multipage quiz
- How to hide the answers from the student using JavaScript

Understanding Assessments

Assessments evaluate how well a learner understands the material you've presented in your eLearning application. Different types of assessments can be delivered via an eLearning application:

- **Pretest**—This type of assessment evaluates the initial knowledge that the learner has about the topic. This data can then be used to present only those subtopics that the learner doesn't already understand.

- **Self-evaluation exercises**—This type of assessment presents feedback to help the learner benefit from both correct and incorrect responses they make to questions. These assessments can also serve as practice for a later graded quiz.

- **Graded quiz**—This type of assessment tracks the learner's answers and usually gives a single try per question.

- **Certification exam**—This type of assessment requires proctoring and is usually at odds with the "on my time" and "anywhere" benefits of eLearning. Most certification exams are offered separately from eLearning applications.

Assessments can be created in two ways: as a single Web page containing multiple questions, or as multiple Web pages. To score the assessment, you need to add up all the individual scores to give the learner a final score. When all the questions are on a single Web page, all the data you need is contained on that page. It's more complex, requiring additional planning and coding, to score an assessment contained in multiple Web pages.

Introducing CourseBuilder Variables

When you create assessment questions with CourseBuilder interactions, CourseBuilder has a set of JavaScript variables that hold the learner's data. You can access these variables to add up the learner's score and display it. CourseBuilder captures learner data for every interaction. A learner's data is available from the following JavaScript variables:

- **correct**—Contains the value true if the learner answered the question correctly and false if he or she did not.

- **totalCorrect**—Contains the total number of correct responses the learner selected.

- **totalIncorrect**—Contains the total number of incorrect responses the learner selected.

- **possCorrect**—Contains the total possible correct responses.

- **possIncorrect**—Contains the total possible incorrect responses in the interaction.

- **score**—Contains the value entered in the Score attribute in the CourseBuilder Interaction dialog box for the answer the learner selected for the interaction.

- **tries**—Contains the number of attempts the learner made to submit an answer to the question.

- **triesLimit**—Contains the number of attempts allowed by the Tries Limit attribute in the CourseBuilder Interaction dialog box.

- **time**—Contains the amount of time the learner took on his or her last attempt to answer the question.

- **timeLimit**—Contains the amount of time allowed by the Time Limit attribute in the CourseBuilder Interaction dialog box.

When you have multiple CourseBuilder interactions on a page, each interaction tracks each of the variables in the previous list. So, how can you tell the score of the multiple-choice interaction from the score of the text entry interaction? You use *dot notation* to differentiate between the variables of the different interactions. Dot notation is a method of addressing members of an object hierarchy. Using dot notation enables you to reference the score of the multiple-choice interaction—G01.score, for instance—as different from the score of the text entry interaction—G02.score, for example. The Course-Builder interaction object G01 is different from the object G02.

CourseBuilder gives each interaction a unique identifier. This identifier is contained in the object attribute of the <interaction> tag. The identifiers are named G01, G02, G03, and so on. To find the unique identifier of a CourseBuilder interaction, select the interaction and turn on Code view, as shown in Figure 12.1.

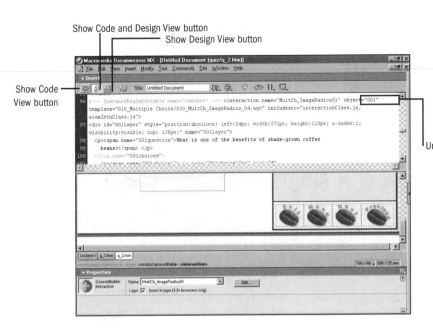

Show Code and Design View button

Show Design View button

Show Code View button

Figure 12.1

The unique identifier for a CourseBuilder interaction can be found in the HTML code.

Unique identifier

The <interaction> tag should be selected in the code, and you should easily spot the unique identifier as something like object="G01". Now you know that this interaction is G01, and its score can be referenced as G01.score. You also can see that objects within the interaction used the unique identifier in their names too. You might be able to spot the unique identifier in the tag selector.

Displaying CourseBuilder Variables

Now that you know what variables are available and how to differentiate variable values between interactions, what do you do with the variables? Because you want to display a total score for an entire quiz, you'll want to calculate a total score by adding up all the individual scores. You'll also want to display that score to the learner.

To display the contents of a JavaScript variable in CourseBuilder, you place the variable name in curly braces ({}). CourseBuilder resolves the variable name to whatever value the variable contains. To display a total score in a Popup Message action, you enter a calculation contained in curly braces, as shown in Figure 12.2.

Power User Tip

Many of the elements involved with the interaction, such as layers and images, are named by using the identifier. Do not ever rename these objects or modify any CourseBuilder JavaScript code by hand because you will likely impair the interaction's functionality.

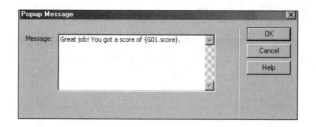

Scoring a Single-Page Assessment

When you create a single-page assessment, you can choose to give learners feedback as they answer each individual question, or you can give the feedback at the end of the quiz. CourseBuilder is able to implement either feedback method.

Practice using CourseBuilder by creating a new Web page and adding five questions created with CourseBuilder. You can use some of the questions from the content in the previous chapters or make up your own. The next section explains how to copy and paste Course-Builder interactions into a single-page assessment.

Copying and Pasting CourseBuilder Interactions

When you added CourseBuilder interactions to Web pages, Course-Builder named each one G01 because they were the first interaction added to the page. The naming might be slightly different if you deleted interactions from the page or added multiple interactions. When you combine the interactions on a single page, each one needs a unique name.

You can copy CourseBuilder interactions by selecting the interaction and using the Copy command (Edit, Copy). When you paste the interaction, CourseBuilder automatically increments the unique identifier so that it's not the same as other identifiers on the page. To copy and paste a CourseBuilder interaction, follow these steps:

1. Create a new blank Web page (File, New). Save the page as **quiz.html** in the quiz directory of your site.

2. Open the original multiple-choice question. Select the interaction and copy it.

3. Paste the multiple-choice question into quiz.html. If there is an existing CourseBuilder interaction on the page, be sure you do not paste the interaction within the existing <interaction> tags (examine the tag selector).

4. Open the question to edit it.

5. Select the General tab, and change the attributes as shown in Figure 12.3: Change the Judge Interaction on a Specific Event, uncheck the Reset button setting, and set the Tries Limit attribute to 1.

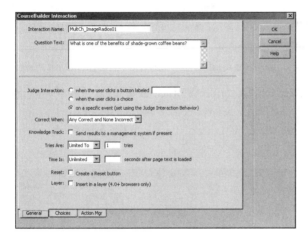

Figure 12.3
Change the General tab attributes to reflect that the interaction is now part of a quiz.

6. Select the Choices tab, and confirm that the correct choice has a score of 10.

7. Select the Action Manager tab, and delete all the segments.

8. Insert a horizontal rule under the question to separate it from the next question (Insert, Horizontal Rule).

Repeat these steps to add other questions to the quiz page.

Using the Action Manager Interaction

You've created an example of every category in the CourseBuilder Gallery except the Action Manager category. The Action Manager interaction doesn't appear onscreen or present any content to the learner. This special interaction controls other interactions on the

Web page. You'll use the Action Manager interaction to judge all the other interactions and present the score to the learner.

The Action Manager interaction can be thought of as the collector of data from the other interactions on the page. The Action Manager interaction has only two tabs: the General tab and the Action Manager tab. There are no default segments in the Action Manager, so you need to add the code yourself. Add an Action Manager interaction to your quiz Web page by following these steps:

1. Place your cursor at the bottom of the quiz Web page, and insert a CourseBuilder interaction (Insert, CourseBuilder Interaction).

2. Select the Action Manager category in the Gallery, and then click the only icon available, the ActionMgr interaction.

3. Select the General tab, and set it up as shown in Figure 12.4. Set the Judge Interaction to trigger when the learner clicks the Score the Quiz button. Leave all the other choices unchecked.

Figure 12.4

The General tab in the Action Manager interaction enables you to set the button name for the quiz.

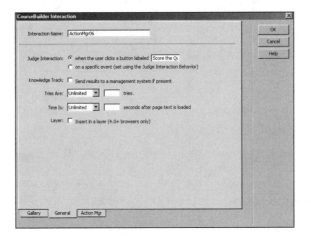

4. Select the Action Manager tab. Add a new segment called Segment: Judge Interactions.

5. Beneath the segment, add a Judge Interaction action for each question in the quiz, as shown in Figure 12.5. If you have five questions, you'll add five of these actions, selecting a different question name from the drop-down list for each.

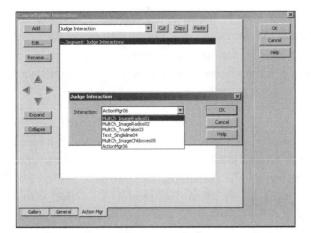

Figure 12.5
Select the interaction to be judged from the drop-down list.

6. Rename each of the Judge Interaction actions by clicking the Rename button. Name them **Judge Interaction 1**, **Judge Interaction 2**, and so on. This is so you can tell each action apart.

7. Add another segment beneath the segment you just created, and name it **Segment: Score Quiz**.

8. Add a Popup Message action with the message **Your score is {G01.score + G02.score +G03.score + G04.score + G05.score}**, as shown in Figure 12.6. Make sure you include the score for each question in the quiz.

9. Click the OK button to save your changes. Check the functionality by previewing the Web page in the browser.

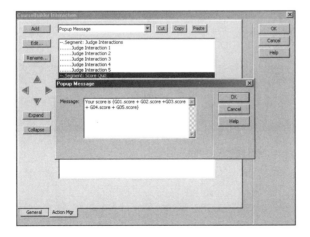

Figure 12.6
Embed JavaScript variables into a Popup Message as feedback for the learner.

When you click the Score the Quiz button, all the quiz questions are judged, and the total score is displayed to learners. Because this type of quiz is usually intended for learners to confirm their knowledge, you should add additional feedback about which questions are correct and which are incorrect.

Did you receive lots of feedback after you scored the quiz? That's because you set each interaction on the page to be judged on a specific event. When the Action Manager CourseBuilder interaction triggers, judging all the questions, the feedback for each individual question is displayed. When you are using an Action Manager interaction to display feedback for an entire quiz, you must delete all the learner feedback code in each individual interaction on the Web page.

Edit the quiz to prepare to add more feedback for the learner. First, inside the existing form containing the Score the Quiz button, add a text field (Insert, Form Objects, Text Field). In the Property inspector, set the Char Width attribute to 3, and name the text field **Quizscore**, as shown in Figure 12.7. You'll load the score into this text field.

Figure 12.7
Set text field attributes, such as Char Width and the name, in the Property inspector.

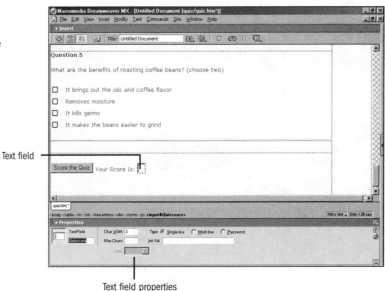

Text field

Text field properties

You should also insert text fields beneath each question. After learners score the quiz, you'll load feedback into the text field so that they can review whether they answered the question correctly. When inserting a text field, you can place the text field into an existing form or click the Yes button when Dreamweaver prompts you to add a form tag. Give the text fields unique names, and make each text field a multiline text field with a Char Width attribute of 50 and a Num Lines (height) attribute of 5, as shown in Figure 12.8. Dreamweaver MX enables you to also add multiline text fields using the Textarea object.

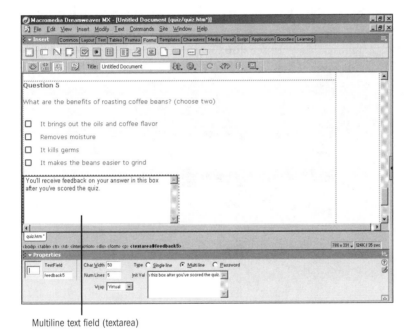

Multiline text field (textarea)

Figure 12.8
A text field can appear with multiple lines by setting the Num Lines attribute.

You can offer the learner a message in the Init Val attribute of **You'll receive feedback on your answer in this box after you've scored the quiz.** The multiline text box will scroll if the feedback you eventually send to the text field is longer than the five lines that are visible.

In the Action Manager interaction, you created a segment to judge the quiz and a segment to calculate and display the score in a pop-up message to the learner. Now you'll edit the scoring segment, sending the score to the text field you just created:

1. Select the Action Manager interaction, and open the Course-Builder Interaction dialog box to edit it.

2. Delete the Popup Message action under Segment: Score Quiz using the Cut button.

3. Add a Set Text of Text Field action under Segment: Score Quiz.

4. Select the Quizscore text field from the drop-down list at the top of the Set Text of Text Field dialog box, as shown in Figure 12.9. Enter **{G01.score + G02.score + G03.score + G04.score + G05.score}** in the New Text text box.

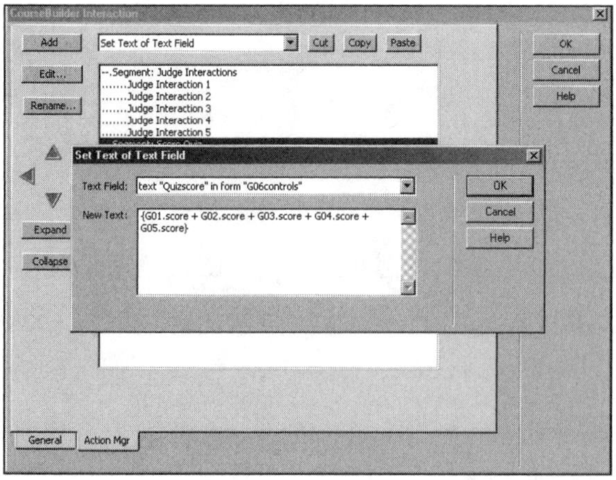

Figure 12.9

The Set Text of Text Field dialog box enables you to send text, including variables, to a text field on the Web page.

In addition, you'll add individual feedback for each question on the Web page. CourseBuilder will send one text message to the multiline text field beneath the question if the learner got the answer right and a different text message if the learner got the answer wrong. Continue editing the Action Manager interaction:

1. For now, collapse the two existing segments by clicking the Collapse button.

2. Select Segment: Judge Quiz Interactions, and add a new segment beneath it. To add a new segment, select Segment from

the Actions drop-down list menu and click the Add button. Name the new segment **Segment: Question 1 Feedback**. Set it to Always Evaluate from the Beginning.

3. Add a condition under the new segment. Select Condition from the Actions drop-down list menu and click the Add button. Name the condition **Question 1 Correct**.

4. Select Interaction from the Type drop-down list at the top.

5. Select the first question on the Web page from the Interaction drop-down list.

6. Select Correct State from the Property drop-down list.

7. Select Equals from the Equals/Does Not Equal drop-down list.

8. In the Type drop-down list at the bottom, make sure the Select option is showing.

9. In the last drop-down list, select Correct. The Condition Editor dialog box should look like Figure 12.10. Click the OK button to save your settings.

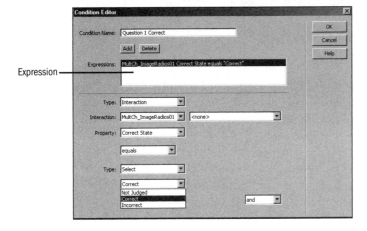

Figure 12.10
Use the Condition Editor to create a condition judging whether the learner answered a certain question correctly.

Now you need to add an action that will be triggered when the question is answered correctly. This is when you send feedback to the text field under the first question on the Web page. You'll also need to add code to the Action Manager judging whether the question was answered incorrectly. Because there are only two answer states, correct or incorrect, you can use an Else statement to trigger feedback for an incorrect answer. Continue to edit the Action Manager to add correct and incorrect feedback for Question 1:

1. Add a Set Text of Text Field action under the condition you created.

2. Select the Feedback text field beneath the first question in the Text Field drop-down list at the top of the dialog box. It's important that you send the feedback to the correct text box.

3. Enter the feedback text in the New Text text box. This feedback will be specific to the question, reinforcing that the learner got the answer correct. Click the OK button to save your settings.

4. Add an Else action beneath the Set Text of Text Field action.

5. Copy the Set Text of Text Field action (using the Copy button) and paste it beneath the Else action (using the Paste button). This action contains the feedback that's displayed if the learner does not answer the question correctly.

   You could make this quiz much more informative by adding conditionals for each potential answer the learner could choose. This example gives only generic incorrect feedback for any incorrect answer.

6. Edit the Set Text of Text Field action for the incorrect feedback (using the Edit button). The Correct text field should remain selected. Change the text in the New Text text box, and then click the OK button to save your settings.

7. The Action Manager tab should look like Figure 12.11. Click the OK button to save your settings for the Action Manager interaction.

Preview the Web page in the browser and check the functionality of the interaction, making sure that the proper Question 1 feedback appears in the Correct text field. Add a condition and feedback for each of the questions on the Web page by repeating the preceding steps. Remember, you can copy Segment: Question 1 Feedback, paste, and then edit the content for each of the questions.

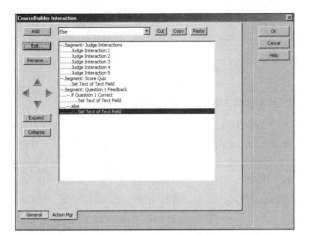

Figure 12.11
The Action Manager contains feedback for each question.

Whenever you need to perform actions on multiple CourseBuilder interactions, you use the special Action Manager. To create a standard quiz-scoring interaction, modify the Action Manager interaction and save your custom version to the Gallery. You can embellish this interaction by, for instance, disabling the interactions (the Set Interaction Properties action), displaying the amount of time it took the learner to answer the quiz, or displaying a hyperlink to additional information for incorrect answers (the Go To URL action).

Scoring a Multiple-Page Assessment

An important limitation of Web pages is the inability to *maintain state*—in other words, to retain user-specific data across multiple Web pages. When you view a Web page scripted with plain HTML or with a combination of HTML and JavaScript, a connection isn't maintained with the Web server. Your browser downloads the Web page to the browser's cache folder on your hard drive. So are you viewing the Web page on the Web? No, you are actually viewing a Web page on your hard drive. After you've requested a Web page and it's downloaded from a Web server, the anonymous connection is broken.

Because Web pages do not maintain state, an assessment over multiple Web pages must contain a method to record learners' score tallies as they progress from page to page. You can keep track of a score on a single Web page, like the one you created earlier in this chapter, but when the learner leaves that Web page for another page, the data is lost. There are three ways to record learner data: frames, cookies, or server-side scripting. The following sections discuss the pros and cons of each method.

Using Frames to Keep Score

Frames are a method of presenting multiple Web pages in a single browser window, as shown in Figure 12.12. There is a Web page for each frame and one additional Web page, called a *frameset*, that defines how the frames fit together in the browser window. You've probably noticed frames in Web sites that you have visited; they are less popular than they once were. Frames may or may not have borders defining them; if borders aren't present, you might not even notice that frames are used.

Figure 12.12
Frames present multiple Web pages in a single browser window.

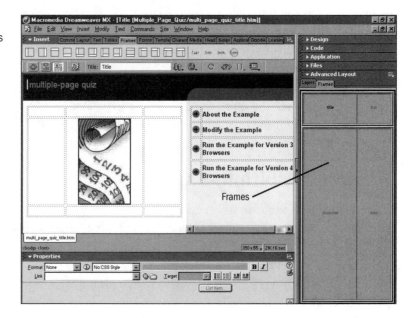

Frames are useful when you need a single Web page to remain visible while another portion of the window changes. For instance, one frame holds the table of contents of a report containing links to the report sections. The user selects a link in the table of contents and loads a portion of the report in a different frame. The table of contents Web page is not reloaded until the user leaves the frameset.

CourseBuilder installs an example of a multiple-page quiz in the CourseBuilder\Help\Show_Me\Multiple_Page_Quiz\ directory. Open the frameset page multi_page_quiz_mainframe.htm in your browser. This page contains four frames, shown in Figure 12.13. The top two frames remain fixed, and the larger two frames at the bottom load different content.

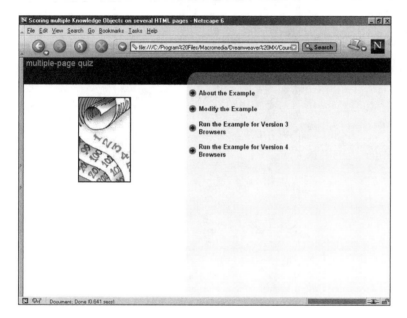

Figure 12.13
The multiple-page quiz example loads four frames.

Run the example by clicking on the red arrow button next to Run the Example for Version 4 Browsers. When you run the example, another frameset is loaded into the frame on the left of the browser window; the frameset is nested in the bottom-left frame. The nested frameset contains two frames: The top frame presents the question, and the bottom frame contains the navigation and JavaScript code that records the question score and time for each question. I'll call the lower frame the *tracking frame*.

The question frame can communicate with the tracking frame via JavaScript. Open the nested quiz frameset in Dreamweaver by opening multi_page_quiz4.htm. Open the Frames panel (Window, Others, Frames), and you'll see a representation of the two frames, as shown in Figure 12.14. Notice that both of the frames have names; the top frame is named "main," and the bottom frame is named "nav." The frames communicate with each other by using these names to *target* the other frame.

Figure 12.14
You modify and change the properties of frames by using the Frames panel.

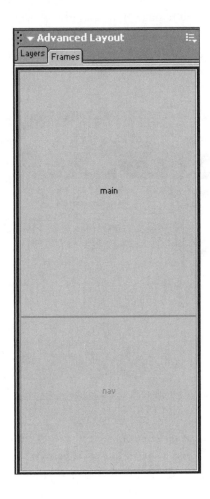

The concept of targeting is important when working with frames. You add the target property to a hyperlink, as shown in Figure 12.15, to cause the URL referenced in the link to load in a frame different from the one that contains the link. The same idea is used when storing user data in a tracking frame. Instead of storing the data in the question frame, which will be replaced when a new question loads in the frame, the code sends the user data to the tracking frame, which does not reload.

Figure 12.15
The target property directs the URL in a hyperlink to load in the targeted frame.

This multiple-page quiz example is designed as an example that you can use to create your own multiple-page quiz. The JavaScript that controls the scoring and tracking for the multiple pages is contained in the tracking frame. To modify the example, you'll need to make sure you name the frames so that they are referenced correctly by the code.

You've seen the major advantage of frames in presenting a quiz: You can maintain the score for multiple pages in a static tracking frame. However, there are major disadvantages to frames, too. If learners happen to reload the Web page, all their data is lost. Even if you remove the browser's standard buttons, some learners may know the shortcut key for the reload command. There are also usability issues with frames, and some learners might not understand how they work.

Using Cookies to Keep Score

The second way to maintain learner data across multiple Web pages is to use *cookies*. Cookies are small bits of data that the browser stores on the user's computer. A cookie is specific to the computer, not necessarily the user. Because a Web browser cannot maintain data, a cookie is another way to track small amounts of data from page to page in a Web browser.

You write and read cookies by using JavaScript. Cookies contain three bits of data: a name, a value, and an expiration date. If you don't give a cookie an expiration date, it expires when the browser is closed. The browser stores the cookies in memory until the browser is closed, so the cookie data will be deleted if you don't set an expiration date.

The cookie you create in this chapter will be used to hold the ongoing score of a multiple-page quiz. At the end of the quiz, you can read the cookie value for the final score and display it for the learner. You could make this example more complex by adding more information to the cookie value. However, this is a simple example of writing a JavaScript function, writing a cookie, and reading a cookie.

Writing a JavaScript Function

To use cookies to capture the learner's score, you'll need to write a JavaScript *function*, a group of JavaScript statements that together form a procedure. You'll add a function to the learning.js file you created from Dreamweaver functions. Then you'll add a *function call*, a JavaScript request to run the function, to each page of the quiz.

In Dreamweaver, open learning.js, which is stored in the scripts directory of your site. At the top of the file, enter the following code for the function that will control the cookie:

```
function addToCookie(score)    {  \\function to add to score cookie
    var score_cookie=document.cookie;
    //Figure out the start of the cookie value
    var start=score_cookie.indexOf("=",score_cookie) + 1;
    //Figure out the end of the cookie value
    var end=score_cookie.indexOf(";",score_cookie);
    if (end == -1) {
        end = score_cookie.length
    }
    //Get the substring of the cookie that is the value and
    //use the parseInt() function to convert it to a number
    var cookie_value=parseInt(score_cookie.substring(start,end));
    var cookie_value = cookie_value + score;
    document.cookie="score=" + cookie_value;

//the line below displays the current
//cookie value in a JavaScript alert box.
//make sure you comment out this line in
//the final version by placing two slashes
//in front of the statement.
    alert(document.cookie);
}
```

Comments in JavaScript are preceded by two forward slashes (//). Notice the second-to-last line in the code: alert(document.cookie);. This statement pops up a JavaScript alert window, the same type that Dreamweaver's Popup Message behavior presents, displaying the current contents of the score cookie. This line is included to help *debug* the code—to make sure it works properly. You'll want to delete this line or comment it out by adding the two forward slashes at the beginning of the line.

On the first page of the quiz, you need to create the cookie to hold the score. Again, this is done with JavaScript. You can place JavaScript in the <head> of the quiz's first page to create and initialize the score cookie. Open quiz/1.html and view it in Code view. At the top of the Web page, below the references to the external JavaScript files (<script language="JavaScript" src="../scripts/behActions.js"></script>), enter the following JavaScript:

```
<script language="JavaScript">
<!--
document.cookie="score=0";
//-->
</script>
```

The JavaScript create a new cookie with the name "score" and initiates its value to 0. Because you did not set an expiration date, the cookie is available only during the current browser session. If learners close their browsers (or they crash) in the middle of the quiz, their scores cannot be retrieved. Also, if another learner uses the same computer and the browser software has not been restarted, the score value could be retained. However, because you initialize the score cookie on the first page of the quiz, the previous learner's score is overwritten.

CourseBuilder judges each of the quiz questions you created in Chapter 10, "Including CourseBuilder Interactions and Controls," when the learner clicks the Check Answer button. When the learner clicks this button, you also trigger the addToCookie() function that you added to the main external JavaScript file. You'll use the Call JavaScript behavior triggered by the button's onClick event to update the score cookie. The Call JavaScript behavior offers an easy way to add a simple JavaScript statement without editing the code.

When you call a JavaScript function, you need to be aware of any *arguments* that the function expects. Arguments are pieces of data that the function needs passed to it so that it can complete its procedure. You can easily identify arguments because they are listed in parentheses after the function name. Because the function you added is named addToCookie(score), this function expects a single argument named score. When you call the function, you need to pass this single argument to the function. The addToCookie() function needs to receive the learner's score for the current question so that it can be added to the existing score value.

To update the score cookie after the learner answers the question, follow these steps:

1. In Design view, click the Check Answer button. Make sure the Behaviors panel is open.

2. Notice that there is already a behavior attached to this button. The Judge Interaction behavior triggers the judging of the CourseBuilder interaction. Select the Call JavaScript behavior by clicking on the + button in the Behaviors panel.

3. The Call JavaScript dialog box appears, as shown in Figure 12.16. Before entering this code, you'll want to confirm that the interaction on the page is named G01. Enter the function call's code into the JavaScript field:

   addToCookie(G01.score);

Figure 12.16

Enter a single JavaScript statement into the Call JavaScript dialog box.

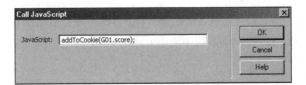

4. Click the OK button to save the settings in the Call JavaScript dialog box.

5. Make sure the onClick event appears in the Events column.

Preview the Web page in the browser. When you select the correct answer, the score should add 10 to the total score (the setting in the CourseBuilder Interaction dialog box). When you select an incorrect answer, the score should remain at 0.

The preceding steps for function calls must be added to each of the Check Answer buttons on each page of the quiz. While you are setting up the quiz, you can leave the score's Popup Message behavior to check that the quiz is working properly. Then comment out the code when you've finished.

To create a Web page displaying the score that's contained in the cookie, follow these steps:

1. Create a Web page called score.html, and link the last quiz question page to it.

2. Add the text Here are the results of your quiz:, and insert a text field (Insert, Form Objects, Text Field). Add a form around the text field if prompted.

3. Name the text field **finalScore**.

4. Select the <body> tag in the Tag Selector, and then open the Behaviors panel. If you created this page from a template, you'll need to detach it from the template (Modify, Templates, Detach from Template). Confirm that <body> Actions is displayed in the title bar of the Behaviors panel.

5. Click the + button in the Behaviors panel, and select Set Text of Text Field from the Behaviors drop-down list (in the Set Text submenu).

6. Select the text field finalScore from the drop-down list.

7. In the New Text text box, enter JavaScript code in braces that will display the cookie's contents:

   {document.cookie}

8. Click the OK button to save your settings. Confirm that the onLoad event is listed in the Events column. This loads the score into the text field when the page loads.

When all the quiz pages are linked, test the quiz and the final score page. Make sure the cookie is displayed in the text field. Note that you would have to add JavaScript coding to parse out the score cookie, dividing its name, score, from its value. It's easiest to display the whole cookie in the text field.

Using Server-Side Scripting to Keep Score

The most robust and useful way to score a quiz is to use server-side scripting. This requires the learner to create a unique session with the Web server. The learner's score can be stored in *session variables*, which are similar to cookies stored on the server, or the score can be stored and retrieved from a database on the server. Chapter 13, "Creating and Tracking a Dynamic Web Site," covers creating Web pages that include server-side scripting.

Hiding the Answers from Learners

One of the disadvantages of assessments in Web pages is how easy it is for the learner to gain access to the answers. Many Web users know how to look at the HTML code for a Web page in their browsers. When they examine the code, it isn't too difficult to identify the answers in a CourseBuilder interaction.

When it is necessary to create a secure assessment, the only way to maintain security is to use server-side scripting to compare the learner's answer to the correct answer stored in a database. Achieving this and tracking results will be explored in Chapters 13 and 14.

There are a couple of ways to thwart all but the most clever learners from finding the answers:

- **CourseBuilder Code in an External JavaScript File**—You can cut the CourseBuilder code containing the answers, paste it into a blank file, and save it as an external JavaScript file (.js). You must add a reference calling the file to the Web page that you cut the code from.

- **Disable Right-Click in the Browser**—If you've loaded the quiz pages into a window without menu bars, the learner cannot view the source by using the menu bar. However, you can right-click in browsers to get a context menu containing a command to view the HTML code. The next section discusses how to disable the right-click that displays that menu. Unfortunately, the learner might still know the keyboard shortcut for the command to view the source.

Disabling the Browser's Right-Click

To disable the learner's ability to right-click on the browser window, you again have to use JavaScript. You'll add a new function to the main external JavaScript file for the learning site, learning.js. Open this file and add the following code at the top of the page:

```
function disable_right_click(e)    {
    var browser = navigator.appName.substring ( 0, 9 );
    var event_number = 0;
    if (browser=="Microsoft")
        event_number = event.button;
    else if (browser=="Netscape")
        event_number = e.which;
    if ( event_number==2 || event_number==3 )
        {
        alert ("Right Mouse Button Is Disabled");
        return (false);
        }
    return (true);
}
```

At the top of each Web page that contains an assessment question, you need to add the following function call:

```
<script language="JavaScript">
<!--
document.onmousedown=disable_right_click;
//-->
</script>
```

You can add this JavaScript code between existing <script> tags, if you prefer. This makes the code a little cleaner. You might also want to add a comment above the code telling future developers what the code accomplishes. The ideal way to implement the function call code is to add it to a quiz question template during template development.

Summary

In this chapter, you grouped several CourseBuilder interactions into a quiz. For a single-page quiz, you used the Action Manager Course-Builder interaction to judge the interactions as a group and give individual feedback on each one. You learned how to place feedback into a form's text fields. For the multipage quiz, you learned about framesets and how to insert JavaScript into the frames to track the results from several Web pages. You also learned how to hide quiz answers from learners using JavaScript.

Part V

Tracking the User

chapter 13

Creating and Tracking a Dynamic Web Site

WITH DREAMWEAVER MX, YOU CAN USE A SERVER technology to

create Web pages based on data from a database. *Dynamic* Web

pages contain elements written to the page immediately before

it is served to a learner via a Web server. Whether you're dis-

playing the learner's name, are computing the learner's score, or

are logging a learner into the course, the server processes the

Web page and displays dynamic data within the page or inserts

data into a database.

Dreamweaver MX incorporates the dynamic Web page creation previously available only in Dreamweaver UltraDev; now there is a single version of Dreamweaver instead of two separate versions. So far, you have created what Dreamweaver considers regular Web pages, pages without dynamic, database-generated content. Dynamic Web pages are completely different from the Dynamic HTML (DHTML) that you used earlier in the book. The word *dynamic* means two different things in these two instances.

If you have never worked with server technologies, it can be intimidating. This chapter guides you through weighing the server technology choices, setting up your Web site, and creating and testing some basic dynamic Web pages. Often the most difficult part of using server technologies is setting your site up correctly.

In this chapter, you will understand the following:

- The differences between the server technologies available in Dreamweaver MX

- How to configure your Web site definition to test your site on a local or a remote server

- How to authenticate the learner by using Active Server Pages

- How to create a simple report by using Active Server Pages

Defining a Dynamic Web Site

How do you choose which application server technology to use for your online learning project? You need to answer a couple of important questions about the server, software, and database before you can add dynamic Web pages to your project in Dreamweaver MX.

Exploring Server Technologies

Dreamweaver produces Web pages scripted to the most popular server technologies:

- Microsoft Active Server Pages (ASP and ASP.NET).

- Sun JavaServer Pages (JSP).

- Macromedia ColdFusion, which writes ColdFusion Markup Language (CFML). Allaire, the creator of ColdFusion, merged with Macromedia in 2001.

- Hypertext Pre-Processor (PHP).

All server technologies require application server software to translate the server-side scripting produced by Dreamweaver MX into a Web page. You need to specify which application server technology (ASP, ASP.NET, JSP, ColdFusion, or PHP) your site will use. If you are creating dynamic pages using Dreamweaver MX, you need to solidify server requirements well in advance of the development phase of an online learning project.

Dreamweaver automatically scripts your Web pages with the server technology you select. For example, if you choose JSP as your server technology, Dreamweaver adds JSP code to your Web page. When you create a Web page in Dreamweaver MX, you can view the *server-side code* in Code view. If you were to view the code after the JSP application server software has processed it, you would see only plain HTML. The application server processes the server-side code, removing it from the Web page, and inserts any data specified by the server-side code as plain HTML.

When deciding which server technology to use, you also need to identify the following:

- The application server that will run your online learning application.

- The database that will be used to house the data.

- How you are going to connect the application server to the database.

Which operating system will be running on the server? The two most popular server operating systems are Windows (NT, 2000, or XP) and various flavors of Unix. If you are serving your online learning application from a Windows server, it's easy to use ASP as the application server because Internet Information Server (IIS), the Web server software included with Windows, automatically processes ASP. Using ASP on a Unix server requires that you purchase third-party application server software. ColdFusion and various JSP and PHP servers also have versions that run on a Windows server.

Some of the application servers run on multiple operating systems. ColdFusion, for example, has server versions for most popular operating systems, enabling you to develop Web pages that can be served on a variety of platforms. There are JSP servers, such as IBM WebSphere and JRun, that work on different operating systems. PHP can also run on Windows or Unix and has a version that runs on Mac OS X. Mac OS X, unlike previous Mac operating systems, is a flavor of Unix; most everything available for Unix or Linux has been made in a Mac OS X version.

Choosing a Server Technology

In Chapter 4, "Creating a New Web Site Definition," you initially indicated in the Site Definition Wizard that the site would not use a server technology. Now you can edit the site definition, adding the information that is required when defining a dynamic Web site. You can modify the site definition without damaging any of the existing Web pages in the site.

Edit your site definition (Site, Edit Sites) to select a server technology. Select your online learning site, and click the Edit button to open the Site Definition dialog box. With the Basic tab selected in the Site Definition dialog box, select the radio button indicating that you want to use a server technology on the second page of the Site Definition Wizard, shown in Figure 13.1.

The following sections discuss the four different server technologies available in Dreamweaver MX: ASP, JSP, ColdFusion, and PHP. This discussion is complicated because it involves multiple operating systems, servers, and development machines. If you already know which server technology your project is using, you can jump directly to that section to see how to set up Dreamweaver.

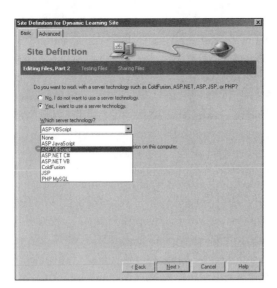

Figure 13.1
Select a server technology in the
Site Definition Wizard.

Selecting ASP as the Server Technology

The engine to run Microsoft Active Server Pages (ASP) is contained in the Internet Information Server (IIS) Web server software, available free from Microsoft. This technology's cost (free) and ease of use have been the main driving forces behind its popularity. You can run dynamic ASP pages on a Windows server running IIS or on a Unix server with Sun Chili!Soft ASP installed (www.chilisoft.com).

You can install IIS on any computer running Windows NT, 2000, or XP. The software is available on the operating system installation CD-ROM or as a free download from Microsoft. If you are using Windows 95, 98, or Me, you need to download and install Personal Web Server, an application available free from Microsoft at www.microsoft.com/msdownload/ntoptionpack/askwiz.asp. After you install the Web server on your computer, start the server by using the Personal Web Manager, shown in Figure 13.2. You can launch the Personal Web Manager from Start, Programs, Administrative Tools (Windows 2000 and Windows XP) or from the Control Panel (Windows 98).

Note

Selecting ASP as the server tech-nology gives you a great deal of flexibility. ASP is popular and easy to deploy and test because it is integrated into the Web server that comes with Windows. ASP, however, is a proprietary technol-ogy designed to work on Windows only. You can purchase Chili!Soft to enable ASP to work with vari-ous versions of Unix, but ASP is usually deployed on Windows servers. Be aware that, as of this writing, Windows server products have had serious security holes. If you decide to use IIS, be sure you download and install the security patch updates when they are posted on the Microsoft Web site.

Dreamweaver MX enables you to use ASP 2.0 or ASP.NET to create dynamic Web pages. To use ASP.NET, first download and install the .NET Framework. ASP pages have the .asp file extension, and ASP.NET pages have the .aspx file extension. ASP code appears between <% and %> in Code view. When a browser requests a dynamic Web page—mypage.asp, for example—the Web server uses the ASP processing capabilities to translate the scripts, perform any logic, and insert data from a database.

When you select ASP as the server technology, Dreamweaver enables you to specify VBScript or JavaScript as the scripting language it will use. VBScript is a Microsoft scripting language based on Microsoft Visual Basic, and JavaScript is a standard Web scripting language originally developed by Netscape. If you are using ASP.NET as your server technology, Dreamweaver can generate scripts in Visual Basic (VB) or C# (pronounced "C sharp"); both are object-oriented pro-gramming languages. Dreamweaver creates scripts in the language you select. You should select the scripting language you are most familiar with; because ASP is a Microsoft technology, VBScript is the most popular selection for ASP 2.0.

Figure 13.2

Use the Personal Web Manager to start and configure IIS or Personal Web Server.

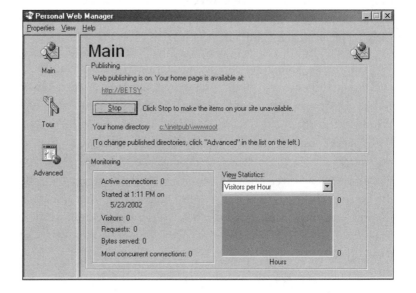

Selecting JSP as the Server Technology

Another popular server technology is JavaServer Pages (JSP). The Java Servlet Engine enables servers to translate JSP code into dynamic Web pages. These *servlets* are compiled Java code that process JSP on the server. Java is a flexible and popular programming language that runs on a variety of servers and operating systems.

JSP Servers

When you use JSP, your server must have software installed to translate the JSP code into a dynamic Web page. JSP code resides between <% and %>. Although new products are coming out all the time, as of this writing, these are the most popular JSP servers:

- **JRun**—Macromedia JRun (formerly from Allaire, which merged with Macromedia) is a JSP server that runs on Windows or Unix. You can download a developer version (runs on your development machine for a single user) from Macromedia at www.macromedia.com/software/jrun/trial/.

- **Tomcat**—A free, open-source JSP server that works with any Web server that supports JSP and servlets. It is usually used with the popular free Web server software, Apache. More information is available at java.sun.com/products/jsp/tomcat/faq.html.

- **WebSphere**—IBM's JSP server, WebSphere, is part of a family of middleware software products. The WebSphere server is available for Windows and Unix. More information is available at www.ibm.com/software/webservers/appserv/. A trial version of IBM WebSphere is included with Dreamweaver and is available to download from the WebSphere Web site.

- **iPlanet**—The iPlanet Application Server serves JSP on Unix. You can get more information at developer.iplanet.com/.

Like ASP, if you want to test your JSP pages on your local machine, you must have one of the JSP application servers installed and working on your computer. The JRun Management Console, running on my development computer, is shown in Figure 13.3. If you do not want to install the application server on your local machine, you can simply upload your pages to the remote server for testing.

Figure 13.3
You manage users and settings for JRun in the Management Console.

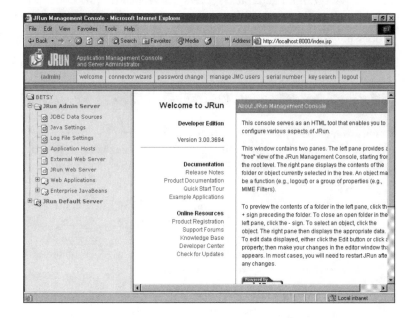

Selecting ColdFusion as the Server Technology

Yet another server technology is Macromedia ColdFusion (formerly Allaire ColdFusion), which uses tag-based code for dynamic Web page development. The ColdFusion server works with most operating systems and Web server software. ColdFusion's flexibility and ease of use has made it a popular application server.

You can install the ColdFusion server that comes with Dreamweaver onto your local machine to test your online learning application locally. After you install the server and test your installation, the ColdFusion server administrator looks like Figure 13.4. You can set up and test data sources and even specify an e-mail server to facilitate handling e-mail via ColdFusion tags.

The ColdFusion language, called ColdFusion Markup Language (CFML), looks similar to HTML. For example, to select records from a database using ColdFusion in Dreamweaver, the <cfquery> tag is used:

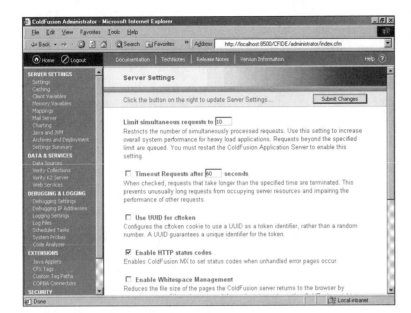

Figure 13.4
You administer the ColdFusion server via the browser.

```
<cfquery name="rsMfg" datasource="cfExample">
        SELECT * FROM tblMfg
</cfquery>
```

Of course, Dreamweaver writes most of the code for you, but you will want to understand the way ColdFusion works in case you need to add complicated functionality.

Selecting PHP as the Server Technology

Hypertext Preprocessor (PHP) is a popular open-source server technology available for most operating systems. Dreamweaver creates PHP scripts that work with the popular open-source SQL database MySQL. Open-source software is available free on the Web; you can download PHP at www.php.net and MySQL at www.mysql.com.

The PHP scripting language syntax is similar to C, Java, and Perl. PHP code resides between <? and ?>. Dynamic PHP Web pages usually have the file extension .php, .php3, or .phtml.

Specifying Your Site-Testing Location

Creating dynamic Web pages by using a server technology, such as ASP, JSP, or ColdFusion, requires that you view the Web pages you create via a Web server. You can no longer simply select the Preview in Browser command and preview a Web page from your hard drive. For this reason, storing and viewing your dynamic Web pages from an appropriate location on a server is important.

The third page of the Site Definition Wizard, shown in Figure 13.5, asks you to define how you will work with dynamic Web pages during development, which is when you store and test the pages.

The Site Definition Wizard offers four different preview choices:

- **Edit and Test Locally**—You install Web server software and application servers on your local development computer and test the Web pages there. You need to use a server technology that runs on the operating system you have on your development computer.

Figure 13.5

The Site Definition Wizard enables you to select how you will preview dynamic Web pages created with Dreamweaver MX.

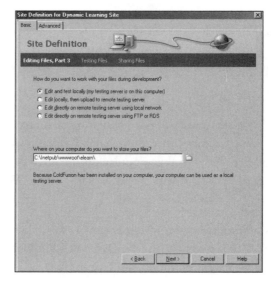

- **Edit Locally, Then Upload to Remote Testing Server**—This method doesn't have the overhead of running a Web server on your development machine. Before testing a dynamic Web page, you must send it to a remote server and access the page via a URL (www.mycompany.com/staging/) or an IP address (216.22.45.120/staging) for testing.

- **Edit Directly on Remote Testing Server Using Local Network**—This method works when you are on a local network where you can access the directories of a Web server via a mapped drive. You will edit the dynamic Web pages on a mapped network drive (such as U:\inetpub\wwwroot\staging\) and then access the pages for testing via a URL or the Web server's IP address.

- **Edit Directly on Remote Testing Server Using FTP or RDS**—When you select this method, you can select a check box specifying that Dreamweaver should automatically upload the Web page to the remote server every time you save. This method is like the local network method except that the files are uploaded via FTP (File Transfer Protocol) or RDS (Remote Development Services); RDS is available only when you work with ColdFusion as the server technology.

If possible, I prefer to test the dynamic Web pages I develop right on my computer. This method requires installing both a Web server and an application server on your development computer. I prefer to run a Web server and an application server on my local computer so that I can create and test dynamic Web pages without constantly transferring the files to the server. The local computer mimics the final Web server environment, using similar settings so that you do not need to modify the dynamic Web pages later.

After you've selected where you will test your dynamic Web pages, you need to enter that location into the text field at the bottom of the Site Definition Wizard. Use the folder button to the right of the text field to select the directory (your site root) containing your files.

Setting Up a Server on the Mac

If you are using a Mac running Mac OS X, you can fully develop dynamic Web pages in Dreamweaver MX and test them using the built-in Apache Web server. You need to turn on the Web server capability in the Sharing panel of System Preferences, as shown in Figure 13.6. Click the Start button under Web Sharing to start the built-in Apache server.

You can store a dynamic Web site in your personal site root, based on your username. Your personal site root is located in the Sites folder within your Users folder; mine is located at /Users/betsy/Sites/. I can access the contents of this directory by using the URL http://127.0.0.1/~betsy/ or http://localhost/~betsy; the IP address 127.0.0.1 is the default IP address for the current computer, as shown in Figure 13.7. This default address works only when accessing the Web server from the computer that's running it. For others to access your Web pages, you need to give them a public IP address, such as http://*domain_name*/~betsy/.

Power User Tip

In Mac OS X, you can find your IP address in the Network category of System Preferences.

If you'd prefer not to use the username preceded by the tilde (~), you can place the Web site directly within the server's root, called the DocumentRoot. This directory is found in the /Library/WebServer/Documents/ directory, as shown in Figure 13.8. Replacing the index.html file in this directory replaces the default home page at the root of the server.

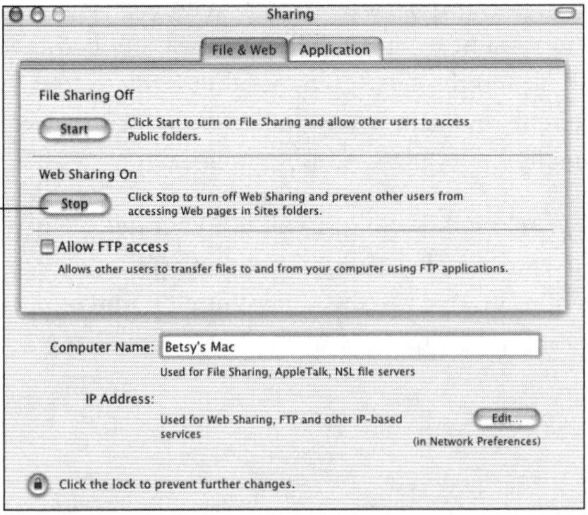

Figure 13.6
Turn on the built-in Apache server in Mac OS X in the Sharing category of System Preferences.

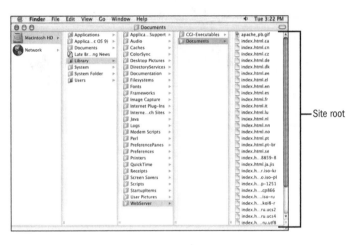

Site root

Most Mac developers should use one of the server technologies that are popular with Apache users. The Tomcat server described previously is a free Apache add-in that processes JSP. There is also a popular free PHP add-in for Apache that works with the MySQL database (also free). To install Tomcat on your Mac, check this URL: developer.apple.com/internet/macosx/tomcat1.html. To install PHP on your Mac, check this URL: developer.apple.com/internet/macosx/php.html.

Setting Up a Server in Windows

If you are using Windows, you can install a Web server, such as Microsoft IIS or Personal Web Server (PWS), on your local machine to preview your work locally. You administer the Web server via the

Personal Web Manager application shown in Figure 13.9. You need to start the Web server before you can serve Web pages on your computer. The default way to view your local Web server is with the URL http://computer/; computer is replaced with the name of your computer (my computer is named BETSY, as shown in Figure 13.9).

Figure 13.9
Manage the Web server on your development computer with Personal Web Manager.

Local server URL

Start/Stop server button

Home directory

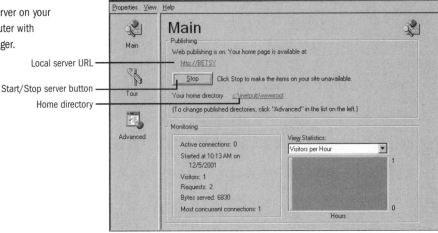

Power User Tip

You can also use the URLs **http://127.0.0.1/** or **http:// localhost/** to access your local server.

Both IIS and PWS create a root directory for the server called www-root (the path is usually c:\inetpub\wwwroot\). Other servers, such as the IBM HTTP server (available from www.ibm.com/software/web-servers/httpservers/—click on the Downloads link on the left), might call the root directory htdocs. Read the server documentation to find out where the root of the server is located. I find it easiest to store dynamic Web pages within the root directory because the correct file permissions have been set for you.

However, you do not have to store your dynamic Web pages within the root directory. If you store your Web pages outside the root directory, you must define the directory as a *virtual Web directory*. Virtual Web directories enable the Web server to serve the Web pages in this directory as though they were stored in the server's root directory. To create a virtual directory, you can use Personal Web Manager with IIS or PWS. Select the Advanced view, shown in Figure 13.10, by clicking the Advanced icon in the left side of Personal Web Manager. This view shows all the directories that are active on the Web server, both physical (within the wwwroot directory) and virtual.

To create a new virtual directory, follow these steps:

1. In the Advanced view of Personal Web Manager, click the Add button to open the Add Directory dialog box, shown in Figure 13.11.

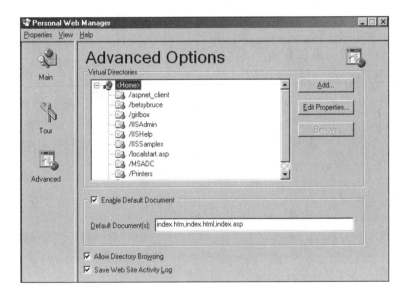

Figure 13.10

The Advanced view in Personal Web Manager enables you to view all the directories, both physical and virtual, that are active on IIS or PWS.

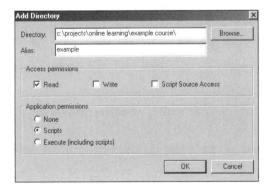

Figure 13.11

Add a virtual directory, specifying the path and the alias, by using the Add Directory dialog box.

2. Browse to the directory that contains the online learning application and give the directory an alias. The alias is the name appended to the URL to access the directory; it does not have to be the actual name of the directory. For example, you could map c:\projects\myclient\course1\ to client_course1, and when you preview http://localhost/client_course1/, you will see the files in this directory.

3. Select the Read check box in the Access Permissions section. This limits public users, people viewing the page via the Web, to reading the Web pages, not changing them. You don't want to give too many access permissions to anonymous users, and they need only read permissions to view the pages.

4. When creating dynamic pages with ASP, JSP, or ColdFusion, you need to select the Scripts radio button in the Application Permissions section. This gives the application server permission to run your ASP, JSP, or ColdFusion scripts in the directory.

5. Click OK to save the new virtual directory.

Back in the Advanced view of Personal Web Manager, some additional settings are useful and apply to all your Web directories. Specify the *default document names* (the filenames of the pages that load automatically when only the directory is given in the URL) and confirm that the default document is enabled. You might want to deselect the Allow Directory Browsing check box. If a certain directory does not contain a default document, such as index.html, anonymous users will be able to view your entire file structure if Allow Directory Browsing is enabled. It is safer to disable this option so that mischief-makers on the Web cannot meddle with your files.

When you have finished setting up your virtual directory, make sure your server is running, and type **http://*computername*/**, replacing *computername* with the actual name of your computer. Add the name of the virtual directory at the end of the URL. If you have one of the default documents (index.html, for instance) in that directory, it should load into the browser. Otherwise, you have to specify an HTML filename as well in the URL.

Specifying the Testing Server URL

The Testing Files page of the Site Definition Wizard asks you to enter the URL that Dreamweaver will use when you preview the Web pages in a dynamic Web site. This URL depends on the name of the server and the directory where your files are stored. If you opted to test your files remotely, you might enter a URL such as http://www.companyname.com/staging/courses/management/. If you are serving your test site from your local development computer, you might use a URL such as http://127.0.0.1/courses/management/.

Click the Test URL button, shown in Figure 13.12, to have Dreamweaver test the connection to the URL. Dreamweaver displays a message stating that it either connected successfully or did not connect to the URL. If Dreamweaver didn't connect successfully, check your spelling. Also, check whether the permissions are set correctly, either on your computer or on the server. In my experience, many Web server problems are caused by incorrect permission settings.

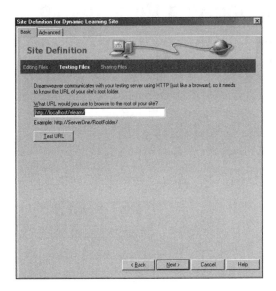

Figure 13.12

Enter and test the URL to the testing server in the Site Definition Wizard.

You have entered the necessary Site Definition Wizard settings for a dynamic Web site. To see these settings in a single view, select the Advanced tab of the Site Definition dialog box, and then select

Testing Server in the Category list box, as shown in Figure 13.13. You can also edit the settings in this tab.

Figure 13.13
In the Advanced tab, you can view and change all settings in the Testing Server category at one time.

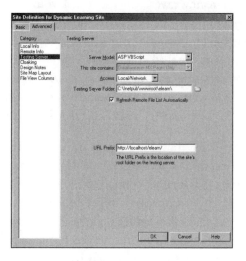

Connecting to a Data Source

You've defined your site to handle dynamic Web pages, but there are still a couple of items to set up before you can begin creating pages. First, you should become familiar with the Application panel group, shown in Figure 13.14. These panels are used only when working with dynamic Web pages. You'll also use the Live Data View button (the fourth button from the left on the toolbar, with a lightning bolt icon) to view dynamic pages, including real data from a database right in Dreamweaver MX.

Figure 13.14
Dreamweaver MX has panels that are used only when creating dynamic Web sites.

Notice that the panels (except Components) initially contain a checklist of four items. You should have already successfully completed three of the four, as indicated by the checkmarks beside them. If any of the first three items do not have checkmarks, click the link within that item and add your settings.

Select the Databases panel to set the fourth item on the list: Create a Connection. This setting controls how your dynamic Web pages connect to a database. You'll explore two popular ways to connect to databases: using an ODBC driver (Data Source Name) and using a custom data string.

Using ODBC to Connect to a Data Source

When developing dynamic Web pages using ASP on a Windows computer, it's common to connect to a database by using Open Database Connectivity (ODBC, a standard developed by Microsoft for database connection). To use ODBC, you select Data Source Name (DSN) from the Databases drop-down list, as shown in Figure 13.15. You can set up a connection to a DSN for a database located on your local development machine or on a remote server. Even if you are using a local Web server, you can still connect to a remote database.

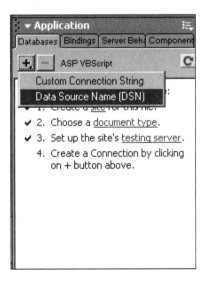

Figure 13.15

Select the type of database connection from the Databases drop-down list.

The Data Source Name (DSN) dialog box opens, where you set the connection information for the database. First, name the connection. If you have previously defined the ODBC driver for the database (you'll explore this in a minute), you simply select the DSN from the drop-down list in this dialog box. If you need to define the DSN, click on the Define button to open the ODBC Data Source Administrator.

Select the System DSN tab, as shown in Figure 13.16. You need to create a systemwide DSN so that the application server can access it to process your dynamic Web pages. A User DSN does not give the server privileges to access the DSN definition and driver.

In this example, you can use the database created by the Learning Site extension covered in Chapter 14, "Tracking with Learning Site." This is an access database containing tables that track student progress through an eLearning application. This database is covered in more depth in Chapter 14. Click the Add button, select the Microsoft Access Driver (*.mdb) from the list, and click the Finish button.

Figure 13.16

Add a System DSN so that the DSN is available to the application server.

System DSN tab

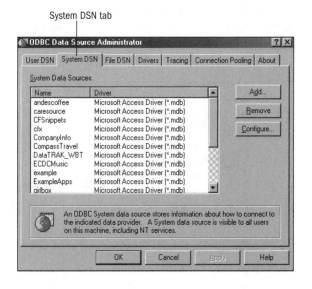

Enter the Data Source Name in the text box at the top, and enter an optional description of the connection. Click the Select button to select the Access database file with the .mdb extension. The ODBC Microsoft Access Setup dialog box should look similar to

Figure 13.17. Click the OK button to close the ODBC Data Source Administrator. Select your newly created DSN from the drop-down list in Dreamweaver's Data Source Name (DSN) dialog box. Click the Test button to make sure that Dreamweaver connects successfully with the database.

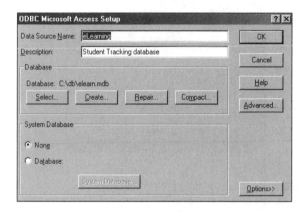

Figure 13.17
You create a new DSN using the Access database driver in the ODBC Data Source Administrator.

The beauty of ODBC is that you can connect to different databases on different computers as long as the ODBC connections use the same DSN. So I can test my dynamic Web pages on my local development machine by using the DSN "eLearning" connecting to an Access database. Later I can load my dynamic Web pages onto a remote server. The dynamic Web pages will work, as long as the remote server has a DSN with the same name as the one I used during development. The DSN can even connect to a different type of database (Microsoft SQL Server, for instance), and as long as that database has the same tables structure, everything will work fine.

You've just configured a connection to a local DSN, so the Data Source Name (DSN) dialog box should have the Using Local DSN option selected. If you had connected to a DSN defined on another computer, you would select Using DSN on Testing Server. Click the OK button, and Dreamweaver adds a directory to your site root called Connections. This directory contains a single ASP file defining the connection.

Now your database connection is active, and you can view the structure and fields available in the database tables in Dreamweaver's

Databases panel. Expand the database you just defined by clicking on the small plus (+) sign next to its name. Then expand the Tables view in the same way. Expand one of the tables to see the fields it contains, as shown in Figure 13.18.

Figure 13.18
Dreamweaver displays the tables and fields in the connected database.

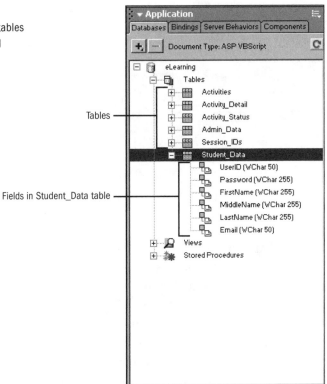

Tables

Fields in Student_Data table

Using a Custom Connection String to Connect to a Data Source

As long as you know the correct parameters to enter, you can also connect to a database by selecting Custom Connection String from the Databases drop-down list. This connection method to the database can be much quicker than an ODBC connection. You'll need to consult the Dreamweaver documentation or the documentation for your database to figure out what to enter as the connection string. This is the connection string to the database example used earlier:

```
Driver={Microsoft Access Driver (*.mdb)};DBQ=C:\db\elearn.mdb
```

The choices available for connections vary, depending on the server technology you selected when setting up your site. Figure 13.19 shows the Databases drop-down list for a site configured to create JSP pages on the Mac.

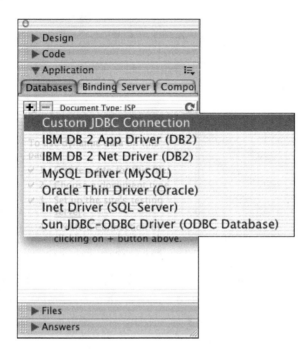

Figure 13.19
The Databases drop-down list presents choices based on the server technology your site is configured for.

Selecting the MySQL driver opens a partially filled-in dialog box, shown in Figure 13.20. In this example, the server is located on another machine accessed by its IP address (240.13.41.15) at a specific port (1520). The name of the database is courses.

Figure 13.20
You'll need to specify the URL to the MySQL server location and the appropriate driver for the database in the MySQL driver dialog box.

Authenticating Users

Now that you've defined all the preliminaries for dynamic Web pages, you can add a login page to your site. The login page collects a user ID and password from the learner and checks it against the database. This exercise assumes that you've set up the database used with the Learning Site extension described in Chapter 14. You can jump ahead to that chapter now, or you can follow along, creating the ASP page and then test it after you've completed Chapter 14.

After the learner has been authenticated by successfully logging in, each Web page in your site needs to have code added to check for an authenticated user. After you create the login page, you'll add the authentication code to each page. When this code has been added, you need to log in to the Web site every time you test a Web page, so this step should always be your last one when developing an eLearning application.

In the rest of this chapter, you'll explore using some of the *server behaviors* that come with Dreamweaver MX. Server behaviors are blocks of code prescripted to perform an operation on a dynamic Web page. Server behaviors are scripted in whatever application server scripting language you specified in your site definition. So if you are creating a site in JSP, Dreamweaver MX enters JSP code, and if you are using CFML, that's the language inserted into your Web pages.

Creating a New User Form

Power User Tip

Dreamweaver MX doesn't have authentication server behaviors available for ASP.NET or PHP.

First, create a page for registering a new user. Create a new Web page (File, New), selecting the Page Designs category in the New Document dialog box. From the Page Designs column select UI:Register as the page design. Save this Web page as newuser.asp. The new page contains a form with a number of text fields where the new user can enter information to be placed in the database. You might not be able to see the form delimiter (a red dashed line), but you should see the

`<form>` tag in the Tag Selector when you select one of the text fields. In the following steps, you'll modify this form and add a server behavior to enter the new user in the database:

1. Select the three rows at the bottom of the table that contain fields for Gender, Birth Date, and the generic Yes/No radio buttons, and delete these rows. The easiest way to select the three rows is to place your cursor in the top left cell and drag along all of the cells. Right-click (Command click on the Mac) and select the Delete Row command from the Table submenu of the context menu.

2. Change the label User Name to UserID, and then change the name of the text field to UserID in the Property inspector, as shown in Figure 13.21. The names you use aren't random; they are the names of fields that exist in the database. Remember that capitalization is important: UserID isn't the same as userID.

3. Select the text field next to the label Password and name it Password. Change its type in the Property inspector to Password so that any characters typed into the field are replaced with asterisks.

4. Select the text field next to the label Confirm and name it Confirm. Change its type to Password, too.

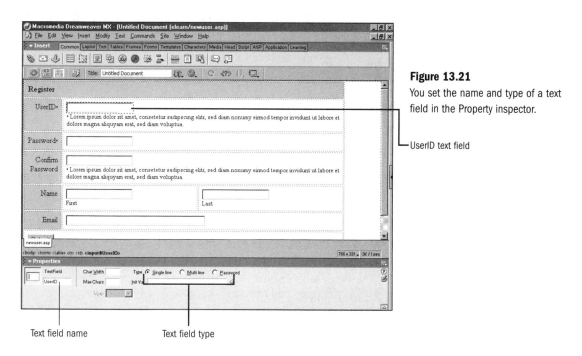

Figure 13.21
You set the name and type of a text field in the Property inspector.

UserID text field

Text field name

Text field type

5. Add a new column to the row containing the Name label (for the middle name) by clicking in the right column and inserting a column (Modify, Table, Insert Column). Copy the first or last name text field and label (Edit, Copy), and then paste it (Edit, Paste) into the new cell. Change the label to Middle.

6. Select the text field for the first name and name it FirstName. Name the middle name text field MiddleName and the last name text field LastName.

7. Select the email text field and name it Email.

8. Make sure your Web server is running before you preview the Web page in the browser. Preview the Web page in your browser, but don't click the Submit button yet (you haven't set that up yet). If your site definition is set up correctly, you should see the page displayed in the browser and an absolute URL beginning with http:// as the file location. If you receive errors, check your server connection and file permissions. Also, examine the error for any line numbers and check the code in your Web page for anything that looks unusual on the line.

9. Open the Server Behaviors panel, click the drop-down menu (+), and select the Insert Record behaviors. In the Insert Record dialog box, select the eLearning connection you defined previously, and select Student_Data as the table where the data will be inserted. Click the Browse button to select index.html as the page where the user inserts a record.

10. The bottom half of the Insert Record dialog box enables you to select which form element goes into which field in the database, as shown in Figure 13.22. Because you named your text fields the same as the fields in the database, Dreamweaver is good at matching them up. You'll need to double-check that Dreamweaver has matched fields correctly, and make sure that all the fields are submitted as text.

The Confirm text field should be set to <ignore>. This is the field where the user enters their password a second time. You'll use a form validation behavior next to make sure that the Password and the Confirm text fields match. You don't need to submit the Confirm text field to the database because the Password text field is submitted.

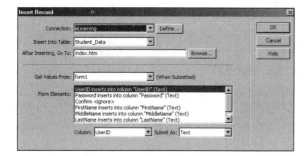

11. Click the OK button to have Dreamweaver insert the code into your Web page.

You can preview your Web page in the browser, and then create a new user, if you'd like. You can check whether the record was actually created by opening the Access database (if you have Microsoft Access), or you can wait until you create the login page in the next section. If you insert a record without any errors, it is likely that you successfully added a new user to the database! Remember to write down the user ID and password so that you can use them to log in later. If you need to make changes to the Insert Record server behavior, simply double-click to open it in the Server Behaviors panel.

There are two additional issues to deal with in your new user form. You have to add code to the page that checks whether the two password entries match. You also need to check that the user ID does not already exist in the database. You download an extension from the Macromedia Exchange to check the passwords and use a Dreamweaver MX server behavior to check the user ID.

Although Dreamweaver MX comes with a Validate Form behavior (a behavior, *not* a server behavior, available from the Behaviors panel), it will not check whether two text fields within a form match. There is a Check Form behavior that does the trick. It was created by Jaro von Flocken, and you can download it free from the Macromedia Exchange (search for the name in the Search box on the main page). Download and install the Check Form behavior using the Extension Manager (you'll need to restart Dreamweaver MX). Sorry, Mac users but this extension is only available for Windows.

You'll attach the Check Form behavior to the Submit button so that
the two password entries are checked when the learner clicks the
Submit button. Click the Submit button, and pick the Check Form
behavior from the Yaromat submenu in the Behaviors panel. The
Check Form dialog box opens. Select the Password field in the list at
the top. Select the Text Must Be the Same radio button, and then
select the Confirm text field from the drop-down list, as shown in
Figure 13.23. Add an error message at the bottom of the dialog box,
and then click OK. Make sure that onClick is listed as the triggering
event in the Behaviors panel.

Now you need to finish the form by adding the Check New Username server behavior to the page. First, create a new Web page (File,
New) stating that the username already exists. This is the Web page
that the Check New Username server behavior will redirect the
learner to if they pick a username that exists in the database. Save
this page as nameexists.htm.

In newuser.asp, open the Server Behaviors panel. All the server behaviors involving logging in the user are listed in the User Authentication submenu of the Server Behaviors drop-down list. Select the
Check New Username server behavior. Select UserID as the Username Field, and select nameexists.htm, the page you just created, as
the page to go to if the user ID exists. Preview your Web page, and
try adding the user ID that you created earlier; you should be redi-
rected to the nameexists.htm Web page.

Figure 13.23

The Yaromat Check Form behavior
enables you to add code to compare
two text fields.

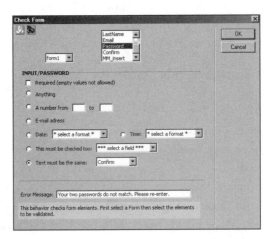

Creating a Login Page

Now you'll create the page where learners will log in each time they enter the eLearning application. First, you'll need to create a couple of Web pages:

1. Create a log in page using one of the Page Designs. Open a new Web page (File, New), select the Page Designs category, and select the UI:Login design. Save this page as login.asp.

2. Create another new Web page that learners will go to if they are unsuccessful during the login. Call this page notfound.htm.

In login.asp, change the label above the top text field to UserID, and then select that text field and change its name to UserID in the Property inspector. Name the other text field Password. Notice that the type of this text field has already been set to Password. Select the Log In User server behavior from the User Authentication submenu of the Server Behaviors drop-down list. Configure the Log In User dialog box as shown in Figure 13.24.

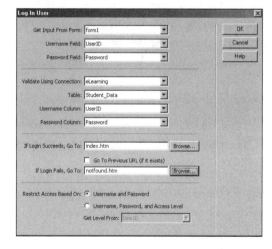

Figure 13.24
The Log In User server behavior enables you to set where the user goes after the login.

Restricting Access to Web Pages

Unless you restrict access to Web pages, your authentication efforts are useless. You need to add code to each Web page checking to see if the learner has already been authenticated and is authorized to view the current page. Otherwise, anyone can continue to view any of your Web pages. If your eLearning course requires a fee, includes confidential information, or requires authentication for some other reason, you will need to restrict access to each Web page.

To restrict access to only authenticated users, you must make each page in your eLearning application a dynamic Web page. In the example in this book, that means you need to rename each page with the .asp file extension. You also need to apply the Restrict Access to Page server behavior to each Web page. Before you modify any pages, create a simple Web page indicating that the user is not authorized to view the Web page and save it as notauthorized.htm.

To add authentication to a Web page, follow these steps:

1. Rename a Web page with the .htm file extension with the .asp file extension.

2. Open the Server Behaviors panel and select the Restrict Access to Page behavior from the User Authentication sub-menu of the Server Behaviors drop-down list.

3. The Restrict Access to Page dialog box opens. Select the Username and Password radio button to require both a username and password to authenticate the learner. If you create a Web site that requires various levels of authentication (such as administrator and user levels), you can have an access level if you have an access level field in the database.

4. Enter notauthorized.htm in the text field at the bottom of the dialog box, as shown in Figure 13.25, as the page to go to if access is denied.

When testing authentication, remember that you might have opened a session with the server previously. It's always a good idea to close the browser and reopen it to continue testing authentication functionality. Open your login page and log in to the application. You should successfully proceed to the home page. Also try logging in incorrectly.

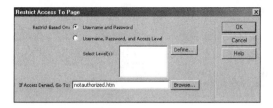

Figure 13.25
You must add the Restrict Access to Page server behavior to every Web page in your Web site to restrict access.

Creating a Report

After you've collected data in a database, you create a report to view the data. You can create reports on quiz scores, enrollment, and check to see how long students are spending in the eLearning application. You can create reports that draw data from the database and display it in a Web page. There are many different ways you can display data. This example displays a table containing all the student information in the Student_Data table.

Creating a Recordset (Query)

Creating a dynamic Web site with Dreamweaver MX requires that you understand at least a little bit about databases and *SQL* (Structured Query Language, the language of database programming, usually pronounced "sequel" or as the individual letters "S-Q-L"). You'll create a *recordset* in Dreamweaver MX, a group of database fields extracted from the database by sending a SQL statement to the database.

To create a recordset, you'll use the Bindings panel. This panel displays the fields available in the recordset and enables you to use those fields in a Web page created in Dreamweaver MX. This panel is called the Bindings panel because the process of connecting Web page content to the recordset is called *binding* data.

Open a new Web page and name it report.asp. Create a recordset by opening the Bindings panel and clicking the Bindings drop-down list. Select the Recordset command to open the Recordset dialog box. This dialog box has two modes: simple and advanced. Make sure you are in simple mode (the Advanced button is at the right of the dialog box). Configure the Recordset dialog box as shown in Figure 13.26, naming your recordset rsStudentInfo and selecting the Student_Data table. Click the Test button to see all the values from the Student_Data table.

Figure 13.26

The simple view of the Recordset dialog box enables you to select a single table and the fields that you will use for your report.

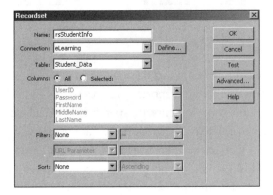

If you click the Advanced button, you can see the SQL statement you have just created. It should look something like this: SELECT * FROM Student_Data. This statement tells the database to return all the values (*) from the Student_Data table. As you learn more about application servers and need to perform more complicated tasks, you can use the advanced mode of the Recordset dialog box. Click the OK button to create the recordset. Expanding the recordset in the Bindings table displays all the recordset's values plus a few special values useful for displaying pages of data.

Select the Application tab of the Insert bar. These objects are all special objects that you can use when working with a dynamic Web site. Select the Dynamic Table object (also Insert, Application Objects, Dynamic Table). This object enables you to create a table displaying all the records in the recordset, dynamically creating a new table row for each record.

In the Dynamic Table dialog box, select the rsStudentInfo recordset and click the option to Show All Records. You can leave the border at 1. Click the OK button to save your settings; the page should look like Figure 13.27. Dreamweaver MX puts data field placeholders in each of the cells. Preview the Web page in your browser to see the report results.

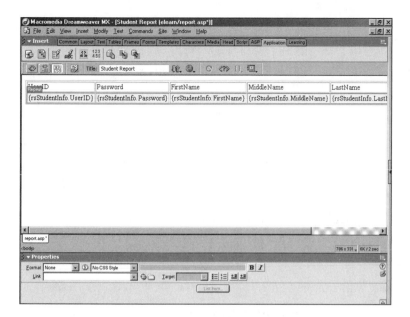

Figure 13.27

Placeholders appear on the Web page where data will be placed by the application server.

Previewing Dynamic Pages Using the Live Data View

When you properly set up local or remote previewing using the browser, you can also preview your final pages right in Dreamweaver by using Live Data view. Clicking the Live Data View button on the toolbar or choosing the Live Data command on the View menu supplies the dynamic pages with live data from the database. This view enables you to modify the data's layout while immediately seeing the results of your edits on the appearance of the live data.

Summary

In this chapter, you explored all the server technologies you can use with Dreamweaver MX. You learned about the issues you need to consider when selecting one of the technologies and how to configure your site definition for the chosen technology to work. You learned how to connect to a database and create a recordset (query). You also learned how to use several of Dreamweaver MX's server behaviors to insert a record into the database and authenticate users. You also created a report using one of the application objects and viewed data from the database in Dreamweaver MX by using Live Data view.

chapter 14

Tracking with Learning Site

LEARNING SITE, AVAILABLE FREE on the Macromedia Exchange,

is designed to construct, track, and administer an eLearning

application. In Dreamweaver MX, Learning Site can create a

tracking Access database along with Active Server Pages (ASP)-

coded Web pages ready for you to track and administer students'

activities with the eLearning application. This extension offers an

inexpensive method of tracking a small number of students.

Even if you are implementing a large-scale eLearning effort using an LMS (covered in Chapter 15, "Using a Learning Management System"), you might want to begin your project by developing a prototype with Learning Site. This gives you a chance to handle potential standards-compliance issues when dealing with the Learning Site Access database, developed based on the Aviation Industry CBT Committee (AICC) guidelines (covered in Chapter 15). Because the standards are designed to create eLearning applications that work on any compliant tracking system, you should be able to easily transfer your eLearning applications over to the LMS when it is available.

You don't need to use Learning Site to create your entire eLearning application. Although the extension is certainly capable of helping you construct an entire Web site and its navigation, you could simply create a portion of your application—a quiz for instance—using the extension.

In this chapter, you will understand the following:

- How to configure Learning Site
- How Learning Site tracks to a frameset
- How to track CourseBuilder interactions
- How to administer the eLearning application using Learning Site

Using Learning Site

The Learning Site extension's tracking capabilities are only a portion of what the extension offers. It actually offers a user interface complete with built-in navigation and various interface designs. This section introduces Learning Site functionality.

In Chapter 2, "Assembling the Team and Collecting the Tools," you learned about the Macromedia Exchange, Macromedia's repository for extensions to Dreamweaver (www.macromedia.com/exchange/dreamweaver/). To use Learning Site, you'll need to download it from the Learning category of the Exchange. There are versions for both Windows and the Mac. This extension is free and was created by Macromedia.

After you've installed Learning Site, you'll see a new menu under the Site menu (actually in all the Site menus: in Dreamweaver MX's menu bar, in the Site menu in the Site panel, and in the Site menu of the Site window). This new Learning Site submenu, shown in Figure 14.1, contains the commands that enable you to add the Learning Site functionality to a current Web site (with Web pages already developed) or a new Web site. The menu contains commands to create a learning site, edit an existing learning site, and add administrative ASP files.

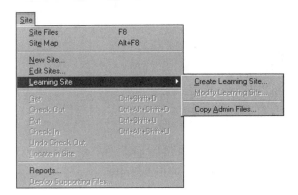

Figure 14.1
The Learning Site submenu contains the commands to add Learning Site files to your defined site.

Choose Site, Learning Site, Create Learning Site from the menu to open the Learning Site dialog box. You might see a warning message if you issue this command within a Web site that already contains files. Learning Site adds files to your site that could overwrite existing files. For instance, the default name of the learning site home page is index.htm. If you already have a file named index.htm in your site, Learning Site will overwrite it.

The Learning Site dialog box has a tabbed interface, shown in Figure 14.2, that walks you through creating a learning site. When you use this extension with Dreamweaver MX (or UltraDev 4 for those of you who have not upgraded to Dreamweaver MX), you have the option to create ASP tracking pages. If you don't plan to use the tracking capabilities of Learning Site, you can clear the Data Tracking check box in the Site tab. This disables the last three tabs: Tracking, Login, and Results.

Figure 14.2

The Learning Site dialog box has a tabbed interface like CourseBuilder's.

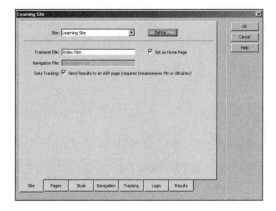

At the top of the Site tab, you can select an existing Web site or create a new site definition for your learning site. Click the Define button to create a new site definition or select an existing site from the Site drop-down list. If you are planning to use tracking, you need to configure the site definition as described in Chapter 13, "Creating and Tracking a Dynamic Web Site."

Exploring the Learning Site Frameset

Learning Site creates a *frameset*, a Web page that defines several frames, each containing a Web page. Using a framed interface enables the Web site to *maintain state* across multiple pages in your eLearning application, meaning you can track information to one of the Web pages because it stays loaded in one of the frames. One of the difficulties when tracking eLearning applications is that Web pages are served to anonymous users without an easy means of tracking who that user is.

By default, Learning Site creates a frameset containing three frames stacked one on top of each other, as shown in Figure 14.3. The top frame, named navFrame, contains the navigation. The middle frame, named mainFrame, displays the pages in the eLearning application. The contents of this frame are replaced each time the learner clicks a navigation button to move to a different Web page. The bottom frame, named cmiresults, is an empty frame, invisible to the learner, which is used to store tracking data.

Frames have several characteristics that make them useful in eLearning applications:

- **Continuous content display**—You can display the content in a frame, such as the navigation frame, without reloading it when the learner navigates to another page. This keeps the Web page loaded in the browser so that the learner doesn't see the slight delay while images and other elements reload into the browser.

- **Targeting**—You can have a hyperlink in one frame load content into a separate frame.

- **Continuous tracking**—You can have frame content, such as the cmiresults frame, that remains continuously loaded in the browser window. Other frame content can update variables and read user data from this frame, maintaining tracking records.

Power User Tip

Learning Site creates a frameset, but that isn't the only way to track multiple pages. Instead of tracking to the frames, you could track each interaction on the server by creating a session. A session begins when the user visits the first ASP page in your eLearning application, and data from each page they visit can be stored in session variables. Session data is tied to a specific user and can be retrieved without accessing a database. Session data is similar to cookies except it is stored on the server.

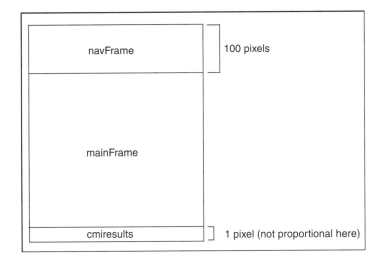

Figure 14.3
The frameset used to create a learning site contains three frames.

You can view a Web page's frame layout in the Frames panel (Window, Others, Frames), shown in Figure 14.4. You can select a frame in the Frames panel and modify its properties in the Property inspector. Figure 14.4 shows the properties of the navFrame that Learning Site creates. Note that the cmiresults frame doesn't appear in the Frames panel because it is too small.

The easiest way to select a frameset so that you can view and edit its properties is to select the <frameset> tag in the Tag Selector. The frameset created by Learning Site contains a nested frameset that contains the bottom two frames. Frameset properties, shown in Figure 14.5, enable you to set the frame size and border properties.

Figure 14.4
Dreamweaver displays the frameset in the Document window and the frameset configuration in the Frames panel. Note that you cannot see the cmiresults in the Frames panel because it is too small.

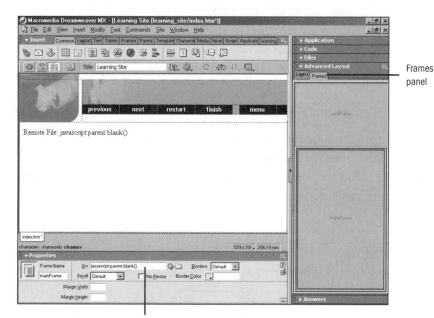

Frames panel

Frame properties

Figure 14.5
Select the **<frameset>** tag in the Tag Selector to display the frameset properties in the Property inspector.

You can modify the frame configuration to suit the visual layout you prefer. You must be careful to maintain the same frame names (the code depends on those names). Also, you need to leave the code in the Web pages intact because there are many interdependencies between the frames.

Designing the Learning Site (the Site Tab)

This section covers the first four tabs in the Learning Site dialog box: Site, Pages, Style, and Navigation. You use these basic tabs whether or not you've enabled tracking. (Learning Site's tracking capabilities are covered in "Exploring Tracking with the Learning Site," later in this chapter.)

Power User Tip

If you close the Learning Site dialog box, you can open and edit your Learning Site configuration by selecting the Modify Learning Site command (Site, Learning Site, Modify Learning Site).

The Site tab is where you set the filename of the Web page containing the frameset. Naming gets a little confusing when working with frames because you have both filenames and frame names (two separate names). You can leave the default name as index.htm or change it to another name. If this page will be your site's home page, make sure the Set as Home Page check box is selected. You'll want this page to be the home page if you are designing an entire eLearning application with Learning Site. If you are just designing a quiz, or part of an application, you can leave this option unchecked.

Adding Content to the Learning Site (the Pages Tab)

The Pages tab of the Learning Site dialog box enables you to load or design the pages that the site contains. If you already have pages of eLearning content in the site, you can load those pages into the Pages list box at the top. Otherwise, you can have the Learning Site dialog box create new pages for you, specifying a filename, title, background color, and type of page.

First, try loading existing Web pages into the Pages tab. They could be pages you created earlier in this book. To add an existing Web page to the Learning Site, click the + button. Learning Site adds an untitled document to the Pages list box. You can ignore the Page Is radio buttons because they are used only for creating new Web pages with Learning Site. Load an existing page by clicking on the folder icon next to the Page File text box and selecting an existing page in your Web site. Figure 14.6 shows three existing Web pages loaded into the Pages list box. You can delete pages from this list by clicking the - button, or reorder the entries by using the up and down arrow buttons.

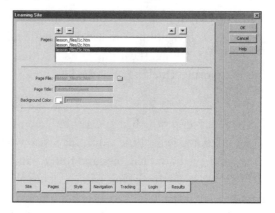

If existing Web pages contain CourseBuilder interactions, those interactions need to have the Knowledge Track check box selected (in the General tab of the CourseBuilder interaction). In the Tracking tab of the CourseBuilder Interaction dialog box, the weight of the question needs to be set to at least 1. The interactions can also have score settings for the correct choice(s).

When you create a new page in Learning Site, you can choose to add three different types: Blank, Media, or CourseBuilder Interaction. When you add a new page to the Page list box, you select the type of page by selecting the corresponding radio buttons. Select Blank and simply add a filename, title, and background color; you can modify the Web page later. Select Media to add an Authorware, Flash, or Shockwave object to the page. You select the object file to include in the page along with size attributes, as shown in Figure 14.7.

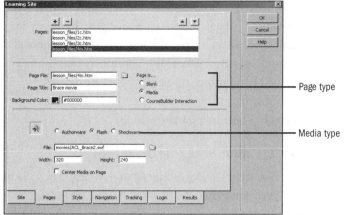

Figure 14.7
Create new pages in the Pages tab. The pages can be blank, or they can include CourseBuilder interactions or other media files, such as Flash.

Page type

Media type

You'll need to have the CourseBuilder extension installed to take advantage of adding a CourseBuilder interaction directly in the Learning Site dialog box. Select the CourseBuilder Interaction radio button, and the Learning Site dialog box displays a list of available CourseBuilder interactions, as shown in Figure 14.8. Select one of the interactions from the list; you set up the interaction by opening the page and editing it. If you haven't added the CourseBuilder support files to your site yet, the Learning Site dialog box prompts you to add them when you save your settings (by clicking the OK button).

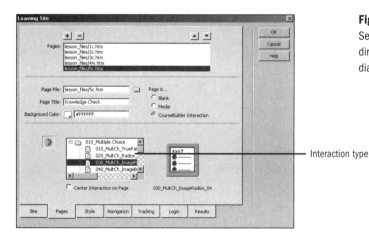

Figure 14.8
Select a CourseBuilder interaction directly in the Learning Site dialog box.

Interaction type

Later, when you've completed the Learning Site dialog box setup, the extension creates the new Web pages for you. Each page will include all the code necessary to track and navigate through the eLearning application. Consult the Learning Site documentation, available by clicking the Help button in the Learning Site dialog box, if you plan to track information from Flash movies; you'll need to complete some steps in Flash to enable tracking.

Applying a Layout Style (the Style Tab)

Learning Site offers five prebuilt layout styles. You can use one of these styles or your own custom styles. The styles, which you set in the Style tab of the Learning Site dialog box, set the background and button images in the navigation.htm Web page.

When you select the Custom layout style in the Style tab, text boxes appear, as shown in Figure 14.9, that enable you to set up six different buttons. Click the folder icon to browse to the button's up state. You do not need to enter the dimensions of the button images because the Learning Site dialog box calculates them for you. You simply load the up state of the buttons into the Learning Site dialog box, but you can open navigation.htm later and add the other states, as described in Chapter 6, "Constructing the Interface."

Figure 14.9
Select a prebuilt layout style or custom-build it with your own images.

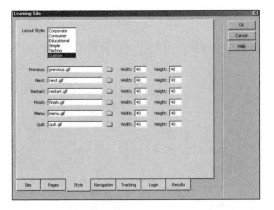

Learning Site copies the images you specify in the Style tab to the images directory (created by CourseBuilder or Learning Site). This is one of the support directories you explored in Chapter 10, "Including CourseBuilder Interactions and Controls." Don't be alarmed by the URLs beginning with file:///; Learning Site will use a correct relative URL for the buttons in navigation.htm.

Learning Site configures the buttons with the correct JavaScript calls. You are not required to use all the button types available in Learning Site. You can always delete buttons by editing the navigation.htm file in Dreamweaver.

Configuring the Learning Site Navigation (the Navigation Tab)

Learning Site offers several navigation choices and adds the complicated JavaScript for you. You should consult the course specifications you defined in Chapter 3, "Establishing the Course Specifications," to confirm how the course should work. What happens when learners quit the eLearning application? What happens when they click the Next button on the last page? Those questions are examples of the types of navigation behaviors you specify in the Navigation tab. The six choices available in the Learning Site Navigation tab are shown in Figure 14.10.

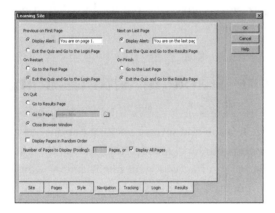

Figure 14.10
You configure the navigation through using the Navigation tab's settings.

The Navigation tab enables you to configure these settings:

- **Previous on First Page**—When learners are on the first page and click the Previous button, you can display an alert message (like the Popup Message behavior) or take them back to the login page. You'll explore the login page later in the section "Exploring the Login Page (the Login Tab)."

- **Next on Last Page**—When learners are on the last page and click the Next button, you can display an alert message or take them to the results page. You'll explore the results page later in the "Exploring the Results Page (the Results Tab)" section.

- **On Restart**—When learners click the Restart button or reload or refresh the Web page with the browser controls, you can take them back to the first page or the login page.

- **On Finish**—When learners click the Finish button, you can take them to the last page or the results page.

- **On Quit**—When learners click the Quit button, you can take them to the results page or a specific Web page in your site, or you can close the browser window.

- **Display Pages in Random Order**—This setting enables you to randomly present quiz questions. You can also create a random pool of questions by electing to display only a certain number of questions to the learner.

If you plan to delete any of these buttons from navigation.htm, you do not need to configure them here. For instance, if you are not presenting a quiz, you probably do not need the Finish button, which controls completing a quiz.

Exploring Tracking with Learning Site

There are various reasons to track a learner's progress through an eLearning application and several tracking options. At one extreme, your application could include a certification exam requiring vigorous supervision. Alternatively, you might simply want to create a login so that unauthorized users do not access the course. The first example requires intense monitoring by a tracking system (and probably a human proctor), but the second example tracks very little information about the learner.

In Chapter 12, "Scoring an Assessment and Hiding the Answers," you explored tracking within the browser using JavaScript. After the learner closes the browser, or even goes to another Web site, all the tracking data is lost. Using cookies to track learners enables you to maintain data from browser session to browser session, but cookies are browser specific, not learner specific. The data isn't available if the learner moves to a different computer (or even a different browser version on the same computer!).

In Chapter 13, "Creating and Tracking a Dynamic Web Site," you explored how Dreamweaver MX allows a Web site to connect to a database, enabling you to log in learners and track information about them. You used server behaviors to have Dreamweaver MX create dynamic Web pages for you. With Learning Site, many of the necessary dynamic Web pages and even the database are created for you automatically!

This section explores the remaining three tabs in the Learning Site dialog box. You'll also become more familiar with the table structure of the database the Learning Site creates.

Creating a Tracking Database (the Tracking Tab)

Learning Site creates the Web pages that enable tracking the learner to a database using ASP. You use the Tracking tab to set up the data connection. You can define an ODBC connection and specify a DSN, all in this tab, and the information is added to the site definition. Remember, when previewing your site using a Web server on your local machine, it is easiest to save your site in the server root directory.

At the top of the Tracking tab, shown in Figure 14.11, you specify an activity ID and name. This information is used in the database to identify the results of this particular learning activity (the current Web site). Select the Include Results Page check box if you plan to display quiz results to the learner.

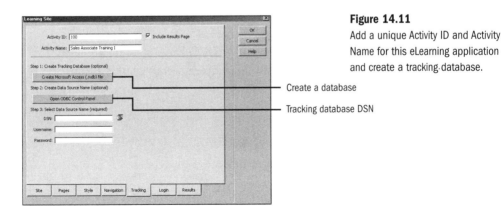

Figure 14.11
Add a unique Activity ID and Activity Name for this eLearning application and create a tracking database.

Create a database

Tracking database DSN

An important consideration when tracking learner activities is the level of *granularity* that you want to track. Granularity is the degree of detail something can be broken down into. In an eLearning application, granularity is defined by the number of content chunks. The current Web site is considered a single activity (defined by the Activity ID) by the tracking database. So do you want to create a new site definition for each lesson in your course so that it is tracked as a unique activity? Or will it work for your eLearning application to track the entire course as a single activity?

Create the database by clicking the Create Microsoft Access (.mdb) File button. Save the database on your computer. If you are developing on a Mac, you can save the database and transfer it to a Web server running on Windows. You do not need to have Microsoft Access to create this database, although you will need Access to open and look at it.

It isn't a good idea to save a database in a directory that has permissions set to be available over the Web. These public permissions may allow people to view the data in the database. Sometimes, databases used for eLearning applications have sensitive information, such as Social Security numbers, test scores, and telephone numbers. I usually save databases in a directory called "db" that is not within the server root or in a virtual Web directory. If you are previewing your dynamic Web pages using a local Web server, the database probably isn't available to anonymous viewers over the Web anyway.

If you need to define a new DSN, click the Open ODBC Control Panel button. As you learned in Chapter 13, you need to select the System tab of the ODBC Data Source Administrator and create a new DSN, using the Access driver linking to the database you just created. Close the ODBC Data Source Administrator, saving your settings.

Select the DSN for the learning site database by clicking on the small globe icon to the right of the DSN text box. Select the DSN from the list and click the OK button to insert the DSN into the text box. Add a username and password if your database requires it. (The default learning site database does not require a username or password.)

Exploring the Learning Site Database

The Access 97 database that Learning Site creates has six tables: several that track learner activities, one that maintains records of student data, and one that maintains records of administrator data. The database is constructed to be compliant with the Aviation Industry CBT Committee (AICC) guidelines (AICC version 2.0). This is one of the major tracking standards, and you'll learn more about it in Chapter 15. The Access database may be viewed in more recent versions of Access but will have to go through a conversion process to be edited in a more recent version.

The first four database tables described in Tables 14.1 through Table 14.4 are used to track the learner. References are made to the corresponding CourseBuilder settings when appropriate. Remember that interactions can be tracked by using the individual tracking methods for Authorware, Flash, Shockwave, and other files.

The Activities table, shown in Table 14.1, creates a record for each Dreamweaver Web site you define as a learning site. For instance, a single quiz defined as a site in Dreamweaver would be a single activity.

Table 14.1   The Activities Table

Field	Data Type	Description
ActivityID	Text	A unique identifier for the activity, entered in the ActivityID text box in the Tracking tab (refer to Figure 14.11).
ActivityName	Text	A unique name for the activity, entered in the Tracking tab.
ActivityURL	Text	The URL of the activity.
ActivityDescription	Memo	A description of the activity. There is no place to enter this information in the Learning Site dialog box.

The Activity_Detail table, shown in Table 14.2, creates a record for each Dreamweaver Web site you define as a learning site. For example, a single quiz defined as a site in Dreamweaver would be a single activity.

Table 14.2 The Activity_Detail Table

Field	Data Type	Description
ActivityID	Text	Corresponds to one of the activities in the Activities table.
UserID	Text	Corresponds to the UserID of one of the users in the Student_Data table.
Question	Text	Records the Interaction ID entered in the Tracking tab of the CourseBuilder Interaction dialog box.
UserResponse	Text	Records the user's response (the answer choice). This is the value in the Name text box in the Choices tab of the CourseBuilder Interaction dialog box.
Result	Text	Records whether the user's response was correct , incorrect (w), or not judged (n). This value corresponds with the selection in the Choices tab of the CourseBuilder Interaction dialog box.
QuestionTime	Text	Records the time (hours, minutes, and seconds) the question was answered.
QuestionDate	Text	Records the date (month, day, and year) the question was answered.
TypeInteraction	Text	Records the AICC code for the interaction type: m means a drag and drop interaction, t means a button interaction, f means a text interaction, and c means any other type of interaction.
CorrectResponse	Text	Records the name of the correct answer (specified in the Choices tab of the CourseBuilder Interaction dialog box).

Field	Data Type	Description
ResponseValue	Text	Not currently used, but might be used in future versions.
Weight	Text	Records the value entered in the Weight text box in the Tracking tab of the Course-Builder Interaction dialog box. Weight specifies how much the interaction's score affects the total score.
Latency	Text	Records the latency value, the amount of time users spent on the interaction (the difference between the time they entered the Web page and the time they completed the interaction).
ObjectiveID	Text	Records the value entered in the Objective ID text box in the Tracking tab of the CourseBuilder Interaction dialog box.

The Activity_Status table, shown in Table 14.3, creates a record with information about completing the group of activities. For a quiz, this information would be the total score and total time for each user.

Table 14.3 The Activity_Status Table

Field	Data Type	Description
ActivityID	Text	Records the ActivityID corresponding to an activity in the Activities table.
ActivityName	Text	Records the ActivityName corresponding to an activity in the Activities table.
UserID	Text	Records a UserID corresponding to a user in the Student_Data table.

continues

Table 14.3 Continued

Field	Data Type	Description
TotalTime	Text	Records the total time users spent in the complete activity, from the time they entered the first Web page to the time they clicked the Quit or Finish buttons.
ActivityDate	Date/Time	Records the date the activity was performed.
Score	Number	Records a total score for the entire activity, based on the weight and score the learner received on each interaction. The scores are converted to a percentage value, with 100% being a perfect score.
Location	Text	Records the last page the learner entered before finishing (clicking the Finish or Quit buttons) the activity.
Status	Text	Records whether the learner completed the activity (reached the last page of the activity). The value c means complete and i means incomplete.

The Session_IDs table, shown in Table 14.4, creates a record describing a current session for a user. This record is updated each time a student logs in.

Table 14.4 The Session_IDs Table

Field	Data Type	Description
SessionID	Autonumber	A unique value automatically assigned by the database for a user session.
UserID	Text	Records a UserID corresponding to a user in the Student_Data table.
ActivityID	Text	Records the ActivityID corresponding to an activity in the Activities table.

The tracking tables opened in Access look like Figure 14.12.

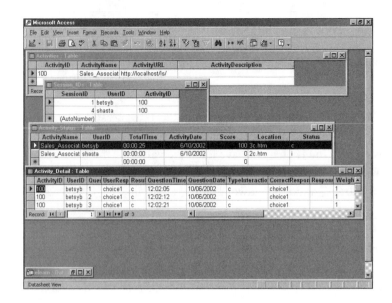

Figure 14.12
The tracking tables display student activity records in Access.

The Student_Data table, shown in Table 14.5, creates a record with data for each student. Each record must have a unique value for the StudentID field, the value that the student uses to log in.

Table 14.5 The Student_Data Table

Field	Data Type	Description
UserID	Text	A unique value entered in the Add New User form (adduser.asp) that identifies a student. The user logs into the activity using this value.
Password	Text	A password value entered in the Add New User form. The user logs into the activity using this value.
FirstName	Text	The first name value entered in the Add New User form.
MiddleName	Text	The middle name value entered in the Add New User form.

continues

Table 14.5 Continued

Field	Data Type	Description
LastName	Text	The last name value entered in the Add New User form.
Email	Text	The email value entered in the Add New User form.

The Admin_Data table, shown in Table 14.6, creates a record with data for each administrator. The database can have multiple administrators, and each must have a unique value for the AdminID field. This table is created with a default administrator: the AdminID value is "admin" and the Password value is "admin."

Table 14.6 The Admin_Data Table

Field	Data Type	Description
UserID	Text	A unique value entered in the Add New User form (adduser.asp) that identifies an administrator. The administrator logs into the Admin Menu dialog box using this value. A record with the value admin is available so that you can log in the first time.
Password	Text	A password value entered in the Add New User form. The administrator logs into the Admin Menu dialog box using this value.
FirstName	Text	The first name value entered in the Add New User form.
MiddleName	Text	The middle name value entered in the Add New User form.
LastName	Text	The last name value entered in the Add New User form.
Email	Text	The email value entered in the Add New User form.

The user records tables opened in Access look like Figure 14.13.

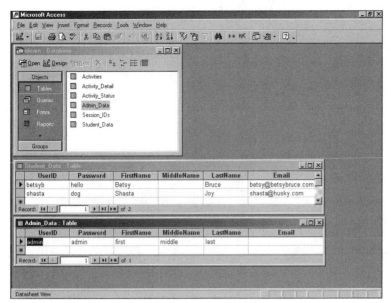

Figure 14.13
The user records tables display student and admin data in Access.

Exploring the Login Page (the Login Tab)

The Login tab of the Learning Site dialog box enables you to set the filename, title, and layout style of the student login page, the page where all learners will log in to the eLearning application. Enter a filename and title, as shown in Figure 14.14. You can select one of the existing layout styles in the Login Logo list box, or you can select Custom and navigate to your own logo. Remember, you can always modify this Web page in Dreamweaver later.

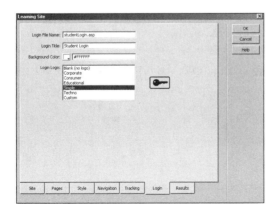

Figure 14.14
Configure the login page's filename, title, and layout style in the Login tab.

If you modify the student login page, you need to be careful not to change or delete the existing code. There are a number of server behaviors and code objects in the Web page, shown in Figure 14.15. You can change layout attributes (such as colors and alignment), add CSS styles, and create layout tables, but be careful not to disturb the existing code.

Figure 14.15
You can modify the ASP pages in Dreamweaver MX as long as you do not change the code.

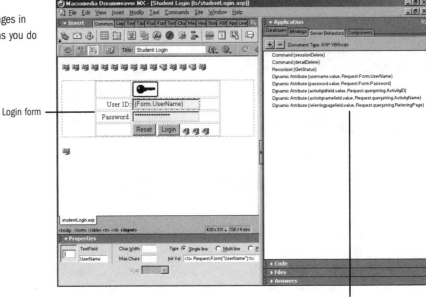

Login form

Server behaviors

Exploring the Results Page (the Results Tab)

The results page is presented to learners after they've completed the entire activity defined in this learning site; they can click the Finish or the Quit button to see the results page, depending on how you've set up the navigation. Like the Login tab, you set the filename, title, and layout style for the results page in the Results tab of the Learning Site dialog box, shown in Figure 14.16.

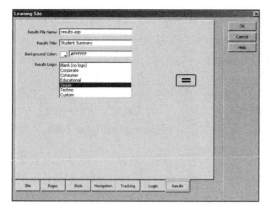

Figure 14.16
Configure the filename, title, and layout style of the results page in the Results tab.

The results page displays several fields from the Activity_Status table at the top of the report (ActivityName, Score, TotalTime, and ActivityDate), as shown in Figure 14.17. At the bottom is a dynamic repeating table row displaying data from the Activity_Detail table. The table displays the Question, UserResponse, Result, and Latency fields.

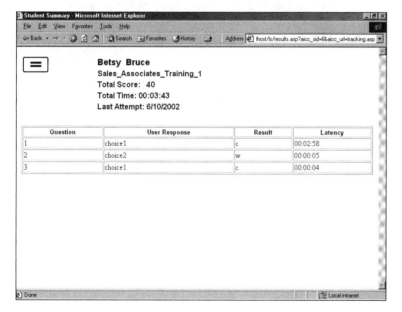

Figure 14.17
After the learner finishes the activities, the results report displays the score information.

Adding Learning Site Administration Files

To complete the learning site, you must add the administration files enabling you to add new users and view reports about eLearning application activities. Select the Copy Admin Files command (Site, Learning Site, Copy Admin Files) to add the following files to your site in the site root:

- **adminLogin.asp**—The login Web page for the administrator. Initially, you can log in using the user ID "admin" and the password "admin." You'll want to add a more secure administration user and delete the default user.

- **adminmenu.asp**—The Admin Menu is displayed after you log in as an administrator. It enables you to add and modify users, display reports, and search for students or activities, as shown in Figure 14.18.

Figure 14.18
The Admin Menu enables you to administer the eLearning application when using Learning Site.

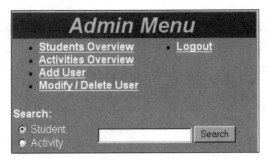

The Copy Admin Files command creates a Reports directory containing the following files:

- **activities.asp**—Displays a list of all activities in the database. Each activity requires a separate learning site eLearning application. Click the Activities Overview link in the Admin Menu.

- **activitysummary.asp**—Creates a report displaying the individual user results for a certain activity, including the average, high, and low scores. Click an activity name in the Activities Overview report.

- **adduser.asp**—A form enabling you to insert a new student or a new administrator. Click the Add User link in the Admin Menu.

- **deleteuser.asp**—Deletes a student or an administrator record. Click the Modify/Delete User link in the Admin Menu, and then click the Delete link next to a user record.

- **modify.asp**—Modifies an existing student or administrator record. Click the Modify/Delete User link in the Admin Menu, and then click the Modify link next to a user record.

- **modifydisplay.asp**—Displays a list of all students and administrators along with a link to modify or delete the record. Click the Modify/Delete User link in the Admin Menu.

- **searchResults.asp**—Displays a list of records that meet the search criteria you enter in the Search area of the Admin Menu.

- **studentdetail.asp**—Displays the results of the last activity attempt for a student. Click the Student Overview link in the Admin Menu, click a UserID link in the Students Overview report, and then select an activity name in the Student Summary report. This report is similar to the results.asp report learners see after they complete an activity.

- **studentsPlus.asp**—Displays the Students Summary report listing an activity summary for a student. Click the Student Overview link in the Admin Menu and click a UserID link in the Students Overview report.

Summary

In this chapter, you learned how to use Learning Site to navigate and track in an eLearning application. You explored the tracking frameset and the database tables that Learning Site creates. You also learned how to turn on tracking in a CourseBuilder interaction and explored the administration forms and reports available with Learning Site.

IN THIS CHAPTER

chapter 15

Using a Learning Management System

YOU MIGHT BE INVOLVED WITH AN ELEARNING project distributed to learners via a *learning management system* (LMS). An LMS is an application that administers the use, management, and tracking of eLearning applications. Whether or not you were involved in choosing this system, developing eLearning applications managed by an LMS will make you intimately familiar with the way it works. An LMS is also sometimes called Computer Managed Instruction (CMI).

Even if your project is not currently being launched by an LMS, you'll still want to be familiar with major learning standards (AICC and ADL SCORM, for example) and how to implement them in your eLearning applications. Building in compliant functionality during your initial development (in the templates, for example) can save a lot of time later if the organization ends up using an LMS.

Standards are important because if you develop eLearning applications that use a standard method of collecting data into an LMS, you can move those eLearning applications to any standards-compliant LMS with little reengineering. If you develop eLearning applications for a proprietary LMS, you are stuck with that LMS and its way of collecting data. Although the standards are still evolving, most LMS applications recognize and adhere to one or several of the standards, at least to minimum requirements.

This chapter features a popular LMS program called WBT Manager, available from Integrity eLearning. This LMS was the first to be certified as Aviation Industry CBT Committee (AICC) compliant (more about AICC compliance later in the chapter). This Web-based LMS has similarities with other LMS systems in that it collects and reports on data, administers students and courses, and enrolls learners. You'll need to read the documentation on your system to see how it works with Dreamweaver MX and CourseBuilder.

In this chapter, you will understand the following:

- What a learning management system is
- What the major learning standards are
- How to collect information from a multiple-page quiz and send it to an LMS
- How to use Knowledge Track with an LMS

What Is a Learning Management System?

Numerous popular LMS software packages are available today. The applications widely vary in their functionality and features, but the majority of LMS applications have these capabilities in common:

- **Administration function**—The LMS manages students and course listings.

- **Enroll learners**—Most LMS applications enable you to enroll students or allow them to self-enroll.

- **Collect and store data**—The LMS collects and stores data about students' progress and success in individual courses.

- **Reports**—The LMS offers prebuilt and (usually) ad hoc reports on student and course data.

Learning management systems are expensive software applications that should be evaluated carefully before purchase. Companies that provide this software often offer a hosting option, in which they provide the LMS hosting on their server for your content. This can be a good choice for organizations that don't want to devote IT resources to maintaining a server and database application. LMS applications are usually priced per student user; you buy a license for, say, 100 users or 10,000 users or whatever you need.

The LMS you use can run as a LAN-based client-server application or as a Web-based application. Some LMS applications have components for both server types, enabling you to deliver both traditional computer-based training (over a LAN) and eLearning applications (over the Web). Most LAN-based LMS applications require installing a client program on each student's computer.

WBT Manager, the LMS used as an example in this chapter, is a Web-based LMS that runs through a browser. Web-based LMS servers don't require any software installation on a student's computer because they run over the Web. Not only does the student access eLearning applications over the Web, but the LMS can be administered over the Web, too, as shown in Figure 15.1.

Power User Tip

I'm not in favor of LMS applications that have time expiration periods for students, limiting the amount of time they can view a course. It's acceptable to require that a student complete a course within a certain period; however, most training courses should be available to students for review and reference whenever they need them. The obvious exception would be certification assessments.

Figure 15.1

WBT Manager from Integrity eLearning is an LMS that runs in a browser and can be administered over the Web.

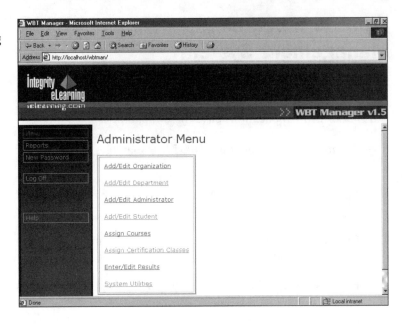

Power User Tip

Check Appendix A, "Resources," for a link to download a trial version of Web Manager.

You can use LMS applications to manage both off-the-shelf and custom courses. It's important that all types of courses can interact easily with the LMS. The way courses interact with LMS applications is described in various LMS standards (discussed in the next section, "Exploring Learning Standards").

If you haven't made a decision on which LMS you are going to use, here are some basic capabilities to look for in an LMS:

- **Standards**—It's important that an LMS adhere to one of the major LMS standards. LMS applications adhere to standards at various levels.

- **Templates**—The availability of templates and examples of eLearning applications that work with the LMS will considerably shorten your development time. It's especially useful to get Dreamweaver and CourseBuilder examples from your LMS vendor.

- **Ease of eLearning application integration**—It's best to determine how easy it is to add your eLearning application to the LMS so that students can take the course. You might be importing your course multiple times during testing phases, and understanding the complexity of the steps required to accomplish this is important.

- **Interface with other systems**—Some LMS applications can interface with human resources databases and other enterprise-type databases. This capability is useful for large organizations that want to enroll and track learners via their employment information.

Exploring Learning Standards

Several learning standards address the issues of integrating eLearning applications (and other types of learning applications) into LMS applications. The common standards are created by committees who formulate technical recommendations. The standards organizations can also certify that an LMS or specific learning applications are compliant with their particular standard.

In the past, the most common type of LMS has been a custom application that an organization creates to manage its own courseware. The developers create a custom method of storing and passing data to and from the learning applications. Unfortunately, an organization is locked into this application because any change would mean it needs to redevelop all the courseware to work with a new system.

An important role of LMS standards is defining LMS and courseware interoperability so that an organization can switch to a different LMS that adheres to the standards with minimal or no impact on courseware. The standards do this by defining a set of variables and communication methods for passing information between the courseware and the LMS. After you've developed courseware with the standard variables, you can launch and manage it from any LMS that works with the same LMS standard.

LMS standards describe the *meta-data* involved in the course definition. For instance, the author, title, objectives, and course structure can be meta-data that can be read from a file. eXtensible Markup Language (XML) is the language of choice for meta-data because of its flexibility and popularity.

The Manifest Maker for ADL SCORM extension, developed by Macromedia's Tom King, creates the meta-data necessary to create an ADL SCORM v1.2 Course Manifest. Some LMS applications use this manifest to organize and control an eLearning application. You can download the Manifest Maker, shown in Figure 15.2, from the Macromedia Exchange for Dreamweaver at www.macromedia.com/exchange/dreamweaver. You open the Manifest Maker dialog box from the Commands menu (Commands, Manifest Maker).

The Manifest Maker creates several documents, including imsmanifest.xml, shown in Figure 15.3. This document, created in XML, defines the course's structure and file locations. You should consult your LMS documentation to see whether it supports this document and how you should configure the Web site to work properly with the LMS.

The learning standards do not stand independently; instead, they work together to create open standards that interrelate. Members of standards organizations are often members of other standards organizations, too. There are four major LMS standards:

- **Aviation Industry Computer-Based Training Committee (AICC)**—The AICC is an international association of technology-based training professionals that develops guidelines for the deployment, delivery, and evaluation of training technologies. The AICC pioneered the most widely accepted interoperability standards for computer-based training and eLearning applications. The relevant publications for standards are called AICC Guidelines and Recommendations (AGRs). See AICC AGR 6 and AICC AGR 10 for information on content interoperability and Web-based communication. You can find more information at www.aicc.org.

- **Advanced Distributed Learning (ADL or ADL SCORM)** — ADL is an initiative sponsored by the U.S. Government to facilitate instructional content development and delivery using current and emerging technologies. The ADL SCORM (*SCORM* stands for Sharable Content Object Reference Model) project focuses on the next generation of open architecture for eLearning applications, including standards for runtime communication, course structure, and content meta-data. You can find more information at www.adlnet.org.

- **IMS Global Consortium (IMS)**—The IMS is a nonprofit corporation that began with a focus on higher education. Today,

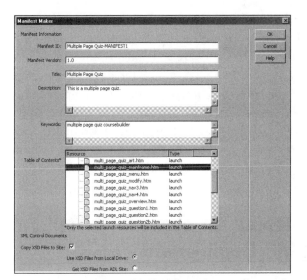

Figure 15.2
The Manifest Maker extension enables you to create ADL-compliant manifests used to configure eLearning applications within some LMS applications.

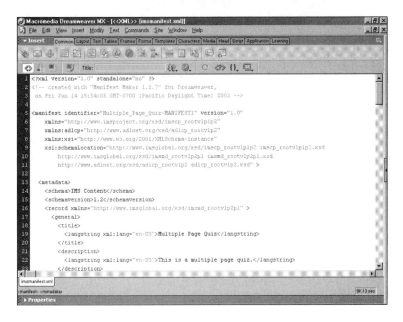

Figure 15.3
A manifest file, created by the Manifest Maker extension, uses XML to define course structure and file locations.

it's expanded its specifications and projects to address corporate and government training, K–12, and continuing education. The IMS is concerned with an open standard for locating and using educational content, tracking learner progress, reporting learner performance, and exchanging student records between administrative systems. You can find more information at www.imsproject.org.

- IEEE Learning Technology Standards Committee—The IEEE LTSC develops technical standards, recommended practices, and guides for software components, tools, technologies, and design methods that facilitate the development, deployment, maintenance, and interoperation of computer implementations of education and training components and systems. LTSC has been chartered by the IEEE Computer Society Standards Activities Board. You can find more information at http://grouper.ieee.org/groups/ltsc/.

Developing an eLearning Application for LMS Deployment

In Chapter 12, "Scoring an Assessment and Hiding the Answers," you explored the multiple-page quiz example installed with CourseBuilder. Again, it is located on your hard drive in the Dreamweaver directory at CourseBuilder\Help\Show_Me\Multiple_Page_Quiz\. This example tracks CourseBuilder interactions over multiple pages using a frameset. In this section, you'll explore this example further and see how to modify it to work with your sample LMS, WBT Manager.

In this section, you'll work with the three HTML files that make up the 4.0 browser version of the multiple-page quiz example: multi_page_quiz4.htm, multi_page_quiz_overview.htm, multi_page_quiz_nav4.htm, and multi_page_quiz_summary4.htm. The multi_page_quiz4.htm page contains the frameset that defines the configuration of multi_page_quiz_overview.htm and multi_page_quiz_nav4.htm as frames. You should copy these four files into a new directory and then define a new Dreamweaver site (see Chapter 4, "Creating a New Web Site Definition," if you need a reminder about the steps for defining a site).

You can also copy all the Web pages you've created with CourseBuilder, along with the associated images and scripts, into the new directory. Rename multi_page_quiz4.htm as index_frame.htm and multi_page_quiz_nav4.htm as navigation.htm. You'll eventually delete multi_page_quiz_overview.htm after you've replaced it with the first page of your eLearning application. Rename multi_page_quiz_summary4.htm as summary.htm. If you open navigation.htm, you'll notice that some images are missing. That's fine for now because you'll replace the images with the button images from the Kup-a-Coffee interface used earlier in this book.

These Web pages depend on an external JavaScript file named navigation.js. This file must also be copied and saved into the site's scripts directory. The JavaScript contained in this file is discussed in the "Understanding the Tracking JavaScript" section of this chapter.

Using a Tracking Frameset

Because the tracking frameset maintains navigation in a separate frame, any content Web pages you create for the tracking frameset will not have any navigation in them. You can remove navigation from the templates you used to create pages in the eLearning application. Begin by editing the template, removing button images and any editable regions involving buttons. The easiest way to do this is to right-click (Control-click on the Mac) on the editable region, and choose Templates, Remove Template Markup from the shortcut menu.

Save your changes to the templates and update all the pages that are linked to the template. Dreamweaver will prompt you to tell it what to do with the editable regions you removed. The Inconsistent Region Names dialog box, shown in Figure 15.4, enables you to map editable regions in existing pages to other editable region names, or remove them, which is what you want to do. Select Nowhere from the Move Content to New Region drop-down list to delete the content from each page.

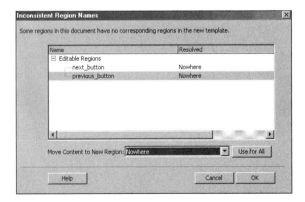

Figure 15.4

Update your Web pages linked to templates by removing editable regions content.

Open navigation.htm, and modify the navigation buttons. The four buttons in the navigation Web page are Restart, Previous, Next, and Finish. These buttons are actually contained in an Explore CourseBuilder interaction. Open the interaction (by selecting the <interaction> tag, and then clicking the Edit button in the Property inspector) to load new button graphics, as shown in Figure 15.5. After you've closed the CourseBuilder Interaction dialog box, you can add extra button states, as described in Chapter 6, "Constructing the Interface."

The Action Mgr tab of the Explore CourseBuilder interaction shows a Call JavaScript action (see Figure 15.6), when each button is selected. The functions called in this action are already in the navigation Web page. You'll explore these JavaScript functions in the next section of this chapter. For now, click the OK button to save your changes to the CourseBuilder interaction.

Figure 15.5

Modify the interaction in the navigation Web page with your custom buttons.

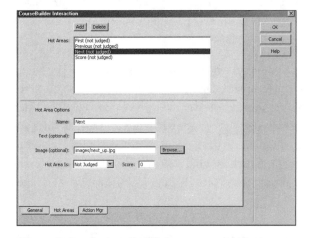

Figure 15.6

Call the JavaScript functions included with the multiple-page quiz example by using the Call JavaScript action.

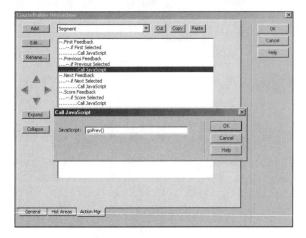

To make the navigation Web page look like the content pages, you need to attach the external cascading style sheet that you created in Chapter 5, "Defining Cascading Style Sheets." Click the Attach Style Sheet button in the CSS Styles panel and link to the external style sheet (.css). After you've finished your edits to the navigation Web page, close the page and save your changes.

Open the Web page defining the frameset, index-frame.htm, and load the first page of your eLearning application into the top frame (named main in the Frames panel). To load a Web page into an existing frame, use the Open in Frame command (File, Open in Frame). Load the navigation.htm Web page into the bottom frame.

Now you'll change a few properties in the frameset and frames so that the two frames blend seamlessly into one another. In the Frames panel, select the main frame to display its properties in the Property inspector. Turn off the scrollbars by selecting No from the Scroll drop-down list. Leave the border properties at their default settings in the individual frames because you'll change them in the frameset.

Select the frameset by clicking one of the frames in the Frames panel and then selecting the <frameset> tag in the Tag Selector. Turn off the borders by selecting No from the Borders drop-down list in the Property inspector. Also, enter 0 into the Border Width text box. With the frameset selected, change the title of the page in the toolbar. When you preview the frames in the browser, you shouldn't see any division between the two frames.

Understanding the Tracking JavaScript

The multipage quiz example provided with CourseBuilder works because of the JavaScript functions included in the navigation Web page. You used functions in Chapter 8, "Creating Interactivity with Behaviors and Animations," when you added JavaScript functions to your Web pages by using Dreamweaver behaviors. A *function* is a named procedure that performs a service. The function is always structured in the same way:

functionName(arg1, arg2, arg3, ...)

The function name is followed by parentheses, enclosing any *arguments* that the function might need. Arguments are values that you pass to the function for it to do its job. For instance, if you are using a function that adds two numbers, x and y, you need to pass the values of x and y as arguments. I like to think of functions as little factory assembly lines. The arguments are the raw materials that you send to the factory. After they go through processing, you receive a product that you can use.

If you examine navigation.htm in Code view, you'll see a lot of JavaScript in the page. At the top are all the linked external JavaScript files (.js) necessary for CourseBuilder interactions to work. Under that, you'll see the JavaScript that enables the multi-page quiz to work.

First, you'll explore the *array* that contains all the pages within the "quiz." An array is a group of objects with the same attributes that can be addressed through an *index value*. The index value corresponds to a position in the array. Note that not all these pages must have a CourseBuilder interaction; they can simply be informational Web pages.

When you use this tracking frameset, you must list each Web page in order in the array. The quiz array (appears on lines 39 to 44 in my navigation.htm) has index values of 0 to 5; the first item in an array begins with an index value of 0. You'll replace the array code with the pages that you'd like to navigate through, adding or deleting lines in the array. It should look something like this:

```
quiz[0] = new quizPage("lesson1/1.htm")
quiz[1] = new quizPage("lesson1/2.htm")
quiz[2] = new quizPage("lesson1/3.htm")
quiz[3] = new quizPage("lesson1/4.htm")
quiz[4] = new quizPage("lesson1/5.htm")
quiz[5] = new quizPage("lesson1/summary.htm")
```

In addition to the array code, there are a number of JavaScript functions defined in navigation.htm. Here's a description of each JavaScript function:

- **quizPage(src, time, timeLimit, tries, score, completed)**—This function creates a separate quizPage object for each page in the quiz. It is called by the array for each Web page listed in the array. This is where the learner data is stored for each page in the quiz.

- **goNext()** and **goPrev()**—These functions increment or decrement the index value of the array, moving the learner forward or backward through the pages in the quiz.

- **goFirst()** and **goLast()**—These functions take the learner to the first or the last page in the quiz (in the array).

- **initPage()**—This function initializes the page in case it is reloaded.

- **handleNNResize()**—This function refreshes the page if it is resized in Netscape 4.x.

- **restoreQuizObjects(storage)**—This function is called by the initPage() function to restore objects on the page.

- **saveQuizObjects()**—This function saves quiz data into persistent storage created as a hidden form in the navigation page. It is called when the values from the quiz are saved.

- **setTries(URL, tries)**—This function is called after the learner completes an assessment question and stores the tries in the array.

- **setAsDone(URL)**—This function is called after the learner completes an assessment question and stores a completed value in the array.

- **setTimes(URL, time, timeLimit)**—This function is called after the learner completes an assessment question and stores the times in the array.

- **setScores(URL, score)**—This function is called after the learner completes an assessment question and stores the scores in the array.

- **resetObject(URL)**—This function resets the tries and score values for an entry in the array.

- **findPage(URL)**—This function locates an entry in the array by the given URL.

If you look at the end of the page in Code view, you'll see a form that's contained in a hidden layer. This is the form that stores the persistent values described in the preceding list in the saveQuizObjects() description. You do not want to change or remove this code.

Now you've modified and explored the navigation.htm page. This page will remain loaded in the browser while other pages in the eLearning application are loaded in the main frame above it. The navigation page will collect and maintain the data until you tell it to send the data to the LMS.

Tracking Data to a Frame Using JavaScript

You'll need to add two JavaScript functions to each page in the eLearning application that is tracked by using the tracking frameset. The first function is also included in the navigation.htm Web page: initPage(). You can add this function to your Snippets panel, shown in Figure 15.7 so that you can easily add it to each page.

Figure 15.7

The Snippets panel enables you to save and reuse sections of code.

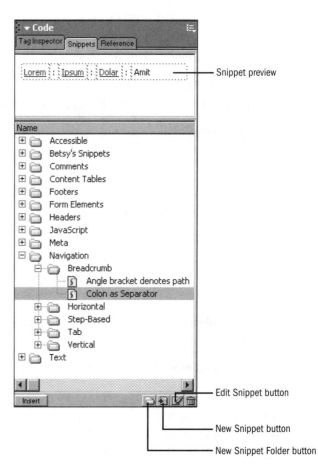

Select the initPage() function in the Code view of navigation.htm. You create a new snippet by clicking the New Snippet button to open the Snippet dialog box, shown in Figure 15.8. In the Snippet Type section, select the Insert Block radio button, and the Code radio button should be selected for Preview Type at the bottom of the Snippet dialog box. Or you can add this function to the external JavaScript file (.js) that's included in every page of your eLearning application.

Each page in your quiz must call initPage() when the page loads. The way to add that behavior is to call the function in the <body> tag on the onLoad event. You can edit the <body> tag in your template, adding the function call like this:

<body onLoad="MM_initInteractions();initPage()">

Note that on this page, the onLoad event already was being used to call the MM_initInteractions() function for initializing CourseBuilder interaction. You simply add the new function call, separated from the first one by a semicolon.

To facilitate the tracking of CourseBuilder interactions, you need to add a JavaScript function to the <head> section of each page with a CourseBuilder interaction. This function, called updateQuiz(), sends the results of the CourseBuilder interaction to the navigation page.

Select the snippet type —

Select the preview type —

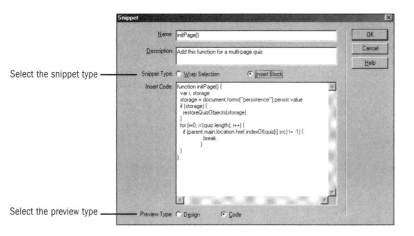

Figure 15.8
Create a snippet for code or objects that you'll use frequently.

It calls three of the functions in the navigation page: setTries(), set-Times(), and setScores(). You'll call this function from Course-Builder's Action Manager. Here is the code (it must be entered exactly as it's listed here!):

```
function updateQuiz() {
    parent.nav.setTries(document.URL, G01.tries);
    parent.nav.setTimes(document.URL, G01.timeLimit);
    parent.nav.setScores(document.URL, G01.score);
}
```

The code in updateQuiz() specifically refers to a CourseBuilder interaction named G01, the CourseBuilder interaction's unique identifier that you explored in Chapter 12. Therefore, it's important that the interaction on each page is actually named G01. The first CourseBuilder interaction added to a page is always named G01, so you need to be careful when deleting or changing interaction types; it's best to completely delete an unwanted Course-Builder interaction and then add a new one so that it is named G01 instead of G02.

You call the updateQuiz() function from the CourseBuilder Action Mgr tab. You need to add a function call for both a correct and incorrect answer. Select the Call JavaScript action from the Action drop-down list and click the Add button to add this action beneath the if Correct and if Incorrect conditions, as shown in Figure 15.9.

Figure 15.9

Add the **updateQuiz()** function call, using the Call JavaScript action, to both the correct and incorrect answer sections.

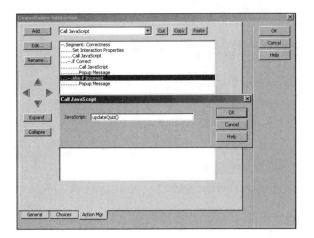

Sending Data to the LMS

You'll need to construct the final summary page as described in Chapter 12. The summary page is the page that actually calls the LMS, initiates communication, and passes data. This page contains code specific to your LMS.

WBT Manager provides two external JavaScript files containing functions for communicating with the LMS along with the template examples for Dreamweaver. You can simply modify the example, adding your own course content, and easily connect with the LMS. I've seen similar templates available from other vendors.

Using the LMS

Using an LMS requires that you divide your eLearning application into logical trackable units. The AICC standard calls these units *assignable units* (AU), the ADL standard calls them *Sharable Content Objects*, and others call them simply "learning objects." Usually these objects are what you'd consider lessons or smaller sections within a course.

WBT Manager has an administration tool that configures a group of learning objects into a course. You set course properties in the Course Properties dialog box, as shown in Figure 15.10. Properties can include whether students can self-enroll and whether the course status is set as "completed" on entry. You can add course structure through this utility or import the course structure by using the AICC standard format for a course description (a file with a .crs file extension).

You enroll students in a course by using the Web-based administration program, as shown in Figure 15.11. You can enroll students, or you can enable them to self-enroll as well as enter a start date and a completion date for the course.

You can also run reports on student progress, as shown in Figure 15.12.

Power User Tip

After you've added the LMS code, you will encounter errors if you test your eLearning application without launching it from the LMS. You might want to add this code toward the end of development so that you can easily test it on your own computer.

Figure 15.10

You administer the LMS by using an administration tool.

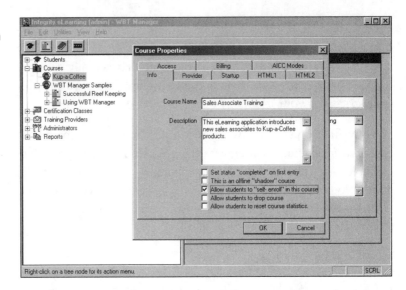

Figure 15.11

Student enrollment can be accomplished over the Web-based WBT Manager administration page.

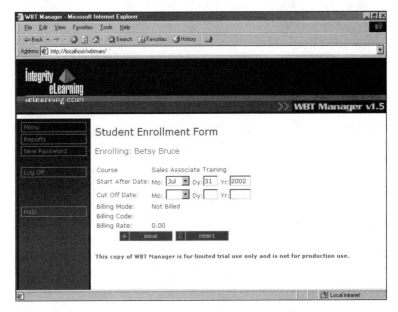

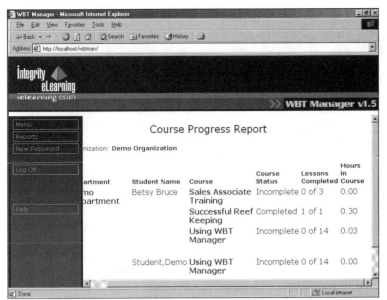

Sending Data Using Knowledge Track

Some LMS applications, notably Lotus LearningSpace, use the Knowledge Track options available in CourseBuilder. To interact with these LMS applications, you need to select the Knowledge Track option in the General tab of the CourseBuilder Interaction dialog box. In the Tracking tab of the same dialog box, you must also enter the Interaction ID, Objective ID, and Weight settings.

There are two ways to trigger judging an interaction: selecting one of the Judge Interaction choices in the General tab of the Course-Builder Interaction dialog box, or using the Judge Interaction action. If you plan to use the Judge Interaction action, select the third choice, On a Specific Event, in the Judge Interaction section of the General tab. When you turn on Knowledge Track in a CourseBuilder interaction, you will automatically trigger actions no matter which triggering method you use for judging the interaction.

Power User Tip

Ideally, the Knowledge Track system works with any AICC-compliant LMS. There is still variation, however, in the LMS industry, so make sure you test this functionality with your LMS (or, better yet, the LMS that you haven't purchased yet!) before starting development.

When you've enabled Knowledge Track, you send the following AICC-compliant information to the LMS every time an interaction is judged:

- Date the student exits the interaction (DD/MM/YYYY)
- Time the student exits the interaction (HH:MM:SS)
- Interaction ID (set in the Tracking tab)
- Objective ID (set in the Tracking tab)
- Type of the interaction (c for multiple choice, f for fill in the blank, and u for all other types)
- Correct answers
- Answer selected by the student
- Whether the selected response was correct or incorrect (w)
- Weight (set in the Tracking tab)
- The latency (time it took for the student to answer the question, formatted as HH:MM:SS)

If you aren't testing your interaction from an LMS, you will receive error messages when using CourseBuilder's Knowledge Track. You need to launch the interaction from the LMS, initiating the LMS connection, and then send information to the LMS.

You might have noticed that judging the interaction does not send scoring information to the LMS. You need to use the Send Score action in Action Manager or the Send Score behavior from the Behaviors panel to send the score to the LMS. When adding a Send Score action, you can select to send a score for a particular interaction on the Web page, or you can choose to send custom information, as shown in Figure 15.13. You can embed JavaScript variables into any of the Dreamweaver actions.

Figure 15.13

The Send Score action enables you to send scores from a specific interaction or a custom score to the LMS.

There are other tracking actions you can use to send required data to the LMS. Consult the LMS documentation on what types of data it requires and use these behaviors to supply that data. These are the tracking actions:

- **Send Core Data**—Sends data complying with AICC standards. Enter the data or variables into the Send Core Data dialog box, as shown in Figure 15.14.

- **Send ExitAU**—Send the ExitAU command to the LMS, signaling the end of an assignable unit to an AICC-compliant system.

- **Send GetParam**—Sends the GetParam command to comply with AICC standards. This command requests data from the LMS.

- **Send Interaction Info**—Sends information about a specific interaction.

- **Send Lesson Status**—Passes information about the status of a lesson to an LMS. This action sends the same status values as shown in Figure 15.13 for the Send Score action.

- **Send Lesson Time**—Passes information about how long the user took to complete a lesson, or group of interactions, to the LMS. You can send the time of a single interaction or send a custom value.

- **Send Objective Info**—Passes information about the objective along with the status of the interaction.

Although you will probably use the tracking actions in Course-Builder's Action Manager most of the time, you can also use these actions from the Behaviors panel. When you install CourseBuilder, all the tracking actions, along with Judge Interaction, Reset Interaction, and Set Interaction Properties, are added to the Behaviors drop-down list, as shown in Figure 15.15. You can attach these behaviors to any object in your Web page. For instance, you can have users click a button when they are ready to submit their final score to the LMS.

Figure 15.14

The Send Core Data action enables you to send the interaction status, location, score, and time to the LMS.

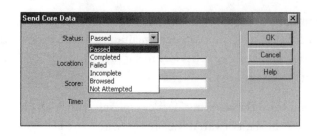

Figure 15.15

The Behaviors drop-down list displays all the tracking actions plus the Judge Interaction, Reset Interaction, and Set Interaction Properties options for CourseBuilder interactions.

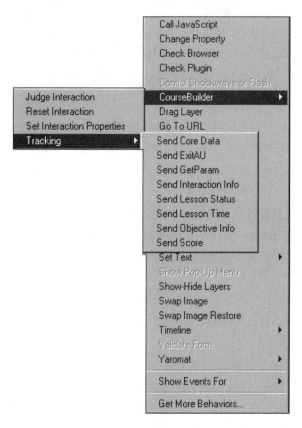

Summary

In this chapter, you explored creating a multiple-page quiz-tracking frameset, using the example that comes with CourseBuilder. You explored how the frames communicate with one another and learned the JavaScript functions you use to track a score. You investigated how learning management systems work and the standards that are wide-spread in today's learning industry. You also examined the actions and behaviors available to send information to certain LMS applications by using CourseBuilder's Knowledge Track functionality.

Part VI

Collaboration and Optimization

chapter 16

Safely Collaborating and Sharing the eLearning Site

To SHARE YOUR ONLINE LEARNING SITE with others, you must transfer the files from your local site to a remote site. You can use Dreamweaver's transfer commands to accomplish this; however, most professionals use some collaboration method to guard against overwriting the other's work. Dreamweaver has a built-in collaboration system, and it connects with some external collaboration methods, too.

When collaborating with others, you share the remote site with your team and maintain a local site for your individual work. Two issues are addressed by the collaboration methods discussed in this chapter: *overwrite protection* and *version control*. In a team environment, you'll need to institute a system of overwrite prevention to keep more than one person from working on a document at a time. You also might want to use version control in case it's necessary to restore the file to an earlier state.

Although this chapter focuses on collaboration in a team, a lot of this information is useful for solo workers. When you develop an online learning application, you eventually have to share it with your learners, so you'll need to understand how to safely transfer files to a public place. Often, solo workers interact and share files with clients and subcontractors, too. It's important that you have a transfer method that works, that maintains the integrity of your online learning site, and that is easy to use.

In this chapter, you will understand the following:

- How to configure a remote site
- How to transfer and synchronize files between the local and remote sites
- How to set up and use Dreamweaver's built-in check in/out system
- How to set up and use WebDAV with Dreamweaver
- How to set up and use Visual SourceSafe with Dreamweaver

Connecting to a Remote Site

You'll share your online learning application files with other people, either learners or your team members, as shown in Figure 16.1. To share the files, you must upload them to a remote location. This remote site, which mirrors your local site *exactly*, is located somewhere else—for example, on a server accessed over the Internet or on a network drive. The remote site could be your public Web site, but is most likely a private staging area for your team to share files.

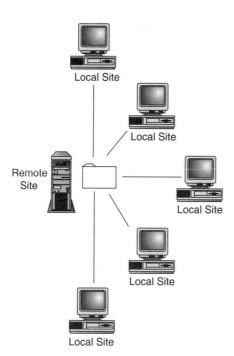

Figure 16.1
Each Dreamweaver developer has a local site on his or her hard drive and connects to a common remote site on a server.

Local Site

Local Site

Remote
Site

Local Site

Local Site

Local Site

The way you access remote files depends on your team's working environment. There are five ways to connect to the remote site in Dreamweaver: File Transfer Protocol (FTP), Local/Network, Remote Development Services (RDS), SourceSafe Database (VSS), and Web Distributed Authoring and Versioning (WebDAV). The first three methods, FTP, Local/Network, and RDS, are discussed first. These are the most commonly used transfer methods.

- Use FTP, a way to move files over the Internet using the *File Transfer Protocol*, if your remote site is accessible over the Internet only.

- Use Dreamweaver's Local/Network access if your remote site is available over your *local area network (LAN)*.

- RDS is used when you are transferring files to Macromedia ColdFusion server. An RDS connection enables you to browse database structures on a ColdFusion server.

The other two methods, SourceSafe Database and WebDAV, include overwrite protection. This system creates archives of every version of every file uploaded onto the server. It also maintains a check-in and check-out system so that only one person may make changes to a file at a time.

You set up each remote file access method differently. You can use multiple methods during different phases of your project. For example, you might develop initially using a remote site on your team's LAN, so your remote site is initially defined by using the Local/Network settings. At a later phase, you might be required to transfer the site to a corporate site available over the Internet. You can then edit your site definition, changing the access method to FTP, or you can create a new site definition for FTP remote access.

Editing Your Site Definition

In Chapter 4, "Creating a New Web Site Definition," you used the Web Site Definition Wizard to quickly set up your site definition, skipping the file transfer sections. You also reopened your site definition and edited it using the properties available on the Advanced tab of the Site Definition dialog box. In this chapter, you'll edit the site definition, adding information about the transfer method and server location where your remote site is located.

Remember, to edit your site definition you can choose the Edit Sites command from the Site menu or simply double-click the name of the current site showing in the Sites drop-down menu. This menu is located in the toolbars of both the Site panel and the Site window.

In the Basic tab of the Site Definition dialog box, click the Next button until you return to the Sharing Files section, the section where you specified "None" in Chapter 4 as the connection method to the remote site. The next sections describe configuring a remote site connection for FTP, Local/Network, and RDS. You'll explore the configuration settings in the Site Definition Wizard and in the Advanced tab of the Site Definition dialog box.

Accessing the Remote Site Using FTP

After selecting FTP as the access method, follow these steps to set up FTP access. Enter the information for a valid FTP server, a server where you have an active account. If you do not have an FTP account anywhere, simply read through these steps to familiarize yourself with the process, and go on to the next section to set up a Local/Network remote site.

1. Enter the FTP server in the FTP Host text box. Enter the URL without the protocol (in other words, do not add ftp:// to the FTP server name): **ftp.*mycompany*.com** or **www.*myhostingservice* .com**.

2. Enter the directory where your course will reside in the Host Directory text box. This might be the most difficult step. Ask your network administrator for the path; it will depend on the server operating system, your login privileges, and directory names. You can try leaving it blank and see where you end up. Often, the administrator has configured your account so that you automatically enter your default directory on the FTP server when you log in.

3. Enter your username in the Login text box. Using "anonymous" as the username won't work here. You must be an authenticated user on the FTP server.

4. Enter your password in the Password text box. Select the Save check box to save your username and password on the system if you're not concerned about others inappropriately accessing the remote site from your computer. A completed example is shown in Figure 16.2.

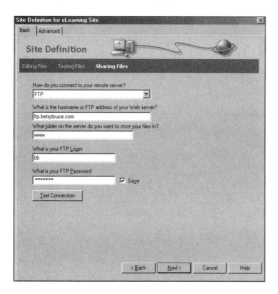

Figure 16.2

The completed Remote Info category defines the remote site on an FTP server.

5. Click the Test Connection button to see whether your FTP connection is configured correctly. Dreamweaver keeps an FTP log that you can investigate if you have FTP connection problems. Choose the Site FTP Log command from the Site menu (in the Site panel or Site window). The FTP log, shown in Figure 16.3, opens in the Results panel group and shows the error messages the server returns to Dreamweaver. It might say that you have an incorrect password or that you don't have permission to log into a directory.

When you select the Advanced tab, other FTP settings are available:

- Select the Use Passive FTP check box if you are behind a firewall that requires using passive FTP. A passive FTP connection is more secure, enabling the FTP client (Dreamweaver, in this case) to control the flow of data. Consult with your network administrator for more information. If you are not sure, leave this option unchecked.

- Select the Use Firewall check box if you are behind a firewall. You'll need to set up firewall preferences (the firewall host and port) in the Site category in Dreamweaver's preferences. You can get this information from your network administrator. Again, if you're not sure, leave it unchecked.

- Select Use SSH Encrypted Secure Login to enable you to use the Secure Shell Protocol (SSH) to connect securely to a server. This setting is available only in the Windows version of Dreamweaver MX. To create this functionality on a Mac, download an application called MacSSH from www.macssh.com. Again, if you're not sure, leave it unchecked.

Figure 16.3

The FTP log helps troubleshoot your FTP connection if you are having problems connecting.

eLearning with Dreamweaver MX: Building Online Learning Applications

You should ignore the Check In/Out settings for now. You'll explore checking files in and out in detail later in this chapter.

Accessing the Remote Site with Local/ Network Access

Using Local/Network access is the simplest of all the remote access methods: You share remote files on a directory somewhere on a network. This directory can serve as a common repository for your team to share files with each other. It can also reside on a Web server where you'll be able to view the remote site in a browser.

When using Local/Network access, you might be tempted to skip defining a remote site and just define the network site as your local site. Don't do it! Dreamweaver works best when you define both a local and a remote site. You can run into version control issues when working with others from a common directory.

If you did not set up your remote site in the previous section using a valid FTP server, set it up using Local/Network access. If you aren't currently working on a network, create a directory on your local hard drive and pretend it's a directory on the server. Create a directory anywhere on your hard drive called remote_site to serve as your remote site.

After you select Local/Network as the access method in the Site Definition Wizard, follow these steps to set up your remote site:

1. Select the remote_site directory you just created as the remote folder.

2. Be sure the Refresh Remote File List Automatically check box is selected. You'll see updates right away if team members add files to the remote site.

A completed example appears in Figure 16.4. There are no additional settings in the Advanced panel for a Local/Network connection.

Figure 16.4

The completed Remote Info category defines Local/Network access to a LAN.

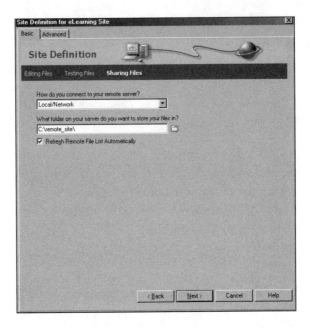

Accessing the Remote Site Using RDS

If you are working on an application using Macromedia ColdFusion as the application server, you can use ColdFusion's RDS to access the remote files. The advantage of RDS is that you cannot only access and update files on the server, but you can also view databases. You'll need to ask your server administrator for the values to place in the following settings:

1. Enter the name of the host computer where your Web server is installed. This will be an IP address or a URL, for example **localhost, 127.0.0.1,** or **www.*mydomain*.com**.

2. Enter the port that accepts HTTP requests. This is usually port 80.

3. Enter the directory path to your remote site directory on the server. For example, c:\inetpub\wwwroot\elearning_site\.

4. Enter your ColdFusion username in the Username text box.

5. Enter your password in the Password text box. Select the Save check box to save your username and password on the system if you are not concerned about others inappropriately accessing the remote site from your computer.

A completed example appears in Figure 16.5. There are no additional settings in the Advanced panel for a RDS connection.

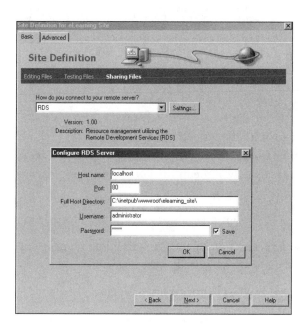

Figure 16.5
Enter the server address, directory, and login information to create an RDS connection to a server running ColdFusion.

Transferring Your Files To and From the Remote Site

Now you'll explore actually transferring the files to the remote site. To transfer files, Dreamweaver borrowed some standard FTP command names: Get and Put. The Get command moves files from the remote site to the local site. The Put command moves files from the local site to the remote site. Dreamweaver uses these command names whether you are using FTP, Local/Network, RDS, or the other access types you'll explore later in this chapter.

Be sure you have Dreamweaver's Site window open so you can see both the local and the remote sites. The toolbar contains the commands you'll use to transfer files. You explored the toolbar view buttons, the three buttons on the far left side, and used the Site drop-down menu to change sites in Chapter 4. The following are the other buttons in the Site window toolbar (see Figure 16.6):

Figure 16.6
The Site window toolbar offers easy access to the transfer commands.

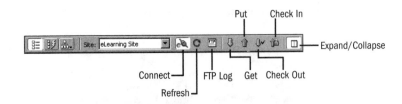

- The *Connect* button establishes a connection with the remote server. All the access methods except Local/Network require you to initially connect to the remote site. Connection to a remote site with Local/Network access is unnecessary because you are usually authenticated on the network when you log on to your computer.

- The *Refresh* button redisplays the list of files in your site.

- The *FTP Log* button opens the FTP Log report. This button is available only when FTP is the access method.

- The *Put* and *Get* buttons transfer files to and from the remote site.

- The *Check In* and *Check Out buttons* also transfer files to and from the remote site, marking them as checked in or checked out by you. You'll explore this overwrite protection system later in this chapter.

- The *Expand/Collapse* button (Windows only) collapses the Site window into the Site panel. A mini version of this toolbar (minus the view buttons) is available in the Site panel.

Power User Tip

Check the Dreamweaver Help files for more tips on troubleshooting your FTP connection. You'll find excellent information regarding firewalls, operating system differences, and figuring out the correct path to a directory.

If you set up your site using Local/Network access, you are already connected and ready to transfer files. If you set up your site using FTP, choose the Connect command to start a session with the remote server. After you connect to the remote site, you'll see a list of remote site files, and the green light in the Connect button on the toolbar will be lit. Unless you've experimented with FTP on your own, you will probably have an empty remote site directory.

Cloaking Directories and Files

It's important that the remote and local sites mirror each other exactly. There shouldn't be any extra files or directories in the remote site. If there are extra files or directories, you should select a different remote directory for your remote site.

You might have files or directories in your local site that you don't want to upload to the remote site. For example, you might have a directory containing all the original images used to produce the optimized GIFs and JPEGs used in your site. If you're using Macromedia Fireworks (see Appendix B, "Using Fireworks" for more information), it's handy to maintain your original Fireworks files within your site so that you can automatically update images from Dreamweaver.

Dreamweaver MX enables you to *cloak* files or directories, excluding these files from all site operations including transfers to the remote site. By default, cloaking is enabled when you define your site. You disable cloaking in the Cloaking category of the Site Definition dialog box (under the Advanced tab), shown in Figure 16.7. You can also instruct Dreamweaver to cloak files with a particular file extension, such as .png (Fireworks file) or .fla (Flash file).

Figure 16.7
Enable cloaking in the Advanced tab of the Site Definition dialog box. You can also instruct Dreamweaver to cloak files with a specific file extension.

You cloak files and directories by selecting the Cloak command from the Cloaking submenu of the Site menu (in the Site panel or Site window) or the context menu that pops up when you right-click (Control-click on the Mac). This menu, shown in Figure 16.8, enables you to cloak selected files.

Figure 16.8

Cloak specific files and directories by selecting the Cloak command.

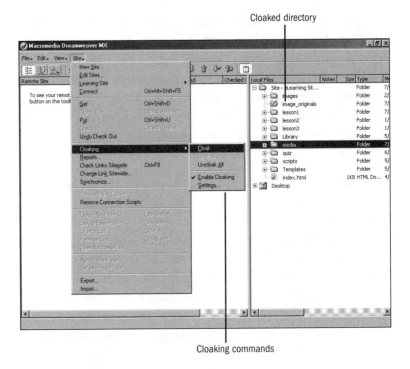

Cloaked directory

Cloaking commands

Cloaked files are excluded from the following:

- **Transfer commands**—The Get, Put, Check In, Check Out, and Synchronize commands, used to transfer your files to and from the remote site, ignore files in your site that are cloaked. You'll explore these commands in the next section.

- **Assets panel**—Cloaked files to not appear in the Assets panel.

- **Template and Library updates**—Dreamweaver excluded cloaked files created from templates and files containing Library items from update. However, cloaked template and library files still update all their instances even when they are cloaked.

- **Site maintenance operations and reports**—Cloaked files are excluded from sitewide link updates, search-and-replace operations, and reports.

Using Get and Put

Transfer your entire local site by selecting the top line in the local site, the line listing the path to your local site directory. Selecting this top line effectively selects the entire local site, even though not all the files are highlighted. Transfer the files to the remote site by choosing the Put command (either on the toolbar or from the Site menu). If Dreamweaver displays a dialog box asking whether you really want to use the Put command on the entire site, answer Yes.

The status message box appears on top of the Site window, displaying the transfer status of your files. These messages might show onscreen quickly or slowly, depending on how fast your connection is to the remote site. Click the Cancel button to stop the transfer process.

The Site window interface enables you to drag and drop files between the local and remote sites to start a transfer; however, I don't suggest doing this. It's too easy to accidentally place files into the wrong directories. I suggest using the Get or Put commands or the Synchronize, Check in, and Check out commands that you'll explore later in this chapter. In Windows, I prefer to handle most of my transfers using the Site panel.

Try out the Get command by selecting a file or a couple of files (use the Shift or Command keys while you click to select more than one file) in your remote site. Choose the Get command (Site, Get) or click the Get button on the Site window toolbar. Although you can actually select files in either window to use the Get and Put commands, it's more logical to select the files in the window where the files originate, and then perform a command on them. I suggest selecting files in the local site to perform a Put and selecting files in the remote site to perform a Get. Obviously, if you're using the Windows Site panel, you can only see the files in the current view (selected from the drop-down menu).

Synchronizing the Local and Remote Sites

Use the Synchronize command to make sure that both the local and remote sites are up to date. The Synchronize command compares file-modified dates on the remote and local sites. If a team member has modified a file and moved it to the remote site, it will have a more recently modified date than the file in your local site. Use this command to make sure both the local and remote sites have the most recent file versions before making changes or reviewing the project on the server.

This command is a little scary at first but will save time after you understand how to properly use it. Many new Dreamweaver users are concerned that the Synchronize command will somehow destroy the file structure of their sites and prefer to trust themselves to manually synchronize the local and remote sites. I prefer to use the Synchronize command and have never had it "misfire" and cause issues with my site. The command gives you a preview of the transfers it's proposing so that you can review the list before synchronizing the site.

If you selected Local/Network as your access method, you can simulate someone changing a file on the remote site. To accomplish this, you can't open the file in the Dreamweaver Site window because that simply retrieves the file and opens it from the local site (even if you select it from the remote site). Open a file from your remote_site directory with Dreamweaver's Open command, change something about it, and then change it back so that you don't mess up the page. Dreamweaver still thinks you changed something (it's only a software application!), and then saves the page. This simulates a team member modifying the file and then saving his changes up to the remote site on the server.

Now, your local and remote sites are no longer synchronized. When you examine the modified dates in the local and remote sites in the Site window, you can see that the file you changed has two different times, as shown in Figure 16.9. Using this manual examination method during development would be difficult for a lot of files, but the Synchronize command automatically examines the modified dates for you.

Select the Synchronize command (Site, Synchronize) in the Site panel or the Site window. The Synchronize Files dialog box has two settings: Synchronize and Direction.

Use the settings from the Synchronize drop-down menu to control the scope of the site synchronization. Synchronize the entire site right now by choosing Entire eLearning Site, or whatever your site is called. Dreamweaver will also synchronize only the files you have selected in the Site panel or Site window if you select that setting.

Remote modified time

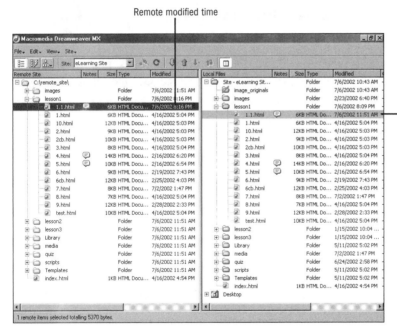

Figure 16.9

Files must be synchronized when the modified times differ between the local and remote sites.

Local modified time

The Direction drop-down menu controls whether you Get only, Put only, or perform both a Get and Put. Select Get and Put Newer Files to have Dreamweaver analyze both sites for newer files.

Click the Preview button to see the list of files that need to be synchronized, as shown in Figure 16.10.

Figure 16.10

The Synchronize command compares the local and remote sites and the preview window shows which files need to be synchronized.

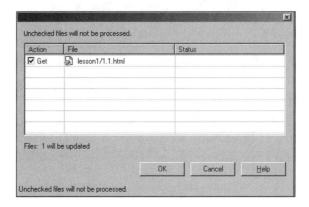

In the Preview window, Dreamweaver suggests an action—Get or Put—depending on whether the local or remote site has an updated file. You should review this list to see whether it looks like what you expected. To reject the suggested synchronization actions, deselect the check box beside the filename. When you click the OK button, Dreamweaver synchronizes your site, transferring files between the local and remote sites, making sure that both are up to date.

See, that's not so scary! This is a valuable command when you aren't sure whether your local site or the remote site contains newer files.

Q: Dreamweaver keeps giving me errors when I try to synchronize my site with the remote site on our FTP server. What's up?

A: The problem probably stems from your permissions on the server. (In my experience, permissions cause most of the problems involved with servers.) To detect the server's time and compare the modification dates, Dreamweaver needs to quickly create and delete a directory. If you do not have the appropriate permissions set to create directories, this function will not work.

Understanding Dreamweaver's Check In/Out System

Dreamweaver includes an overwrite protection system, enabling team members to check files in and out of the remote site. Dreamweaver's built-in system isn't completely secure because it's possible, although difficult, to overwrite files in the remote site. Dreamweaver's built-in system, the *check in/out system*, is adequate control for most small to medium-sized teams to use for online learning application development.

Dreamweaver's check in/out system works with either FTP or Local/Network access to the remote site. After you enable check in/out in the site definition, you'll be required to check out files from the remote site before working on them. You'll also be able to tell which files are checked out by your team members.

Dreamweaver's check in/out system works by simply creating small .lck files in remote site directories. These files are not visible in Dreamweaver's Site panel or Site window. If someone looks at the site files from outside Dreamweaver, she'll see one file with the .lck extension for each file that is checked out. The .lck files contain the name and e-mail address of the person the file is checked out to. If your team intends to use Dreamweaver's check in/out system, everyone on the team must be using Dreamweaver.

Turning On Check In/Out in the Site Definition

To turn on Dreamweaver's check in/out system you must edit the site definition (Site, Edit Sites). After you've specified a connection method to the remote site, the next page in the Site Definition Wizard asks whether you want to enable Dreamweaver's check in/out system. When you select the radio button next to Yes, Enable Check In and Check Out, additional fields become available.

The second set of radio buttons lets you determine what happens when you attempt to open a file that you do not have checked out. I suggest choosing the radio button next to the I Want to View a Read-Only Copy option so that you can quickly view, without editing, the content of a file without checking it out. Sometimes I simply want to view a file without making changes to it. If you select the Dreamweaver Should Check It Out option, Dreamweaver checks the Check Out Files when Opening option in the Advanced tab.

Enter your checkout name and e-mail address, as shown in Figure 16.11. You need to enter a checkout name that is unique within your team. When you enter your e-mail address, your name will appear as a hyperlink to others on your team, enabling them to send you an e-mail message from Dreamweaver about any file that you have checked out.

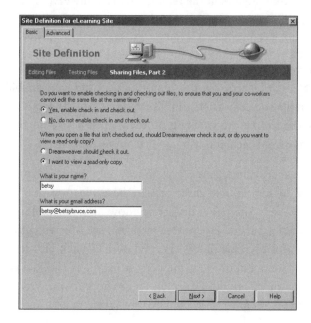

Checking Out Files

Check out a file from your remote site by highlighting a file from the local site and clicking the Check Out button on the toolbar. You can do this from either the Site panel or the Site window. Dreamweaver gets the file from the remote site to make sure you have the most recent version. You do not need to use the Get or Put commands when you are using the check in/out system because the functionality of those commands is built into the Check In and Check Out commands. Notice that a small green check mark appears next to the file you checked out, as shown in Figure 16.12.

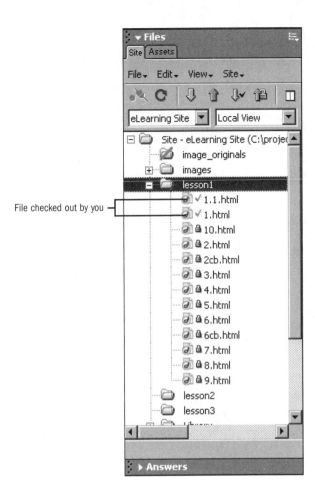

File checked out by you ⎯

Your checkout name appears beside the checked-out file. Anyone who connects to the remote site can see that you have this file checked out. Your checkout name appears as a hyperlink (a mailto link) that launches an e-mail message when clicked. The subject line of the e-mail message references the selected file (including its path) and the defined site name, as shown in Figure 16.13. This feature is useful for team members to communicate via e-mail about a certain Web page in an online learning application.

Figure 16.13

E-mail messages launched from the Site window reference the file and site names.

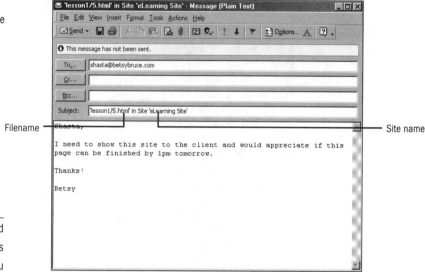

Filename ————— Site name

Power User Tip

Dreamweaver might ask you if you'd like to include dependent files when you check out files. If you respond positively, Dreamweaver downloads any images, movies, and other files that are linked to the files you have selected for download. This can cause the download to take much longer because of the additional files. Often in eLearning projects the media files are created prior to development and do not change, so continually downloading them is a waste of network bandwidth and time. I usually respond negatively to this dialog box, checking the Don't Show Me This Message Again check box so that it disappears forever.

When a team member has a file checked out, it appears in your local and remote sites with a red check mark beside it. The red check mark is a visual cue telling you that the file is not currently available for you to check out. If someone has a file checked out and you try to check it out, you'll receive the warning message shown in Figure 16.14. You can override the check out—if the team member has gone on vacation, for example—by clicking the Yes button. Obviously, overriding a checked-out file defeats the overwrite protection and should be used only in very unusual situations.

The file checkout process starts when Dreamweaver gets the file from the remote site. Dreamweaver creates an .lck file on the remote site, and the checkout name appears beside the file on the remote site as a hyperlink. Dreamweaver removes read-only attributes from the file in the local site so that you can make changes. A green check mark appears beside the files you checked out.

Figure 16.14

Dreamweaver displays an error message when you attempt to check out a file that someone else has checked out.

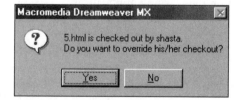

Checking In Files

When you've finished your work on a Web page, you save your changes and check the page in to the remote site using the Check In command. The check-in process uses the Put command to transfer the file to the remote site, deleting the .lck file. Your name is no longer listed next to the file, so the file is available for other team members to check out. Dreamweaver sets the file attributes of the local file to read-only so that you cannot save changes to the file. To make changes, you must check out the file again.

Check out some files in your Online Learning App site. In Chapter 17, "Using Reports," you'll run reports on your site that tell you which files are checked out by whom. Just to make that reporting a little more interesting, you might want to edit your site definition and create a different checkout name to simulate working on your project with other people.

Using WebDAV and Visual SourceSafe

Dreamweaver's built-in check in/out system is adequate for some online learning application projects. However, large, enterprisewide teams might want to use more robust overwrite protection and version control systems. Of course, small teams can also decide to invest in the software and hardware necessary to use these systems.

Dreamweaver enables connection to the remote site via the WebDAV protocol, an extension of HTTP. Many believe that WebDAV might eventually replace FTP because of the security risks FTP poses to servers. WebDAV offers overwrite protection, controlled by the server, and the protocol will eventually provide version control, too.

Microsoft Visual SourceSafe (VSS) is version control software that runs on your team server. Along with strong overwrite protection, this software saves copies of all file versions. As you can imagine, maintaining copies of all files takes up a lot of disk space, so it's necessary to make sure the server has plenty of extra space for multiple copies of the same files.

Power User Tip

Because e-mail messages reference the site name you enter in your site definition, it's important that all team members use the same site name. By following this guideline, the site name can be interpreted correctly when team members receive e-mail messages.

Power User Tip

Dreamweaver automatically transfers design notes to the remote site when a file is checked in. You can communicate with team members through design notes attached to files. You control the design notes in the Design Notes category of the site definition. You turned the design notes on for this site in Chapter 4 when you created the site definition.

Using WebDAV

WebDAV is an exciting new protocol used to collaborate over the Internet. WebDAV is a nonproprietary protocol—actually an extension to HTTP, the protocol that controls the Web—and it is supported by many types of servers and computers.

Although the WebDAV specification defines file version control, at this time that feature hasn't been implemented in any software. As of this writing, all applications that support the WebDAV protocol implement only the overwrite protection portions of the specification. This evolving protocol eventually will handle version control, though, so stay tuned!

For the server, the example in this book uses the built-in WebDAV capabilities of IIS 5, the Web server that comes with Microsoft Windows 2000. Previous versions of IIS do not support WebDAV. WebDAV support is part of the Mac OS X operating system and can be added to the open-source Apache Web server for Unix. To enable WebDAV on a server, the server administrator might need to download special additions to server software. Your server administrator must give you complete access to any remote directory you access from Dreamweaver by using WebDAV. The directory you access must be available via HTTP, meaning it must be on a Web server and be accessible from a URL.

Setting Up WebDAV Access

When you are collaborating using WebDAV, you select WebDAV as your access method in the remote site definition for your site. Dreamweaver will be the client application interacting with WebDAV on the server housing the remote site. Complete these steps to edit your remote site definition to enable WebDAV:

1. Click the Settings button to open the WebDAV Connection dialog box.

2. Enter the complete URL to the WebDAV folder that parallels your local site. You must enter complete path and port information.

3. Enter the username and password your server administrator gave you.

4. Enter your e-mail address. Dreamweaver uses this information to turn your checkout name into a mailto link in the Site window.

5. Select the Save Password check box if other people accessing this site on your computer isn't a concern.

6. The WebDAV Connection dialog box should look like Figure 16.15. Click the OK button to save your WebDAV setup.

Notice that you didn't turn on check in/out functionality when using WebDAV access because checking files in and out is built into the system. WebDAV handles this functionality on the server. In this book's example on an IIS 5 Web server, the ownership of a file on the server changes from person to person as it is checked in and out.

Transferring Files with WebDAV

You transfer files with WebDAV in much the same way you transfer files by using Dreamweaver's check in/out process. Start by clicking the Connect button to create a connection to the remote server. The four transfer buttons work similarly, too. Here's what they do:

- **The Get command**—Gets the most recent file version from the remote site. If you want to view a file but you do not need to edit it, you choose the Get command to move the file to your local site without checking it out. The file properties are marked as read-only.

Power User Tip

Some Web administrators prefer to allow access to WebDAV via an alternative port, instead of the default port 80 used for HTTP. This enables an extra level of security because access to WebDAV requires a user to have a high level of access. You might be told to access your remote site via WebDAV on port 81 (or some other port). When using any port other than the default port, you need to add the port to the URL directly behind the domain name: for example, http://www.yoursite .com:81/.

An advantage of WebDAV is that it can be used via a Secure Socket Layers (SSL) connection, a secure way to connect over the Internet. SSL connections begin with https instead of http.

Figure 16.15
The completed WebDAV Connection dialog box enables WebDAV access to the remote site.

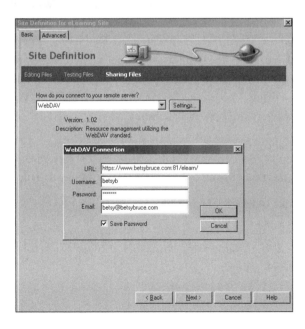

- **The Put command**—Puts a checked-out file on the remote site without checking it back in. This command is useful if you want to share a file with your team but need to continue editing it.

- **The Check Out command**—Gets the most recent file version from the remote site and gives you ownership of the file. The file is blocked from being checked out or replaced by anyone else until you check it back in. You check out a file while you are editing it.

- **The Check In command**—Puts a file on the remote site and removes your ownership of the file. The files are free to be checked out by someone else on your team.

Using Microsoft Visual SourceSafe

Microsoft Visual SourceSafe is a popular version control software package that enables development teams to tightly control files. If you are using Windows, you must have a licensed copy of the Visual SourceSafe (VSS) client installed on your local machine to use VSS with Dreamweaver. Microsoft Visual SourceSafe Server and client are components of Microsoft Visual Studio.

If you're using a Macintosh and want to access a Windows-based VSS server, you need to purchase and install MetroWerks Visual SourceSafe for Macintosh. You also need ToolServer, an application available free from the Apple Developer's Site. See Appendix A, "Resources," for more information on both of these products. Also, as of this writing, VSS on the Macintosh requires VSS 5 (VSS 6 is the most recent version of the software).

VSS version control is used for the following:

- Ensures that only one person is making changes to a file at a time.

- Tracks older versions of files.

- Tracks cross-platform and reusable code—not important for Web development, but this tool is used for all sorts of development.

Setting Up Visual SourceSafe Server Access

If your team uses VSS, you configure the SourceSafe database as your remote site in Dreamweaver by following these steps:

1. Select SourceSafe Database as the access method in the site definition.

2. Click the Settings button to open the Open SourceSafe Database dialog box.

3. Click the Browse button to locate the srcsafe.ini file on your local hard drive in the VSS client directory. This file describes the path to the SourceSafe database.

4. Add the project name in the Project text box. Leave the $/ symbols at the beginning of the project name, as they signify the root folder in VSS.

5. Enter your VSS username and password in the appropriate text boxes. Select the Save check box if inappropriate access to the remote site from your computer isn't a concern.

6. The Open SourceSafe Database dialog box should look like Figure 16.16. Click the OK button to save your SourceSafe database setup. Again, you didn't turn on the check in/out functionality when using VSS access because checking files in and out to VSS is built into the system.

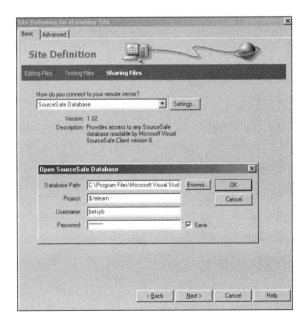

Figure 16.16

The completed Open SourceSafe Database dialog box, pointing to the srcsafe.ini file with the correct project name.

Transferring Files with VSS

When you transfer your files to the remote site with VSS, a new copy of your file is saved on the remote site if you've made changes to the file. You use the same buttons and commands you use with Dreamweaver's check in/out system. Start by clicking the Connect button to create a connection to the remote server.

The Get and Put commands work identically to how they work with WebDAV. There are a couple of differences, however, with the Check Out and Check In commands.

The Check Out command gets the most recent file version from the remote site and marks it as checked out to you. The file is completely blocked from being checked out or replaced by anyone else until you check it back in. You check out a file while you're editing it.

The Check In command puts a file on the remote site, checking it in to VSS. If changes have been made to the file, a copy of the new file is added to the VSS project. The check mark indicating that the file is checked out to you is removed, and the file is free to be checked out by someone else.

Power User Tip

When using Visual SourceSafe, Dreamweaver doesn't have access to the server's timestamp. Therefore, the Synchronization command is not available. You might receive a warning telling you this the first time you connect to VSS. You'll want to check the box on the warning dialog box telling Dreamweaver to no longer show you the message.

The process appears to work just as it does with Dreamweaver's check in/out system: You check out a file, make the appropriate edits, and then check it back in. All your team members can see that you have the file checked out and they can see, when your name is no longer next to the file, that you checked it back in. Note that your name next to a file is not a hyperlink, so team members can't automatically send e-mail to you by clicking on your name as they can with Dreamweaver's check in/out system or with WebDAV.

When your team uses VSS, you have the VSS client installed on your machine. If you were not using Dreamweaver—if you were developing an application by using a C++ compiler, for example—you would use the VSS client to check files in and out of the VSS project. You can use the VSS client (see Figure 16.17) instead of Dreamweaver if you need to. This method is especially useful for sharing files that are outside the scope (and file structure) of your defined site (such as storyboard files, scripts, analysis documents, and so on).

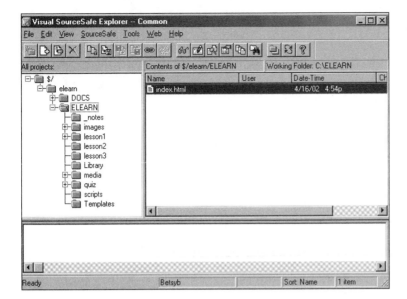

Figure 16.17
The Visual SourceSafe client enables you to view checked file status and check files in and out of VSS.

When you check files back into VSS from Dreamweaver, an Add Comment dialog box appears, prompting you to enter a comment. This comment is attached to the version of the file you check into VSS. You should enter information about the changes you've made to the file, and then click the OK button. Note that the comments can be viewed only from within the VSS client, not through Dreamweaver.

Summary

In this chapter, after adding an access method to your site definition you learned how to synchronize your local and remote sites manually and automatically. You explored Dreamweaver's built-in check in/out system, WebDAV, and Visual SourceSafe. You learned how to set up your site and to check files in and out with each of these access methods.

IN THIS CHAPTER

chapter 17

Using Reports

DREAMWEAVER COMES WITH SEVERAL USEFUL reports that

you'll use to manage your online learning applications. It's impor-

tant that your Web pages be robust and abide by Web standards.

Many of the Dreamweaver reports enable you to check that all

the pages in the Web site have been formatted correctly, and

overall, Dreamweaver reports simply make life easier by enabling

you to seek out errors or provide documentation for your project.

In this chapter, you'll try several reports that will prove useful to your online learning application project. You'll also install some Dreamweaver extensions to add extra reports to Dreamweaver. You can save the results of any of the reports into an XML file that you can import into a database or display by translating the XML into an easily viewable format.

It's important that you do not wait until your online learning application project is almost complete to run many of these reports. You want to use the reports to identify problems, such as broken links or missing alt text, early in the project. Some of the reports, such as Design Notes and Checked Out By, can be used throughout the project to maintain a record of your project.

In this chapter, you will understand the following:

- How to define the scope of a report
- How to use the reports that come with Dreamweaver and how to install additional reports
- How to fine-tune your report results using the report settings
- How to save report results as an XML file and display the report results

Understanding Reports

A report is a detailed account of characteristics of your eLearning site that helps you locate potential problems or document your efforts. Reports can be run on a single file or multiple files. Some reports, such as Checked Out By, aren't very useful on a single file (it's easy to figure out who has a single file checked out without running a report). Other reports, such as Missing Alt Text, might yield overwhelming results when run on an entire site. Luckily, it's easy to run reports multiple times until you figure out the most meaningful *scope* for your report.

The Reports command is under the Site menu in Dreamweaver's Design window or Site window. This command launches the Reports dialog box, shown in Figure 17.1. You select the scope of the report in the Report On drop-down menu at the top of the dialog box. You can select the current document, the entire local site, selected files in the site (you must be in Site window to use this choice), or a certain folder. If you set the scope of the report as a folder, you'll need to click the folder icon to browse to the folder you'd like to report on.

Dreamweaver reports have two main categories: Workflow and HTML. Expand and collapse the reports in each category by clicking the small plus or minus icons next to the category folder. To run a report, select the check box next to that report. The Report Settings button becomes active when some reports are selected. When you click the Report Settings button, a dialog box opens enabling you to enter parameters for your report. The parameters depend on which report you've selected.

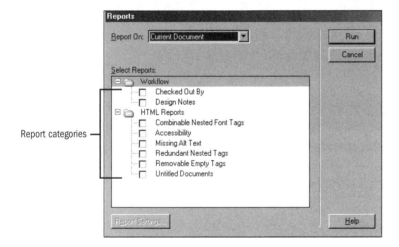

Report categories

Figure 17.1
Select the report type and scope in the Reports dialog box.

Exploring the Workflow Reports

The Workflow reports—Checked Out By and Design Notes—can be especially useful to project managers and team leaders. These reports return results on the files in your online learning site and are probably of the most value when run on the entire site. In the following sections, you'll run a report on which files are checked out by which team members and another report on the design notes contained in the online learning application site.

Finding Out Which Files Are Checked Out by Whom

If you use Dreamweaver's check in/out system, you can run the Checked Out By report to find out who has which files checked out. Simply select the Checked Out By report, set the scope to Entire Local Site, and click the Run button to generate a report showing all the checked out files in your site (shown in Figure 17.2).

Limit the report results to a single team member by adding report parameters. Prepare the report as in the preceding paragraph, but before you click the Run button, click the Report Settings button at the bottom of the dialog box. Enter a team member's check-out name in the Checked Out By text box, click the OK button to save your report settings, and click Run. Now the report is limited to files checked out by only one person.

Figure 17.2
The Checked Out By report shows all the files in the site that are checked out and who has them checked out.

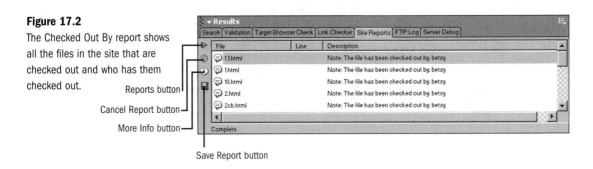

Reports button
Cancel Report button
More Info button
Save Report button

The Site Reports panel displays a list of files as the report results. The Site Reports panel displays columns of information including the file name and a description. Open files listed in the report results directly from the panel by double-clicking the line in the results. You can open only files that you already have checked out.

Investigating Your Site's Design Notes

The Design Notes report lists the existing design notes in your site. You can run the Design Notes report on a single file, but you'll experiment with running the report on your entire site. Go ahead and run the Design Notes report on your entire site, and the Site Reports panel should look like Figure 17.3.

Just as you used the Report Settings section to limit the Checked Out By report to a single person, you can run a Design Notes report that shows only certain design notes. To do that, you enter up to three search parameters to limit the results of your search, shown in Figure 17.4, in the Report Settings section.

Run a report on the Developer design note you created in Chapter 4, "Creating a New Site Definition." Enter the name of the design note, Developer, in the left column. Search for a design note value containing a specific developer by entering his or her name as the design note value in the right column of the Report Settings section.

Power User Tip

The Checked Out By report cannot access Visual SourceSafe or WebDAV remote sites, so this report will not work if you are using either of those access methods.

Power User Tip

If you've limited the report to a single team member, after you run the report, you should remove the name you entered in the Report Settings section. Dreamweaver remembers this data, a feature that can be helpful if you run a report on the same person most of the time, but it might offer an incomplete report in the future if you forget you've limited the report to a single person.

Figure 17.3
The results of the Design Notes report list the name and value pairs contained in Dreamweaver's design notes.

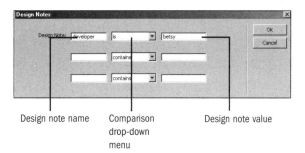

Design note name   Comparison drop-down menu   Design note value

Figure 17.4
Up to three search parameters can be used to limit the results returned by a report.

The Comparison list box, located in the middle column, specifies the relationship between the left and right columns. It includes the following selections: Contains, Does Not Contain, Is, Is Not, and Matches Regex. Select the Contains option. Click the OK button to save your report settings, and then run the Design Notes report.

The report returns a listing of all the design notes that contain the specific developer. If you search for only a first name, selecting Contains in the drop-down list returns all notes with that first name. If you had selected Is in the Comparison list box, the search would return only files with design notes that match exactly. Note that you can also run reports using Does Not Contain and Is Not.

The Comparison list box enables you to use regular expressions by selecting the Matches Regex setting. With regular expressions, you can use special characters to perform wildcard-type searches. A list of common regular expressions is available in the Dreamweaver and UltraDev Help files.

For example, if you need to search for all the design notes named Notes dated the 15th of any month, you would enter this regular expression: \d+/15/\d+ (as shown in Figure 17.5). The \d means "any digit character," and the + after it means "search for any digit occurring one or more times." The slash separating the month from the day is next, followed by 15, the day you are searching for, followed by the slash separating the day from the year. The expression ends with another \d+.

Figure 17.5
Use regular expressions with the Matches Regex comparison to perform wildcard searches.

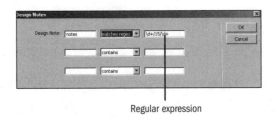

Regular expression

---

eLearning with Dreamweaver MX: Building Online Learning Applications

Exploring the HTML Reports

The reports available in the HTML Reports category help you maintain and correct the HTML code in your eLearning Web site. Two of the reports in the HTML category are important to run on your online training application. The Missing Alt Text reports images that do not have the alt text attribute. The Untitled Documents report helps you discover which documents do not have titles.

Some of the reports in the HTML Reports category are most useful when importing a site created by either hand-coding HTML or after using an HTML editor other than Dreamweaver. I am not going to cover the Combinable Nested Font Tags, Redundant Nested Tags, and Removable Empty Tags reports. These reports clean up sloppy HTML and are very straightforward to run.

Uncovering Missing Alt Text

Alternative text, or alt text, is contained in the alt attribute of an image. An image's alt text contains a textual description of the image, relating important ideas and information that the image represents. Alt text is an often forgotten attribute of an image that enables visually impaired learners to hear a description of an image, through special software that reads a Web page. In Netscape and Internet Explorer 4.0 and higher in Windows, the alt text is displayed as a ToolTip over an image.

Select the Reports command and run the Missing Alt Text report on a file in your site (pick a page with images in it). After you run the Missing Alt Text report, the Site Reports panel lists all instances of images that do not contain the alt attribute. When you double-click on a line in the report results, Dreamweaver opens the file and selects the image that is missing the alt attribute. The Document window opens in split view, showing both design and document views with the <image> tag selected. To add the alt text, simply type a description of the image in the Alt text box of the Property inspector, as shown in Figure 17.6.

Power User Tip

Regular expressions can also be used in Dreamweaver's powerful Find and Replace command, found under the Edit menu, enabling you to use the wildcard searches to find and replace portions of your online learning application.

If you aren't a UNIX guru or used to coding in a certain language, regular expressions (also called regex) might seem very strange. Regular expressions are powerful ways to search for patterns in data. See Appendix A, "Resources," for Web sites you can use to learn more about regular expressions.

Figure 17.6

Enter text in the alt text attribute of an image in the Property inspector.

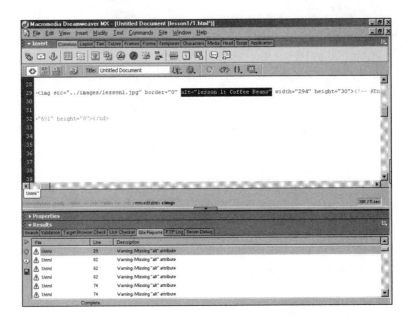

Catching Untitled Documents

To search for all files missing a title, run the Untitled Documents report. This report works just as the previous reports do. When you encounter a file that does not have a title, enter a title in the Title text box on the toolbar.

In a public Web site, it's extremely important that all your Web pages have titles. The document title appears in the browser's title bar and is the name of the favorite or bookmark the user saves in the browser. The document title is also used by search engines to find and rank the Web page. In online learning applications, some of these issues are not important, but it's still important that your Web pages have titles and conform to the standards for a well-structured Web page.

Using the Accessibility Report

Section 508 requires that United States Federal agencies' electronic and information technology be accessible to people with disabilities. Accessibility regulations for United States government purchasing officers make accessibility a concern for many Web developers. Online learning applications created for United States government agencies are subject to the accessibility specifications.

With the recent implementation of Section 508, the United States government is committed to delivering Web pages to those with physical, visual, and hearing disabilities. If you aren't subject to these regulations, it's still a good idea to be familiar with accessibility recommendations; you might be tasked with creating online training applications that serve those in the disabled community. You can learn more about Section 508 at www.section508.gov.

Dreamweaver not only includes a report that will test your Web site for accessibility, it includes prompts that you can turn on in Dreamweaver preferences (Edit, Preferences), as shown in Figure 17.7. When enabled, Dreamweaver will prompt you to enter the necessary attributes to make your Web site accessible.

When you select the Accessibility report, the Report Settings button enables you to fine tune the type of items the report lists, as shown in Figure 17.8. Expand the individual categories to view the long list of items that the report checks.

Power User Tip

See Appendix A, "Resources," for the URL to the Macromedia Accessibility Resource Center, where you'll find information on creating accessible sites with Dreamweaver. There's even a free accessibility test check.

Figure 17.7

Accessibility preferences enable you to turn on prompts to help make your Web site compliant with government accessibility guidelines.

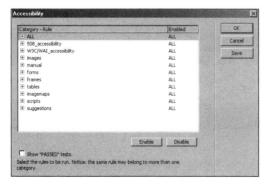

Figure 17.8

The Report Settings enables you to fine tune the type of accessibility report you run.

The Accessibility report runs a report against both the Section 508 guidelines and the W3C Web Accessibility Initiative (WAI) guidelines. If you expand these two guidelines in the Report Settings section, you'll see the elements that are reported on for each one. The Report Settings parameters also divide these report elements into categories such as images, frames, tables, and so on. If you turn off one of the report elements in one category, it's turned off in all the categories.

After you run the report, the results show the items that are missing by displaying a red × next to pages that have failed to meet the guidelines. The results descriptions even reference the exact section of the guidelines that address with the failed item. If you run this report using the same modified report settings, be sure you save the report settings for next time.

When you double-click one of the entries in the report results, you open the Web page to the portion of the code that the report is referencing. Instead, if you click the info button with a report entry selected, you'll open the UsableNet Accessibility Reference in the Reference panel, as shown in Figure 17.9. This reference helps you understand the standards, explaining the guidelines and details of the problem encountered in the Web page.

Figure 17.9

The Results panel Info button opens the UsableNet Accessibility reference in the Reference panel.

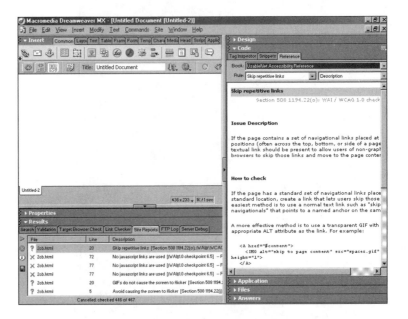

Using the Site Summary Reports

Macromedia provides the Site Summary reports extension that includes many useful reports. The Site Summary Reports are also called the Frontpage Migration Kit, meant to help Dreamweaver users migrate Web sites originally created with Microsoft Frontpage into Dreamweaver. These reports are helpful when you need to document your site and to troubleshoot problems, such as broken links. You'll try some of these reports in the next section. First, you'll need to download the free extension from the Macromedia exchange and install it by using the Extension Manager.

Reporting on Files by Creation or Modification Date

The File Creation and File Modification Date Range reports enable you to search for files that were created or modified between two specific dates. Running the report without entering a start date returns all file creation or modification dates. Limit the date range by clicking the Report Settings button and entering a start date, as shown in Figure 17.10. This report is useful if your team has a version control problem and needs to identify the creation or modification date of a file or group of files.

Power User Tip

In the Extension Manager and the Reports dialog box, the Site Summary Reports extension is listed as the FrontPage Migration Kit.

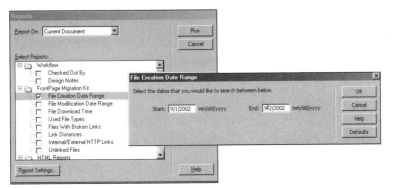

Figure 17.10
Enter a start date and an end date to limit the range of a File Creation or File Modification Date Range report.

Estimating File Download Time

You might find it useful to produce a report detailing the download time for files in your site. The File Download Time report enables you to specify various connection speeds. You can also have the report take into account the size of any media files contained in a Web page. Many companies have standards on the maximum amount of time a single Web page can take to download from their company Web site, so you might need the results of this report to document the download times of the online learning application.

After clicking the Report Settings button for the File Download Time report, set the connection speed. Select the Include Media check box to take into account the time it takes to download any media files displayed in a Web page, too. When you select a line in the Site Reports panel, the detailed description shows the individual sizes of each of the media files displayed in a Web page.

Reporting on Used File Types

The Used File Types report lists the file types included in the scope you set for the report. You'll usually set the scope to Entire Site for this report. The results list the various file types and the number of times the file types appear within the scope of the report. For instance, the report may show that you have 54 HTML files and 14 SWF (Flash) files in your site. Select the More Info button in the Site Reports panel to display a list of the files in the Description dialog box.

The User File Types report might be useful when documenting your Web site. It also might be useful when importing online learning applications that you need to maintain. You might want to know what media types were used (Flash movies, image formats, scripts) and whether there are files, such as design documents, that do not belong in the final site.

Searching for Broken Links

There are four link reports available in the Site Summary Reports (FrontPage Migration Kit) section:

- Files with Broken Links
- Link Distances

- Internal/External HTTP Links

- Unlinked Files

The Files with Broken Links report duplicates the Check Links report that is built into Dreamweaver. The report shows broken links in your site files and lists the files in the Site Reports panel along with the number of broken links the file contains. If you click the Report Settings button before running the report, you can specify the file extensions that you want included in the report.

Run the Link Distances report to find out how many links a user needs to select to get from one point to another in your online learning application. Certain organizations have guidelines on this, so you might have to document your online learning application. Click the Report Settings button to specify the start page, file extensions included, and the maximum number of links, as shown in Figure 17.11. The Site Reports panel lists how many links away from the start page each listed page is.

The Internal/External HTTP Links report lists internal links (links within your Web site), external links (links outside your Web site), or both. Click the Report Settings button and select the appropriate check boxes beside the Internal Hyperlinks and External Hyperlinks settings. The Site Reports panel lists each file and the number of links each contains. Selecting a line in the report results lists the files or URLs in the Detailed Description area.

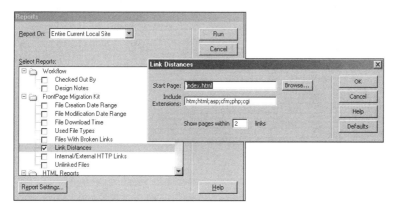

Figure 17.11
The Link Distances report displays how many clicks it takes to get to Web pages in your site from another page.

Unlinked files, also called "orphaned files," are files that are not linked to any other file in the site. These files are usually Web pages that were discarded at some point during development and are no longer necessary to the site. The Unlinked Files report is a duplicate of the Orphaned Files report you can run with Dreamweaver's Check Links command. Click the Report Settings button to configure the file extensions included in the report.

Saving and Displaying Report Results

When you work on a large, important, or tightly managed eLearning site, you might need to produce official reports on the site. It might be helpful to include data produced by Dreamweaver reports. You can actually save report results as XML files to import into other documents or display on the Web.

To save the report results to an XML file, click the Save Report button at the bottom of the Site Reports panel. Dreamweaver prompts you to save the results with the .xml file extension. After you save the report results, open the XML file in Dreamweaver. The results are most easily viewed in Code view, shown in Figure 17.12. These results need to be translated or imported into another application to be archived or usefully displayed.

Figure 17.12

Opening the XML file with the report results shows the format of the results that are saved.

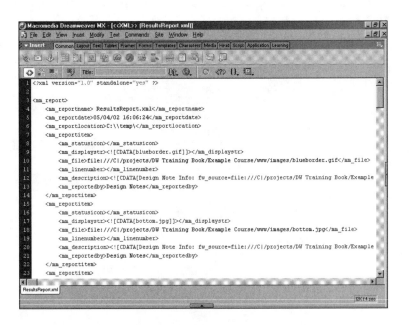

Summary

In this chapter, you used many of the reports that come with Dreamweaver. You created reports on checked out files, design notes, missing alt text, and others. You also installed an extension containing site reports. You explored using accessibility reports to check whether your Web site conforms to accessibility guidelines. You also saved report results as an XML file.

Power User Tip

The easiest way to format the report results XML file is to attach an XSL (eXtensible Stylesheet Language) to define the way your XML file will be displayed in the browser. See Appendix A for a link to a tutorial on how to do this.

IN THIS CHAPTER

chapter 18

Creating Custom Objects and Commands

WHEN EMBARKING ON AN ONLINE LEARNING application project,

you'll want to create custom tools to speed up the development

process. You can create some of these tools before you begin pro-

ducing Web pages, but most likely, you'll discover as you're work-

ing that you're repeating certain objects and procedures and will

want to automate them.

This chapter covers how to create custom objects that are reusable. What is an object in Dreamweaver? Well, Dreamweaver has image objects, table objects, form objects, and so on. Because the Dreamweaver interface is created in HTML, you can easily modify many of the existing objects so that you aren't changing the same attributes repeatedly.

You'll want to practice some of these techniques now, but you'll probably refer back to this chapter after you've started development. This chapter introduces you to simple customizations you can make to Dreamweaver. If you have an experienced JavaScript programmer on your team, you might want to have that person become familiar with the Dreamweaver Application Programming Interface (API) so that he or she can create complicated custom objects and commands for the team.

In this chapter, you will understand the following:

- How to use the Dreamweaver extensible interface
- How to create a custom object and save it to the Insert bar
- How to modify Behavior dialog boxes
- How to record and save commands

Exploring Dreamweaver's Configuration

Dreamweaver's user interface is controlled by files created in standard languages: HTML, JavaScript, and XML. The files controlling the Dreamweaver interface are stored in the Configuration directory, shown in Figure 18.1, under the Dreamweaver directory created when you install Dreamweaver. The extensions you've downloaded and installed in Dreamweaver take advantage of this extensible architecture. When you install an extension with the Extension Manager, it is simply making sure that all the files are installed into the correct directories under Dreamweaver's Configuration directory.

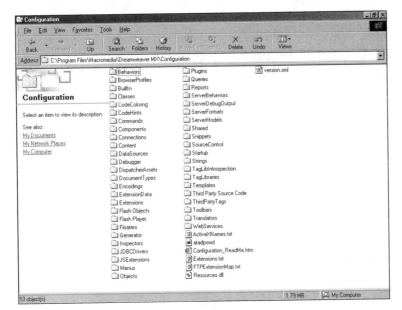

Figure 18.1
The Configuration directory contains the files that control Dreamweaver's program interface.

When you install Dreamweaver MX in the default location, the Configuration directory is located at the following:

- **Mac OS X**—HD:Applications:Macromedia Dreamweaver MX:Configuration

- **Windows**—C:\Program Files\Macromedia\Dreamweaver MX\Configuration

In multiple-user operating systems such as Windows XP, Windows 2000, Windows NT, and Mac OS X, Dreamweaver MX supports multiple configurations. When a new user opens Dreamweaver MX, Dreamweaver creates a configuration directory in the user's individual folder. These folders are located at

- **Mac OS X**—HD:Users:*username*:Library:Application Support:Macromedia:Dreamweaver MX:Configuration

- **Windows 2000 and XP**—C:\Documents and Settings*username*\Application Data\Macromedia\Dreamweaver MX\Configuration

Your team can share a unique Dreamweaver configuration by sharing the configuration files. You can give your team custom tools, specific to your online learning application project, by replacing the default Dreamweaver configuration with the configuration you create. When a new user starts Dreamweaver for the first time, Dreamweaver copies files from these shared locations:

- **Mac OS X**—HD:Users:Shared:Library:Application Support:Macromedia:Dreamweaver MX:Configuration

- **Windows**—C:\Documents and Settings\All Users\Application Data\Macromedia\Dreamweaver MX\Configuration

If you want a specific configuration for each user, you need to modify the files in this directory.

Exploring Objects

Dreamweaver objects are displayed in the Insert bar. Objects insert HTML code and can collect parameters from you, the Dreamweaver user. For example, the table object presents a dialog box asking you for the number of rows and columns you'd like in your table, and then inserts a table object into the Web page. Dreamweaver objects can be added to the Configuration directory.

Open up Windows Explorer or the Macintosh Finder, and navigate to Dreamweaver's Configuration directory. Open the Objects directory. Do the directories in the Objects directory look familiar? Yes, they are the categories shown in Dreamweaver's Insert bar. Create a new category called My Objects by adding a new directory to the Objects directory with that name. If you are working on a multi-user system, or you do not have administrator rights to your computer, you should create this directory in your user folder (see the introduction to this section for the location).

Open the Configuration\Objects\Common directory and look at the types of files in it. The filenames should seem familiar. Each object in the Insert bar has a corresponding .htm file in one of the directories within the Objects directory. The icon representing the object is a 18×18-pixel GIF image that has the same filename as the .htm file. Objects that are more complex have an associated JavaScript file (.js) that controls the design and insertion of the object.

Later in the chapter, you'll create a custom object and save it in the directory you just created. The directory and the object won't be visible in Dreamweaver until you restart Dreamweaver, so that the interface is freshly loaded, or issue the Reload Extensions command. The Reload Extensions command is available by holding down the Ctrl key (Windows) or the Command key (Mac) and selecting the Insert bar's Options menu, as shown in Figure 18.2.

Exploring Browser Profiles

When you run the Check Target Browsers report (File, Check Page, Check Target Browsers) on a Web page, as shown in Figure 18.3, Dreamweaver checks the site against files in the BrowserProfiles directory. Each of these files contains a description of the HTML tags and tag attributes that the browser supports. Dreamweaver compares your Web pages to this list and returns a report listing the tags and tag attributes in your site that are not supported by the target browsers you selected.

Dreamweaver installs with profiles for the following browsers:

- Internet Explorer 2.0, 3.0, 4.0, 5.0, 5.5, and 6.0

- Netscape Navigator 2.0, 3.0, 4.0, and 6.0

- Opera 2.1, 3.0, 3.5, 4.0, 5.0, and 6.0

Figure 18.2
Hold down the Ctrl or Command key and select the Options menu to see an additional command: the Reload Extensions command.

Figure 18.3
The Check Target Browsers report compares Web pages to the browser descriptions in the BrowserProfiles directory.

If your specifications for your online learning application describe delivery to browsers other than those that already have browser profiles in Dreamweaver, you can either create a profile or download and install one that someone else has created. Before you create a browser profile from scratch, check the Macromedia Exchange and search the Internet to see if someone else has already created one you can use.

If there isn't a browser profile for the target browser you need, and if you cannot find one by searching the Internet, you can create a new one by using the browser profile syntax documented in Dreamweaver's online help files. You can edit the browser profile in Dreamweaver or in a text editor, such as SimpleText (Mac) or Notepad (Windows). Save the plain text file in the BrowserProfiles directory with the .txt file extension.

Exploring Behaviors

A Dreamweaver behavior consists of an action and an event. When you explore the Behaviors directory, you'll see it contains two directories: Actions and Events. When you attach any behavior to an object in your Web page, a dialog box appears, as shown in Figure 18.4, prompting you to configure the behavior. Each behavior has its own unique dialog box, which controls the behavior's attributes.

Figure 18.4

The Check Browser behavior dialog box is simply an HTML form that Dreamweaver displays to collect parameters for the behavior.

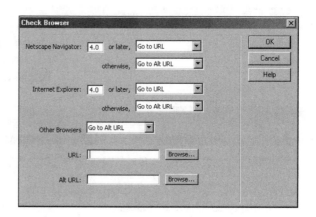

These dialog boxes are created with HTML form elements and are saved in the Behaviors\Actions directory as Web pages. The behaviors also have related JavaScript files that control functionality. I don't suggest extensive changes to these files without a lot of knowledge of JavaScript, but most Dreamweaver users can edit the form elements to alter some of the Behavior dialog boxes. You'll do that later in this chapter.

Exploring Commands

The Commands directory in the Configuration directory houses another group of files that you might need to extend. Later in this chapter, you'll create a custom command that is saved to this directory. You'll use two methods to create a custom Dreamweaver command: command recording and saving history steps as a command.

Exploring Other Configuration Files

You've explored only a few of the directories in the Configuration directory. The Objects, Behaviors, and Commands directories contain the Dreamweaver files that are most commonly extended or edited. These are some of the other directories in the Configuration directory:

- **Dictionaries**—This directory contains the dictionary for the language you specified in the Dreamweaver Preferences General category as the Spelling Dictionary. You can download dictionaries from the Dreamweaver Support Center (find the URL in Appendix A, "Resources") and install them in this directory. The default dictionary is U.S. English.

- **Flash Objects**—This directory contains the Macromedia Generator templates and sample Flash files for Flash Buttons and Flash Text in Dreamweaver.

- **Floaters**—This directory contains the Web pages used for Dreamweaver *floating panels*, also called *floaters*. You launch the floaters from Dreamweaver's Help menu. You can view the examples included with Dreamweaver by choosing the What's New or Lessons command on the Help menu. You can also create your own custom floaters and then edit the menus.xml (after you've made a backup of the file!), adding a command to launch it to the Help menu.

- **Inspectors**—This directory contains custom property inspectors. It does not contain the Dreamweaver Property inspector because that is actually built into Dreamweaver's code.

- **Menus**—This directory contains the menus.xml file that configures all of Dreamweaver's menus. If you change this file, you must create a backup because editing this file could cause problems that require you to reinstall Dreamweaver.

- **Plugins**—This directory contains plug-ins that are used to view external content in Web browser applications. Plug-ins are usually installed in a special directory within the browser installation but can also be installed in the Plugins directory for viewing browser content in Dreamweaver.

- **Queries**—This directory contains saved queries from Dreamweaver's Find and Replace command. You save a query to a .dwr file in this directory.

- **Reference**—This directory contains all the references that are available in Dreamweaver's Reference panel.

- **Reports**—This directory contains the files necessary to run Dreamweaver reports.

- **SiteCache**—This directory contains files describing the site you have defined in Dreamweaver. SiteCache is empty if you haven't defined any sites yet.

- **SourceControl**—This directory contains files describing WebDAV or Visual SourceSafe access in defined sites.

Creating a Custom Object: An Image with Accessible Text

When you insert an image into your page, you use the alt attribute to add a textual description. The alt attribute is read by a text reader application for folks who are visually impaired. Alt text is also useful for those who are viewing your online learning application with a text-only browser, such as Lynx (this is probably not very common).

There is a new accessibility attribute for an image object: the longdesc attribute. This attribute specifies an HTML file containing a comprehensive text description, longer than what should be entered for the alt attribute. Unfortunately, this attribute isn't supported yet in most of the major browsers.

A workaround for the current lack of support for the longdesc attribute is the creation of a *D link*. A D link is the letter *D* (for "description") added as a hyperlink next to an image. The hyperlink signals to visually impaired learners that they can find a detailed description of the image in the linked Web page, as shown in Figure 18.5.

You're going to create a D link object and save it to the Dreamweaver Object panel so that you can easily add it to images. The D link you'll create is the letter *D* surrounded by square brackets, [D]. You'll include a placeholder link consisting of only the # symbol. Creating and using a custom object speeds up development and, most important, makes sure that object presentation is consistent.

Power User Tip

Check the box beside Images in the Accessibility category of Dreamweaver preferences to be prompted to add the alt and longdesc attributes every time you insert an image into a Web page.

D link

Figure 18.5

The D link next to the image launches a detailed description of the image when the link is clicked.

Creating the Custom Object Model

To create a custom object in Dreamweaver, open a new, blank Web page in Dreamweaver. Type **[D]** on the page and format the text the way you'd like all the D links in your site to look. In Figure 18.6, the D link is set to Size 1 so that it's less conspicuous (select the text and set the font size attribute to 1 in the Property inspector). Select the D link text, and enter **javascript:;** in the Link text box of the Property inspector to add a placeholder null link. You'll replace the placeholder link with the link to the detailed description file when you use the custom D link object in a Web page.

Now you've created the prototype for all the D links you'll add to your site by using the custom object. This Web page contains the code that will be inserted into another Web page when you insert this object into the page. However, you have to remove the extraneous code from this page before you can save it as a custom object. Go into Code view or open the Code Inspector. Delete all the HTML code that does not describe the D link. The code should look like Figure 18.7, containing only the D link code.

Figure 18.6

Create the custom object in a new Web page. Each time you use the new object, it will look just like this one.

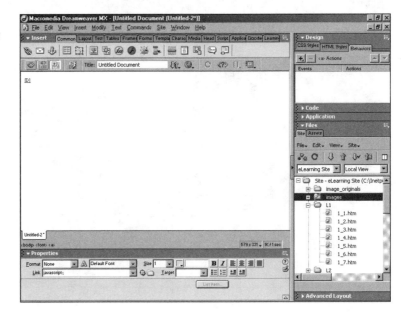

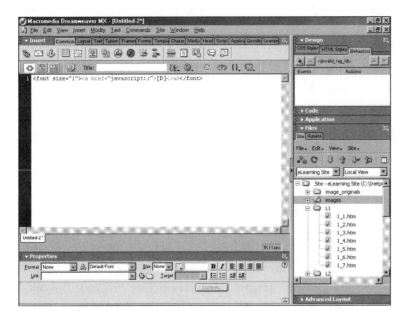

Figure 18.7
A custom object must contain only
the code describing the object, not
the code describing the Web page
body and head.

You'll be inserting the object into a Web page that already contains the body and head tags. If you do not remove the body and head code from the custom object, you'll insert this information into the page an extra time and Dreamweaver will show errors. The object must contain only the HTML describing the object.

Saving the Custom Object

Save the Web page you just created as **DLink.htm** in the Dreamweaver\Configuration\Objects\My Objects directory that you created earlier in this chapter. If you'd like your object to have an icon, copy image.gif from the Objects\Common directory and rename it **DLink.gif** to match the object name.

Before Dreamweaver MX can display your new object, you must add some XML to the insertbar.xml document in the configuration directory where you saved your new object. You edit this file in Dreamweaver MX. You need to copy the way other tabs of the Insert bar are coded in this file, as shown in Figure 18.8. Add a new entry in the file for the My Objects directory, and then add a new entry for the D Link button.

Figure 18.8

Modify the insertbar.xml file to add your custom objects to the Insert bar.

New category code ——

```
<category id="DW_Insertbar_MyObjects" folder="My Objects" showIf="">

   <button id="DW_DLink"
   image="My Objects\DLink.gif"
   enabled=""
   showIf=""
   file="My Objects\DLink.htm"/>

   </category>

   <category id="DW_Insertbar_Layout" folder="Tools" showIf="">
```

Close the custom object page and open a new Web page in Dreamweaver. To use your new object, you have to select the Reload Extensions command. After the extensions reload, your new category and object are available in the Insert bar. Click the object's icon in the My Objects category in the Insert bar, and your D Link is inserted into the page.

Any Web page object with attributes that are changed consistently is an excellent candidate for creation as a custom object. If you always use a horizontal rule set at 80% width, why not save that as a custom object? Custom objects can help you save time and make your Web site objects consistent.

Modifying an Existing Behavior Dialog Box

With a little knowledge of form elements, you can customize Behavior dialog boxes. You might need to make some elements larger or set a different default listing, for example. In this section, you'll modify two different dialog boxes—the Set Text of Status Bar and the Check Browser behaviors.

You can easily create your own extension package files so that others can install objects, commands, and other extensions you've created. There is a link listed in Appendix A, "Resources," to Macromedia instructions for creating an MXI (Macromedia Extension Info) file defining the names and locations of extension files. This file is formatted in XML. The Extension Manager reads an MXI file when you select the Package Extension command and creates an MXP (Macromedia Extension Package) file just like the ones you download from the Macromedia Exchange.

Enlarging a Text Field

I mentioned earlier that the Dreamweaver interface is created with HTML. The fields into which you enter parameters when you add a Dreamweaver behavior are simply form text fields. Sometimes, these text fields are not long enough to enter the amount of information you'd like. You can change the way the Dreamweaver user interface looks by modifying the files in the Configuration directory.

Explore the Configuration\Behaviors\Actions\Set Text directory and open Set Text of Status Bar.htm in Dreamweaver to edit the behavior. Do not change any of the code because you will disable the behavior's function if you do. You simply want to make the text field a little larger.

To edit the text field size, select the lone text field. The Property inspector displays properties for the text field. Isn't it odd that no size attributes are entered? The size of the text field is controlled by the style attribute, which is not displayed in the Property inspector. You'll use the Dreamweaver Quick Tag Editor to edit the style attribute.

Click the Quick Tag Editor icon, shown in Figure 18.9, in the Property inspector. This shows only the code for the selected object, the text field. Edit the style attribute, making the text field 500 pixels instead of the default 300 pixels. You should see the text field grow after you click somewhere else to close the Quick Tag Editor.

Figure 18.9

Use the Quick Tag Editor to edit the code for the text field.

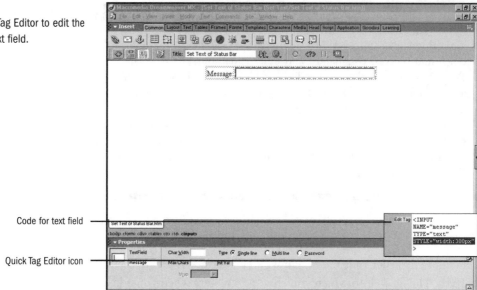

Code for text field

Quick Tag Editor icon

Save the file without changing anything besides the width of the text field. Do not change the name of the file or its location. When you apply the behavior, the text field will be wider.

Changing the Drop-Down Default Values

By manipulating the form objects used in Dreamweaver behaviors, you can enter the default values you commonly use. This is also a way you can limit the values that your team members use, hopefully prohibiting them from using values that aren't ideal for your project. Next, you'll edit another behavior, the Check Browser behavior that controls redirection to a different page, depending on which browser is used to view the page. Explore the Configuration\ Behaviors\ Actions directory and open Check Browser.htm in Dreamweaver.

Let's imagine that you often create a portal page that redirects viewers to a site optimized for either Netscape Navigator or Internet Explorer. If the viewers have neither of these popular browsers or have an earlier browser version, they stay on the current page.

The default Check Browser behavior, shown in Figure 18.10, enables you to set two URLs: the main URL and an alternative URL. You set the browser versions to redirect viewers to one of these URLs. You are going to change the default values so that you don't have to do it repeatedly during your work.

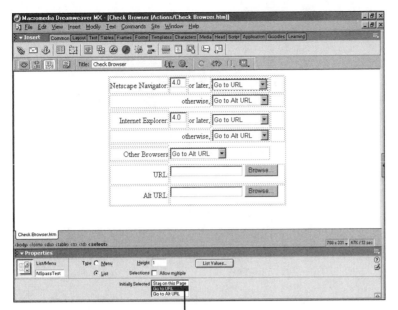

Initially Selected list menu

First, change the default values of one of the drop-down menus in this behavior. Select the drop-down menu next to Netscape Navigator. In the Property inspector, notice that Go to URL is the value selected in the Initially Selected list menu. If you cannot see the Initially Selected list menu, expand the Property inspector by clicking the expander arrow in the lower-right corner. Change the value that will be initially selected by clicking Stay on this Page in the Initially Selected list menu.

Let's say that your Web sites always have an index.html page that has this behavior attached to the onLoad event of the <body> tag, meaning that the behavior takes place when the page loads. You also have two default pages: one for the Netscape-optimized site, index_nn.html, and one for the Internet Explorer–optimized site, index_ie.html. Select the URL text field, and enter **index_nn.htm** into the Init Val field in the Property inspector. Repeat that same step, entering **index_ie.htm** into the Init Val field for the Alt URL. The customized dialog box should look like Figure 18.11.

Figure 18.11

Customize the Check Browser behavior dialog box by changing the initial values of the drop-down menus and fields.

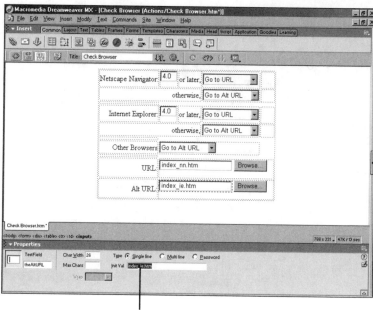

Initial value text box

Save the Check Browser.htm file without making any other changes. When you apply this behavior, the default values will be the ones you modified in these steps. Of course, you can still change the values to reflect the way you'd like the behavior to work.

Recording Commands

You can record a set of steps in Dreamweaver and save them as a command. A recorded command is available only during your current Dreamweaver session; when you close Dreamweaver, the command is erased. Later in this chapter, you'll learn how to save a command to the Command menu for use over and over.

Commands help you automate recurring tasks. Writing a Dreamweaver command from scratch is difficult; however, you can easily create a complex command by using Dreamweaver's capability to record a set of steps. A command in Dreamweaver is similar to a *macro* in other programs. The best application of a recorded command is when you need to apply a set of attributes to objects on a Web page or an entire site. Although there are other ways to automate global changes, such as Dreamweaver's Find and Replace capabilities, recorded commands offer a quick method of repeating a set of steps.

Creating Recorded Commands

To create a recorded command, open a Web page in your site that contains an image file. You'll record the changes you make to this image, and then apply the recorded command to other images. You can't record the selection of objects or mouse movements, so you need to plan to select the object by hand and apply the command. Follow these steps to create a recorded command:

1. Select an image in the page. You'll see the image attributes in the Property inspector.

2. Choose Commands, Start Recording on the menu. You'll know you are recording because the cursor becomes a small cassette tape.

3. Change some of the image's attributes in the Property inspector. For instance, you can add 10 pixels of V space (vertical space) by entering 10 in the V Space text box in the Property inspector.

4. Choose Commands, Stop Recording on the menu. Play Recorded Command is now active in the Command menu. This specific set of recorded steps is playable until you record another command or close Dreamweaver.

Apply the command you just recorded to the other images. Note how quickly the changes are made to the image attributes. You can open other Web pages and continue to use the command as long as you do not close Dreamweaver.

Saving Commands to the Commands Menu

It's nice to be able to record commands, but wouldn't it be great to save useful commands and use them over and over? If you recorded a command for short-term use and you decide that the command would be useful over multiple Dreamweaver sessions, you can save the command. In this section, you become familiar with the History panel and learn how to use it to save a command.

Exploring the History Panel

The History panel (Window, Others, History) records all the steps you perform in Dreamweaver. This panel is useful to back up steps you've completed in Dreamweaver, so you can undo mistakes. To undo steps in Dreamweaver, drag the slider on the left side of the History panel past listed steps. The deleted steps appear grayed out, as shown in Figure 8.12.

Figure 18.12

The History panel enables you to back up completed steps.

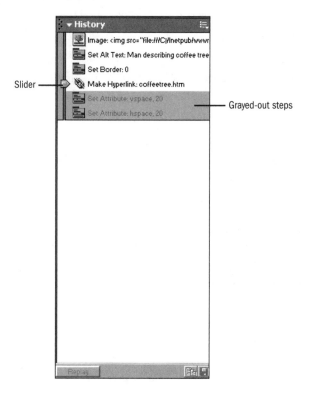

Slider

Grayed-out steps

Open up a new Web page in Dreamweaver, and then open the History panel and type a few letters on the page. The History panel records your keystrokes. Apply some text formatting to the text on the page, and the History panel displays individual steps for each of your activities. You can specify the number of steps displayed in the History panel in the Preferences (File, Preferences) General category; set the Maximum Number of History Steps.

To explore the History panel a bit more, insert a layer in your Web page. Again, Dreamweaver records this step. Pick the layer up by its drag handle and move it somewhere else on the page. With the layer still selected, use the arrow keys to move the layer one pixel at a time. The History panel records all these steps.

However, when you use the mouse to select the text or the layer on your Web page, the History panel does not record the selection. This is why you could not record the selection of the Flash movies when you tried recording a command earlier in this chapter.

Select the text on the page and drag and drop it into the layer. The step listed in the History panel has a red × beside the entry, as shown in Figure 18.13. This red × signals that you will not be able to save this step as a command. Mouse activities, such as selecting objects or performing drag and drops, cannot be saved as commands.

Power User Tip

Move the slider on the left side of the History panel up to undo multiple steps. To redo the steps, move the slider back down. The History menu steps remain editable even after you have saved a Web page. Closing a Web page, however, erases the steps in the History panel.

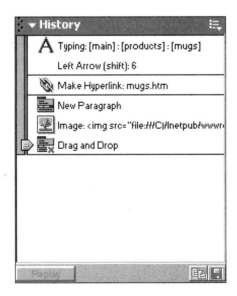

Figure 18.13
A small red × appears beside steps that you are not able to save as commands.

Saving a Command

The History panel has two buttons in the lower-right corner, shown in Figure 18.14, that enable you to copy or save a set of steps. The Copy button copies a set of steps to the Mac or Windows Clipboard, enabling you to paste the steps multiple times or on multiple Web pages with the Paste command on the Edit menu (not the Paste HTML command). The steps remain on the Clipboard until you replace them by copying something else.

Create a command using the History panel:

1. Open a new Web page in Dreamweaver and open the History panel.

2. Type the word **Hello**.

3. Hold down the Shift key and use the left-arrow key to select all five letters of the word. Using the arrow keys to select objects instead of the mouse is a way to get around not being able to record selections. Notice that there is an entry in the History panel for the left arrow keystrokes.

4. Apply the Heading 1 (<H1>) attribute in the Property inspector.

5. To save these steps, shown in Figure 18.15, as a command, select all the steps, and then click the Save button in the History panel. The Save As Command dialog box prompts you to enter a name for you command. This name is what will appear in the Commands menu, so make it descriptive without being too long.

6. Click the OK button to save the command.

Figure 18.14

The Copy and Save buttons enable you to apply a set of steps multiple times or to multiple Web pages.

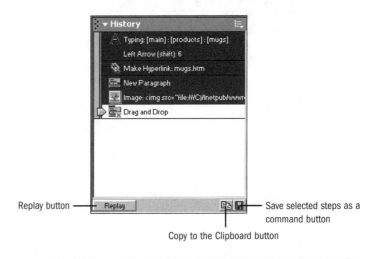

Replay button

Copy to the Clipboard button

Save selected steps as a command button

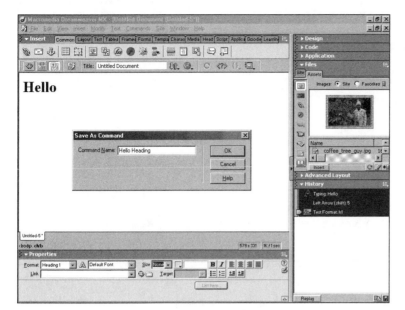

Figure 18.15
Save multiple steps in the History panel to the Commands menu.

Look at the bottom of the Commands menu to view your new command, and try running the command. In the History panel, the command is listed as a single step instead of the multiple steps that were originally shown for the command.

To save the short-term command you recorded earlier, you simply run the command and save it in the History panel. You'll need to run your command on a Flash movie, so open Destinations.html and select one of the Flash movies on the page. Choose Commands, Play Recorded Command on the menu. The History panel lists the Run Command step. Select the Run Command step, and click the Save button in the History panel to save the command to the Commands menu. Now you don't have to worry about losing this command when you close Dreamweaver.

Summary

In this chapter, you familiarized yourself with Dreamweaver's Configuration directory, the key to Dreamweaver's extensible interface. You created a custom object and displayed it in your own custom Insert bar category. You modified the Behavior dialog boxes, and you recorded a command and saved it to the Dreamweaver Commands menu.

Part VII

Appendixes

appendix A

Resources

This appendix lists Web sites, books, listservs, and other resources that can provide additional information on developing eLearning applications.

Chapter 1, "Instructional Design 101"

This section lists resources for learning more about the instructional design process and eLearning strategies.

Books

Marc J. Rosenberg, *E-Learning: Strategies for Delivering Knowledge in the Digital Age,* McGraw-Hill Trade, 2000.
Marc Rosenberg gives a high-level overview and practical advice on using eLearning in an organization. This is an excellent introduction to the business and technological challenges of implementing online training.

Robert Mager and Peter Pipe, *Analyzing Performance Problems: Or You Really Oughta Wanna,* The Center for Effective Performance, 1997.
This is a classic text on recognizing, diagnosing, and addressing performance problems. This easy-to-read book outlines a step-by-step approach to performance analysis. Robert Mager has a number of other excellent books on instructional topics.

Magazines

Training Magazine
www.trainingmag.com/

Online Learning Magazine
www.onlinelearningmag.com/

Web Sites

ASTD (American Society for Training and Development)
www.astd.org/

This professional organization's Web site offers articles, discussion forums, and buyer's guides for training professionals. The ASTD also has local chapters around the world.

Designer's Edge
www.mentergy.com/products/authoring
_design/designer/

This software package walks you through the ADDIE process.

About.com's Instructional Design Links
adulted.about.com/cs/coursedesign/

Chapter 2, "Assembling the Team and Collecting the Tools"

This chapter introduces the roles on an instructional team, including interviews with working professionals. It also introduces the tools used in developing online learning applications.

Books

Lynda Weinman, *Designing Web Graphics.4,* New Riders Publishing, 2002. This book is the classic text on creating graphics for Web sites.

Robin Williams, *The Non-Designer's Design Book*, Peachpit Press, 1994. An excellent introduction to design principles.

Betsy Bruce, *Sams Teach Yourself Macromedia Dreamweaver MX in 24 Hours*, Sams, 2002.
My basic Dreamweaver text that covers in depth the Dreamweaver user interface, inserting images, creating tables and forms, and other Dreamweaver basics.

J. Tarin Towers, *Macromedia Dreamweaver MX for Windows and Macintosh (Visual QuickStart Guide)*, Peachpit Press, 2002.

Contractors

Whether you are looking for a job in eLearning or looking to hire someone, these sites list opportunities and people to fill them.

E-Learning Jobs
www.e-learningjobs.com/

Guru.com
www.guru.com/

Elance.com
www.elance.com/

Macromedia Developer Locator
www.macromedia.com/locator/

Asset Licensing Agencies

PhotoDisc
www.photodisc.com/

Tony Stone
www.tonystone.com/

Sound Dogs
www.sounddogs.com/

Links to Interviewed Professionals

Gateway Learning
www.learnatgateway.com/

MediaPro, Inc.
www.mediapro.com/

19820 North Creek Parkway, Suite 103
Bothell, Washington 98011
425-483-4700
425-402-1441 (fax)

The Boeing Company
www.boeing.com/

Carson Media, Inc.
www.carsonmedia.com/

1689 Laurel St.
San Carlos, California 94070
650-595-2700
650-595-1027 fax

Studio 5 Recording
www.ubsc.com/studio5.html

P.O. Box 4223
Bellevue, Washington 98009
425-643-3930
425-641-2522 (fax)

Macromedia Tool Support Centers

Dreamweaver Support Center
www.macromedia.com/support/dreamweaver/

CourseBuilder Support Center
www.macromedia.com/support/coursebuilder/

ColdFusion Development Center
www.allaire.com/developer/referencedesk/

Flash Development Center
www.macromedia.com/support/flash/

Chapter 3, "Establishing the Course Specifications"

The course specifications guide the development process, providing the parameters that the eLearning application must perform within.

Books

Steve Krug, *Don't Make Me Think: A Common Sense Approach to Web Usability*, Que, 2000.
This books helps you design Web pages that make sense to learners.

Articles

Sheila Paxton, William H. Reilly, and Shawn Snelgrove, "How to Write an RFP for WBT", *Learning Circuits*, April 2000.
www.learningcircuits.org/apr2000/paxton.html

Web Sites

Cookie Central
www.cookiecentral.com/

Chapter 5, "Defining Cascading Style Sheets"

This chapter introduces Cascading Style Sheets (CSS), the standard way to affect the appearance and position of objects on a Web page.

Web Sites

World Wide Web Consortium (W3C)
www.W3C.org/

This group develops the specifications and guidelines for the Web. The Web site is the definitive location for information about CSS.

Jakob Nielsen's Effective Use of Style Sheets
www.useit.com/alertbox/9707a.html

Microsoft IE Filters
www.draac.com/wildiefilters.html

msdn.microsoft.com/workshop/samples/author/dhtml/DXTidemo/DXTidemo.htm

CSS Layout Techniques: for Fun and Profit
glish.com/css/

HTML Writers Guild's Accessibility and Cascading Style Sheets
aware.hwg.org/tips/essay_kb_02.html

Chapter 6 "Constructing the Interface"

This chapter introduces constructing the user interface for the online learning application using tables and layers. This chapter also covers how to implement buttons to use for navigation through the online learning application.

Web Sites

Al Sparber's Project Seven
www.projectseven.com/

Great DHTML menu examples.

Jakob Nielsen's Current Issues in Web Usability
www.useit.com/alertbox/

Jared Spool's User Interface Engineering Group
world.std.com/~uieweb/

Free Buttons

Free button sets for Web Sites
www.freebuttons.com/

Online Graphics Generator
www.cooltext.com/

AAA Buttons: Over 5000 Buttons
www.aaa-buttons.com/

Chapter 7, "Building Reusable Templates and Library Items"

This chapter introduces Dreamweaver templates and library items. These reusable Web pages and objects enable you to speed up development and ensure consistency.

Web Sites

W3C XML School
www.w3schools.com/xml/

Macromedia Templates Download
www.macromedia.com/software/
dreamweaver/download/templates/

These templates were created for Dreamweaver 4 but will also work in Dreamweaver MX.

Chapter 8, "Creating Interactivity with Behaviors and Animations"

This chapter introduces creating interactivity with Dreamweaver behaviors, Dreamweaver's method of adding JavaScript to your Web pages. It also covers animating objects on the screen using timelines.

Web Sites

JavaScript for the Total Non-Programmer
www.webteacher.com/javascript/

Webmonkey's JavaScript How-To Library
hotwired.lycos.com/webmonkey/
programming/javascript/

Chapter 9, "Adding Rich Media Content"

This chapter introduces techniques for adding rich media content to your eLearning application. This content requires player applications to run in the browser.

Books

Matthew David et al, *Flash MX Magic: With ActionScript,* New Riders Publishing, 2002.
Philip Kerman *Sams Teach Yourself Macromedia Flash MX in 24 Hours,* Sams, 2002.

Web Sites

JavaScript Integration Kit for Flash
www.macromedia.com/software/
dreamweaver/productinfo/extend/
jik_flash5.html

Flash Player Census
www.macromedia.com/software/
player_census/flashplayer/

Flash Developer Resources
www.flashkit.com/

Dazzle Technologies Info on Authorware
www.Authorware.com/

Recommended Authorware Books
www.betsybruce.com/books/

Interactive Web Audio
http://www.sonify.org/flashsound/

RealPlayer with Dreamweaver
http://www.realnetworks.com/resources/
extensions/documentation/dreamweaver.html

QuickTime
www.macdesignonline.com/tutorials/
dreamweaver/marapr01_qt.html

Download the QuickTime Object from
the Macromedia Exchange and then
check out this tutorial on how to insert
QuickTime into your Web page.

www.apple.com/quicktime/

Chapter 10, "Including CourseBuilder Interactions and Controls"

This chapter introduces the CourseBuilder
extension to Dreamweaver. It is used to
add interactions to Web pages.

Web Sites

The CourseBuilder Listserv
listserv.cc.kuleuven.ac.be/archives/dwa.html

Chapter 15, "Using a Learning Management System"

This chapter introduces Learning
Management Systems (LMS) and
popular learning standards for LMS
interoperability.

Web Sites

WBT Manager Trial Version
www.wbtmanager.com/wbt/trial/index.cfm

AICC
www.aicc.org/

ADL
www.adlnet.org/

IMS
www.imsproject.org/

IEEE
grouper.ieee.org/groups/ltsc/

Chapter 16, "Safely Collaborating and Sharing the eLearning Site"

This site introduces the collaborative
capabilities of Dreamweaver including
the ability to provide overwrite protection through Check In/Check Out. It also
covers connecting to version control software such as Visual SourceSafe.

Web Sites

Visual SourceSafe
msdn.microsoft.com/ssafe/

Metrowerks SourceSafe
www.metrowerks.com/desktop/MWVSS/

ToolServer for Macintosh
developer.apple.com/tools/mpw-tools/

WebDAV
www.webDAV.org

Goliath (Macintosh)
webdav.org/goliath/

CaDAVer (Unix)
webdav.org/cadaver/

DAVExplorer (Java)
www1.ics.uci.edu/~webdav/

Using WebDAV with IIS 5
iishelp.web.cern.ch/IISHelp/iis/htm/core/
wcwdcp.htm

Macromedia Technote: Setting up
WebDAV Access on IIS5
www.macromedia.com/support/ultradev/ts/
documents/webdav_ud.htm

Chapter 17, "Using Reports"

This chapter introduces various Dreamweaver reports.

Web Sites

Displaying XML with XSL Tutorial
www.w3schools.com/xml/xml_xsl.asp

Webmonkey: The Regular Expression Rundown
hotwired.lycos.com/webmonkey/97/33/index3a.html

Macromedia's Accessibility Resource Center
www.macromedia.com/macromedia/accessibility/

The Extension Installation File Format PDF
download.macromedia.com/pub/exchange/mxi_file_format.pdf

Chapter 18, "Creating Custom Objects and Commands"

This chapter introduces how to modify the Dreamweaver user interface using HTML, JavaScript, and XML.

Web Sites

Introduction to Screen Readers
newmedia.doit.wisc.edu/staff/wolf/intro_scrn_rdrs.mov

Dreamweaver Dictionaries
www.macromedia.com/support/dreamweaver/documentation/dictionary.html

Customizing Dreamweaver MX
www.macromedia.com/support/dreamweaver/custom/customizing_dwmx/

IN THIS APPENDIX

appendix B

Using Fireworks

FIREWORKS MX IS AN IMAGE CREATION AND optimization tool

that is an excellent addition to your Web development Tools

panel. You will need to create and optimize the images that

you use in your Web sites, and Fireworks enables you to

quickly create images with cool effects, such as bevels and

glows. If you do not have Fireworks MX, you can download a

trial version at www.macromedia.com/software/trial_download/.

Dreamweaver and Fireworks are tightly integrated. You can open Fireworks files in Dreamweaver, make changes, and see those changes in the original Fireworks file. You also can export tables, rollovers, and HTML code created in Fireworks directly into Dreamweaver.

Fireworks is a professional image tool that could fill an entire book on its own! This appendix simply touches on some of the important elements and teaches a few image manipulation techniques. There is so much more to learn about Fireworks than is possible in this appendix.

Acquainting Yourself with Fireworks

The Fireworks interface consists of a document window and panels, just like Dreamweaver's interface. The Fireworks document window, shown in Figure B.1, is tabbed with four different displays: Original, Preview, 2-Up, and 4-Up. You create and manipulate an image with the Original tab selected. The Preview tab shows you what the final image will look like.

Figure B.1

The Fireworks document window has four different tabbed displays. Use the Original tab to create and manipulate an image.

Original tab

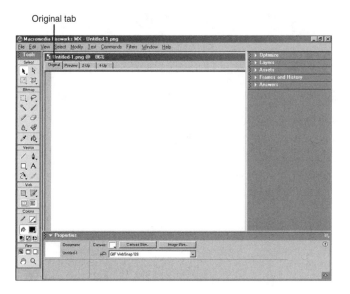

When you're ready to optimize the image for the Web, you can select either the 2-Up or the 4-Up tabs. These tabs display the image either two or four times. Why would you want to display the image multiple times? If you do, you can then optimize the image in different ways and compare how the different versions look, all at the same time. You'll optimize an image later in this appendix.

You can open an existing image in Fireworks or create a new one from scratch. Notice that the Fireworks user interface is similar to Dreamweaver's. In Fireworks, the Tools panel is docked on the left side, as shown in Figure B.2.

Figure B.2

The Fireworks user interface looks similar to Dreamweaver's. The Tools panel is docked on the left side.

Examining the Fireworks Tools

The Tools panel, shown in Figure B.3, contains the tools you use to draw and select objects in the document window. Some of the tools are actually groups of tools. If the tool has a triangle in the lower-right corner of the tool button, it means you can actually select from a tool group.

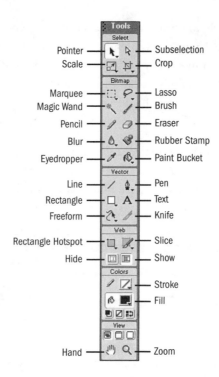

Examining Fireworks Panels

You'll use the Property inspector in Fireworks to set tool options and element attributes. Just like Dreamweaver, Fireworks has tabbed panels, described in Table B.1, that enable you to affect your image in various ways. Also just like in Dreamweaver, the panels can be displayed by selecting them in the Window menu.

Table B.1 Fireworks Panels and Their Functionality

Panel	Description
Optimize	This panel contains all the options to optimize images for the Web. You can select a palette, file format, number of colors, type of dither, and transparent color.
Layers	This panel displays all the layers in the current image. You can create and modify various layers and objects in Fireworks in this panel.
Styles	This panel stores sets of predefined stroke, fill, and effects attributes that you can apply to objects. You also can create and save your own styles.

Table B.1 Continued

Panel	Description
Library	This panel stores symbols, buttons, graphics, and animations that you can use over and over in Fireworks. Symbols are a Fireworks term for objects, text, or groups of objects that are reused. The symbol is the original object. When it is updated, all its linked instances are updated.
URL	This panel stores URLs that you will apply to objects in Fireworks.
Frames	This panel organizes animations created in Fireworks into groups of animation frames.
History	This panel records all the steps you have completed in the current file and enables you to undo them.
Info	This panel provides information about the currently selected object or gives you size and coordinate information for a selection. It also displays the color of whatever the cursor is currently over.
Behaviors	This panel adds behaviors, similar to Dreamweaver behaviors, to a hotspot or slice on your Fireworks image. You can create a rollover, an image swap, a navigation bar, and a pop-up menu, and you can set the text of the status bar.
Mixer	This panel gives you the power to set both the stroke and the fill colors by sight, with the color picker or by using one of the available color models. The color models available are RGB, hexadecimal, HSB, CMY, and Grayscale. You select the color model from the Color Mixer Options drop-down menu.
Swatches	This panel displays color swatches. You can load different palettes from the Swatches Options drop-down menu.

Creating an Image

Now that you've been introduced to the Fireworks interface, you can create a new image from scratch, such as a button graphic that you can use in your Web site. First you create a new file, and then you add some color and text. Next, you apply an effect to make it look more realistic. To create a new file

1. Select the New command under the File menu.

2. The New Document dialog box appears, as shown in Figure B.4.

You set the width, height, and resolution of your new file in this dialog box. Enter 70 pixels for the width and 26 pixels for the height. The resolution should be 72 because that is the standard resolution for images that will be displayed on a computer screen.

Figure B.4

Set the width, height, and resolution in the New Document dialog box. You also set the canvas color here.

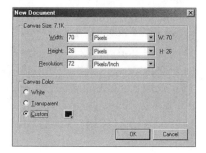

3. Give the button a background color by selecting Custom as the Canvas Color, clicking on the color picker, and then picking a color.

4. Click OK.

5. Select 200% from the magnification drop-down menu at the bottom of the document window, as shown in Figure B.5. This will make it easier to see what you are working on.

Figure B.5

The document window can be magnified using the magnification drop-down menu. The magnification level is displayed at the bottom of the document window.

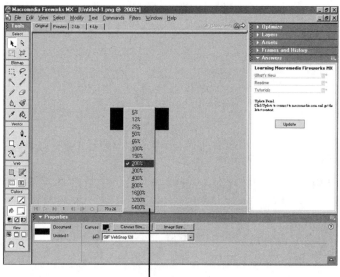

Magnification menu

Adding Text

Now add some text to the button. Fireworks' Text tool enables you to place editable text into the document window. You will turn on guides so that you can judge whether you have the text centered in the button. You can use any font on your system and can apply antialiasing and other text effects.

Add text to your rectangle as follows:

1. Set guides in the middle of the image. Turn on the rulers by selecting the Rulers command under the View menu. The default setting for ruler units is pixels. Because the image is 70 pixels by 26 pixels, one guide will be 35 pixels from the left side and another guide will be 13 pixels from the top. With the rulers on, click within the ruler and drag a guide from the left and then the top. The guides should look like Figure B.6. To get rid of the guides later, simply drag them off the screen or toggle them off using the Guides command in the View menu.

Guides

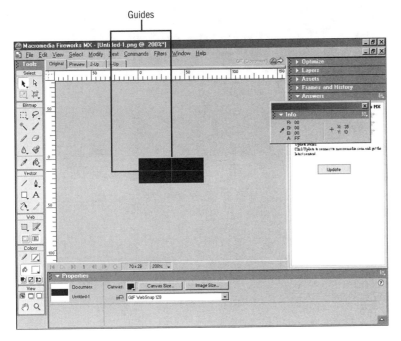

Figure B.6

Add guides to your image so you know where the middle of the image is.

I like to open the Info panel
while I'm positioning guides. The
info panel tells me the guide's
exact position so I don't have to
rely on the ruler.

2. Select the Text tool from the Tools panel.

3. In the Property inspector, select a font, make the font size 14, and choose white for the color (unless white won't be visible on your canvas color).

4. Click on the canvas and enter some text for a button title (try Next for a next button). Leave enough room on the right side for a small arrow.

5. Pick up and position the text object. You can use the arrow keys on your keyboard to fine-tune the positioning while you have the text selected. Select the text with the arrow tool. The button should look something like Figure B.7.

Figure B.7

Create a text object and set the font, font size, and font color.

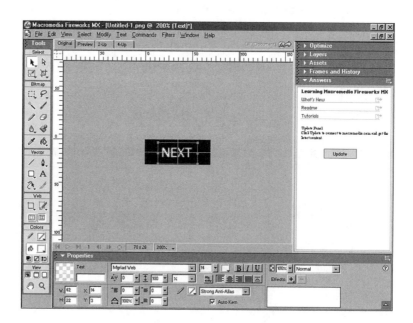

Adding a Shape

Fireworks has tools to draw any type of shape you might want using *vector graphics*. Vector graphics are graphics drawn using mathematical formulas to define the lines, arcs, and colors in the graphic. Vector graphics often create very small files and are easy to edit. Now you'll create a triangle shape to the right of the text that will look like an arrow. After you create the triangle, you can modify the stroke (the outline) and the fill. To create a triangle

1. Select the Pen tool from the Tools panel. The cursor becomes an ink pen. The Pen tool adds points to create a shape.

2. Click to create one point in the triangle. Hold down the Shift key while you click to create a second triangle point. This should force the creation of a straight line. Hold down the Shift key and click on the original point to close the shape. This last line might not be perfectly straight, but you can adjust it.

3. There are two arrow tools: the Pointer tool and the Subselection tool. The Subselection tool (the white arrow tool) can select a single point in your triangle. Use this tool to select any of the points, and then press the arrow keys on your keyboard to fine-tune the position of the points so that the triangle is even.

4. Be sure the triangle object that you just created is selected (in case you clicked your cursor somewhere else after step 3!). You will see the three points when it is. If the triangle is not selected, select the Pointer tool from the Tools panel, and click on the rectangle to select it.

5. The Stroke settings are in the Property inspector. Select None from the Stroke category drop-down menu, as shown in Figure B.8. Notice that the stroke color picker now has a red line through it signifying that this object does not have any stroke attributes applied.

6. The Fill settings, shown in Figure B.9, are directly to the left of the Stroke settings in the Property inspector. Select Solid from the Fill category drop-down menu, and select a color (I suggest white) from the color picker.

7. Underneath the Fill settings is the Edge property. Be sure that Anti-Alias is selected so that the edges of the triangle will blend nicely into the background.

Power User Tip

You might want to reduce the magnification to 100% so you can see what your button will look like in its final size.

Figure B.8
Set the stroke in the Property inspector.

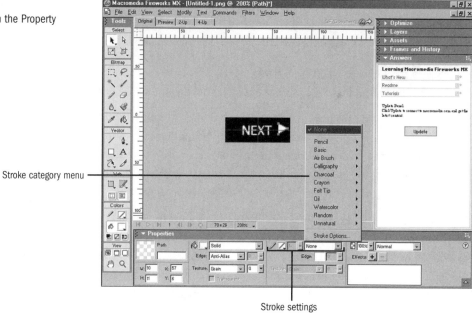

Stroke category menu ─

Stroke settings

Fill settings

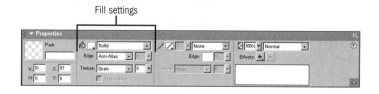

Figure B.9
The triangle now has no stroke and a solid fill.

Creating a Rollover Image

It's easy to use Fireworks to create rollover images. You'll create a rollover version of the button that glows with a green color. When the user places the cursor over the button, the other glowing image will load. To begin creating a rollover image

1. Open the Frames panel. Add a new frame by clicking the New/Duplicate Frame button in the lower-right corner of the panel (the button with the plus sign).

   When you click on Frame 2, you see a dim version of your button that's on Frame 2. This is called *onion skinning*, and it shows a dim version of the content of the other frame so you can line it up with the current frame's content.

2. Select Frame 1 and select everything by using the Select All command (Control+A or Command+A). Copy the contents of Frame 1 (Control+C or Command+C), click on Frame 2, and paste the contents (Control+V or Command+V). Now you have an exact copy of Frame 1 in Frame 2.

3. Select the text on Frame 2 with the Pointer tool. The text attributes appear in the Property inspector. Change the text color to a bright green. Remember which green it is because you'll use it in a few minutes for the arrow.

Adding an Effect

Fireworks has a number of interesting effects that you can easily add to your images to make them look unique and beautiful. Even better, they are very easy to remove if they don't turn out quite the way you'd like. Each time you add an effect to an object, it is listed in the Effects area of the Property inspector with a check mark beside it. You simply uncheck the check box to turn the effect off for that object.

To add an effect to your image

1. Be sure you have the triangle object on Frame 2 selected. You'll apply the effect to this object.

2. Select the Add Effects button (the + button) to drop down the Effects menu, as shown in Figure B.10.

3. Select the Glow effect from the Shadow and Glow menu. The effect is applied to the triangle and the attribute box appears.

4. Select the same green color you applied to the text. If you need to edit the effect, simply double-click it in the list.

You can add bevels, glows, and blurs, and you can emboss images, too. You'll probably want to experiment with the different effects. Usually you can change the colors involved, too. For example, you can make an object glow in yellow from its center or glow from the bottom of the image as if it is on fire. Fireworks effects enable you to get professional image results without having to know all the steps necessary to do the effects with the other tools in Fireworks.

Note

If you have Photoshop, you can use Photoshop plug-ins in Fireworks. Point to the directory that contains the Photoshop plug-ins in the Folder category of Fireworks preferences (the Preferences command under the Edit menu). You'll need to restart Fireworks to load the Photoshop plug-in commands. Fireworks displays the Photoshop plug-in commands in the Effect Panel drop-down menu.

Figure B.10

The Effects area of the Property inspector enables you to select the effect you'd like to add.

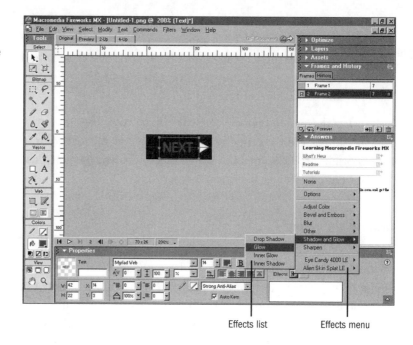

Effects list   Effects menu

To simulate what the rollover effect will look like on the Web page, click between Frame 1 and Frame 2. Does it look good? Now you must complete the final step to export both of the frames as separate images to use in a Dreamweaver rollover image.

1. Select the Slice tool and draw a rectangle completely covering the canvas. The slice appears as a green tinted box over the image. You can toggle slices on and off using the buttons directly beneath the Slice tool in the Tools panel.

2. Right-click (Control-click for the Mac) on the slice you just created. The Slices drop-down menu appears, as shown in Figure B.11. Select the Export Selected Slice command.

3. The Export dialog box appears, as shown in Figure B.12. Name your file next.gif. Be sure the Current Frame Only check box is not checked. Save the buttons in the images directory you created in your Web site.

4. Go to the images directory. You should see two images: next.gif and next_f2. The next_f2 image is the content from Frame 2.

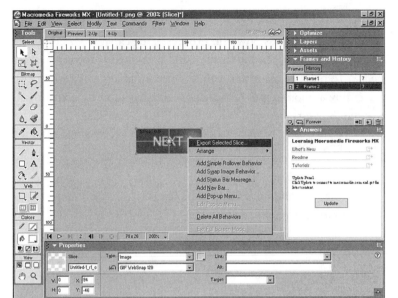

Figure B.11
The Slice drop-down menu enables you to export the frames beneath the slice.

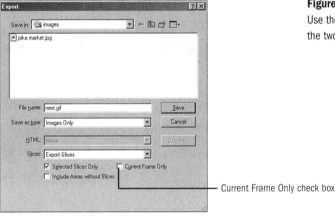

Figure B.12
Use the Export dialog box to export the two frames as separate images.

Current Frame Only check box

So you can make updates or changes to this button, you'll want to save the Fireworks file. All Fireworks files are saved as PNG files. When you reopen the file in Fireworks, you'll have access to change all the text objects, shapes, and other elements of the image. Don't save the Fireworks file inside your Web site; save it in another directory outside the Web site.

Optimizing Images for Use in a Web Page

Another of Firework's powerful features is the capability to optimize an image, showing you the smallest and best-looking format for your image. To practice using this feature, open an image in Fireworks, preferably a photograph. Because your image will be different from the one I'm working with, you will get different results.

To optimize the image and save it for the Web:

1. Select the 2-Up tab, as shown in Figure B.13. This splits the Preview window into two panes so you can compare two different image formats.

2-Up tab   Optimize panel

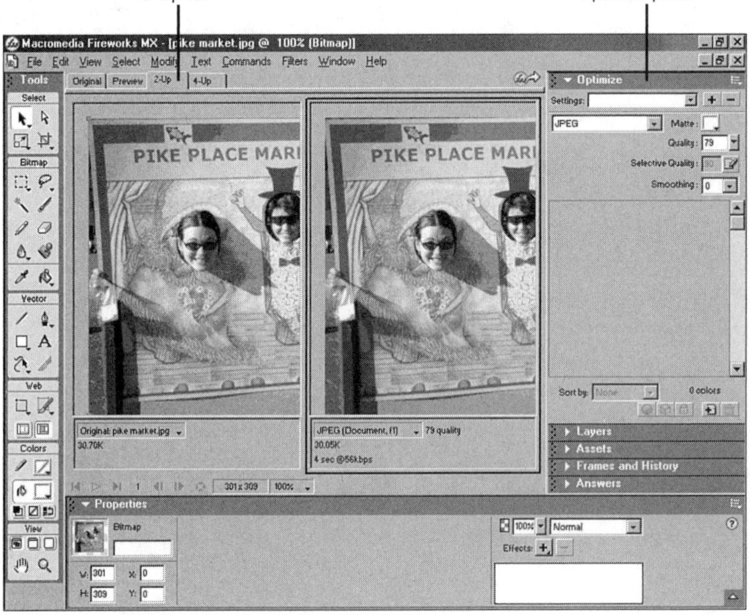

Figure B.13

Split the Preview window into two panes so you can compare two different image formats.

2. Open the Optimize panel.

3. Be sure the right pane is selected. The left pane is the original image. You can tell a pane is selected if it is highlighted with a box.

4. In the Saved Settings drop-down menu at the top of the Optimize panel, select GIF Websnap 256. The statistics on this image format appear beneath the image. This format is much larger than the original JPEG, as shown in Figure B.14.

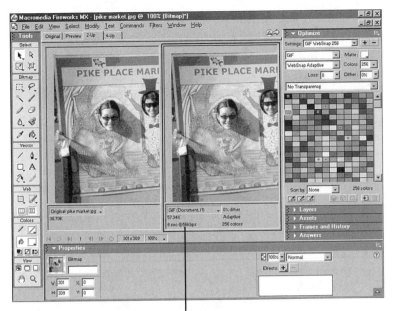

Figure B.14

The Export Preview enables you to compare the file size and download time of different file formats.

GIF file size

5. Select the 4-Up tab instead of the 2-Up tab. Now there are three variations you can compare with the original. Select the image in the lower-left corner.

6. In the Settings drop-down menu at the top of the Optimize panel, select JPEG-Smaller File. This file is much smaller than the original, although it might become a bit blurry. You can adjust the Smoothing in the Optimize panel to a lower number to make the image sharper.

7. Notice that the optimized JPEG in the bottom-left pane is smaller than the original JPEG and takes less time to download. The file size and download time are displayed in each of the panes.

8. Select the version you want to save, and then select the Export command from the File menu to save this optimized version of the file.

9. Enter a name for the file, and select the Save button.

Slicing an Image into Pieces

Fireworks enables you to slice an image into smaller pieces so that you can add interactivity to the individual pieces. You can draw slice objects over an image in Fireworks, and then export the slices as individual graphic files.

To create a sliced image

1. Open an image in Fireworks.

2. Be sure the Show Slices button is selected in the Tools panel.

3. Select the Slice tool and draw a rectangle on top of the image, as shown in Figure B.15.

Figure B.15

Draw slices over the image to create individual image files held together by an HTML table.

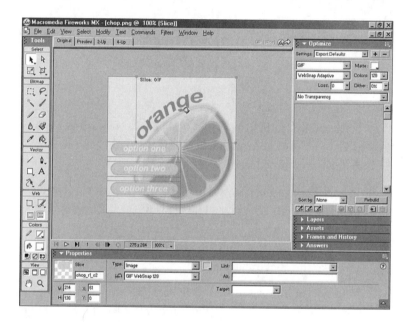

4. Slice up the entire image by repeating step 3.

5. Select the Export Preview command from the File menu. Split the pane and optimize the image as described above.

6. When you click the Export button, Fireworks enables you to export all the slices as individual image files along with the HTML table that will display the images as if they were all one image. Be sure Export HTML File is selected.

7. Select the Save button, and save the HTML file and all the sliced images into a directory.

If you open the HTML file that you just created, you'll see all the slices pushed together as if they were a single image. You can open this file in Dreamweaver and edit it. In a minute, you will learn how to import the HTML into Dreamweaver.

Placing a Fireworks File into Dreamweaver

Dreamweaver and Fireworks are tightly integrated so that you can efficiently use the two tools together. After you've imported HTML created in Fireworks into Dreamweaver, you can edit the HTML in Dreamweaver and update the original Fireworks files, too. Dreamweaver knows when you have inserted a Fireworks file into your Web page, and it keeps track of any edits that you make to the file.

To import the HTML and the sliced images that you created in Fireworks

1. In Dreamweaver, select the Fireworks HTML command from the Interactive Image submenu of the Insert menu.

2. The Insert Fireworks HTML dialog box appears. Select the browse button, and navigate to the HTML file that you saved in Fireworks. Select the Delete file after the insertion check box if you would like the file to be deleted after it is inserted into the Web page.

3. The HTML table and images are inserted into the Dreamweaver document window.

Now the HTML that Fireworks created is in the Web page. Dreamweaver knows that the HTML originally came from Fireworks. When you select the table or the images, the Properties inspector shows that the table or image originated in Fireworks, as shown in Figure B.16. There is also an Edit button that opens Fireworks to make any edits you'd like.

Figure B.16

The Properties inspector shows that the object was originally created in Fireworks and can be edited in Fireworks.

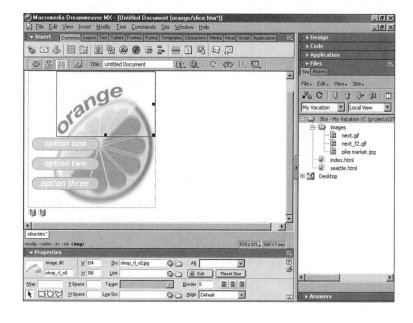

Index

H

handleNNResize() function, 433
hardware, specifying, 81
hash marks (#), 132
Henry, Jennifer, interview with, 38
hidden layers, 217
History panel, 508-509
    saving commands, 510-511
home pages, 88
Hot Areas tab options (CourseBuilder
    interactions), Explore category, 289
hotspots, 229
    properties, 230
HTML
    reports, 481
    styles versus CSS, 140
    support for in browsers, 61
    use in Dreamweaver, 47
Hypertext Preprocessor (PHP), 363, 369

I

IEEE Learning Technology Standards
    Committee, 428
if statements
    nesting, 322
    unnesting, 323
IIS (Internet Information Server), 365
    installing and configuring, 365-366
image maps, 229
    creating, 229
    hotspots, properties, 230
    naming, 229
    tools, 229
images
    animating, 235
    background, previewing, 120
    button states, 170
    creating with Fireworks MX, 525-526
    descriptions, 499
    displaying in Assets panel, 181-182
    effects, creating with Fireworks MX,
        531-533

hotspots, 229
    properties, 230
image maps, 229
    creating, 229
    naming, 229
    tools, 229
inserting into tables, 162
onLoad event, 223
optimizing with Fireworks MX, 534-535
rollover images, creating with Fireworks
    MX, 530-531
slicing with Fireworks MX, 536-537
stretching smaller, 162
swapping, 228-231
tracing, 156, 189
    loading, 157
    positioning, 158
    setting opacity, 157
implementation
    delivering courses, 28
    phase of ADDIE model, 27
importing
    Web sites, 94
    XML into template regions, 199-201
IMS (IMS Global Consortium), 426
index values (arrays), 432
information boxes, 220-221
    dragging, 223
    showing and hiding, 221-222
initPage() function, 433
Insert Corporate MumboJumbo extension, 124
Inspectors directory, 498
instructional design models, 12
    ADDIE, 12
        phases, 13
    benefits, 12
instructional designers, 39-40
    Peppers, Kathleen, interview with, 40
instructional goals, 17
    objectives, creating, 19-20
<interaction> tag, 278, 337
interactions (CourseBuilder), 266
    adding template fix, 270
    browser compatibility, 270-272
    Button, 293

X-Z

DREAMWEAVER MX

New Riders

VOICES
THAT MATTER

HOW TO CONTACT US

VISIT OUR WEB SITE

W W W . N E W R I D E R S . C O M

On our web site, you'll find information about our other books, authors, tables of contents, and book errata. You will also find information about book registration and how to purchase our books, both domestically and internationally.

EMAIL US

Contact us at: **nrfeedback@newriders.com**

- If you have comments or questions about this book
- To report errors that you have found in this book
- If you have a book proposal to submit or are interested in writing for New Riders
- If you are an expert in a computer topic or technology and are interested in being a technical editor who reviews manuscripts for technical accuracy

Contact us at: **nreducation@newriders.com**

- If you are an instructor from an educational institution who wants to preview New Riders books for classroom use. Email should include your name, title, school, department, address, phone number, office days/hours, text in use, and enrollment, along with your request for desk/examination copies and/or additional information.

Contact us at: **nrmedia@newriders.com**

- If you are a member of the media who is interested in reviewing copies of New Riders books. Send your name, mailing address, and email address, along with the name of the publication or web site you work for.

BULK PURCHASES/CORPORATE SALES

The publisher offers discounts on this book when ordered in quantity for bulk purchases and special sales. For sales within the U.S., please contact: Corporate and Government Sales (800) 382-3419 or **corpsales@pearsontechgroup.com**. Outside of the U.S., please contact: International Sales (317) 581-3793 or **international@pearsontechgroup.com**.

WRITE TO US

New Riders Publishing
201 W. 103rd St.
Indianapolis, IN 46290-1097

CALL/FAX US

Toll-free (800) 571-5840
If outside U.S. (317) 581-3500
Ask for New Riders
FAX: (317) 581-4663

New
Riders

W W W . N E W R I D E R S . C O M

VOICES THAT MATTER

www.informit.com